Sweepers Sweepers Man Your Brooms

An enlisted man's story

By Jeff Zahratka
EMCM(SW) United States Navy, Retired

First published by Dog Ear Publishing
4010 W. 86th Street, Ste H
Indianapolis, IN 46268
www.dogearpublishing.net

ISBN: 978-159858-677-0

This book is printed on acid-free paper.

Printed in the United States of America

In loving memory of
Adam Rene Sampson
26 June 1983- 18 August 2007
He inspires me still

On 1 September 1862 Congress ruled that "the spirit ration in the Navy of the United States shall forever cease." While this law abolished "grog" for the enlisted men it did not however, end the wardroom and captain's wine messes. These were closed on 1 July 1914 when Josephus Daniels, then Secretary of the Navy, issued his famous "bone-dry" General Order #99, to abolish these messes. In this country and all over the world the Secretary's order was ridiculed and criticized, but the Secretary was unperturbed. This was noted later when he wrote that "Naval officers always obey orders, whether they like them or not. That is the essence of honor and efficiency." Subsequently to this however, sale of alcoholic beverages has been permitted at shore stations.

While this transition in naval history did not have a direct effect on the occupational structure it did have a rather sobering effect on all Navy men. ***It could have though, with the size of our Navy today, if the tradition had not been abolished. We could in that case possibly have a rating such as "Bartender," or more modernly "Spirit or Grog Technician."***

By Charles A. Malin, Recorder, Rating Review Board, Bureau of Naval Personnel (Pers-A3122), Navy Department, Washington DC, 1971

Foreword

Sea Stories

Every retiring Sailor must pursue a new direction in life and I found it appealing to either write a book or start a sports bar catering to fellow Pittsburgh Steeler fans. The idea of a bar is great when the Steelers win, but oh shit; what if they go 6-10? What if the *Franchise,* Ben Roethlisburger smacks that windshield with the top of his head instead of his jaw? Speaking of jaw; "*God forbid what if the Jaw retires*?" With a book all you lose is ink, the time, and the humility of no one wanting to read your thoughts. But an empty sports bar; I shudder with the lugubrious fear of sheer financial catastrophe. If the Steelers were having a bad year, I could never be traitorous and start a Bengal's bar. I would have to make it a gay bar. "*Whoa tiger; Just kidding Cincinnati*." So its book, not bar, I have chose to pursue; a lucid decision in the end- the attempt is not to be random. This book is about the United States Navy. It's not about fiery battles or the technology of the ships; although a little of that may enter. This book is an enlisted man's trip through the ranks and the accompanying experiences of the 70's, 80's, and the 90's. I know all lives have some moments of unhappiness. I conveniently skipped whatever personal unhappiness I lived through because this book was written to give you a lighthearted moment or two. Although it is primarily based on the author's experiences, it could well be about anyone who ever wore the uniform.

Sailors in general are similar to mongrel dogs. They are faithful, lovable, playful, and smart. But at times they are very guilty of non-cerebral activity. On occasion, these faithful friends will commit underachievement as relational chaos, or to more nautically express that, "*crap on the deck*." When that occurs you just may have what old mariners refer to as a sea story. Is this book primarily for that group of "*Old Salts*" gathering at the local VFW or the Fleet Reserve Association? *Absolutely*, but if you are truly interested in human behavior then this should give you a chuckle or two; regardless of personal acumen. In short, this story is about all of us who served in the three decades that completed the twentieth century. The sitcoms may star different characters, but in many ways this is a microcosm of all those wonderful men and women whom we call Sailors.

If you ever noticed, the most compelling talker around the bar or the hunting camp is quite often an ex -Sailor. So many extraordinary events take place in a Sailor's tour that he is often compelled to share them. They are without doubt the world's most accomplished bullshit artists. Of course this is especially true whenever beer is involved. A Sailor may go to extraordinary lengths to punctuate a good joke. As an example, a now deceased uncle, Bill, was a Navy veteran and a hunter. One hunting season he got lucky, taking down a large 12 point buck in the deep forests of northern Pennsylvania. When the old salt brought the deer into the local tavern dressed in a red plaid outdoorsman jacket, a ball cap on his head, a lit cigarette hanging in his mouth; all the while shielding his dead eyes from the bar lights, (courtesy of nifty dark sunglasses), all thought it amusing. When the dead buck laughed hysterically at the tipsy swab's jokes it was a home run, and brought down the house. The factitious laughing device, surgically implanted in the antlered guest's chest was brilliant, and executed in the highest traditions of naval service. There is nothing more entertaining and socially addicting than a 22 ounce frosted mug of an unadvertised local brew in a room full of "*Old Farts*" swapping sea stories in a cozy tavern, in a town called "(Insert name here)." Sailors are correctly stereotyped for having a learned ability to keep the conversation flowing in neighborhood taverns. They cause patrons to hang around for more beer, and they are directly linked to expanding waistlines in America.

Note: *Several years ago a Navy directive ordered the term Sailor to be capitalized in military correspondence. This script will adhere to that directive*

Part 1

Blue Shirts

Retirement Day

He stood there in Service Dress Blue uniform. He had several rows of ribbons, but less than most master chief petty officers about to retire. Receiving the Meritorious Service Medal and its accompanying ribbon this day would be a special addition to the current group that was pinned to his Dress Blues. He was appreciative and the crew mustered before him felt his sincerity. They were his boys, all of them. Having walked in their shoes gave him credibility. Retirements gave the departing Sailor a forum to speak and reflect. He was most proud of the level playing field that the Navy offered to all men and women, regardless of their background or race. He spoke of the things he was going to remember the most about his twenty six -years. Passing inspections, the technology onboard the ships he served on; these were rendered irrelevant. It was the great Sailors he met and served with who would always be in his heart. He named them by name, outstanding frigate Sailors who worked as a team to make the ship function with a true sense of purpose. To him those men mustered before him were what mattered the most. Most Navy retirement ceremonies reach a point where emotional control is difficult. They mark a tremendous change in life. This ceremony would be no exception. The captain spoke that day about how soon we are forgotten once departed. I believe the point made was that the organization that we call the Navy replenishes itself, much like nature. The Navy is a group inspired by traditions and history. That history is always reinforced and remembered at these retirements. The old master chief, all forty- four years of him, promised the crew that whatever he could do for them or say about them from the next chapter of life, he would do so in earnest and with zeal.

Because this command master chief loved to laugh, and because the frigate crew, were Sailors, who, like all Sailors loved to joke, a final blow was struck at the departing old salt in the name of humor, that addictive elixir that was so important to both. After the emotional scene of passing of the flag, and the presentation of the shadow box, the final benediction was offered. After the prayer and the final piping ashore, some crazy Sailor amplified the *Pittsburgh Steeler Polka, Super Bowl Edition.* The whole crew knew the master chief was a Pittsburgh die- hard to the core. The surrounding ships and the Sailors engaged in busy pier activity were loudly rocked by the sound of *Jimmy's Polka Band* blasting through the busy activity of Norfolk D &S piers. The master chief had a smile on his face as he saluted the Ensign and requested permission to depart the ship for the final time. He knew the Navy would be fine; they still had a sense of humor, and sometimes that's all you have.

Chapter One

Cousin Gary

Gary and I hung out. I had quit school somewhere in the 11th grade because I hated going and I was lazy. I was also in rebellion. Abbie Hoffman's *Steal This Book,* Dylan music, and *Haight Ashbury Street,* all had special meaning to me. All adults in neckties were evil.

The Revolution phase of my existence played out in about a year and a half. By then I was going to night school, and I was killing time with my cousin Gary, a straight laced kid who never really embraced the Revolution. We both held low paying jobs at an Oldsmobile dealer. Girlfriend I didn't have, haircut I did, all to get that low paying job at the Oldsmobile dealer. With our clean cut looks, Gary and I soon discovered we could get served beer at the local bowling alley. Life was good, but truly, life was boring. We spent most of our time cruising around searching in vain for sin and adventure in a place that featured neither. In retrospect, life could have been much worse, and it didn't hurt that Gary was a hoot.

Gary had a sharp wit. He could get on a roll and spew out a steady stream of "what ifs" that could make your stomach ache from laughter. He was funny enough for me to dub him "*King of the Belly Laugh*". He had a great knack for parody; mocking our bosses at the Old's dealer with professional ease. I attributed that to his expertise at picking up the nuances and mannerisms of his unsuspecting victims. He had terrible eyesight and his staccatos of imitations would come at you through these wonderful and impressive thick glasses that made him even funnier. Later in life he pursued laser surgery and completely ruined the entire persona. I loved those glasses. They were a statement of personality. They were memorable. As you will soon discover those heavy duty spectacles were an important segment of the story.

Gary and I always talked about talking to girls. Only we never actually talked to them. We would go to the high school Friday night football games and there we would *observe girls*. We just wouldn't talk to them. We were in short, too chicken and mortified of rejection. We had the testosterone urges of the strutting peacock but the innate shyness of the much lesser fowl, the chicken. So off we would go to the bowling alley, drink pitchers of draft, and debate at length why the girls were so stuck up. All that time in the bowling alley did have a concrete benefit though. *PAC-MAN* arrived as a video game there in 1971 and we became extremely adept *Pacmenarios.*

So there we were, paddling along in the stream of life. Eighteen years old, no burning romances, no exciting nightlife. Neither of us was considering college, especially me. I was a night school student in pursuit of a diploma, and even that was taking an interminable amount of time. I believe it was Gary's mogul of an idea that first crept into our conversation during a random night of cruising in the burbs of Western Pennsylvania. Before joining the Navy became the prodigious decision of our short lifetimes we did conduct an in depth analysis of the personal benefits of naval service. Our conversation went something like: "Gary: "*Jeff, Why don't we enlist in the Navy?"* Me *"Are you shitting me! They have really short h*air." Gary: "*Who gives a rat's ass*?" Me: "*Chicks. They'll think we're a couple of rednecks*." Gary: "*Your hair is already short*." Me: "*But if you enlist it gets cut real short. I think we should join the Coast Guard. They can at least have beards*." Gary: "*But you can't grow a damn beard*." Me: "*Look Dude, I'm working on it*." Gary: "*The Navy is the way to go. They have carriers and you don't get sea sick on a carrier. My brother Rick was in the Navy and told me that."* Me*: "But I know this guy Ron. He was on an ice-breaker in the Coast Guard. They went to Antarctica and crossed the equator on the way. They had to crawl through garbage and shit. It looked pretty gross in the pictures, but it still seemed like they were having a damn good time*." Gary: *Well we ought to go take the test*." Me: "*What friggen test? I ain't takin no damn test*." The subject died for a while and we continued to cruise.

The subject came up again, like an active case of herpes, emerging during a Friday night football game, and we were there alone as usual and wanting to talk to some girls. Of course we could not be so intrepid as to actually engage in a conversation, so we talked to each other about how impressive it would be to be relating to them details of our impending trip to the dangerous jungles of Nam on patrol gunboats. Yes, we would be in danger, but hopefully we would make it back, arriving in glory in our crisp white cracker jacks. Ah yes, ladies would think we were awesome. Gary said, "*Sailors get the girls man. Everyone knows that*." So the idea agitated in our developing craniums for weeks. It would go under then resurface, like a bloated corpse, each time convincing us a little more to take the plunge and go visit that recruiter in Pittsburgh.

At the Oldsmobile dealer, I talked to the body and fender guy that we worked with. His name was Bogey. Bogey, was more than a body and fender guy. He was an artisan of wreckage. He was pure magician, taking crumpled ruins of automobiles and making them whole and pristine again. Bogey was good, maybe the best. Certainly he was the best I had ever seen. I said "I *Bogey, if I were to join the Navy, what job should I go for*?" Bogey had an immediate response. "*Be a fuckin plumber man. Fuckin plumbers got all the money. It's a helluva lot better to be smellin shit than suckin in all these paint fumes. Plumber's the thing man. Best way to go*." Through the insight and good judgment of Bogey, an idea was being born.

I'm not sure when I finally relented to Gary's prodding, but he was certainly the persistent one. In fact, we even began to develop a new tactic with girls, lying. We created tales about our upcoming sea duty as *soon to be members* of the United Sates Navy. Yes, we were probably going to be on gunboats, patrol craft, or swift boats in Nam. I can't tell you if the girls embraced our fabrications. I really can't remember the girls. I am somewhat sure that this all actually took place. I don't believe this was mental invention or illusion, but it could have been. After all 1972 was 35 years ago. But in the overall scheme of things, it was like yesterday, so it must be fact.

Our lying usually gained us a brief measure of pity. There were some good luck back slaps, but it played out quickly, and overall I think our bullshit was detected by quite a few uninterested parties. Our plan left us in the usual place, the bowling alley with a pitcher of beer.

Gary said, "*Now that we told those chicks we were joining, we gotta go to the recruiter*." I said "*Yeah, we'll check it out tomorrow. Pick me up at the house. We'll have to go early though*."I said that knowing Gary would be late. That was it. Our great laid out plans were beginning to unfold.

To my shock, Gary was at my mom's house bright and early the next morning. He was actually going to drag my scrawny carcass down to the recruiter's office in Pittsburgh to investigate the possibility of this great adventure. In Gary's mind he was already manning the gun on a river patrol boat. He was mowing down the enemy, blowing to smithereens anything that moved or twitched. He was heroic, someday vowing to return to a hero's welcome; medals gleaming, muscles bulging, and girls swooning.

In our town it was and still is OK to be military. The Revolution and the protests of Berkeley were strange to most members of our sleepy, little, Western Pennsylvania town. I was swept in previously due to a trip to DC where historical confrontations seemed to be happening by the minute, but I was the exception to most of the youth I knew. People in our town were patriotic. Most adult men were WWII or Korean War veterans. No one protested anything. Hair length and pot were about the only invaders. Polish wedding celebrations were still the high lights of the year. Men worked at the mills, took their allowances for a few Friday night beers, and handed over the rest to their wives. Life was good. It was routine and stable. Nothing much changed. The Pirates were our heroes, and the Steelers were going to lose. That was the summation of 1971 Pittsburgh and the surrounding area.

I can't remember if the drive into Pittsburgh that morning had good or bad weather, so I'll pick good. It was a bright, sunny day. We struggled to find parking. Pittsburgh was a big city, so it was supposed to be hard. With the intertwined labyrinth of one way streets it was intimidating to navigate. We finally parked somewhere. Nervous and anxious we crept up the steps and went in. Life was about to change in dramatic fashion.

If you would have asked me to describe who I expected to see when we entered that office, the last person would have been a Chinese guy. I know now that my recruiter was a Filipino, but in small town Pennsylvania at the time, Orientals were all Chinese. It was doubly shocking to be greeted by a clear Midwestern accent coming out of a voice I expected to be an emulation of a 1930s grade B movie. I wasn't prejudiced, just ignorant.

Rey Barabajabal or something very close to that looked like a warrior from the high seas. His dress blue crackerjacks and perfectly tied neckerchief set off by the white piping and a respectable chest of ribbons made him appear Godlike to us.

We were the easiest enlistments Petty Officer Barabajabel ever had. We did what we had to do and took the test. I believe the appropriate acronym of the era was GCT/ARI test. We both finished with respectably high scores. We only *acted* like dumb shits; it didn't mean we really were. After the test, Rey was genuinely more interested in us than he was when we first entered. Reflecting, I don't believe he envisioned us as high mental category types. But, if nothing else, the high schools of Western Pennsylvania definitely teach with a vengeance. Thankfully some of it stuck.

Rey announced to his new prodigies that we qualified for any rating and associated school that we desired. We picked none. Instead we chose three years, undesignated, buddy system; guaranteed first assignment together, or at least the same home port. Our goal was to be Sailors, in the total classic stereotypical sense of the term. The concept was to become babe magnets in hot uniforms. We would travel, explore the world, and conquer foreign ports. We would someday return to our town in resplendent crisp uniformed glory. Ribbon adorned warriors we would fulfill our destiny and avail ourselves to the women in waiting as twenty something studs.

A return to Pittsburgh for our induction physicals occurred a short week later. I can remember being naked with other young men in a long side to side alignment. A weary looking doctor ordered us to bend over and spread our cheeks. We complied except for one young literal fellow who was bent over with a finger in each side of his mouth, dutifully spreading his cheeks. After his interpretation of the process was corrected the doctor walked the line inspecting for abnormalities of any type. I wondered to myself why anyone would go to school for eight to ten years to be a sphincter inspector, but I guess someone had to do it. Personally, I was just glad I wore crisp clean whitey tighties that day.

We signed about a hundred pieces of paper, none of which we actually read. We were given a time and date to report to the bus for the trip to the airport. We had requested boot camp in either San Diego or Orlando Florida, so of course we were heading to Great Lakes, Illinois, the coldest place on earth in the winter (I *know you're from Minnesota and it's colder there*). We were to report October 25th 1972. The reality of this great adventure was actually beginning in earnest.

After Gary and I finished the preliminary requirements of our contracts, we were compelled to spread the word about our imminent departure. My mother said, "*Good idea there ain't nothing around here.*" My father said "*Learn a trade.*" Most of my uncles and aunts were of the "*Ain't nothing around here" variety.* It was by far the most popular reply. It was a historical point in time when the Pittsburgh steel mills were winding down, victims to union wages and overseas competition. Jobs were scarce. The turn to technology in the Golden Triangle would not occur for a few more years. The foothills bled off a wave of population. Certainly we would have gladly accepted high paying but dirty mill jobs without complaint, but they were no longer there, victims to the economy or progress. The deep blue sea was calling, and Gary and I were answering back.

Bogey, back at the car dealer gave me one profound, final piece of advice, "*be a fuckin plumber man.*" I think the paint fumes made him forget about all the other times he tutored me with that phrase.

Goodbyes were said during the weeks leading up to our departure. We now were the proud possessors of DEPPERS cards, standing for delayed entry personnel. These cards gave us a certain sense of worthiness and made us feel significantly important in our world. Our routine reply as impressive eighteen year old men was that "*we worked for the government.*" We felt on somewhat equal footing now with members of the State Department, FBI, and of course, the Central Intelligence Agency.

As our imminent date of departure drew closer, our sense of apprehension increased proportionally, but still the days sped by, and as October 25th approached, our thoughts were overwhelmed with our impending adventure. After boot camp, Gary and I would be surfing on the North Shore of Oahu, touring the ruins of Pompeii, or running with the bulls of Pamplona. World adventure beckoned, and whatever was to occur in the not so distant future was going to be a sheer blast, or so we convinced ourselves.

I was a very skinny young man. If I turned sideways and stuck out my tongue I resembled a zipper, but I was quite confident that the physical readiness portion of boot camp would not pose a problem. Because of my low body weight I was able to perform a respectable number of pushups. For some unqualified reason, I envisioned that would be the primary physical requirement. The rigors of boot camp physical fitness caused minimal stress in my thoughts. What kept me awake at night was that gnawing excitement of getting in gear and letting the grand adventure begin.

From my family's viewpoint, they were enthralled with my decision. I finally had some direction and a plan. I had survived some trying teenage years but I'll leave it at that. Those days are unto themselves a whole other story.

As the magnanimous day approached we felt our growing impuissance. There was no about face; our derrieres were being signed sealed, and delivered to the United States Navy. We were for all practical purposes the property of the greatest Navy in the history of mankind. We were two out of five hundred thousand. We were .0004 % of the force. We had taken the oath and in the deepest recesses of our young minds was the tentative hope that we would in fact, measure up.

Chapter Two

EM1 Worshick

The final weeks of summer passed and fall began as scheduled. Early in the morning someone drove us to the airport, our day of reckoning had arrived. I was numb. An air of excitement and nervous anticipation hung in the air as we said our goodbyes. Small bags of necessities in hand, we were off, bravely pursuing young men's dreams. This was my second trip on an airplane and I can recall nothing about that flight. As we flew off, leaving Pittsburgh behind, I knew that we would return home for Christmas leave. I felt lucky and more self assured because I wasn't doing this thing solo. It was comforting to know that Gary and I were committing to this adventure as a team. Alone would have been seriously stressful; yep I just loved that "*Buddy System*."

We landed uneventfully in Chicago's O'Hare Airport. A uniform met us there and herded us into a bus with a bunch of other recruits who looked similar to us; tired, yet scared shitless. After the short and extremely grave bus ride to Great Lakes, we were given some direction, none of which was memorable. I only remember being shooed off the bus to a waiting area outside. The complete uniformity of hundreds of pea coat clad men and the funny watch caps that adorned the heads of the alien beings gave the entire scene an eerie appearance. We were herded into a dank old theater with poor lighting. It was cold and unfriendly. In front of us stood an imposing chief petty officer, who began to instruct us in a gravelly and sinister voice. I strained to listen, but the echoes of our dungeon were too much, I heard little. I only remember Gary looking at me through his big thick glasses. He was very nervous, almost in a state of panic and he said "*Jeff, we fucked up*! *We really fucked up*!" I looked at Gary and profoundly said, "*Big time*!" That line and that comment stick with me to this day. A dark day in a cold dark room, surrounded by aliens; it was indeed, scary stuff and a far cry from any image I previously held in my imagination of this moment. This situation seemed surreal and all I could think about was reversing this day back to early morning. I would not be here in this room, I promise you that. Who knew what perils lay ahead?

Eventually we were placed into the proper group which formed our company. There were about eighty of us in all. We were lead to a room when he appeared; the imposing, commanding, and all powerful electricians' mate first class or EM1 Worchick, our inspiring leader for the next nine weeks. He entered the room in all of his dress blue glory. Adorned with ribbons and the amulet of a company commander, he was the perfect Sailor. He looked physically fit. He was lean, like a young cloning of Charleston Heston. He even had Heston's Adam's apple. Maybe they were related. He was *Ben Hurr* in dress blues. When he spoke he even sounded like *Ben Hurr.* This guy was to own our souls for the next nine weeks. When he spoke for the first time, we hung on every word. "*Does anyone here in this group have any college education*?" A spattering of hands went up. "*Good, I want you people to get this place cleaned up. I want the rest of you who haven't had the benefit of college to watch these guys and learn something.*" That said. He walked out.

The days passed quickly as everything fell into a well programmed routine. We marched, did pushups, ran, ate chow, and hand washed our clothes. We even used identical knots when hanging things to dry. We did endless folding, stenciling, cleaning, and classes. Often we were poked with needles, and prodded routinely by tired doctors searching for unknown stuff and quick spreading invasions of bacterial intruders.

Gary and I ended our careers together in the second week of boot camp. Medical decided that Gary had to be ASMOED because he needed a new prescription for his glasses. I have no damn idea what ASMOED stood for. I just know that you got sent back to a holding company waiting for a medical issue to get resolved. So there ended our buddy system plans. The world tour of the *Two Amigos* was not to be. The United States Navy was not listening to our plans and onto the scrap heap went our package deal and preplanned world tour together. We were solo performers on this very strange stage, our destinies diverged, a branching of the best laid plan of our short lives.

Gary and I rendezvoused a few times over the next few years. He served honorably for three years and got out. He was like millions of other veterans. He did his duty, left the service, then went to work, and had a family. Over the years I would see him from time to time. He would usually ask me at the family reunion: "*Are you still in the in the Navy*? *When are you going to retire? You have been there forever.*"

Some of us are meant to remain for the long haul. And some are destined to do their duty and move on. It is virtually impossible to predict what will happen down the road. That is a lesson I would continuously learn in Navy life.

Our boot camp company was #504. Companies competed for flags that they would march with. The company flags demonstrated expertise in a competing area. There was an education flag, a sports flag, drill flags, and others. Our company must have been cerebrally challenged because we didn't win a damn one. The only flag we had was the lonely Company #504 flag. I think this may have irritated EM1 Worshick, because other companies he led had always won *Color Company*. He was competitive and I think having a group of lovable dolts was painful for him to tolerate. However most baseball managers that are successful will usually give credit to having good players. Worshick could not have expected to win the *World Series of Boot Camp*, when everyone in this company was batting .180. We all struggled somewhere far below the *Mendoza line*.

Our company had a particularly difficult time in the education classes and their accompanying forty question tests. If the RCPO, or Recruit Chief Petty Officer (the recruit appointed as company leader) did not pass that test, then his position was passed on to another recruit. We went through a multitude of RCPOs in those first few weeks, as they were anointed and rescinded with weekly regularity.

The guy who slept in the bunk above me was Pagano, a tough guy from Buffalo, New York who had a hard time with the entire team work concept. Worshick would preach to us about unity and team work, and why it was important to help one another. Being an individual was abandoned at the gate. Pagano did his shit the right way and despised getting punished for those who screwed up. One day we were out on the grinder practicing our left obliques or some other maneuver that is filed in my cranium's archive of unrecallable stuff. A few uncoordinated raisins refused to get it. The frustrated Worshick had us drop down in the pushup position to contemplate our woeful performance. Pagano just stood there. Worshick said something like "*Get down Pagano*!" Pagano said, "*No I do my shit right*!" Worshick turned many colors; crimson red, fiery orange, leveling off to a deep purple. I have to give it up to Worshick. He maintained his composure. He was a nuclear power technician from the USS ENTERPRISE. Perhaps his training as a nuke helped him maintain his self control, because he handled the situation as efficiently as an old widow dabbing 12 cards at a Catholic bingo night.

Pagano ended up going to *Happy Hour*. *Happy Hour* in reality made one very unhappy. Going to happy hour was like being a Raider fan after *Franco Harris* caught the *Immaculate Reception*. That is about how happy it made you. Pagano went to many Happy Hours actually. Pagano became the "*Happiest Man on Earth*."

Happy Hour was a time devoted to working out in special sessions with your friend, the piece, a heavy rifle that did not shoot and had no bullets. Drilling with the piece was the name of the game and Pagano was now an expert. Pagano was no longer an individual. He was part of our mystic group of *Great Lakes Raisins*, cruising on, executing the intricate phases of military perfection. He became the unspoken leader of the *Worshick Fan Club*.

Certainly there was occasional time for fooling around and pranks. We were issued sewing kits and one day I creatively decided to stitch Pagano's sheet to his mattress. Upon his discovery of my prank he voiced and grumbled his displeasure in his newly acquired and quite colorful Sailor vernacular. I was surprised when a day later he reciprocated with a little craft work of his own. Pagano smiled at my evident irritation. I swept up his shattered face with a foxtail and emptied it into the barracks shit can. Pagano was now humanized and definitely one of us. He probably stayed in for thirty and made master chief.

That's how it went. We slowly bonded. White guys, black guys, New Yorkers, South Carolinians, a bunch of Pittsburghers; we all started to get along, *cum bye ya*.

We had one truly charismatic character from St Louis, Missouri. He was very black and very funny. He named himself *White Man*. When the company was left to its own cognizance, White Man would analyze each of us. He was the best entertainment we had, due to his incredible skill at mocking our mannerisms and nuances. He memorized how we talked, how we marched, mentally mapping all of our imperfections, which were brilliantly replayed. Whoever screwed up in front of Worshik became the star of the evening entertainment. White Man helped us get through it. He was as important as a letter from home. Just the fact that I can remember him after 35 years says something about him.

One day that winter we were out on the grinder and Worshick was really incensed. His behavior was odd because for a change we had done nothing wrong. He bellowed loudly and barked for us to assume the push up position. Snow was falling but it didn't muffle his expletives. The USS KITTYHAWK just had a race riot and Worchick had to do something about it. So he gave us training. While we were doing our pushups he chewed us out. "*You assholes better never go to my fleet and pull this kind of crap! You better learn how to get along right now*!" Maybe what the Worshiks of the Navy did in retrospect was a correct action. As far as I can recall the Navy never had another riot.

Worshick first noticed me after the third or fourth forty question test. We just had another RCPO flunk it, so looking at the test scores he called out my name. "*ZZ ahraaaatka*." "*Yes sir*!" as I popped tall going front and center. He said, "*You have done really well on these tests. Why don't I know you*?" I had blended in well, undiscovered, unknown; just a pimple on a skin-like crust of pizza. I had managed to miss both accolades and ass chewings. I was happy with that.

Regardless, I ended up being the Assistant RPOC; the last RPOC actually lasted through to graduation. As the Assistant RPOC I had to march at the rear of the company and help call cadence. Although the black guys thought my cadence sucked, they seemed to accept me and White Man had a great time imitating my marching voice. He actually sounded more like *Walter Cronkite* than me, so I was cool with his efforts. One could do worse than be imitated as Cronkite. As we approached the end of our training we were abandoned for an ever increasing amount of time to our own cognizance. We had to be places as a group on schedule. If we were late, we paid.

Service week came. For one week you were basically an indentured servant to some active duty chiefs and petty officers who were either instructors or support personnel. It was the closest thing left to slavery in America. Truthfully, I had a *gee dunk* job during service week. All I had to do was make and pour coffee for some chiefs in an office for a week. I also had to answer a telephone, using the proper telephone etiquette of course. My name was "*Recruit*." That was me. That was all of us. All with the same name, Boot or Recruit.

We finally graduated. We got our dress blues ready, and received our National Defense Ribbons. Everyone was awarded one of those at the time because there was still a war going on. With graduation came boot camp liberty call for the entire company. It was a part of the training to make sure you could actually survive in the world.

Our boot camp liberty was fast approaching and to say we were excited was the understatement of the century. Most of our group chose Milwaukee for liberty over Chicago. There was only one reason for that and that was the drinking age; eighteen in Wisconsin at the time, and twenty-one in Illinois. It was a no brainer for us. Off we bussed to Milwaukee after receiving our due warnings and advise from Worschik.

We were brand new Sailors out and about in a big city; strutting our stuff like proud peacocks, tail feathers spread, looking for adventure. We found our adventure in some bar where most of the company ended up. Their claim to fame was a featured drink called a *Harvey Wallbanger*. Soon we were banging off the walls most likely just like Harvey did when he invented it. That was about the extent of my memory, except for a vague recollection of the song "*Me and Mrs. Jones*" being played in succession about thirty or forty times. I could be wrong but I must say I never had a Harvey Wallbanger again. I have no idea what was in it, but it was brutally effective on a one hundred and twenty pounder with limited drinking prowess.

Somehow with superhuman effort we got through our excursion into freedom without incident. We all returned alive, well, and intact. No broken bones, black eyes, or police arrests. Worshick was secretly pleased I'm sure, but as part of the practiced persona he refused to reveal it.

The day finally arrived to depart Great Lakes. It was just prior to Christmas 1972. There we proudly stood by our expertly packed sea bags in our dress blues. We were Sailors, we had arrived. That's when Worshick called attention. "*Get down recruits. You are scabs out of your mothers' wombs! You think you know something! You know nothing yet! When you get to the fleet, you better realize that!*" We did more pushups in our dress blues over the next fifteen minutes than we did in any block of time over the former nine weeks. Then we were dismissed to board the bus. It was off to Christmas in the Burgh. I had to return to Great Lakes in January for something called Advanced Training Battalion. It was for Sailors who were not headed for an "A" school. But I didn't have to worry about that for two entire glorious pushup free weeks.

I spent my boot camp liberty babbling to anyone who would listen about where I would be ultimately sent. I felt that it would be a slam dunk that I would end up exactly where I wanted, an aircraft carrier out of San Diego; good weather, sunshine, California dreaming. I made the supposition, that aircraft carriers, because they were large and spacious probably had amenities such as carpeted libraries, personal restrooms, and perhaps personal desks. The thought crossed my mind that each Sailor may even have his own quarters. Of course I was only basing my intelligent guesses on the most anecdotal evidence and scuttlebutt. I could not ask these questions directly while in boot camp, some things are to be known intuitively. I was convinced that everyone I met knew all the answers to carrier living standards. I could not ask because I too was supposed to know.

The final event of boot camp leave was a beer gathering with some of the folks I hung out with. We brought in 1973 by singing along with the car radio to Don McLean's *American Pie.* I thought we sounded quite melodious because we were parked in a tunnel with excellent echo; thus ended the year 1972. Now bound by the laws of the Uniformed Code of Military Justice it was time to report as ordered. Worshick had drilled punctuality into our collective brains in such an efficient manner that he should have patented it. Today he would be a billionaire.

Returning to Great Lakes I was confident. I navigated O'Hare International Airport, greeted the *Hari Krishna* Crowd, and jumped on the bus to Great Lakes. I checked into the right place, ahead of schedule I might add. After all, I was superior to most of the thousands of recruits mustering up that day on the Great Lakes grinders. I was a boot camp graduate. Because I had graduated from boot camp in the top ten percent of my class I was informed that I was automatically advanced to E2 from E1. I was now a Fireman Apprentice or FA. I attempted to mentally reinforce all the nautical terms that Worshick had taught us over the past months. Decks, scuttlebutts, shit cans, heads, pissers, shitters, gee dunk, bulkheads, overheads, decks, stanchions, port, starboard, forward, aft, athwart ships, below decks, fart sack, skivvies, quarterdeck, ditty bag, dirt bag, and stairs ain't stairs; they're ladders. These terms get quickly absorbed into a Sailor's vocabulary. They are the normal words of communication, although spouses may on occasion take offense to several and officers normally omit the cussing, for they are, after all, gentlemen. But a Sailor's vernacular must incorporate most of this language in order to lend nautical credibility to salty yarns.

Two major events happened during my two return weeks at Great Lakes. One I purchased my mother a gold four leaf clover. Advanced Training granted regular liberty calls to its students, so of course some fellow adventurers and I seized the opportunity whenever presented. As I passed along a North Chicago street a very nice gentleman from a jewelry store queried me, "*Do you love your mother*?" he asked. I stopped and turned because certainly I loved my mother. This very nice young man soon had me feeling the guilt and shame of a thankless and ungrateful son. I never realized how much I had taken all of my mother's personal sacrifices for granted. I had to get the gold and diamond four leaf clover. It was the perfect gift that would begin to balance the scales towards gratitude vice ungratefulness. If I did not purchase that sparkling jewel, then I would be cast into the evil realm of the unappreciative sons. There was no way I could survive the guilt unless I purchased this shrine to motherhood.

That event was my first experience with the power of credit and the military ID card. My mom loved that clover and wore it often for the rest of her life. It was insignificant that I paid about triple the value for the piece. At least I secured one positive entry in the *Book of Life.*

The other highlight event of the time was the orders I received to an aircraft carrier in San Diego. *NOT!!* No, once again, despite my clearly written preference sheet, I was not assigned to an aircraft carrier in sunny Southern California. I was being signed sealed and delivered to the United States Ship LAWRENCE. The LAWRENCE was an Adam's Class destroyer. When I queried one of the chiefs about the DDG he said, "*Adam's class are good ships*." OK, what is good? The chief said good but what that meant to me and what that meant to him may have some differing points. Time would tell. I did know that I did not wish to reside in Norfolk, Virginia. I was told that the yards were embellished with signs that instructed "*Sailors and dogs to keep out.*" But then again I also heard that most of the folks down there actually held no ill will to the canine members of the community.

Reluctantly, Norfolk Virginia was my destiny. It was January 1973 and I was off to the Fleet, a Blue Jacket in transition. I had to take all the lessons instilled by the mighty Worshick and put it all into my acumen for success and survival. I was about to be a part of that proud tradition of destroyer men that formed the backbone of the US Navy. FA Zahratka was transiting into harm's way. I was apprehensive and yet I was determined to embrace the unknown and to excel. Above all, I figured I could survive if I kept my mouth shut and did exactly what I was told.

Norfolk Virginia is a Navy town above and beyond all other enterprises. It was then, it is now, and it probably will be as long as the sea is used to transport material from one place to another. When I landed there fresh from Chicago and the penetrating winter, I was pleasantly surprised by the milder weather in Southern Virginia. Of course there was a shore patrol liaison petty officer standing by in the airport with a sole purpose of directing poor dumb boot camps and others onto a shuttle; destination NOB D&S piers Norfolk.

I found out soon enough that there was a small problem. The USS LAWRENCE (DDG-4) was a little ways off in a place called Vietnam. Somehow someone talked to somebody and somebody else got Fireman Apprentice Zahratka sent to a temporary holding place on another ship, namely the USS SIERRA, an old destroyer tender or repair ship.

I managed to drag my weary body and sea bag up the brow. I saluted the officer of the deck as Worshick had taught and asked permission to come aboard. Someone must have informed them of my arrival because the messenger of the watch led me down to a berthing compartment deep in the bowels of the ship. They directed me to a rack but provided no locker. I had to make do with binding my canvas sea bag to a nearby supporting stanchion. I fastened it securely with my issued combination lock and hit my pit, the top tree of a three high bunk system. It was my first night on a U S Navy ship and I slept like a baby. That morning the 1MC or general announcing system blasted me out of the rack. "*Reveille, reveille reveille, all hands heave out and trice up. Smoking lamp is lit in all authorized spaces. Sweepers sweepers man your brooms. Give the ship a clean sweep down fore and aft. Sweep down all passageways, ladder wells, and ladder backs. Empty all trash and garbage into the proper receptacles provided for on the pier. Now sweepers" 'Set material condition Yoke throughout the ship. Make Yoke reports to Damage Control Central. Mess gear; clear the Mess Decks."*

These messages were coming at me out of the speaker above my head faster than a hungry hound dog on a bowl of *Gravy Train*. It was an endless barrage of odd verbiage that I had no inkling of the meaning. I was such a rookie. I clambered out of my pit and leapt down to the deck where I surveyed my first ship board shock.

There stood the stanchion with my sea bag still firmly locked, yet slit from top to bottom. Most of the clothing remained but wallet and valuables were long departed. I was devastated and my immediate thought was to head back to the friendly confines of Western Pennsylvania. Talk about livid. A nihilistic view of life crept like an invasive poison vine into my psyche. I was boiling, I was a crime victim my very first night on a Navy ship.

But I could go nowhere. Some despicable scoundrel had my wallet. I had no money, no ID. I felt like a United States Navy refugee. I was stuck in an unfriendly place and as I gazed around I realized that I did not even know how to leave the berthing compartment. I finally queried a few Sailors and the master at arms appeared. I eventually made it to an office where I luckily met up with the heroic PN2 Blass. Fortunately my tiny service record had made it to the personnel office under the care of this PN2. Blass had me retell my story and I could see he was genuinely empathetic to my plight. Several things happened after that. Blass spoke for awhile and discovered that I was from the Pittsburgh area. He informed me that he was the relative of Pirate pitcher *Steve Blass*. That immediately gave PN2 instant credibility of the highest order. We talked a little baseball. He then set it up for me to get a little advance pay from disbursing. Blass got me down to the SIERRA photo lab for a new ID card. He also ensured that me and my remaining things were placed in a berthing compartment with a rack and a locker. He had me assigned to the Chief's Mess for a job and he found out that the USS LAWRENCE was headed home from Vietnam and would return to port in just a few short weeks. Was PN2 Blass a hero? You bet your ass he was. Sailors can become bad eggs and misfits based on those beginning impressions and initial experiences aboard ship. An experienced petty officer who takes the time to help a young apprentice in need is heroic in many ways. That is why to this day, even though I am sure that he holds no recollection of this event, PN2 Blass' name is reverently remembered by me, and I would speculate many others.

My first job on the SIERRA was to keep the Chiefs' head clean. Gleaming shitters, soap scum free shower stalls, or rain lockers, and sparkling stainless steel. The Navy loves shiny metal like koala bears love eucalyptus. As one might expect, the air in my working environment would often present a less than optimum condition, but for the most part head maintenance proved an easy task. Being a very junior Sailor and cleaning are truly synonymous terms. If you join, you will in the beginning clean something. Always be thankful for dirt. It creates employment.

After my bumpy beginning aboard SIERRA, I soon discovered that the tender was a fascinating ship. I loved the smell of their environment. The machinery oil, the burning metal of the weld shop, and the constant racket of lathes and other intricate machinery, was intriguing to me. There were so many people turning to, effectively doing their jobs, keeping a fleet of destroyers, cruisers, and frigates repaired and in fighting condition. Tenders create technicians. Tender Sailors are anything but tender. They have a unique opportunity to really learn their rates whenever assigned as a crew member to one of these bustling ships.

My first memorable job came during my second week aboard SIERRA. Blass assigned me to a week long task assisting a Seabee in building a pavilion for housing motorcycles near pier twenty-one. We bolted that structure together in a few days, and for the next twenty-six years I often bragged to any listener about how I helped put that old rusty thing together. Personally, I believed it was a work of art. It was a sculpture of practicality so to speak, but because I helped to create it, I ranked it right up there with the US Steel Building and Three Rivers Stadium.

I managed an occasional trip home to Pennsylvania for a weekend now and then. It is rather humorous and ironic that so many of us join the Navy to see the world and to get away from home, just to turn around and make great efforts to get back to the place we escaped at every available opportunity. I was no different, and was often a passenger headed up Interstate 64 and 95. I really did nothing special while there. It was justifiable to make the trip though because I was now making an impressive 330 dollars a month. Most of that was mine, except of course for my four leaf clover payment.

I almost began to feel as if I were part of the SIERRA crew when I received word that the USS LAWRENCE was pulling in. Once again the adrenaline kicked in, and I felt the anticipation I had for the high seas adventures in my near future. I was thinking ports of the world, here comes the Z man; destroyer style. I quickly packed up my sea bag and began my SIERRA checkout. When I walked off that brow I didn't look back. I was about to become a *destroyerman.*

Chapter Three:

THE LAWRENCE

I clearly remember that winter day when the LAWRENCE pulled into port from Nam. The ship spent a long deployment running the hostile coast line and providing gunfire support near shore. They had significant shrapnel damage on their starboard side, wounds of pride for being in harm's way. The crew earned a respectable number of ribbons and they were very much ready for the comforts of home. They wanted to stand down about as badly as I wanted to get going. It was 1973 and the war was winding down to its final conclusion. I was going to experience the post-war peacetime Navy of the 70's This Navy would endure its own set of social and economic problems and all of us would be a part of it, but on this day Fireman Apprentice Zahratka was about to report to, "*My Ship.*"

When I trudged up to the LAWRENCE's arriving pier, seabag over the shoulder, there was an impressive crowd gathered for the ship's homecoming. Family members, dignitaries in dress blue uniforms, and other related well wishers were all on hand waiting to greet the crew. This was a scene I would see duplicated many many times over the coming years. It is also a scene that never gets old. One of life's greatest rewards is a return to someone who cares.

The ship rounded the carrier piers shortly thereafter, tugs alongside, the little dynamos determined to bring the ship in. The bow sweep of the Adam's class DDG was gorgeous. The perfect visual of a warship, DDG 4 was an awesome sight. All flags were displayed, while the crew manned the rail in the traditional manner. Family members shrieked with joy whenever they spotted a loved one in the line of blue.

Lines were tossed, and the ship was quickly tied up. Some instructions were barked out on the 1MC and the brow was made fast in record time. There was no delay in getting the men off and liberty call went down quickly. The crew came off that ship like a herd of stampeding cattle. As the crew came down, FA Zahratka and his seabag were going up, and the bony fireman was losing the battle. A jubilant cook shouted as he passed by, "*You are lucky reporting on the ship right now man. We probably won't go anywhere for a year.*" It was a devastating message. I was assigned to a ship tied to the pier for a year. There were a multitude of issues facing the officer of the deck at that particular moment and he justifiably shuffled his newest crewmember momentarily off to the side. Being as confused as Adam on Mother's Day, I stood waiting for direction of some sort. Now, if I had been a more experienced Sailor I would have checked into the ship about two to three hours after it arrived when crowds had departed and the OOD was not heavily engaged in crowd control and immediate ship utility issues. My journey up that brow while a crew of Nam vets were going home for the first time in over a half year would not get me elite membership in the exclusive club of rocket scientists or an invite to a psychology think tank, but it was a boot camp thing to do and the watch section undoubtedly expected it.

Eventually someone escorted me below decks to the engineering berthing compartment. I was directed to a top rack as I believe is the initial lot for all boot camp arrivals. Racks were three high. The senior petty officers earned the middle racks. The junior petty officers inherited the bottom, while the rookies were forced to the top tree. I did not mind. At least I had a base. Top rack holders received a bulkhead mounted locker, while the middle and bottom guys had lift up coffin lockers. Their clothing and personal items went into the coffin, not the Sailor. The mattress covered the top of the coffin rack. Adorning each tiny enclave were a set of pull curtains granting a small measure of privacy. Any way you analyzed it, personal space was at a premium on a DDG. It was occasionally stated that prison inmates received more personal space that a *tin can Sailor*. Unfortunately that statement is true. If you are uptight about the issue of personal area then a U S Navy destroyer or frigate is probably not your most compatible environment.

If the berthing compartment was tight, the head was rather spacious. The only problem was that three separate berthing compartments all used the same head. There was about a half dozen of each item; showers, sinks, shitters, and pissers. But the only time crowding presented a problem was usually right after reveille or immediately after chow.

Although I didn't have a profound sense of knowing right then, I would clean every inch of that head many times over during the next six months. I would know it well. I would be as familiar with the gleaming shower nozzles as a raccoon is with a favorite garbage can. It was I, Fireman Apprentice Zahratka, defender of the Constitution of the United States of America, against all enemies foreign and domestic who was going to execute my duty as head cleaning expert of the USS LAWRENC aft head shower stalls. It was my destiny.

As a fireman apprentice undesignated, I could have been assigned to any number of shops around the ship. Back in 1973 and still in effect today every Sailor that passed through the chow line had to get qualified in general damage control. Every Sailor reporting had to go through an indoctrination period, just so you knew how to get around and what the rules were. There were a multitude of safety issues to be aware of. You had to learn about everyday things such as laundry days, and liberty call. You had to know about the barbershop sign up list, and pay days. There were muster times and mess hours. You had to learn about sick call and request chits. You had to understand what uniforms you could wear aboard ship and what was allowed on the base. Senior crew members taught you about club rules and local alcohol consumption laws. Information came at you faster than the gossip at a wife's club meeting. If a young Sailor remembered ten percent of all the information he was receiving then he was doing fine.

Learning my way around the ship was an ongoing process. There were thousands of nooks and crannies to explore. Nevertheless, navigating the bowels of a ship was a process that was quickly learned. Surprised, I was actually impressed by my own mental prowess with traveling from one place to the next. I often enjoyed watching the very tall guys navigate through a tight passageway with a low overhead. It was as if their heads had a type of *GPS or DOPPLER* system that alerted them to the perfect moment to duck or swerve to avoid a low hanging valve or cable bracket.

My very first LAWRENCE job was buffing a main passageway. The narrow piece of real estate had green deck tile and pea green bulkheads. On the skin of the ship it was haze gray, but the interior belonged to pea green. I made the deck a mirror from end to end. It was a passageway outside of sickbay so those who felt ill could at least be pacified in a squared away environment as they waited for the ship's corpsman, known affectionately on all ships "*the Doc.*"

The LAWRENCE Doc was quite a character. He was a colorful spokesman and was highly renowned in two major areas. One was his venereal disease lecture. It was known to scare people so bad that they would dead bolt their zippers shut in mortal terror. The idea of the burning piss from hell, or even worse, the dreaded chancre of the syphilis spirochete was enough to turn an impressionable fireman into a monk. That driven fear from that lecture probably saved many a young Sailor from the pain of a frightening venereal disease. Doc was also something of a witch doctor. He had perfected a marvelous concoction which he called "*the hangover kit.*" No one knew exactly what was in this famous potpourri of pills and vitamins, but the imbibing sector of the crew swore by it.

Drinking was not a problem in the 1973 Navy. Sailors went out got drunk, came back to the ship, slept it off, no problem. It wasn't until much later in history that ideas started to change. The physical readiness test, body fat standards, healthy environments, and even hearing protection were still struggling into the process of Navy life. Programs that promoted a wholesome healthy life style started to take hold in the 80's, but the 70's were the final death throws of the traditional Sailor stereotype. The girl chasing partying Sailor still held some validity in the overall snapshot of the 1970s post Nam Navy; however; to deem most Sailors as sexy Casanovas was in most cases a wild stretch of the imagination.

Within our small enclave of the real Navy we had a very large group that was there for practical reasons. Many of the LAWRENCE Sailors that I first encountered felt that the comparatively secure environment of a ship was a better choice than a jungle foxhole. What we had was quite a group that thought ocean trumps army. I can't say I blame them. I read *General Frank's* book *American Soldier* and I have to agree that for the most part the Navy got the gravy and the Army got the beans in that war. I write this fully aware that there were numerous exceptions, but overall, the GI and Marine had it tougher than the Blue Jacket; pilots, swift boat crews, and of course POWs notable exceptions.

Most of this group ("*of not intending to stay twenty*"), were knowledgeable professional Sailors. They just weren't real hip on the military obedience issues. Finding opportunity to stretch the rules, they stretched them; like a bored ten year old with *Silly Putty* in a church pew.

One skinny electrician, known as Funny Weed termed any petty officer with at least one four year service stripe a "*Fuck'n Hasher*." That was Weed's endearing term for the careerist. He was a curly haired thin guy with a tough Philadelphia accent that I found out later was, in actuality a Northern Delaware dialect. Somehow he managed to make Delaware a two syllable word that came out *Delware*. It was amazing how much sound could come out of one human being. But he worked hard and while he was running his mouth, he always seemed to be in the process of pulling cable, crimping wire, or lacing a terminal box. Weed was your basic Sailor of the era. There wasn't a chance in Hell that he was ever going to reenlist or make *Sailor of the Quarter*, but some company back in *Delware* was going to get one hell of an electrician once he left the Navy.

At the time I bounced around the engineering department work centers sandwiched between house keeping duties, while I tried to determine what area of work I could engage in. This often presents a very traumatic experience for a young Sailor. Many Sailors chose the wrong rate at the ripe old age of eighteen or nineteen. Many a potential operations specialist or sonar tech got out because he felt trapped in a job that he thought did not suit his abilities. Sometimes schooling and contract obligations required one to stay where they did not wish to be. It was difficult if not impossible to go from a critical job to one less critical, even though you discovered a better fit in another rating.

At that point in history, with a large deep water Navy, all the engineering jobs were critical. So if you were a *snipe*, (the nickname for an engineering rate) you remained a snipe. There was camaraderie amongst snipes. They were normally disrespectful and aloof to *twidgets* and ops types. A twidget is a highly trained electronics technician, a fire controlman, or a sonar tech. Although the Air Force would argue vehemently, they were the best technicians on Earth. But, because the electronics spaces were air conditioned, quiet, and very clean, that deemed all twidgets weak and inept men in the eyes of the snipes. In addition it was often noted that twidgets were so smart as to be determined void of all common sense. Not only was it said that twidgets and nukes were often challenged to walk and chew gum at the same time; they were also accused of using maintenance requirement card steps to change flashlight batteries. If truth be told they were often healthier and better athletes than the snipes because snipes usually smoked the most, slept the least, and rarely received the life enhancing rays and vitamin D of the sun.

On a 1200 PSI destroyer, the fire room was the closest thing there was to Hell on Earth. In comparison, the gas turbine ships of today, with their cool environment engine rooms are luxury yachts compared to the Adams's Class destroyers that operated before them, and later with them in the seventies, and eighties.

There were of course certain members of the crew who demanded one's utmost respect at all times. First and foremost was the all powerful DK or disbursing clerk. The master of pay was to be revered on all "*Small Boys*." One's pay hung in the balance and the disbursing clerk was given tremendous reverent power. Also adding to their elevated status was the fact that most ships had but one.

Of almost equal power were the night baker, and the ship's office personnelmen. The night baker's importance was self evident, while inflaming the wrath of the ship's office could cause all sorts of calamities. Misplacing critical paper has the ability to drive one into a rage of Neptunian proportions. Page two's, inaccurate sea duty calculations, failure to enter qualifications, and shoddy leave accounting have the ability to run vast quantities of cortisol through one's arteries in an ever tightening grip on the blood flow to the heart. The internal stress inferno inside the Sailor's body caused by a callus ship's office was probably the leading cause of early death in the 1970's Navy. Collision at sea ran a distant second.

If your ship had a competent personnel chief he was worth his weight in gold, to be protected like the *Holy Grail.* Luckily for the USS LAWRENCE, all key positions were filled with masterminds. LAWRENCE was blessed.

As I felt my way around the ship, I acquired a better understanding of the actual jobs that were available to me as a striker. The first place I stumbled into was the hull technician's shop. The hull technicians or HTs did both welding and plumbing and I still remembered verbatim Bogey's advice to be a "*fuck'n plumber*." To be honest, I just wasn't feeling it in the HT Shop. It was too crowded, too hot. OK, I guess I was a woos at the time. However, I did enjoy repair division's sense of humor. Of all the engineering divisions they were probably the greatest of the "pranksters." This was evidenced by a major command inspection when the commodore and his staff inspected the ship. R division, primarily the HTs and the electrical types was tasked for a personnel inspection in their Service Dress Blue uniforms. Hidden in defiance below their pant legs were bright red socks. The wily commodore commanded the division to raise their right pant leg. On command a row of red socks was brightly displayed. R division suddenly looked like a row of Vegas showgirls who had overdosed on ugly pills. The young division officer's face was every bit as red as those socks. You really do not want to know the aftermath of the "*Red Sock Incident*."

At any rate, I respected the guys in R division. They were mostly the manly man types. They worked hard and knew how to fix, and engineers were all about fixin. Sometimes a personality flaw could be overlooked when a guy worked all night welding a leaky feed water system. There were trade offs.

I also experienced the hell of the fireroom. The LAWRENCE had two of these, one forward of the crew's mess and one aft. Whenever the plant was lit off and steaming, you had to enter holding the ladder rails with machinery rags to prevent the flesh from burning on your hands. The watch team maintained a close eye on the gauges and steam pressures of the plant, under the saving grace of huge blower motors that kept it all barely tolerable. The 1200 PSI fireroom wasn't for the weak. Not only were the BTs the hardest workers on the ship, they also worked the most hours.

The main engine room or Main Control was manned by the machinist's mates or MMs. The enginerooms were also hot but nowhere near the heated ovens that were the firerooms. MMs were the ship's tear it apart and put it back together guys. Enginerooms were often meticulously clean but incredibly noisy. The guys who worked there longest could usually give you the first and last names of all the nuts and bolts that held the space together. They communicated over loud bullhorn systems amplified to a level required to exceed the decibels of turbines, fans, pumps, motors, gears, and generators. It could be a dangerous place, but at the same time it was an interesting place. The firerooms and enginerooms were simply known as the "*holes*." The men that operated and repaired the equipment in those spaces were the "*snipe*s" Hence the name *hole snipes* aptly labeled the machinists mates and the boiler techs.

I thought about the fireroom as a place to work. It wasn't the work that attracted my attention as much as I just thought the B Division guys were cool. They were always cut'n up and their chief didn't really care what they looked like as long as they kept working their derrieres off, the same way he did. If you were to line the whole crew up on any given day, you could easily pick the BTs out of that line up. They were the *SOS group;* scruffy, oily, and smelly.

The enginemen were fix it guys who perpetually remained in an incessant state of working long hours. They had more maintenance requirements on their equipment than a beaver colony making a move to a new river bend. They were interminably working on everything from evaporators, to galley gear, to small boats. An engineman with nothing to do was an engineman on leave. The nature of the beast in "A Gang" was the perpetuity of the work list.

I thought about the EN rating as a possibility. After all, AC&R guys could end up in a lucrative civilian job after completing their service. This was an industry that was in demand, and would no doubt continue to grow. That was true then and is still true today. For many years the United States Navy has produced highly sought after civilian work force members and it continues to do so today. Sailors make great civilian employees. They bring hard skills to the work force. After working in the environments that they experience, then nothing you task them with in the civilian sector will upset them. If you have the wherewithal to work in cramped quarters, or in a super heated hell that rolls and pitches, while getting your rest in a 120 man bedroom then the remainder of America's employers are unlikely to provoke you with their assigned tasks.

Mulling over my options as an undesignated striker, I moved around from one house keeping job to the next all the while continuing to explore all areas of the ship. One morning I discovered by chance a small scuttle opening below the engineering log room, near the center of the ship just below the gun plot computer room. I passed through that scuttle, and through that hole I entered my destiny.

When I stumbled through that scuttle I knew I was home. It was an innate feeling. I had reached my own personal *Nirvana*, knowing inherently this place was special. It looked important and it was. Granted, the room was small, but it was filled with an impressive array of colorful switches, gauges, meters, and littered with technical looking equipment for electrical and electronic testing. Sailors know this space as the IC Room or Interior Communications Room. It is the home of the ship's electrical gyrocompass, telephone switchboard, and the control panel for the 400 hertz motor generators that supplied power to the ship's weapon's system computers. The lord of this kingdom of components was IC1 Schmidt, a veteran of double digit years and overall one of the third planet's genuine good guys. That day when I discovered Schmidt with his feet up on the top of the Mark 19 Gyrocompass reading a technical manual authored by someone named *Hefner*, I knew that this was the place for me. I had spent quite a few weeks observing a group of the hardest working men in some of the most tasking conditions. All of those jobs had merit, but talking to Schmidt about the IC rating was really the fit I was seeking. When I discovered that the IC Gang was part of engineering then that was it for me. All it took from this point was making a hard plea to the electrical division chief to grant me a shot with the electricians and IC men of R Division. Chief Jones was a fair minded guy and he loved his Sailors. One thing destroyer chiefs have is *juice*. Chief Jones had been in for over twenty years already and it was widely known around the ship that he had what we referred to as "*most juice*." Normally when guys like Jones wanted something to happen: you guessed it, it usually happened. You hear it stated quite often that chiefs run the Navy. Well, believe it, because it is true.

With my case pleaded, coupled with a good track record in my titivation efforts at various locations on the ship as a personal selling point, Chief Jones talked to someone in the chief's mess and I was granted a trial membership in the electrical section of R division. Feel free to guess what my first R division assignment was. I was unceremoniously elected as the division representative and shower cleaning technician to the aft head. I was on the move.

When I was a small boy I would earn popsicles for helping my mother clean our modest brick ranch. Later I would entertain my small army of maternal aunts by telling them I wished to pursue the field of ash tray washing once I grew up. The smoking felines loved me saying that for some reason. However, at the age of eighteen I was surprised to actually be fulfilling that particular destiny. I thought that my future would hold more than a scrub brush and general purpose soap. As a USS LAWRENCE Shower Technician or *LST*, as my self anointed acronym states, I learned a myriad of tricks to employ in the pursuit of cleanliness. I was introduced to the acidic quality of bug juice for metal cleaning, the wondrous properties of the product *Neverdull*, and the application of cigarette ashes to shine metal. The extraordinary uses of vinegar were also a part of the pristine cleaning equation used on my shower stalls.

A ship is all about routine and mine was falling into place. Reveille, shower, breakfast, morning quarters, and off to the showers to do my duty. I would usually have some type of indoctrination class in the afternoon or a general military training session if scheduled. The executive officer's morning inspection brought him into the aft head around 1100. He seemed like a nice enough fellow considering XOs are supposed to be assholes. As a fireman apprentice with less than six months in, I feared the XO.

The XO was fine if the showers were clean and mine always were. It really surprised me that the XO cared so deeply about the cleanliness of my water world there in that small enclave of the aft head. He admired and examined the space as a curator of a natural history museum would admire the new Tyrannosaurus Rex display. He left no rubber floor mat unturned. I thought that I would hate to live at his house. The cleaning that must have gone on there was unimaginable.

The ship was in an ongoing process of getting people back from their long leave periods after the Vietnam deployment, so the swing into a full routine was gradual. For myself, I was just glad that I had the showers to clean instead of the shitters. Not that cleaning shitters was demeaning or anything. No, I felt rather sorry for the shitter guy because he had to put up with the smell of one 1st class petty officer from the supply department who conducted all of his leading petty officer duties from the seat of stall number one. He was a heavy guy, and didn't move around much. He would start the day right there on the pot. Clip board in hand, he would tidy up his daily paperwork, processing chits, ordering supplies, and generally handling his duties quite well. People also knew where to find him so he would be able to direct the subordinate seamen under his cognizance to their assigned tasks. He would flush and abandon his position about ten minutes before the XO would show up for his morning inspection of the space. It wasn't that he was a bad guy or even lazy, he just had a physical thing going on and he dealt with it. As far as shitters go at least we had partitions, although stall doors would be for the next generation of destroyers. One salty old WWII retired master chief, the renowned AOCM Miguel Nunez informed me years later about the head on one of his first ships back in the 40's. He said "*There was just a line of commodes with little space between you and your neighbor. When one wiped he had to be careful just to make sure he got his own ass and not that of his shipmate.*" Perhaps we should have been more appreciative at the time of the habitability advantages that we LAWRENCE Sailors had over our sea service predecessors. With all that, I was still glad I was doing showers until............

All ships I've been told have at least one sick individual that becomes the representative *phantom shitter*. These stealthy but sick individuals actually crap somewhere on the ship. Just not in the normal porcelain place. It is an in house terrorist act designed to maximize the discomfort of the perpetrator's shipmates. It is definitely a person who has slipped through the recruiter's scrutiny to get in the Navy in the first place. The culprit's profile will obviously fit nicely in some chapter of the DSMIV's analysis of abnormal psychology. How he slithers into our ranks I know not, but there he lurks like some latent virus ready to infect the comfort, well being, and sanitation of us all.

I was victimized several times over the course of the next few weeks; Dung in the stall. Putrid and pathetic evidence of his sickness was deposited for me to remove, but we could not make an apprehension, despite the determined efforts of the roving watches and leading petty officers. Crap was occurring in random places. The XO was on a mission to apprehend the *Dungmeister*. He held all hands TV quarters to publicly address the situation to the crew. He discussed the sick phantom defecator that was plaguing us, and he assured us that the abnormal perpetrator would soon experience justice. The next morning the XO discovered a pile outside his stateroom door.

It was random chance when he was caught. An affable BT2 from the forward fireroom was returning late from the strip when he happened upon a smallish man squatting over his neatly placed cowboy boots next to his locker. That young man's military career ended soon after. The next day he was led off the brow, removed from the ship never to return. In an earlier era he would have been marched off the fantail into *Davey Jones's Locke*r to support the carnivorous members of the ocean's food chain. On that day, my guess is that he went to the care of the local naval hospital psychiatric facility. For the crew and myself the scourge ended, my showers glimmered again. No further gifts awaited me at the beginning of my daily routine

Eventually my days in the showers came to a close and I began to integrate with the IC Gang as the interior communications electricians are universally called. Our leader was Schmidt, the petty officer first class or IC1. He had a quick wit, a great sense of humor, and a knack for giving people nicknames. Because of my typically long Czechoslovakian last name I became Zeke. Schmidt was an easy going guy and he allowed me the opportunity to learn all that I could from the two resident petty officers Knight and Horgan. I believe both of those guys were more talented than their rank indicated. Maybe they were there just to do their part because of the war, we never discussed that. They may have been there in the Navy not to be in the Army. IC3 Knight was a superstar. College educated from North Carolina State, he was a well spoken person who had a very polite manner and a very patient attitude. If I had to make a guess abut what he was doing today I would wager college professor or possibly a bank president. Everyone on the ship loved Knight. He was an All American type and exactly the kind of guy the Navy wished to keep in its fold. Of course to an undesignated and very green fireman apprentice such as myself, Knight was not only the macaroni, but also the cheese. Although it would have been easy to ignore an undesignated fireman apprentice, Knight chose the opposite. He actually invested a great deal of time trying to provide me with a basic understanding of electrical theory and the principles that caused that amazing IC gear to work.

Unfortunately, despite Knight's best efforts, electrical theory was completely over my head. To Knight's credit, he gave it a shot and he continued to instruct his prodigy at every opportunity. Knight was always undaunted by my jaw sagging looks of total incomprehension as he launched into explanations of the differences between AC and DC current, or the properties of zener diodes as voltage regulators. I believe he just kept throwing the knowledge in my direction in the heartfelt desire that some of it would stick. What was great about this personable learning process was that one of the most popular and important petty officers on the ship, was truly concerned about the education of a lowly fireman apprentice.

Horgan was a soft spoken serious type from a small town in one of the Dakotas. I'm not sure which Dakota, but if it wasn't South, then it was surely North. Whereas Knight was the communicator and technical theory troubleshooter, Horgan liked to get out and fix stuff. I learned tons of practical knowledge from the handy Horgan. He was at ease with tools and an outstanding troubleshooter. He could make logical sense out of the most bizarre problems.

As for myself, I assisted those two guys, always playing the gopher when required. I also handled a tremendous amount of house keeping duties. I received a lifeboat assignment and a general quarters station. I became the phone talker in a repair locker, under instruction of course. Because IC men repaired sound powered phones, they usually ended up as phone talkers. I suppose someone thought it was a natural fit, although over time I have met many IC men who could fix phones but were hardly *Orson Wells* in their speaking skills.

Finally at some point we got the ship underway. Fireman Apprentice (FA) Zeke got sea sick and all that comes with it, or rather comes up because of it. Schmidt of course exacted great pleasure and glee in witnessing my condition. As a matter of entertainment old salts never tire at the spectacle of a landlubber adapting. After a time we did some operation or other that lead to a rewarding liberty visit to the US port of Saint Thomas in the Virgin Islands. A beautiful place on the island, *Meggins Bay Beach* presents one of the most picturesque places on earth, a true jewel in anyone's estimation. By day that was the location to visit for snorkeling, sunbathing, or gawking. By then the LAWRENCE IC Gang had its newest member on board, ICFA Ray C something, a young guy from one of the square states in the Midwest. My guess is Ohio.

Ray, who somehow had picked up the nickname Snide, became by natural selection my good buddy and co-liberty exploration specialist. That day, liberty call consisted of a very pleasant trip to the idyllic Meggin's Bay Beach. That evening's adventure found us at a very interesting local carnival. The festival was not a tourist affair, but a local event mainly attended by the island residents. We marveled at a very capable steel band for awhile before realizing that it was time to return to the ship.

Returning to the ship meant navigating our way back by street for most of the route; however, there was a short distance that was traversed by a tiny path off the road. By not paying attention to our surroundings, and walking this secluded area alone, meant we were not candidates, nor nominees for the cognitive blue ribbon. *You guessed it.* We experienced a very exciting next five minutes, as the horde of friendly locals relieved us of our money and valuables. The nice young man who robbed me actually stated, "*I don't want your fuuucking ID card Mon, just your fooo..cking money!*" I didn't know he also wanted my pants. We were a sad duo on our way back to the ship, sporting a few bruises and no clothes; yet we still clung to our valid green ID cards. It was a helluva first port. The next morning when Knight saw me he exclaimed "*Damn Zeke you must have had one heck of a good time*!" That I did. That I did.

The LAWRENCE eventually made her way back to Norfolk and there we sat tied to the pier forever, or so it seemed. Being in port was usually quite satisfying for the family guys, but for the wanderlust group it could drag. In 1973 the great evening activity for those of us who lived aboard was drinking beer at the strip. Outside of the destroyer/submarine piers, or D&S gate, Hampton Boulevard led you to the main gate, about a mile down the boulevard to the left. There was also a turn to your left at the main gate that continued down to the supply ship piers. To connect between D&S and NOB you actually had to leave through the gate of one and enter through the other. Today the base is continuous with expanded piers and many new structures. There is no need to travel out of a gate in order to enter the other side of the base.

The strip existed between the D&S pier gate to the main gate, and continued on through the left dogleg, almost the entire distance to the waterfront. It covered well over a mile with establishments located on both sides of the street. It consisted of a long line of bars and honkey tonks that were filled with "*buy me drink girls*" Sailors could get paid, walk to the strip, spend two weeks pay, and return to the ship broke for the next two weeks. Not that I resembled that unfortunate group, but because most young Sailors did not have cars the strip was well attended. There was an alternative, which was catching the base shuttle to the enlisted club, called the *Tradewinds*. For some reason I believe that every Sailor port on earth has a bar with that name. At the *Tradewinds* a Sailor could purchase a 3.2 percent draft beer under the age of twenty-one. That of course has changed. Whether you agreed with that or not is a mute point because that is one law that won't change anytime soon. The strip had its cast of characters, but I mainly remember it as one big "*Dude Fest*, lots of guys, very few women. The ranks were still void of sea going women. The girls in the bars were there to talk their lonely victims out of their paychecks by cajoling the lonely seafarer into purchasing her numerous fruity watered down drinks. At this, they were adept. After teasing their male suitors throughout the evening, in the end they were whisked away at closing time by their long haired live in boyfriends, while the jilted Casanova trudged back to Compartment 3-527-1-L or something like that for a few hours of sleep prior to reveille.

It is natural to assume that lessons are learned from experiences such as these, but alas the lonely heart is a powerful motivator, and many Sailors were doomed to repeat performances again and again. Sailors are after all is said and done, *creatures of routine,* and the Hampton Boulevard strip was a part of that routine for many. I readily recall the awful billboard that greeted you when you left the gate. The message was from a uniform and tailor business; its enticing caption emblazoned with the words *"You can Owe the Big O."* Yes, easy credit followed the fleet and promises of love were right around the corner.

When the strip was plowed under several years later and Hampton Boulevard became a more traffic friendly avenue, some lamented the loss of their favorite tavern. Some rejoiced and bid good riddance to the urban blight. Everyone else just went five miles away to Ocean View.

Often Snide and I, the two shop members who were too poor to live off the ship would spend a great deal of time cleaning or field- daying the IC Room. We would shine the ladder back and the large brass alarm bells. We would fix sound powered phones and use the soldering equipment. We viewed the IC Room in the same manner an astronaut looks upon the control room of a space shuttle, only we had to deal with gravity. To us, it was a very unique place. After our cleaning efforts in the evening, Schmidt would appear the next morning and make a really big deal out of our results.

The IC gear was really fascinating stuff. Most of the equipment consisted of electromechanical devices that provided operations and weapons systems with useful information in heading, ship's speed, wind speed and direction, dial up telephone, and 400 Hertz generated power. The most interesting devices in the IC Room were the 1MC central amplifier, the telephone switchboard, and the Mark 19 Mod 3A electrical gyro compass with its associated control cabinet. The 1MC system or the ship's main announcing circuit had these very interesting gas filled thyratron power tubes that gave a very eerie purple glow whenever the quarterdeck or bridge keyed their remote microphone. The ship's gyrocompass control cabinet had a series of visual red targets that were in a constant state of spin when the ship was underway. These little targets were mechanically bound to the shafts of interesting electromechanical devices called resolvers that provided compensation signaling to the gyro for forces of horizontal and vertical earth rate errors. At that time my training was limited, so to me that equipment worked on the *FM Principal*. We called that *Fuck'n Magic*. As I was to learn there were times that things would break, then there were times when they would function again for no reason. That was always referred to as an *FM* repair.

One thing you could count on as an IC man on a Navy destroyer is that your services were in demand. The shop phone would ring off the hook, the 32 MC would clamor for your services, and the 1MC was constantly paging the duty IC man. At the time Snide and I were learning, Schmidt was doing the leading petty officer administrative duties, while Knight and Horgan, like two squirrels gathering nuts for the winter, were constantly on the go from one end of the ship to the other. They were in a state of perpetual frenzied activity.

Whenever one of the holes called it was a mission that had to be met immediately. Those guys did not like waiting, especially if their amplified went down or a salinity cell to a boiler stage was reading high and did not match the water chemistry test.

The oddity of all personnel who used the engineering amplified circuit, or 2JV as it was called, was that they would all develop a temporary lower Alabama accent, and this was a few years prior to "*Smokey and the Bandit*." Everyone on the 2JV sounded that way, it mattered not whether they were from Maine or Minnesota, get on the 2JV and you transformed into pure lower Alabama. Like a linebacker for *Paul Bear Bryant* one would drawl out "*Main One, Bravo Four, I needda IC Man for slinity cell num'er sic, ya'll*." Once off the amplified it was back to vintage Vermont or the long pronounced vowels of Ohio.

This strange transformation only happened with engineers on their circuits. On the ships maneuvering and docking circuit, or 1JV, the bridge watch's main communication circuit, they made a diligent effort to speak with blue blooded diction. Most of the phone talkers knew that the captain or executive officer may well be monitoring them at any given moment. It was imperative that they be understood. One mistake and someone could end up dead, a victim of synthetic line snap back, collision, or even an accident with the anchor chain. The 1JV phone talker on the bridge usually ended up being a very clear voiced administration type. A good personnelman often ended up in that position. On the LAWRENCE it did not matter what rate you were, there were seaman duties that you participated in without question. You may file records for a living, but you would also pull an underway replenishment cable, or handle a hose on the fire party. The rule has always been Sailor first, rate second, and there were no unions.

Snide was an A school graduate from the IC school in San Diego, California. He knew much more than I did because he had training on the basics. I was trying to learn what I could but the going was tough, especially with liberty call getting in the way. This was a nuisance and tended to interfere with my efforts at on the job training. To my credit, I did take the GED test, which some of my kindly shipmates referred to as the goofball education diploma, and I passed it with flying colors, scoring outstanding in all areas. This seemed to please my mother whom I had (dear soul) put through a period of *accelerated aging* during my infamous "*Revolution Years*."

At that point I had been a LAWRENCE crewmember for several months and I was getting comfortable in the shop, albeit I was the low rung on our little ladder of power. Momentarily I was content just being called an IC man. Having your name associated with a rate was actually a big deal. It sure as hell beat "*Recruit*." Now don't get me wrong, as far as the rest of the engineering rates were concerned we didn't do diddly squat. We were known as a *skate rate*. Not true of course, but IC men were always on that fine line between snipe and twidget, and no one really knew for certain what the hell we did...

I soon began to realize that in order to expand my horizon, it was imperative to gain some formal education. As I contemplated how to do that in the environment I found myself, the worthy (now IC2) Knight continued to obligate his time in a resolute and spirited effort to make me technically adept. The trouble was that it was difficult to understand the operation of magnetic amplifiers, and voltage regulators when to me *Ohm's Law* was something the shore patrol arrested you for. But as I learned, if you clean the ship well enough, don't get in trouble, while acting somewhat amenable to your coworkers, (*not conjunctive to an obsequious oral to rump resuscitator*); good things will usually happen for you in the Navy.

In my case it was a special offer for promising strikers to attend an A school. Because my showers were cleaned well, because I tried to learn from Knight and Horgan, and because I cleaned the IC room at night with Snide, I was deemed a promising striker.

I gave most of my thanks and credit for this opportunity to the strip outside the gate. If I had not routinely squandered my paychecks on the avenue of goodwill then I probably would not have cleaned that IC room at night out of boredom, and I probably would not have been included in the enviable group of "*promising strikers*." But because of my skill with Neverdull, I was called into the XO's sate room, given a motivational speech, and told I would soon be leaving for IC "A" School in San Diego, California. It was 1973. I had only been a LAWRENCE Sailor for a few months and good stuff was happening. I was also informed that this would be a temporary additional duty. I would be returning to the LAWRENCE after school. That was OK with me, because I had discovered by stealth that carriers really didn't have carpeted rooms. I liked the LAWRENCE just fine.

A month, maybe two passed before I left for "A" School and the time went quickly. We got underway sporadically to shake the rust off and it seemed as if the word would pass "*underway shift colors*," and the shit would immediately hit the fan. Knight and Horgan labored like inmates on a Georgia chain gang. I believe they slept, hmmmm…, never. They were constantly fixing alarms, phones, synchros, gyro repeaters, e call buzzers, and synchro amplifiers. Snide and I would usually tag along carrying the tools, but we were probably more pains in their asses than assets or assistants.

Schmidt would keep it real. He had a way of getting phrases moving around the ship. Once we were underway on an operation playing the role of bad guys, or the evil "*red menace of 50 years*." The bridge watch team, in order to get us motivated to participate with enthusiasm would refer to us as "*Comrade*s," on the 1MC. It wasn't long after that until Schmidt just labeled us plain old Communists. The evolution continued until the evolving vernacular settled with all of us being referred to as "*Communist Cockbites*." Our worthy electrician from Delaware expanded this colorful title to include all senior petty officers with over four years of naval service.

I loved the way the old salts talked. Communist cockbite was so much cooler than than I'm hip, or far out dude, the slang traveling around the strip. A hippie on the honky-tonk trail stood no chance with a tin can gunner's mate when it came to jacking the jaws. Give me that match up any time and I win ten out of ten in any verbal confrontation.

The day for "A" school finally arrived. I was packing up my seabag and getting ready to boogie. Knight was really pleased about the opportunity I was getting, as was Schmidt. Surprisingly Horgan really irritated me. He said, "*Zeke all you're going to do out there is screw around and have a good time because you don't give a crap about anything except partying.*"

I was more than slightly PO'd about Horgan's remarks. I left the quarterdeck thinking just one thing, one overpowering thought permeated through my young brain, "*I'll show Horgan who's going to succeed*!" I vowed to make Horgan eat his words. I was going to kick ass and take names, screw him. You know, that Horgan was one smart son of a bitch. His words motivated me more than anything else could. He knew it then, I knew it later.

I got to San Diego in warm weather. In San Diego it was always warm weather. It was a truly attractive place to be but I knew I was there to work. Besides, I was under the age of twenty-one and California had some very strict drinking laws. I would be doing very little socializing over the next few months. I checked into the barracks set aside for the "A" School students and was assigned to a room with a guy named Chris, a genuinely friendly young man from the LA area.

School started with a self- paced program of basic electronics and electricity referred to as *BEEP* School. You had a certain number of weeks to complete the program or you were awarded extra hours of supervised training. The decision was made for you that you were going to complete the program. I was on time. There was a metamorphosis occurring within me about then. Getting acquainted with technical terms was laying a foundation of confidence that was invigorating. I felt I was accomplishing something important. I did not wish to return to the ship and sit there listening to technical talk and not know beans about what was going on. Education was now something concrete and visible. I witnessed knowledge and training at work with Horgan and Knight. That was the goal, to be on a par with those guys. I was slowly becoming someone with a direction and it was a good feeling. This Navy I was involved in had a way of capturing and directing your energy into a goal. My old long haired friends from back home would have called it *brain washing*. Sailors called it *calibrating*. I was a fireman in the process of being calibrated. Filled with a jargon of technical terms that we only began to understand, my 'A" School peers and I impressed each other with discussions about impedance, inductive reactance, and the different configurations of transistor amplifiers. Magnetic amplifiers, Boolean logic, and multivibrators were discussion points shared to demonstrate our understanding to one another.

In the class room we had tremendous competition with each other. We had good instructors, boring instructors, and some fun instructors. One IC1 with an insect name such as Roach was enamored with shit can basketball. Juice and milk cartons flew into the shit can with dedicated precision. We had shit can basketball tournaments throughout that week, until the senior chief IC Man shut us down. I'm certain the IC1 had a few bites missing out of his derriere that day, but he was a good instructor and he sported an excellent left hook.

There was occasional liberty. Many movie theaters existed in San Diego at the time and the buses were very reasonable. *American Graffiti* hit the theaters that summer and I loved that movie ever since. To this day that sound track remains a classic in most Baby Boomer collections. That nostalgic movie must have affected someone on the top floor of the adjacent barracks as that sound track blasted through his kick ass stereo for weeks thereafter. The music provided a pleasant ambiance outside. For a few hours each evening the streets jammed with the *Wolfman*. No one complained, not even the shore patrol. The music was excellent and fit well in the cool California evenings.

A friend of mine from back in PA was stationed on a ship from 32nd Street in San Diego, and after I had been there for a month or two he discovered through the home front grapevine that I was there and he came looking for me. I'll tell you it is always a good thing to make a connection with a home boy. Mark and I had a couple of laughs talking about home stuff, but one of the big things Mark did for me was to introduce me to the young evolving Pittsburgh Steelers of the early seventies. Mark knew they were on local television there in San Diego that weekend and he suggested we hit the TV room in my barracks. I said "*you gotta be kiddin, the Steelers suck.*" Mark said "*No way man, these guys are actually pretty good.*" I was doubtful, but relented. We went into that barracks TV lounge and I witnessed these demons in black and gold assaulting some unfortunate team into a state of pathetic surrender. I watched this exciting fellow called Green chase people down like a junkyard dog after a filet mignon. I thought, "*holy hell, who are these guys*?" This was the beginning of a life long devotion to a great sports team. To me the Pittsburgh Steelers would from that day forward symbolize my connection to a city I would only visit sparingly in future years. The Steelers were always the banner that said home. They played the way Pittsburgh people acted. They were hard workers with heart. They became great in the future and I reveled in their glory from a distance. People who love the Steelers never change. They are what they are; die hard and faithful. But oh what a run that team of the seventies did indeed have.

The day when Mark introduced me to that talented team of 1973 I became hooked forever on the Pittsburgh Steelers. It was nice to be three thousand miles from home and watch your home town team kick ass and take names. I was to become from that point on what my shipmates disdainfully and often enviously referred to as an *obnoxious Steelers fan.*

Mark was an HT on one of the ships. He was truly a good guy and I thoroughly enjoyed the few liberties we had in San Diego. Very tragically he was killed in a hideous motorcycle accident a few short years later while back in Pennsylvania. I will always give Mark credit for turning me into a crazy Steeler fan for life.

As school drew to a close we pushed ourselves through intramural softball, then basketball. In class we traveled through solid state devices and blue print reading. In the four to six months I was in San Diego there was only one opportunity for a long excursion to see what was out there. During Thanksgiving weekend, a bubblehead (submarine Sailor) classmate and I rented a car and decided to tour Southern California. The mileage was limited so we had to disconnect the odometer cable for the trip. We ended up in the snow at Mount Palomar. We then cruised to the Salton Sea. Working our way to Palm Springs, we somehow coaxed the little car up the steepest mountains I had ever seen... California has that geographical diversity thing going on and it was clear how people got caught up in the whole "*California Dreamin*" mindset. For me, although it was still the USA, I was seeing the world and getting a close up view of those photos I had only known in my high school geography books. I had always harbored a secret inner fear that I would never get the opportunity to see these places I had read about. Each time I visited a famous historical place or saw an important geographical landmark I felt like joining the Navy was a good decision. I wasn't crazy about my short hair, but everyone on the base had short hair, so it was no big trauma. Thus far I felt like the Navy was doing me a world of good. Soon I would be returning to the USS

LAWRENCE. I was freshly trained, armed with months of electrical knowledge, calibrated and ready to take my place as a fully functioning member of the LARRY IC Gang.

Graduation at "A" School arrived, classmates high-fived, and bid each other farewell. Most of us would never cross paths again. I graduated with a respectable average in the top twenty percent of the class, and as I left for the airport I thought of Horgan and how he would have to eat his words. I thought of the technical jargon of the super tech Knight, and now I felt confident that I could at least communicate with him about the details on a blue print. I was eagerly looking forward to getting back and I was ready to roll. I had just over a year in and now I had Class A School under my belt. I thought I was ready to fix, and on a destroyer in engineering it was all about fixing equipment. I was determined that Schmidt would take notice that I now possessed talent that exceeded cleaning skills with a scrub brush.

When I arrived back at the ship I was to learn a very sound lesson. Situations on ships often change in the blink of an eye. What was today could be very different tomorrow. Being on sea duty and being predictable were about as synonymous as Newark, New Jersey and summer vacation spots.

When I finally made my triumphant return to the USS LAWRENCE, the Officer of the Deck greeted me with a "*Fireman Z, Petty Officer Knight is going to be glad to see you.*" I thought…*OK,* and made my way to Engineering berthing where I found out that E division had been moved to weapons berthing. I relocated there, unpacked, and settled in. Change was positive so far. I now had a coffin locker instead of a bulkhead mounted standup unit. The coffin locker was sectionalized and had a lot more room. One had about 70 plus inches of length, all for uniforms and personal stuff. The top propped up like the hood of a car, except instead of displaying a 400 cubic inch four barrel, it displayed your *Bryle Cream, High Karate*, and just for show *Trojans*.

I found Knight in the IC room and he was genuinely ecstatic to see me. He queried me at length about what I had learned and he seemed impressed that I did so well. Then he dropped the bomb about all that had happened in the past months...

Schmidt had decided to get out at mid career and to take a position in the gyro shop as part of shop 51 in the Norfolk Naval Shipyard. Horgan, who had been a short timer got out and went back to North or South Dakota. Snide was the strangest story of all. It seems that Snide, who was in reality an eccentric character anyway, became involved with a group that believed the *Comet Kahoutek* was going to crash the Earth reeking havoc on all of civilization. So the last thing that anyone could recall was Snide purchasing a survival book and heading off to the mountains. Kahoutek came and went but Snide stayed gone, leaving behind his legendary tale of a true natural survivalist. I never saw Snide again.

The very noble, yet exhausted Knight was making a valiant effort of going it alone. One man trying to maintain all that equipment was a monumental task at best, and Knight was spreading himself thin. He was making a valiant effort to hold down the fort until the cavalry arrived. It takes the bureau a little while to catch up when manning issues develop for unexpected reasons, submarine force excepted. Reliefs would be identified and sent, just not right away.

The IC shop was in shambles. Equipment and parts were scattered from one end to another. Knight was barely getting sleep, and he could not afford to take the time to field day. It then began to dawn on me that for now, I was the only cavalry that Knight was going to get. I was the posse riding in to save the brave and heroic Knight as he battled the IC gremlins of no mercy. "*Oh shit*", I thought. To add fuel to the whole inferno, Knight had about two weeks left before his enlistment ran out. Now, I was about to be up to my neck in alligators, and luckily, I was too naive for any of that to register just yet.

Knight spent his final two weeks lavishing upon me as much wisdom as he could about our gear and how it worked. We spent a significant amount of time of time going over the operating procedures of the Mark 19 gyrocompass, the lowering and raising process of the rodmeter for ship's speed data, and the items that required certification on our underway check off list. As one of the two remaining IC men, at least I was temporarily excused from any department housekeeping assignments. I felt as if my shower technician duties were finally behind me.

The learning curve I was experiencing in those few weeks was fast and furious. Finally Knight left forever. It seemed like ten minutes after I arrived and not the actual two weeks that had passed. Knight spent his last two days onboard basically talking to himself. He maintained a great deal of composure and class, but I knew he was more than ready to head to Raleigh. He had done his time and he was ready to get on with his life. Knight was one of those rare *Super Star Sailors*. I knew the chief's mess had pushed hard to keep him in the Navy. But in the end the Navy lost him as it did a lot of great Sailors in that decade. The pay at the time was not keeping pace with the civilian sector, and there was discontent as the so called transition to a peacetime Navy was in process. As long as our life long nemesis the Russian bear was making ships and planes the whole idea of a peace dividend ended up as some politician's wishful thinking. As this conflict of thought was taking place, many Navy professionals were feeling underpaid and over worked. Many people in mid career, people such as Schmidt were packing their seabags and moving on.

At the time, little of this big picture stuff was registering with me at all. I was a one year guy and I was having a pretty good time. I wasn't seeing all the other stuff. I knew there were some pot heads and general non military types around me, but they were everywhere at that time. At any rate there wasn't much I could do about it. I knew that many Sailors were partaking of the *heathen devil weed*. It was a part of that time. At any rate, who would know unless they were caught red-handed? So it was there, it was being smoked, and more than a few drug busts occurred on the ships of the seventies through locker searches, and Naval Investigative Service plants.

Personally, there I was, all alone in the shop, a force of one. Chief Jones was still there as the electrical chief. It wasn't that the electricians were unwilling to help me out, they often did, but those guys were also short handed and often they too were at work many hours after liberty call was passed. It wasn't that electricians and IC men could not do each other's jobs given the opportunity, but the opportunity had to avail itself for effective cross rate training.

Time was ticking for me and I was doggie paddling in a whirlpool that was sucking me down a drain. I thought that I would burn out, but just as I was being overwhelmed by the constant calls for service, be it sound powered amps in the holes, gyro repeater alignments on the bridge, or grounds occurring in the 2JV, my cavalry started to arrive. Not as a force of several which was needed desperately, but rider by rider, one at a time.

Chapter Four:

Keesey, Steve, and Mr. Spencer

Steve Parrot was the first to arrive. As I was to discover over time, one could not be creative enough to make up the swashbuckling, red neck, sportsman hunter, NRA card holding, right wing, beer drinking, cycle riding, verbose, and frugal Steve Parrott. Steve was to be a best friend for years. His amazing skills on economizing were…well……. legendary. Steve was an ICFN like me, fresh out of school and coming to his first duty station. From Woodbury, New Jersey, he did not quite project that distinct South Jersey diction. He spoke clearly and directly, and he was very outspoken. With that trait he was very South Jersey, with what you see is what you get. He maintained no facades. Steve had one great passion, guns. Bring up the subject of Rugers, Smith and Wessons, muzzle loaders, or shot guns, and he could talk like a fire arms technical manual editor. He was adept at tearing them apart and putting them back together. From what I observed, Davey Crockett didn't have shit on Steve as far as marksmanship was concerned. Steve didn't really fit in with the pot smoking peaceniks that were in our midst. He was more of the vocal "*I hate fuckin dopers*" type.

Another great event occurred about the same time as Steve arrived. We were blessed with the addition of our new division officer, the memorable Ensign Sam Spencer. Ensign Spencer was just like us. This was his first ship, and we were his first subordinates. He also had all of R division under his control. Ensign Spencer was a human form nautical version of *pure energy.* Possessing a very sharp wit; tactfulness did not maintain a place of high esteem with the ensign. Screw up and he would let you have it swiftly and without hesitation. He was all about production. He had a distinct voice, probably due to the high frequency of the vibrations of the atoms of which he was composed. He was the tallest person on the ship, overlooking even the great HT Italian *Mount* Polermo. He was somewhat of an athlete; lean and fit looking. Piss him off and he could be from his stateroom to your face in 3.06 seconds, blowing your hair back with an enthusiastic rendition of a NASCAR driver who ran out of gas at Daytona. When we first got underway together for a few short days of training operations he told Steve and I that it would be a good idea not to work more than eighteen hours in a given day. We should ensure that we get at least six hours of sleep per night. Of course this excessive benevolence overwhelmed us. Mr. Spencer took charge from day number one. Someone surely forgot to tell him that ensigns were supposed to just listen in the beginning until they knew something, but Ensign Spencer was full throttle from the moment he stepped on the brow for the first time. If he would have been under Robert E Lee at Gettysburg he would have kicked Picket's ass and charged up that hill first.

There were times despite my work with Knight and Horgan, and despite our A school training that Steve and I were overmatched by malfunctioning gear we had never even heard off. Often we had to work hard just to find out how to secure the power to the equipment. Maybe it was covered in A school, maybe we didn't remember it. After all, A school was for the basics. A patient and knowledgeable leading petty officer provided the real training and we didn't have one. Calls came in to the shop and off Steve and I would go to check out some strange electromechanical device, not having a clue about what it did or how it worked. On occasion we could wing it, but more often we just became frustrated. It was tough to learn by trial and error, and we ran the risk of causing further damage with our lack of experience.

We routinely found ourselves staring into things like dead reckoning analyzers and indicators, NC2 plotting systems, or dead reckoning tracers. These were ingenious pieces of equipment that were invented and manufactured in the days of gears, motors, transformers, and a slight sprinkling of transistors. The fifties technology permeated the Adam's class ship. Circuit card electronics were slowly being integrated into systems, on LAWRENCE they hadn't yet arrived as a function of a shipalt or an equipment update. Vacuum tubes were still a part of many amplifier circuits. These devices were actually more thought provoking to repair than the circuit card electronics that were then integrating into the new systems of electronics. We couldn't swap circuit cards to fix a fault; we had to look into gear assemblies and small motor brushes, or search for pinched interconnecting wiring. It was a challenge for two green fireman and we often chased our tails in frustration.

He arrived without fanfare. We received no prior warning of his arrival. He was just there one morning sitting in the IC Room. He may have ridden in on a nor'easter. He had the look of the old salts of the 1800s. A giant cup of coffee in his grasp, he looked to be maybe forty, or maybe seventy, it was impossible to tell behind the gray beard he sported. His dungarees weren't new, but they were meticulous with perfect creases. This guy looked like he could have been right off *Captain Ahab*'s whaler. I was floored at Steve's first comment, "*Wishbone*." What a hoot. Wishbone the cook from *Wagon Train,* old Charlie Wooster himself, was there in our shop. When he spoke he had a powerful way of communicating. He told us he was IC1 Keesey. I had no inkling of the effect that this guy would have on me, but today I can tell you that IC1 Donald W Keesey was the most influential person of my entire naval career. Everything I would need in order to be successful in the years ahead would be provided to me by Keesey. Over the next two years Keesey was going to be that old term *Sea Daddy* to a new group of young IC men. Steve and I were the first, but more were coming.

At that moment, he was *Wishbone from Wagon Train*, and we were very curious as to what he was about. He was reporting to the LAWRENCE from shore duty in Iceland. He let us know that he had been stationed on about fifty ships. Keesey looked like a Sailor. Maybe it was the beard, maybe not... He must have received some type of run down from Mr. Spencer or Chief Jones about our situation.

He let us talk. We unloaded our status report on all of our equipment trying to keep the conversation as technical as possible. He just nodded with a little smirk as we talked. After that he told us to take off and go on liberty. I said we have to check out with the division officer. Keesey said, "*Not anymore. I run liberty.*" That was that. Keesey was boss, and we were not. End of story, not really?

Reveille was at 0600. We usually nestled in our racks until about 0645 then rushed to the head and off to morning chow, speeding to beat the line closing. At 0555 the next morning I heard this gravelly voice saying "*Zeke, get up, reveille.*" I think I smacked my head on the bottom of the rack above as I sat straight up. For the next two years I woke up every morning to that voice, "*Zeke, reveille.*" You didn't argue with Keesey. He was a stickler for punctuality. He maintained a pace. It was the Keesey pace. Officers couldn't rush him, and subordinates couldn't slow it down. He was steady as a rock. He could be a hoot, or he could be as cranky as Sweet Pea with a diaper rash. One thing was unarguable though; Keesey was the *Guru of IC gear*.

Keesey had certain ways he wanted things done. Maybe they were quirky, maybe they were for a reason, but our process was definitely the Keesey method. He was a stickler for organization and cleanliness. He was big on tool accountability and maintaining test equipment. The ship had a phone system and we were tasked with maintaining it. But we didn't use it much. Keesey referred to phone calls as the *lazy man's way*. If we got a trouble call we had to show up at the scene. If we needed something we had to come back and get it. I didn't consider it then, but the wily old salt was teaching us to be prepared. We got into a habit of carrying tool belts at all times. Steve's tool belt also carried a trademark custom knife and fork set. When moving through the mess decks it wasn't unusual for him to stab at a displayed chunk of cheese as the cooks were preparing for lunch. Once, when assigned to a working party, Steve pilfered a huge cheese which he stashed in an air ventilation system. He was also addicted to red hot food and he would maintain a large jar of chili peppers in an obscure fan room.

Sometimes kicking and screaming and bitching like fat Boy Scouts who ran out of candy, our work habits became organized, and it happened quickly. It was part of the Keesey pace. If we wanted to go on liberty and hit the strip, then you had to turn to. Keesey kept it simple. Keesey understood and competently absorbed the information in technical manuals, but his true skill lied in his innate ability to tear things apart, put them back together again, and make it all work perfect. I would observe his efforts then and I yet to witness anyone duplicate his skill since, and I have seen a multitude of Navy techs over the years. Perhaps the legend I hold of IC1 Keesey has morphed over the years, but that guy knew his rate like Santa's head elf knows toys. He was the "*god of gears*." He was an electromechanical mad scientist in his DDG laboratory and we were his *Igors*.

Once we learned how to deal with Keesey the rest just fell into place. All that was required was a little gamesmanship and you would be fine. Get up on time, don't look like crap in uniform, keep the shop clean, personally investigate trouble calls, take the tools and prints you would need with you, and don't sit on your ass in the shop after morning quarters. That last one was huge. *BK (Before Keesey)* it was natural to meet up in the IC Room for coffee and then get the morning into a gradual roll to action. Not with Keesey. If you were down there after he arrived then you went into fox tail battle mode. You were going to clean and shine. So the way to avoid it was to grab your tools and move out quick.

Now to say Keesey had us learning at a fast pace was like saying the Titanic was leaking. It was the understatement of the decade. He would never give you the answer; only lead you in the right direction. It could be an epiphany to one as young as me to actually succeed on a job he sent me on. Keesey would say, "*It's all right to break something as long as you're learning*."

During this phase of the *Navy Bureau of Restocking Sailors to the LAWRENCE IC Gang* we received our next addition, an Alabama intellectual named Jeffrey T. Rodgers. He was a totally devoted married guy; young, cerebral, but with a good sense of humor. He was also a pretty big guy. He was trained at the Stromberg Carlson telephone school prior to reporting for duty as a telephone technician. When he arrived he promptly explained to his new boss, Keesey that telephone maintenance was to be his primary function. This, he explained is what he was told by his "C" school instructors. Phone techs were to be just that, they should be left alone with their special alignment gear and unique test equipment to work their magic.

Keesey sent Rogers off to clean the head for the next week. Welcome to "*Keesey's World.*"

When Rodgers got back from his duties with the toilet brush he was more amenable to the Keesey method of employing duty assignments. It helped that the three of us all got along so well. Rodgers had yet to move his wife to Norfolk so the three of us would be out and about most often, given the opportunity. However, we all suffered from the same syndrome, lack of transportation. With that obstacle out and about usually meant the base bowling alley. Hmm, pitchers of beer at the bowling alley; history certainly has a way of repeating itself, that is for certain.

There we were; four strong and Keesey had us moving in the direction he wanted. Supplies were getting ordered, we were gaining experience, and the IC men were moving fast, wearing tool pouches, and we were gaining a reputation for being industrious workers. If you walked fast while wearing a tool pouch people would get out of your way in a hurry. Acting like a man on a mission would cause people to part like the Red Sea giving way to Moses. Steve would often get tremendous urges with all the peppers and cheese he consumed. As he traveled to the aft head at the speed of light the crowds in the passageways would give way and often remark at how the IC men were working their asses off. Yes, it was the tool belt and its impressive contents of Stanleys, crescents, diagonals, spin tights, and crimpers, coupled with our signature power walk that made believers out of our ship mates. I suspect our derrieres were still in their full form, but with the help of the Steve hot pepper effect, we gave an overall impression of a busy and dedicated work force.

It was about 1973 when it was revealed to us that we were going to deploy the following year on a UNITAS. I had no idea what UNITAS stood for. I only knew that you circumnavigated South America, hit a lot of ports, and partied like New York socialites at a New Years Eve bash. It sounded like the best possible cruise available; tons of liberty and amazing sights to see. Even though it still remained a year away, the crew was excited about this particular deployment.

The Vietnam era guys were trickling off to their civilian destinies and the new adventure seekers were taking their places. The ship was beginning to gain certain camaraderie as it went into a cycle of deployment preparation. It was about this time that our fourth complimentary IC man arrived, Vic Pratt from the Cincinnati, Ohio area. Vic was a long legged thin guy who was prematurely balding. He was soft spoken, but very funny and animated. He could do great slapstick. He was immediately nicknamed the "Bean." Why in the world we gave him that name I'm not sure, but I don't think anyone ever called him Vic again. For the entire time he was a LARRY Sailor he was Bean Pratt, or simply, the Bean.

Bean had a tremendous talent with his constant companion, a very expensive twelve string guitar. He was dedicated to that guitar and all said he was quite an accomplished musician. He was constantly stashing that thing. Keesey wasn't fond of clutter. I knew Bean was happy when we all got together for our first crash pad. It became one of his eccentric habits to buy a twenty-five piece bucket *of Kentucky Fried Chicken* along with four big bottles of *Coca Cola*. He would then lock himself up in a room on a Friday night with his twelve string, chicken, and cola, and we wouldn't see him again until sometime Sunday or when the chicken bones created a stench, whichever came first. Bean could play anything from *Earl Scruggs* and Blue Grass, to *Jim Croce*. I wouldn't be surprised to find out that today he was in a band strumming out some originals. Hell, he may even be in Nashville with the *Grand Ole Opry*; it wouldn't be a shock. Bean was a dedicated guitar player and an all around interesting piece of the shop mosaic.

Keesey's crew was beginning to come together as a group. We were all quite diversified from each other, but we were forming a team that could keep the fecundity of ship's interior communications gear running smoothly, without big headaches up the chain.

The Keesey-Spencer relationship was riveting entertainment in the *Clash of the Titans*. They were two strong personalities in the constant process of head butting. Ensign Spencer was a fast moving do it now bottom line guy. Keesey was about pace and rhythm, everything done with an eye towards craftsmanship. Ensign Spencer earned the nickname "*Sooner,*" that being his normal comment when given a status report on when something broken would be back in operation. Keesey liked doing things methodically, with great planning, at the Keesey pace. A typical exchange between the Ensign and Keesey would go like this:

Spencer: *"Hi Keesey, What are you working on?"*

Keesey: "*Alarms.*"

Spencer: "*What alarm system is that?*"

Keesey: "*This one.*"

Spencer: "*Keesey, that orange wire; why are you hooking up that one, instead of the brown one?*"

Keesey: (No acknowledgement, he keeps on working)

Spencer: "*Keesey, Why don't you make the orange wire brown, and stick it in there?*"

Keesey: (Gets down from the overhead junction box sits down after grabbing a ball peen hammer, and crosses his leg.)

Spencer: "*Keesey, What are you going to do with that hammer?*"

Keesey: "*I am going to smash this knee cap of mine so I can go to the hospital so I can be left alone.*"

Spencer: "*OK Keesey, keep working, I'm outta here.*"

The Ensign then shoots through the scuttle and disappears off to his next work center.

Ensign Spencer was everywhere. He knew the entire crew by name and he would turn up when you least expected him. You could be on your hands and knees in the aft air conditioning equipment room to take a gauge reading and there would be Ensign Spencer checking to see if you were making your watch rounds.

Keesey did have one super human power which even the ever moving swift Spencer did not possess. Keesey had the ability to dematerialize just as *Captain Kirk* crew leader of the *ENTERPRISE* starship, reappearing seconds later at a remote location somewhere else within the skin of the ship, usually pissed off and right next to your face.

I experienced this once first hand while working in the combat information center or CIC. Engrossed in the repair to the dead reckoning table located there, I called the IC room, where Keesey answered the phone by growling his last name. I said, "*Keesey, could you look in the print drawer and tell me*?" Right there Keesey cut me off with a "*Using the phone is a lazy man's way, if you need!*" Right then I hung up the phone on Keesey. He chafed me with his reply. I was in the middle of an important job. When I hung up I turned around and was immediately greeted by a hydrophobic form of foaming Keesey about 1/8 inches from my face. I felt the singe of fire across my hair line as I received the greatest verbal assault since General George S. Patton rode a tank. Hanging up on Keesey was probably not the most intelligent course of action I could credit myself with.

As we prepared for the upcoming cruise, I began to experience the many virtues of being an adept IC man. The ship was connected by thousands of cables for literally hundreds of circuits. The intricate labyrinths of electrical and sound powered circuit cables were connected in some fashion to sound powered jack boxes, switches on a control panel, or to an associated communications switchboard. These cables often intersected in terminal boxes where repairs or circuit additions could be made to the wiring. The cerebral engineers who thought these complex systems up usually provided spare wires in a cable in order to effectively make repairs to wiring that may open or decompose causing a grounded or open circuit. Mapping a path by studying cable routes in isometric wiring diagrams enabled a sharp IC man to reroute things such as ship's entertainment circuits or shore telephones to a junction box near his rack, via spare pairs of wire in designated cables. Thus did I manage to have the captain's phone line available for my personal use from the secluded comfort of my curtain drawn rack in the weapons berthing compartment. I would simply use my telephone hand test set, clip on the spare cable leads upon which I had routed the captain's telephone line, and, *Wahlah*! dial tone. I would tell you what Keesey did to me when he caught me, but truth be told, I was never caught.

Our final puzzle pieces were starting to fall into place as far as personnel needs. We acquired a young guy from Georgia named Matt Faulkner. He was our shop athlete and the favorite of females. He enjoyed a good time, and it didn't hurt the IC shop's credibility to have the ship's best softball player. Rogers gave Matt his nickname, and he was christened Flash Faulkner. Flash, due to Matt's unique ability to fall immediately asleep on a hard rubber matting surface, but it stuck, and Flash liked it.

Our final crew member prior to gaining our full complement of IC men came from New Jersey. His name was Joe Drebbit. He was a soft spoken guy, and slightly younger than the rest of us. He must have come from a household where his mother really knew how to cook. I know that Frog as he was unceremoniously dubbed due to the rhyme scheme of Drebbit with ribbit, had a very difficult time with the typical LAWRENCE offerings of floating meat, and saucy food served mainly in earth tones. The happiest I ever saw Frog was after a liberty call where he discovered the best of restaurants. He would describe at length the sheer joy of a filet mignon wrapped in bacon, with a baked potato the size of one's head, smothered in sour cream and topped with a sprinkling of chives. Getting underway was dreadful to Frog, and it was all about the chow.

Prior to our UNITAS cruise we were going to get ramped up with a short two month jaunt to the North Atlantic and Europe. This was very exciting to us. The idea of seeing Europe was always a check in the box for places I wanted to go. Prior to the cruise Keesey managed to obtain some further schooling for several guys in the shop. Steve became trained as the fix it man in the NC2 Plotter, a very thought provoking submarine tracking device. It was located prominently in the combat information center. Now Steve, tough guy that he was usually turned a little green in rough weather. Our trip to the North Atlantic was a little rough. Neptune was in one of his routine cycles of extreme agitation. That was normally something that *tin can Sailors* could bet money on and our journey was no exception.

IC equipment only breaks at the worst possible moments. So when greening queasy Steve crawled to CIC on the plotter trouble call the stage was set for disaster. Steve did manage to get the side panel off of the equipment just before we absorbed a major roll to starboard. With excellent timing Steve blew his beans deep into the interior of the component filled device creating fresh paths of low resistance throughout the machine. If it wasn't broke before it certainly was now. That plotter didn't work again for a rather long time. In Navy jargon the Steve spew caused a CASREP. From that day forward the operation's specialists in CIC kept a very wary eye on any of Steve's incursions into their darkened domain.

It was during that North Atlantic cruise that that we all became the famed *Blue Noses* of nautical lore. We were traveling north of the Arctic Circle which was the qualifier. For accomplishing this feat we were ungraciously hosed down with cold salt water at about 100 plus pounds per square inch as we crawled towards our objective on the bow. There to greet us was the blue faced and incredibly hideous *King Neptune* who graciously painted our snot lockers with a blue dye concoction. After that we were granted a ceremonious swipe on the bull nose with some good Navy quality blue paint. We were thus good to go, certified *Blue Noses, Great Salts of the Arctic*.

The North Atlantic had a few excellent ports: Cherbourg, France, Rotterdam Holland, Travemunde, Germany, Arendahl, Norway, and Portsmouth, England. Each place was unique. Our IC gang was dedicated to having a good time and they accounted themselves well on these visits. As always we were great ambassadors for the *American Way*.

When we pulled into the Dutch port there was a US Navy frigate already tied up to the pier. Steve and I went over to give them some repair assistance on their NC2 Plotter which they requested on their message traffic. Steve had the NEC and it was a common practice to help each other out when the need arose. It was a voluntary mission.

We arrived early that morning and were escorted to the frigates IC room where we were greeted to the sight of several IC men sound asleep on the deck's rubber matting. The shop's first class IC man, a robust fellow with a sad air was shaking his head from side to side in an obvious state of mental anguish. "*What am I going to do? What am I going to do*?" He just kept repeating the phrase over and over again. We had to inquire about the strange scene spread before us. "*Well*," he said. "*I took my whole shop out last night to Wally's* Sex *Club' and charged the whole thing on my Master Card! I just don't know what my wife is going to say when she gets the bill for this*." For this we had no suggestions, his goose was cooked. He was to be sacrificed by his wife on the *Altar of Montezuma* and we knew of no recourse. I hope he didn't suffer and may he rest in peace. In my opinion, just tying the name *Wally* with the word *sex* was too weird. Steve couldn't fix the NC2 because of a lack of parts, so we departed the sad scandalous scene. It was *bad karma*.

In Rotterdam we were wondering the streets at night in the lively city when we came across an inviting tavern with strange music escaping into the street. We ducked in and gathered around the bar. On the floor were some dancers performing a folk dance of considerable skill. The talented dancers we soon discovered were Greek and that was the theme of the tavern we were in. We continued to be entertained and to our amazement the bar's patrons would down a shot of a clear liquid. They would then toss the glass to the dance floor, all the while the dancers continued on with their precise and practiced moves on the shattered glass. There must have been some folk lore significance to this, but I have no idea what it was. It looked like fun and at the time seemed like the right thing to do, so we began to toss our glasses on to the dance floor also. We probably shattered about half of the tavern's glasses when we started to think about heading back to the ship. What we were unaware of was the friendly bartender adding in the cost of each glass, with the customary Yankee mark up included I'm certain. Between the four of us we were well short of the final tally. We were contemplating running for it when one of us spotted our first class gunner's mate walking by.

They say that God takes care of children and fools and I believe that as long as we include young Sailors into that group also. This was one of those times. Lucky for us, the gunner bailed us out of the situation and saved our bacons. We owed the gunner for that one.

We had a very memorable evening in Lubeck Germany during that cruise. We entered one of those vintage European taverns in the center of the town. Inside were a group of lively senior citizens. Although their English wasn't the best and our Deutsch was practically non existent, they were very friendly and engaging to us. Being American Sailors gave us some sort of celebrity status with these folks. I just took it that American ships didn't visit this port that often, but as chance would have it several of these folks were Nazi death camp survivors and they liked Americans. These were great citizens of the world, proving that whenever in Europe it was very likely that an unpredictable adventure could occur. I was definitely seeing the world and getting my money's worth.

Arendahl Norway, and I realize that many of these ports have probably changed over the years, was a picturesque ski village, or so it appeared. The XO was on the 1MC and tried to down play the port. He said the beers were very expensive there. He implied that they were probably four dollars a piece. That was big money for a brew in the early seventies. But being Sailors we went anyway. What the XO failed to mention was that the four dollar beers were eleven feet tall. Okay, exaggeration, but one did not need a whole lot of those mega brews. Norwegians were big people, and their beers were Viking size.

Keesey encouraged the shop to take liberty. He was strict, but overall fair minded about time off. He himself was a non drinker. Maybe once upon a time, but he no longer drank. He smoked though, and back then I believed we all did, except for Rodgers and Frog. The great anti-smoking campaign had yet to begin.

Keesey had one of those expensive single lens reflex cameras and I suppose he was finalizing his final career years with some photographic memories. He often resembled a prosperous tourist, touring and tooling around, snapping away photos of the world. Keesey wasn't anchored to the ship, although he was very zealous when there.

We all stood sounding and security watches on our days in port. We were tasked to rove the ship, carrying both a pistol and a sounding tape. Our primary duty was to measure water levels in the engineering and auxiliary spaces; and then to pump it out as necessary with the installed eductor systems. The gun, I speculated was for whoever tried to steal our anchor chain. Actually, I never figured out why we needed the pistol. I do know it was better off in the hands of the weapons guys and that is where it eventually ended up through review and evolutionary changes in the watch process. Eventually the sounding and security watch became only a sounder, even though we were no longer doing armed security rounds we still maintained the title sounding and security watch.

As Ensign Spencer became more familiarized with the role of division officer he created the famous *Turkey List*. Fittingly, the high profile ensign came up with an idea for tracking those of us who exacerbated him in some special way. Once on the Turkey List, a subordinate had to accomplish many positive feats of working gallantry to get erased from the evil easel. Ensign Spencer had an elaborate hierarchy established within the turkey structure. One could be on for a minor infraction as a T*emporary*

Turkey. More heinous deeds could elevate one's status to P*rime Turkey*. Some could even manage to achieve P*ermanent Turkey*. However, only the IC men ever received the ultimate distinction of *ALL TIME TURKEYS*.

I am not stating that we IC men did not deserve this distinction. Most assuredly, we did. We were known as pranksters throughout the ship. People coming to the IC Room to drop off sound powered phones would usually leave shaking their heads, and cursing in disbelief as they muttered, "*IC men are some crazy sons a bitches*," or some similar adjectives. Invading our lair could mean getting treated to a friendly W*et Willy*, a P*ink Belly*, or often a *Melvin*.

The IC gang would often pull a prank with little thought or debate about repercussions. We were not renowned as deep thinkers, being total sellouts for a good joke. By virtue of *group think* we would often act in unison on many things we would fear to singularly execute.

We had kicked around the idea about a sound powered phone generator fire and decided to pull it on the ensign while he was officer of the deck while underway. Now for those who are unfamiliar with the phone systems aboard ship; sound powered phones are exactly as stated, powered by sound. You speak into a transmitter and the vibration of your voice travels through the ships wiring. The sound is formed in the earpiece of receivers at remote stations plugged into the jack boxes of that particular circuit. It is a great system of communication because of its evident simplicity. If a ship were to lose power, communication still takes place.

Now if the ensign thought about it for even a moment he would have detected the prank, but we were banking that we could catch him on the excitement factor. We cast the bait and reeled in our fish. It began.

"Bridge, Main Control. We have a Class C fire in Main Control, in Compartment 5-111-0-E. Away the duty electrician, and away the scramble squad." Off went the whole scene. The ensign was very much the pro, demanding regular status reports, and forwarding those reports directly to the captain (who was totally in on it), and ensuring all involved were taking the proper damage control measures. The whole scenario ended with the cause of casualty being a frozen bearing, estimated time to repair two weeks until the receipt of parts. The top watch had the messenger deliver a warmed up rusty bearing to the bridge. The ensign said, "*I'll take that*!" He was relieved from watch and took the bearing proudly to the wardroom where he was greeted by the captain and the assembled department heads.

A short time later we heard our names being called on the 1MC to the DCA's stateroom. There were our names topped off as the *All Time Turkeys*. There was no chance in hell of parole. For the rest of our

LAWRENCE years we were gobblers, forever forlorn, left to scratch and peck as engineering fowl of ill repute.

Now please don't get the wrong idea about Ensign Spencer. He was high energy. He could be on the bridge as the underway OOD in rough weather and everyone around him, the helmsman, the quartermaster of the watch, and the lookouts would be blowing their beans in an accommodating shit can. Spencer would be standing there binoculars on his neck with a smile on his face, loving every minute of it. He seemed to thrive in adverse situations. He also had a great talent for verbal snap back. When he didn't like your answer about equipment status concerning time for repairs, his reply; "*Fix it! Sooner*," actually became his nickname. At least among the IC men it was. I'll put it in this perspective, there were a lot of tough personalities that Spencer as a young ensign had to deal with, and I never saw him back down to anyone.

Now Spencer and Keesey would fight like rabid dogs at times and we in the IC room thought that they just didn't like each other. Once upon a time Keesey angered Steve. Steve pulled lint out of his belly button and flicked it on the deck. Keesey made him field day the entire IC room. Rogers was upset because he thought he should only be working phones and Keesey thought differently. I was against his no phone calls to the shop policy.

So we, as a group went to complain about him to Spencer. Spencer listened to our complaints, looked at us then picked up the phone and dialed Keesey. He said in front of us "*Keesey the IC Men are up here and they are fuck'n with you.*" That was it. We had severely misinterpreted the relationship between the two. Oh hell no, they probably never went out partying together, but Spencer knew Keesey was just what we needed. If Keesey was annoyed by us he didn't show it. It was all about the work.

Keesey was an electromechanical wizard. He had this unique blood vessel in his nose that he would energize with a snort and swallow. It was analogous to booting a computer. The vein would slightly pop and he was locked in on his task. Tearing down thought provoking mechanical gear trains, expertly, and effortlessly, or so it seemed, putting it all back together, new part in place, system restored. Keesey was Merlin in blue jeans and a chambray shirt. Yes Merlin had returned from King Arthur's realm to reappear as the IC1 on the lovable LARRY. Whatever we thought about Keesey, his technical skills were unmatched.

Keesey however, had a great deal more to offer than his dexterity at repairing equipment. He knew how to organize, delegate, and scold appropriately. He was hard but fair. Keesey didn't drink, he smoked but all enlisted guys smoked back then. The officers had quit for the most part, but the enlisted crew still burned them up. Keesey had a girl friend from Massachusetts he called his *Portagoose.* So Keesey didn't party or raise hell like a lot of his peers did. He did have that gigantic camera of course, complete with a ton of gadgets, and he became talented as a late career photographer.

We had some other characters on the ship, in addition to the IC gang. Cressy was a holdover electrician from the Vietnam crew. He was a short guy with a very funny demeanor, enhanced by a slight lisp. He was a master of the hair slick down process; managing to hide tremendous swaths of hair under the grease only to have it wash out in the evenings into a style that fit in with the current civilian trend. He had a very fast Corvette so most people thought he was naturally cool. Cressy was sent mess cooking where he was assigned to the scullery to help out with dishes and trays. While underway Cressy thought he could lighten his work load by tossing a few dishes and trays over the side. The method seemed to have an effect over time as we began to see our meals served more often on paper plates. Plan of the day notes began to appear about missing mess gear. Soon thereafter Cressy's time came to a close. He got out and drove his Vet back to Connecticut or to some state similar to Connecticut.

A big country boy electrician from West Virginia was enamored by that song from the seventies, *The Streak*. I'll withhold his name to protect him from the wrath of his wife. This hill hopper executed the famous lunch time streak of the LAWRENCE. Certainly it would have been a much greater offense had we had female crew members at the time. But at that time, male only was the norm. At 1135 that morning, out of engineering berthing he came, like a resurrected Greek from 1000 BC, except for the ski mask over his head. Down the main passageway he fled, right through the lunch crowd and into Main Control. Then out he came back tracking through the mess decks as the crew cheered. He streaked to the berthing compartment, reappearing fully clothed and undetected by the command monikers of military deportment. He had succeeded in his mission of exhilaration. He became famous in the LAWRENCE underground circles as the *Mushroom Man* due to his white stem like legs and his mushroom button buns. One significant item that episode accomplished, no one ate the bratwurst that day.

IC men had an added benefit to their rate. We controlled the ship's movies. At the time movies were distributed to the Navy Motion Picture Exchange down on the waterfront.
The IC men repaired the 16 millimeter projectors so we were naturally tasked with picking up the flicks at showing them to the crew at 2000 each evening. The IC men could watch them in the shop whenever they liked at

night. This was a great benefit to nocturnal creatures such as the Bean. Whenever the ship was underway there was considerably less control about movie selection. They just circulated among the ships that were out there with you via vertical replenishment deliveries. Although we were allowed to leave port with quite a collection, we would run through the allotment very quickly. Bad movies and massive repeats were very depressing to the crew so the IC men throughout the fleet would leave codes written on the movie guide books and inside the green movie boxes. GFF was good fucking flick. SFF was shitty fucking flick, and Good T&A was obvious. Getting a good T&A was always welcome because we could show those many times over without complaint.

Our process was to drag our projector to the mess decks each evening getting all the reels rewound for presentation to the crew. The *Bruce Lee* Kung Fu movies could be very dangerous due to the large stanchion we had right smack in the middle of the mess decks. Bruce would be high kicking, and knocking the snot out of the evil enemy, snapping their necks with a vengeful twist as he sent thousands off to *Neverland.* His lethal spins, kicks, and hand chops inspired the LAWRENCE crew to combat, as they battled our lone stalwart stanchion, practicing LAWRENCE karate chops and high swooping kicks on the silent steel pole. The pole had been there supporting a portion of the upper level since 1957 and had never given way. The stanchion would not be defeated by martial artists in their infancy. The stanchion stood there silent in defiance, never losing one bout despite having no arms or high flying feet to defend itself. On the other hand Doc provided ice packs to many a swollen hand or foot to the aggressive attackers of our stalwart stanchion.

Steve was a frugal young man. Don't get me wrong, he would spend a fortune on a high quality fire arm. Guns were a true necessity to Steve. Once he moved off the ship to a trailer in a remote location in rural North Carolina. His first purchase for his new home was for reloading equipment. But for all other purposes Steve was rather frugal and proud of his methods of economizing. One Steve method was his soap collection process. He would enter the shower stalls in the morning, collecting all the little left behind soap fragments developing them into his own personal kaleidoscope of a cake. He loved the thrift stores and all you could eat buffets had magnetic appeal to him. His careful use of funds resulted in a purchase of an arsenal of weapons that could arm a small third world country. Steve could talk about weaponry with the same knowledge and verve that a modern geek can talk about the variations in different styles of hard drives and modems. He could speak endlessly about stopping power, rifle ranges, scope accuracies, hollow points, and wad cutters. He was extremely knowledgeable about what guns were best to kill whatever, or whoever, from wherever. He was like a spokesman for *Smith and Wesson,* or a feature writer for *Guns and Ammo*. How he finally settled down in Madison, Wisconsin, near that liberal campus I'll never know. Perhaps he is just there to provide some right wing balance or to irritate the local *PETA Chapter*.

Steve made some of his shipmates a little wary. He had no use for dopers and he had no problem talking about how *fuckin dopers ought to be shot*. He had two favorite lines he often drew on. "*All I want is a license to kill*." The other was "*fifteen cents*." Now the fifteen cents statement referred to Steve's theory that a problem would be solved for that amount, as fifteen cents was the purchase price of one round that he could use to whack whoever grated on his nerves. Because of these public pronouncements, those who didn't know Steve were reserved. Those of us who knew him thought he was a *hoot* and totally harmless. He may have been frugal, but Steve was never selfish. He always paid his fair share for beer and I am sure that if I had asked, Steve would have shared his soap cake with me.

Whereas Steve could have a temper, Rodgers was a mellow man. He was a smart guy, and a very dedicated family man. He did maintain a firearm at home, once his wife moved from Alabama north to Norfolk. Rodgers was very true to his marriage. He often said if anyone ever accused him of cheating on his wife then he would kill him. Well it so happens his wife was teasing him one day and told him that good ole Steve had let it be known that he, Jeff, had fooled around in one of our liberty ports. Now Jeff, being a man of his word loaded his pistol and waited patiently in his recliner for Steve to arrive. Steve just happened to be coming for dinner that day. His wife became frantic but Rodgers couldn't be swayed, and he was going to put Steve six feet under and that's just the way it was. His wife begged and pleaded to get him to believe that it was all just a joke. It was a dumb test on her part to see if he would react. In the end maybe her tears got to him, but finally he relented and decided to let Steve live. When Steve finally arrived at the Rodgers and heard about his near death experience he paled in fear. But all was well and all that remained was the soon to be embellished tale of how Jeff almost whacked Steve.

We were all beginning to get a bit excited about our adventurous trip to South America. We were doing operations locally and then we were underway to the Caribbean for further training. At Roosevelt Roads Puerto Rico we pulled into port for fuel and other issues prior to a gunfire support exercise. The ship sponsored a picnic on the beach the very next day. I had rat holed my personal inflatable raft which I broke out for this type of occasion and hauled it down to the beach. The beach at Roosevelt Roads is a gorgeous little jewel with excellent snorkeling. Located within the perimeter of the base, it provided a vast world of underwater tropical sea life. I learned a harsh lesson that day about Caribbean sunshine when I fell asleep in that raft and woke up about three or four hours later. I returned to the ship resembling a freshly dipped merlot pickle. I wasn't feeling enchanted by the tropics at that point and I came very close to be placed on report for malingering. It was a painful lesson and since that event I have always cautioned Sailors about the sun. I should be hired as a spokesman for *Johnson and Johnson.* I certainly made many sales for that company's sun block products. The Caribbean sun is a sneaky beast and will fry you like a catfish at a Mississippi cookout. I learned another lesson the hard way and Keesey was not a great pity advocate in the department of doing dumb stuff.

On one occasion we were underway on operations and were engulfed in a severe storm. Mr. Spencer was probably the only one on the ship enjoying the moment. The rest of us were turning the hue of our pea green bulkheads. A cruel cook, as a sinister joke manufactured some split pea soup and more than one of us lost our lunch. Occasionally on a down pitch it would cause a chain reaction of hurls. In addition to the weather, there are always a few sympathetic pukers. It was indeed, nasty stuff, and quite slippery for the unsuspecting passerby. There were a number of ships out with us on that particular operation. I believe it was titled *Solid Shield.* But realistically the only thing we were longing for right then was solid ground. During that heavy storm the ship's anemometers, or wind birds as we called them took flight off the end of the yard arms and just flew off searching for better weather. Hell, if I could fly I would have gone too. Even the anemometers were the IC men's equipment so we were going to have to deal with putting in new ones very soon.

A short period after the end of that exercise we were rolling into another one that required shooting an ASROC or anti submarine rocket. We knew that a wind input was a requirement for that ballistic trajectory. We were temporarily faced with the scenario of no wind birds, no ASROC shot, and any time you can not fire a weapon system captains become agitated. Somehow Ensign Houdini Spencer did his magic. Between his casualty reporting and bird dogging the supply line, he managed to get us new wind birds. Mr. Spencer would always do whatever it took to get the job done. In this instance he acquired new wind birds. I believe if we needed an aviary that Mr. Spencer would have found a way to get us one. With him no was never an option. Bean Pratt was our high place or aloft guy. I suppose that growing up with an abundance of flat land in Ohio made him truly appreciate a perch of great heights with a spectacular view.

With Keesey's guidance and expertise, the wind birds were installed, and the ASROC shot was a huge success. The captain personally thanked the IC men for their efforts by making an announcement on the 1MC. Receiving a public *Bravo Zulu* the IC men were permitted to bask in the aftermath of the positive recognition.

As the great ship LAWRENCE inched ever closer to that deployment date, the inspections came and went. Pour out any acronym from a bowl of Alphabets and we probably had an inspection from that group of letters. There were always people coming to assist us in discovering our deficiencies and training inadequacies. Like the IRS they were the government, and they were only there to help.

I can remember many of the folks on that ship but I have a difficult time remembering the inspections. It wasn't that we received any great accolades from our inspection results on the LAWRENCE. We were an old DDG and it was a tremendous amount of work to keep us going. We were a clean ship though, and we always looked squared away. Our motto came from a War of 1812 hero. James Lawrence, a true swashbuckler who commanded one of the great early Navy frigates, the USS CHESAPEAKE. He was struck down in a battle with the British at sea but he spoke some dying words that became a national rallying cry and provided great motivation to our fledgling fleet. Lawrence's dying words were, *"Don't Give up the Ship"* It was our motto on LAWRENCE, his namesake and the fifth ship to bear the name. It was part of our coat of arms. Some of us would use the name DGUTS as a nickname for LAWRENCE. That term had a macho ring to it that we found attractive. One creative Sailor created his own motto based on the LAWRENCE cleanliness standard. He artistically created a bucket on canvas with a crossed broom and swab above it. Across the top was emblazoned his personal motto, *Go Clean Up the Ship,"* He had DDG 409 stenciled on his bucket. Hence, whereas we were DGUTS he had his personal motto, GCUTS.

Hair was an issue of vast importance in the early seventies. Today's Sailors do not appear vastly different from their civilian counterparts. Back then we stood out like infected nose pimples. Most Sailors felt that women would reject them because of the important issue of hair length. Ladies of the era may deny it, but they were right. Young folks have a general desire to look like their peers so Sailors went to great lengths to try and hide as much hair as possible. The greased down look was the most popular. A tremendous amount of hair could be hid deeply impacted in a bed of molten *hair grease*. The ship's master at arms force was in a constant battle to get folks to the barber shop. Beards presented another issue. The styles and types of acceptable beards were posted on drawings around the barbershop. Frankly, many Sailors just did not look that good with a beard. Then again, many of those guys did not look that good without a beard. Grooming standards were tough to enforce mainly because the young folks detested the look that they had to adhere to. I believe the Navy lost many potential reenlistments specifically due to the hair issue. For many young Sailors the Charles Manson look was OK but the old salts just couldn't bear it. It was a push pull social issue.

Admiral Zumwalt was now in as Chief of Naval Operations or CNO and he made a multitude of social changes. A lot of it was resented by the old salts, and it wasn't enough change for the young crowd. A giant pay raise probably would have eased much of the dissention, but that wasn't a part of the plan.

The LAWRENCE continued its track, continuing preparations for deployment. Several crew members, including myself were enrolled in a college Spanish class in order to communicate with the South American locals. I purchased *Fodor's* latest travel guide to study some of the places we would visit. I was thinking about Rio and the Copacabana with string bikinis, the Straits of Magellan, the Inca ruins, or perhaps there would be an excursion to the world's highest elevation inland lake, Lake Titicaca. After reading that book, I was ready for what promised to be an exciting adventure. As much fun as the other ports had been, this sounded exponentially better. My personal wanderlust was alive and kicking.

The ship had at least one more inspection to get through and that was an in depth material condition inspection called INSURV. This was a team of very scary individuals who came aboard the ship and really took a hard look at every nook and cranny. They weren't just called experts, they really were experts. These guys were brine encrusted old salty officers and senior enlisted chief petty officers who knew just where to look and what to look for. There were no skeletons left undetected in one's closet with this group. These guys found out that we had pig iron for ballast and it was rusting out. A novice would never know that. There is one thing you have to maintain as a U S Navy Sailor and that is flexibility. It was going to be a huge time consuming process to upgrade that ballast, but what had to be, had to be.

The bottom line was that our UNITAS trip to South America was lost. We were rescheduled for a nice trip to the Middle East at a slightly later date. So *FODOR's* was out, and saving money on a long cruise with very few ports was in. There was a general disappointment because a lot of scuttlebutt went around about how much fun a UNITAS cruise was for a destroyer crew. Now we were off to Bandar Abbas and burkas, instead of Rio de Janeiro and string bikinis, *ya hoo*!

There were a thousand little itineraries taking place before the deployment. Uniforms had to get stocked and Keesey gave us all a seabag inspection. He cheated by skipping the skivvies counting. He wasn't too keen on handling our underwear even if it was allegedly clean. We inventoried and repaired scores of sound powered phones. Keesey had us zero and align all of our servo systems including gyro repeaters, speed indicators, wind direction indicators, and rudder angle indicators. We replaced all broken sound powered jack box covers, and checked all the indicator lights of our bridge equipment. Keesey was like the *World Book Encyclopedia* of shit to do.

Personally, we stacked up on junk food, cameras, film, and personal items. Allotments to wives or to family members were started. Hopefully, no one would give his bar room sweet heart a power of attorney. That was a sea story told all too often on many a deploying ship. We were roaring to go when the time for underway shift colors finally came to pass.

There was a major historical event that was developing about the time of our departure. The Arab oil embargo smacked us right into a complete course correction and itinerary change in route to the Middle East. The Egyptians made many of my ship mates happy with the closing of the Suez Canal to United States ships. At our deck plate level that meant Shellback initiation was now on the horizon. With the ship now tasked with circumnavigating Africa in route to the Persian Gulf we would not only be toasted as Shell Backs, but as *Royal Diamond Shellbacks.* We would pass right through the crossing point of 0 degrees latitude and 0 degrees longitude off the coast of West Africa. In addition we would do our crossing of the Atlantic from the vantage point of the Brazilian East Coast, where the city of Recife rests at the hump of the continent. This meant that South America was back on the burner at least for one port visit. In addition we added a travel port at Trinidad in the West Indies and a fuel stop at my favorite cove for roasting my carcass, Rosy Roads, Puerto Rico. I stocked a large supply of sun block for this trip. Steve and I did a great deal of sale shopping in preparation for the deployment. Steve, frugal man that he was, was a verifiable master of finding cheap stuff. I purchased a pair of blue and white plaid pants and a pair of white slip on loafers at a thrift store for about a dollar fifty. It was hideous attire at any stretch of the imagination. Steve protested the purchase, interjecting that I paid way too much. We stocked up on clearance items, such as shaving cream and body powder. We really did not need all that we bought, but at substantial discounts we envisioned ourselves as body powder business moguls, or the merchants of *Mennon.* On LAWRENCE every tiny bit of space had stuff. Mercifully, whenever we had zone inspections we could hide our spare parts in Mr. Spencer's stateroom. For personal items we were on our own. The regular method was to run things from one space to another. Once an inspector left a space then the IC man would vacuum in behind, laden down with things to stash. It was tough but doable. Bean was a streak with his twelve-string, traveling throughout the gamut of IC spaces. Steve thought about bringing some guns. He would have raised some suspicions running around the ship, hauling a rifle from space to space, and in the end he relented to reason and opted for off ship storage.

Eventually the calendar said get going. It was underway, shift colors. Despite all of our preparation, IC trouble calls came pouring in like a break in the Hoover Dam. *"Duty IC man, Bridge, IC Room Main Control, I gotta a ...",* and on it went. Keesey just stood there calmly taking the calls and pointing to an IC man and off we went. Steve stared at the suddenly erratic underwater log and said "*It's a fuckin curse*!" That's what made Steve so insanely comical, the serious way he presented ridiculous assumptions. Did Steve really believe the LAWRENCE was cursed? It was maybe yes, maybe no. No one was certain.

As irritating as a bunch of broken equipment can be, counter balancing the whole situation was the presence of Keesey. As grumpy and cantankerous as the old salt could be, we always understood that Keesey knew his craft. He was our "*ace in the hole,*" even though we, as rebellious young folks often thought he was just an *ass hole*. Certainly our grizzled wizard never granted a laziness allowance. When someone attempted to skate, the old fart always knew where to find you. Except for Bean, that is. Bean had supernatural powers and had the ability to blend into the bulkhead or deck matting without detection. It was truly a gift. Keesey trained IC men really learned how to fix from their mentor. He knew thousands of unique little troubleshooting tricks. He could strip a switchboard in a nanosecond to isolate a ground. He could usually analyze a closed servo loop just by hearing about a malfunctioning indicator's symptoms. Keesey could often tell you to open the cover of a sync amp and check for the voltage on the stator leads of the 400 hertz synchro transmitter. He was often dead on the money. Steve thought at times that Keesey truly was a wizard. After all, he looked like Merlin. He believed Keesey had psychic powers. Keesey certainly agreed with Steve's evaluation. If Keesey believed you were giving him some reverent power, then he wasn't about to turn it down. After all, it could come in rather handy someday. One could seldom predict when the skills of the warlock needed to be called upon.

As time passed, the trouble calls slowed down and we fell into our routine of maintenance, watches, drills, field days, and training. One thing I always noticed about the 1200 psi steam plant on the LAWRENCE was its reliability after it settled down. Once the hole snipes got it up and steaming, it seemed to work efficiently, a thousand different systems, whirling, winding, spinning, pumping, and steaming, with the great heat blasts from the fire room always a reminder of what made the shaft turn.

We uneventfully pulled into Roosevelt Roads, no sunburn this time. Then it was on to Port of Spain Trinidad. Liberty there was interesting. The IC men got lost of course as we were walking about. Steve wasn't about to invest in anything as extravagant as a taxi cab. We stumbled upon a garage band set up outdoors on a suburban lawn where they were holding a practice session. There was a long legged white guy on the key boards and some interesting locals jamming away at their rendition of the current hit *Kung Fu Fighting.* They were so good I thought they might actually be the guys who originated the song. In a matter of minutes the entire neighborhood came to life and the impromptu affair turned into a miniature Caribbean block party. When we glided out of there the band was still going strong, fueled by their neighbors' enthusiasm. All in all I have had much worse times and the people of Port of Spain were actually quite friendly.

When we departed Port of Spain steaming out of the Caribbean and into the Atlantic, the ship began a series of closed meetings among many of the old salts. They were mainly comprised of chiefs and a sprinkling of the senior officers. There was also a fair representation of first class petty officers, Keesey certainly being one of them.

This sinister group were the nefarious *Shellbacks* who were planning our demise within the next day or so, and evil little smiles began to appear on their "*I'm gonna get you*" baleful, and for the most part unattractive little faces whenever we questioned them about the upcoming event.

In addition, hideous devices were being constructed with wood and canvass in the HT Shop and bos'n locker, while the senior stew burners were stashing some galley originated compost on the fantail. The substance reeked with a sour smell and it sported a sickly and lumpy earth tone hue. Even when the chief commissary man came near to add to its contents, he could only approach the offal for a short duration before his olfactory sense was overcome by the grisly paste.

The evening before the equator crossing, Davey Jones was on the 1MC threatening us *Pollywogs* with our impending fate. Unfortunately our commanding officer got on the 1MC and freely admitted that he too would have to join in the fate of his fellow Pollywogs.

We slept as soundly as some Tombstone horse thieves awaiting a hanging; which is to say fitfully at best. At least I didn't have a watch that night as I remember it. The morning of the crossing arrived and reveille was weird. Rather than my customary Keesey greeting of "*Zeke get up*, It was a mean nasty "*Get up low life wog*!" Bright lights were shining in our faces as we dressed in the day's attire.

T-shirts were inside out and backwards. Pants were also inside out and backwards with skivvy shorts over top of the pants. Shoes were worn right shoe on left foot and left shoe on right foot. The Royal Shellbacks were dressed in varying degrees of pirate attire. The HT1 had a heart tattoo on his well defined bicep with an arrow protruding through. Inside was the graphic phrase "*Suck Me*"

The wogs were rounded up and forced to crawl from weapons berthing to the mess decks. Nasty little shalalees manufactured from short pieces of fire hose moved us along. Our valiant Pollywog captain was on all fours as the Shellbacks had him filling out a meal evaluation. Everything was checked outstanding, our skipper was no fool. Breakfast itself, was doctored up into peculiar green things, and creatively served in such a manner as to appear totally inedible. The forced fare was slightly better than it looked. We were forced to partake of these victuals prior to continuing our crawl to the bow. The *"Inside Out Wogs"* as we were ungraciously nicknamed gathered in our humble horde on the focsle. The ship's mast was flying the skull and cross bones, the Jolly Roger was in control of the ship.

The wogs were attempting a revolt led by the dynamic Spencer. The ensign was determined to carry us to victory over the arrogant minority of Shellbacks. However, the revolt was quickly halted with the Royal Shellbacks counting coup, as we were kicked back with 110 psi of fire main pressure, supplied by pure equatorial sea water. As we fell to the deck in soaked submission the heroic long lean Ensign Spencer, now adorned in an odd red helmet, was instructed to begin sweeping the horizon. So broom in hand, our great hope for a victorious Pollywog revolt, was humiliated, forced to sweep the horizon, all the while announcing his activity to the horde of bleating wogs, and adding to animated piratical glee expressed by our jubilant oppressors. This visual quickly transformed the leader of our revolt into a harmless, tall, and gangly buffoon, certainly stated with all due respect to the ensign. Hence we, the defeated wogs were now dutifully bound to obey our sadistic masters. The Shellbacks lined us up on our hands and knees, and we crawled like slow moving mutant insects along the starboard side to progress to our ultimate goal of fantail frolics.

As we crawled through the fire hose wielding pirates, we were increasingly annoyed with various substances. It was literally a "*smear campaign."* We finally neared the Royal Court of King Neptune. King Neptune, Master Chief Reid, was a living nightmare, and Chief Jones was the ugliest Queen who ever sailed the seas. The abominable transvestite would have made the *Sea Hag* proud. We were ordered to kiss the queen's foot. Naturally, the foot was covered in a poop like adobe, very harsh and putrid. The sonar senior chief as the Royal Baby was down right disgusting. It was bad enough just seeing that guy in a diaper, but we had to kiss the Royal Baby's belly as well. The kiss placed on that belly was a challenge to the most stalwart of the wogs. The ample belly was covered with an unimaginable muck, of which there was no substance on earth with which to compare, unless a method was perfected to pass a plump road kill through a blender. We finally made it to our goal, the fantail and to the wogs' credit, no one was mortally afflicted. As I began my approach to the garbage filled contraption, a Royal Shellback decided that I required to be justly sweetened. Pancake syrup in the backside did the trick. It was pounded home by his handy little shelelee and I uncomfortably continued my crawl to the final grotesque objective.

Soon I was at the entrance to the tunnel of putrid crap. The large stitched vinyl enclosure provided pure joy from one end to the other. Bacteria must have loved it. In we went, slithering like worms through the decayed matter. It was the tunnel of terror. As we exited we were led to a home made swimming pool constructed on the fantail. Two large Shellbacks began to dunk us under and ask us who we were over and over until we understood wog was no longer the answer. *We were Shellbacks. We had survived.*

I can attest that the clean up for the initiation took forever; first us, then the ship. A hundred or two hundred Sailors were taking salty fantail showers just to get clean enough to enter the berthing compartments; fortunately, no cruise ships passed by. We would have appeared quite strange with two hundred naked dudes taking a community shower. The best news was everyone lived.

Ricife Brazil is a large South American port and huge tropical trees were everywhere in the town. At that time there was also a very prominent military presence consisting of troops with machine guns on all the busy street corners. As I looked around I observed no one that appeared threatening, unless they were hiding behind those huge trees. It was my first view of a place that was not in keeping with our way of life. The North Atlantic countries were politically free, and except for beer size and the fact that Norwegians speak better English than we do, their way of life was very similar. You got the feeling here that you would do just fine as long as you minded the government line. Go against that and it would be anybody's guess. The entire concept of soldiers on the street struck me as very unnerving and ominous.

That aside, Recife was a party town and fronted a festive atmosphere. Our port visits were usually about two days in duration, then gone. Recife was soon left in our wake as we set a course for the West Coast of Africa. It did take a day or two to recover from Recife's special culinary delight, meat on stick offerings, which were purchased from street vendors in little carts. I had no idea what biological life form the kabobs stemmed from, but it would not have surprised any of us if they originated from a four legged rodent or bat species. Whatever they were, they were not in tune with the LAWRENCE Sailors' digestive tracts. A day or so and the offending fare was a historical footnote of minor value, soon forgotten as we sailed on to further unknown adventure, our health thankfully restored.

The LAWRENCE was far away from Norfolk, Virginia as we made way at a steady sixteen knots to the African coast. I recall at some point we ended up in the company of a Knox class frigate, the USS ELMER MONTGOMERY. I was amazed at how smoothly everything was working. Our major equipment continued chugging away. I can not remember the LAWRENCE losing electrical power at any time during the entire deployment unless it was for a basic engineering casualty control exercise. The LAWRENCE was definitely giving the taxpayers their money's worth thus far. Being that we were in a high heat environment we were permitted to relax attire somewhat, and many of us developed that well tanned salty look. We were soon the definitive swarthy crew. It was interesting so far. As we passed through the specific spot where 0 degrees longitude met 0 degrees latitude at the equator we were now officially *Royal Diamond Shellbacks.* No further initiation took place. The one in South American waters was it for the time being. With that behind us, passing through this coordinate was a mere footnote, albeit a rare one.

We arrived in the formerly French administered country of the Ivory Coast in the port city of Abidjan. It would prove to be a very unique place. The first thing I noticed about Abidjan, were the vast multitudes of iguana type creatures. Steve wished he had his shotgun. He envisioned a mountain of lizards laid to waste. But the amphibians seemed harmless enough. None attempted to explore us through our pant legs, and they demonstrated no desire to bond with their western human intruders. As for the people of Abidjan, most were tall and slim and many of the women displayed unusual head attire. We were at an out door café and a young street vendor had ventured to the area of our tables hoping to make a sale with the Americans. A watchful constable quickly whipped out a nasty little black jack type of device and whaled away on that poor kid. That took us aback and was rather horrifying to be quite frank. The kid was only trying to make a living. It's really strange for an American to witness someone getting punished for trying to work. We were gaining an understanding as to how the third world operated. To experience that exchange first hand was an eye opening event as we became less naïve and more soberly educated about the ways of the world.

On an upbeat note, a large contingency of Girl Scouts came and visited the ship. Yes, the Ivory Coast had Girl Scouts. We fed them large quantities of chocolate chip cookies, chocolate milk, and our own special bug juice. They were quite thrilled with that and they left the ship supercharged and full of good old Yankee sugar with positive thoughts of the sweet vessel LAWRENCE.

Liberty call was granted for several days as we took on fuel so off we went tripping around the city eager to explore what was out there. Shopping was the thing in Abidjan. The craftsmen had no idea how valuable their carvings were. They were true artisans, and the cost for the fruits of their labor was ridiculously low. One could purchase masks, elephants with ivory, warrior figurines, and many other themes. The detail in the wood was excellent. I approached a kiosk type shop with a large elephant carving selection. In this tropical location we dressed for the weather and I was sporting my nifty blue checked pants and the white shoes. If I were to see that outfit today I would probably regurgitate. To this day I have an awful time just watching movies from the seventies because of the outrageous clothing men wore in the disco era. Hopefully none of it will ever return to acceptable style. It was… well…, ghastly.

There I was, traversing the streets of Abidjan with my fancy dude pants and *Liberac*e looking shoes. I was immediately spied by the elephant vendor, a very tall thin man, perhaps six feet four or six feet five inches tall. He called out to me, "*My American friend what change can we make for those pants and those shoes*?" I replied, "*How about that one right there?*" I pointed to a large elephant with tusks of ivory (fake for certain). "*However I can't go back to the ship with no clothes*," I said. He said, "*My friend we can exchange our clothes*." This I declined. I wasn't about to try out his duds. He spoke then, "*Bring back the pants and shoes and we trade*." So off we went back to the ship. I peeled off the duds and returned eager to give up my fine western attire. The vendor believed he had made the steal of the century as he presented me with one of his finest pieces of art. Thrift store pants and shoes for a total cost of one dollar and fifty cents for a genuine hand carved elephant of African teak, at least I thought it was. Even the frugal Steve had to applaud my skill on that deal.

As for the recipient of my western finery, he quickly dropped his laundry right there in the public domain and suited up in his new duds. Luckily the shoes fit. The pants were OK in the waist but finished just a tad below the knee. It did not seem to matter though, as the crowd gathered around him, admiration and envy in their eyes as they awarded accolades to his new fashion statement.

As I was lugging my huge elephant back to the ship we discovered Keesey and Rodgers near one of the busy shopping areas. Keesey had his awesome camera out and was enthusiastically snapping photos of his surroundings. He stood out like Abe Lincoln's wart on Mount Rushmore. There he was, *Wagon Train's Wishbone* in Africa. I will say that Keesey dressed better than the television Wishbone, but with his distinguished gray beard he was drawing the same kind of attention that my blue and white checked pants had garnered earlier.

An ever increasing number of children began to gather around the visitor from the West. They were enamored with Keesey's wise look and the fascinating camera around his neck. To their way of thinking he was an American of great omnipotence. He was the wisest of the wise. They began to chant in unison as they gathered around him. "*My Father, my Father, Take my picture! My Father, my Father please take my picture*!" The chant increased as Keesey obliged, but as they edged in to touch the great Wise Man of the West, Keesey became cantankerous with all the closeness and his newfound notoriety, so he began to Keesey the kids as he would on occasion Keesey us. Keesey's brashness elevated minute by minute, but Rodgers, who was in hysterical laughter as he too joined in the chant of "*My Father My Father, take my picture*!" finally gained his composure and wrestled Keesey away from the growing horde. Just then one of those very effective constables appeared, and like the iguanas that coexisted with them the youth scattered in a flash. For the remainder of the cruise whenever Keesey appeared with the camera his fellow shipmates would chant, "*My Father, my Father, Take my picture*!"

Our memorable visit to Abidjan ended and we were content as we slipped further south along the African coast. We spent a great deal of time stashing our treasures in various nooks and crannies throughout the ship. Our cruise was still in its infancy yet we already had stuff galore. But once in the Persian Gulf the port opportunities would assuredly dissipate.

Our next stop was in Mossamedes Angola. I am not certain if they were in a civil war or just about to have one. I did know that Fidel Castro was dallying there with his mercenaries in order to export his irritating revolution under the guidance of the ever lurking and opportunistic Soviets. It was a one day stop for fuel. I had duty so Angola did not get added to my memorable list of ports. Some of the folks that did get off the ship said that walking around the area they viewed a great deal of spray painted graffiti displaying dissatisfaction and anger of some sort. It was an obvious trying time for this country. I did not particularly mind missing this troubled port after analyzing some of the feedback.

That was to be the end of the port visits for quite a while as we prepared to steam around the Cape and on into the Indian Ocean. We followed several hundred years in the wake of Portuguese explorers Vasco Diaz and DeGama, but at least LAWRENCE was a helluva lot faster and had movies. Frog didn't like the ship's chow, but it was probably better than the salt pork that our Portuguese predecessors had for fare.

On we sailed. The storied albatross, *Diomedea Epomophora,* actually circled our wake around the Cape of Good Hope, just as the legends told. They were huge birds with giant wing spans, fabulous gliders. The ELMER MONTGOMERY, constantly on our flank provided great silhouette photos as the sunsets came and went in their timeless routine.

As we rounded the Cape message traffic alerted us that we were about to get a photo op on an important Soviet warship. As Cold War warriors, this was our forte. The KIEV, a large Soviet carrier had not been seen for a long spell. It had undergone an in depth overhaul in a Soviet shipyard and we were instructed to make an observation up close and personal when we gained their proximity. When the large ship approached we were on the decks viewing them, cameras in hand. The ELMER MONTGOMERY made a beautifully choreographed cowboy maneuver as it turned a hard over across the Soviet stern and cut a perpendicular incision into their wake. We passed them on our port side. Steve and I decided that it would be very Yankee like to moon the Russians. And without hesitation we executed operation *Double Full Moon.* Although our mission was enacted with impulsive abandon we felt that the questions raised as Soviet scientists studied the glowing gadgets could cause concern about a new secret weapon system on United States DDGs. Miraculously our ship's master at arms didn't catch us, but the important thing for us was having our asses displayed on microfilm in the Kremlin archives.

We continued on our journey right into the Indian Ocean and finally arrived at a liberty port that was interesting and rare for American ships to visit. The island of Mauritius with its small city of Port Louis was unique in its diversity as an Indian Ocean island. Most of the population was Indian in appearance, but there were also a large number of Chinese inhabitants. The two ethnic groups also appeared to be unassimilated, which was curious on a small island. The streets were narrow and crowded and the locals seemed to be enamored with us. A small café we entered had a large poster of American President John F. Kennedy hanging on the wall. In Mauritius there were obviously some fans of America's most famous family, and I could always understand the popularity of a former Sailor. They were very interested in the jobs we did aboard the ship. When we explained that we repaired telephones they were genuinely thrilled about that. Now we also took company that day with one of our gunner's mates, a tough Pennsylvania guy. When he told them he was a gunner, they immediately became unthrilled. They started talking a little louder and their mannerisms and gestures were not generating the warm fuzzies we had been receiving earlier. Wisely, we made a mutual decision to move on down the road and depart the company of our agitated hosts.

During our visit we ambled into one of those classic Chinese gambling dens. One could not have created a Hollywood set with greater authenticity than this place. Going on was some type of Chinese dice game where a cup was involved and perhaps some beans. The room was full of smoke; the single hanging light bulb was focused on the center of the gaming table. The dealer was an ancient Chinese man, with a meticulous little beard. He was totally focused in the play. The smoke created little indoor thunder clouds that hung in the air as if they would start throwing out lightning bolts any second. We studied the game for awhile. It was curious that as weird westerners we created no visible interest among the patrons at all. We unanimously decided that we could out fox the Chinese bean guy. Yes you could call us fatuous, *dumr'n a stump* could also fit. At any rate we sat and bet small coins and did really well raking in the big coins. When we departed having reached our limit of carcinogenic smoke we were proud of the accomplishment. We had accumulated an impressive stack of coins. When we dropped into a local café for a beer, our winnings enabled us to buy three drafts. It seems that the big coins were worth their weight in lima beans or some similar dried vegetable. So it was an early night that evening as we trudged back to the ship, victims of the wise Chinese Bean Guy.

We discovered that Mauritius had one other group that added to the island's diversity. It was a vacation spot for well-heeled French aristocrats. They were known to keep themselves isolated at a resort on the other side of the island so certainly we had to gather our remaining resources and go on a mission to the French resort. Wisely, we had the foresight to get all duded up in our finest attire. Coat and tie on an isolated island in the Indian Ocean while hob- nobbing with the old money French. You really can't make this stuff up. The taxi got us there in a reasonable amount of time. The patrons at this opulent palace were consonant, we were not. Even in sports coats and ties we were still your typical loud Americans. At least we weren't wearing sneakers with the sport's coats. The patrician French were quiet and measured in their movements. They barely glanced at us but they knew we were there. They were sporting what I have come to term the classic *"weaned on a pickle look,"* It appeared to me that each patron of this country club style restaurant must have just finished a long love affair with a 12 ounce *Heinz Kosher Dill.* We had a light dinner and I mean light because the menu prices required a home equity loan and the only real estate we possessed were four by six coffin lockers. Except for Flash, he had a top rack.

It was obvious that for us to eat our fill here we would need a cosigner. I had a bowl of pheasant soup. I savored that fowl. After all, if a ring neck pheasant from Latrobe, Pennsylvania (I thought all pheasants were indigenous to Western Pennsylvania) sacrificed its life to be plucked, frozen, and shipped to France, only to be redirected to a small island in the South Indian Ocean, then by golly it should be savored. This was especially true since the pheasant and I had a common birth place. So I savored my fowl pheasant soup with great appreciation, glad to have robbed the pleasure from the wealthy French, at least for this one instance.

Then I spotted the slot machine near our table. I walked over to that machine deposited a coin and pulled the lever. The machine spun, stopped, and appeared to blink its eyes before it began coughing out coins like a dying cowboy with the whooping cough. The coins gagged their way out of there for an eternity.

The French patrons who had filled this machine in the recent past through unlucky donations looked on with their puckered smirks that indicated to us that it would be wise to bail out. We came, we saw, we conquered. The possibly wealthy descendents of the Marquis de LaWhatever were no longer enamored with our presence. We gathered our winnings, leaving the blue collared waiter a generous tip and hastily departed for the seedier island locations.

We left Mauritius and Port Louis in our wake, knowing that our next stop was going to be at our prescribed location in the Middle East. So far we had no serious behavior problems for the entire cruise. Everyone was alive, functioning, and no international incidents transpired, our microfilmed derrieres in the KIEV incident excepted.

The ship acted like a brand new model, not one who had its keel laid in 1957. For certain there was the constant barrage of sound powered amplifier problems, high salinity cell readings, but turbines and boilers, and main switchboards had no huge faults. We continued on our mission unabated.

Different shops were more than willing to mess with each other in spirited jest. As IC men all other snipes referred to us a *skate rate.* We had a clean air conditioned shop. Hell we even lived in weapons berthing. So we were the bastard children of the department. Engineering officers hated dealing with us because they did not want to discuss gyrocompasses or synchro signal amplifiers. They were already up to their armpits in alligators such as evaporators, galley gear, generators, forced draft blowers, and the multitude of main propulsion equipment. The job of the chief engineer was a nightmare on a destroyer. As far as the IC men and their gear, we were a headache that most preferred not to have. When these strange creatures with tool pouches, meters, and hand sets with clips would show up in a fire room, there would usually be some banter to follow.

One day during the cruise we were sent down to forward fire room to fix a sound powered buzzer system. We had our Simpson 260 multimeter with us. It was a battery operated device designed for measuring resistance, voltage, or amperage in a low power electrical system. Now Rogers pulled one on the fire room messenger of the watch. He took the red meter lead and touched it to my neck. I jittered in a convincing manner and blurted "*Damn you Rogers, quit shocking me you asshole*!" Whereas Rogers shocked me one more time and I jumped two feet off the deck shouting "*Damn it, Quit*!" This was all totally phony as the multimeter carried only a small signal charge for measuring circuit resistance. At this point Rogers slowly turned toward the messenger. "*Crazy IC Men, You are all friggen nuts, man*!" Rogers, with an evil gleam in his eye began to chase the terrified BT all over the fire room with his multimeter.

For quite a while we had some B Division guys thinking our Simpson 260s were deadly weapons, similar to today's taser weapons. They gave us a wide berth until their chief spilled the beans on us. It seems that the forward fire room wasn't calling in their IC trouble calls so we wouldn't electrocute them with our deadly multimeters.

The Keesey Spencer relationship was so much fun that we would kill time by making cassette tapes of the interaction between the two of them. Steve loved playing the part of Mr. Spencer and I usually did Keesey. We were quite talented thespians and our Spencer Keesey tapes were very popular until the day Mr. Spencer came down the shop ladder and busted us. Just as the tape was saying "*Keesey make the orange wire brown stick it in there*!" Mr. Spencer just shook his head and said, "*Keesey good luck with this bunch.* " Mr. Spencer knew that Keesey had a handle on us. So even though we were *All Time Turkeys,* the Keesey factor meant we could be ignored except for emergencies.

When we pulled into Bahrain we required fuel and food. It was a bullets and beans stop. We also received a lot of back mail. All was fine on the Western Pennsylvania front. Bahrain was host to a U S Navy base and we had some rented space there. It was good for a formaldehyde beer and a little shopping, but we were in the Gulf and now on patrol. At my level I had no idea what we were patrolling for. As always, I guess it was watching the Soviets and knowing they were watching us.

So began our endless mission of churning up real estate in the gulf. We all had our cameras and any opportunity for a photo was welcome. There was a particular island that we steamed past and I snapped a photo shot of it. During the ensuing weeks I was able to shoot many interesting islands, all of which were somewhat similar in size and topography. It was not until several days after our return from deployment that I realized my assortment of island photos were entirely comprised of the same island. It was probably worth one photo shot, but it certainly not warrant an entire roll of dedicated film.

That particular stretch of patrol lasted about two months before we made a port call in pre terrorist infested Karachi Pakistan. Liberty call there was all about sights and sounds, and strange things to observe. In Karachi it seemed that everyone drove two cycle gas and oil burning vehicles so the air was ripe with tissue killing carcinogens. Poverty was everywhere. If you gave something away it attracted a multitude of beggars, usually poor women and children.

The restaurants were inexpensive, as was the shopping. From a monetary perspective a Sailor dollar could stretch like a fat woman in spandex. The IC Gang, lazy types as we were, were riding along aristocratically in a horse drawn cart, taking in the sights when a bicyclist streaked by grabbed the knit Schlitz Beer hat off my head and peddled off into the pollution filled smog. Ultimately, he deserved that hat. He displayed a skill that Manhattan bicycle messengers would envy. Those skills were also demonstrated on a bicycle that would have been on the trash heap of any suburb in America. For pure foreign country entertainment value, a Pakistani bicycle magician zooming through the streets of Karachi adorned with a white yarn knitted Schlitz beer hat, how cool was that? He had to be the macaroni and the cheese of Karachi for the life of that hat; well done fleet thief, well done!

We came upon a zoo on our excursion. A zoo, not a big deal you may think. But, the interaction between the animals and patrons in a Karachi zoo is much different than the interaction one experiences in the USA between people and animals. Now Rodgers, the macho yet intellectual man from Huntsville, Alabama received the opportunity to play *Lawrence of Arabia from the LAWRENCE* on the back of a camel at this zoo. He actually had the *Peter O'Toole* look going on, perched high up on the hump of the primeval beast.

I expressed my desire to view the largest snake. When three guys carried out the eleven miles or so of python I became slightly apprehensive. That feeling was extrapolated when they draped the formidable reptile around my shoulders, adorning me with a living serpent shawl. I maintained composure long enough for a few memorable photos and that was the end of that. Once in a while a Sailor must stop and ask. What the hell am I doing in Karachi Pakistan wrapped up in a snake? Is this making me a more world-wise person? Only Sailors and the traveling staff of *National Geographic* get these opportunities. I also understand that until recently a beloved Australian would take everyone on these insane adventures that most folks could only think about. World adventurer *Steve Irwin* met his death in an unfortunate accident but at least he lived life to the fullest. So here in a Pakistani zoo many years prior to cable television, we too were able to dabble in similar excitement. It would not surprise me at all if the renowned Australian had spent some time in the Australian sea service prior to his takeoff as a television star.

When LAWRENCE got underway again we commenced our usual scramble to store our treasures and purchases. Lockers were filled with brass figurines, camel saddles, and various hand made items, such as carpets and tapestries. LAWRENCE was beginning to emulate a treasure ship. If we were to sink and then be rediscovered a century later, we would be a great find to treasure hunters.

But instead we steamed on, with each repaired trouble call progressing us ever closer to the technical excellence that Keesey demanded. Keesey's greenhorns were actually becoming skilled at the IC game. We were a confident bunch and being a captive audience for months on end made us even better.

A brief interlude occurred in our predictable routine when we slipped into the midst of a huge anchorage of Soviet Navy ships. There was a large flotilla resting there at anchor enjoying Soviet style fun and relaxation. Wow, they had political indoctrination, work, and no liberty, *whoo whoo, where do I sign*? What a nasty system their sailors had to sail under; join the navy and see the ocean. Maybe the lucky ones got to do a little sun bathing on a Cuban beach now and then, but I am sure that it wasn't a political priority to get their crews R&R.

The USS LAWRENCE, in true DGUTS fashion had the audacity to steam right through the middle of this group. We had a young OPS type lieutenant who supposedly spoke Russian. He blared over the 1MC topside speakers hailing their ships. The Soviets quickly replied in good, but slightly accented English. "*Your Russian is awful! Please leave the area.*" We took our sweet old time and deliberately made our way through letting them know that the watchful eye of the LAWRENCE was ever in focus on them.

Our deployment made it over the hump or past the half way point as Christmas approached. This year would be an Iranian Christmas. New York, London, Paris, and Bandar Abbas, Iran, we were quite lucky to get one of the four greats. Our mission was good will to the Iranian people, to ensure the future generations of Iranians would continue to love and admire the Western ways of their American friends long into the future.

At the time LAWRENCE visited we were all good buddies. The Iranian Navy even had a few of our old fram cans they kept in good working order with the help of a few wizardly old Yankee machinist mate retirees. The Iranians possessed some old movie projectors which they desperately wanted repaired. They also wanted to view a few fresh American movies. Ambassadors of good will that we were, the Iranians were quickly accommodated by the Keesey boys. Repairs were made and we even showed them a few flicks. Bean volunteered as the projectionist and the IC men were granted heroic status by the Iranian crew. They really became enamored with Flash. I think they just enjoyed saying his name, FFLLAssh, FFLLAssh! Bean was also a big hit and the two were like Elvis on tour in Tupelo. They didn't get their pictures on any Iranian coins or bills because Pshaw Pahlavi had a monopoly on all of that. Nonetheless, the red carpet was rolled out for the DGUTS IC men.

A few Iranian sailors invited us out to one of their clubs so we accepted and went out with the boys. The Iranian club was a true dude fest in every sense of the expression. The music was OK, but the guys dancing together were a little much for us and we made it a rather early exit.

We did go to a theatrical play there that was sponsored by members of a local community working for one of the oil companies. The home grown thespians actually did a very professional job and it was quite enjoyable for us. I believe the foreigners working there just enjoyed having some new folks to talk to. We were an innocent and enthusiastic bunch, if not a polished group, and the oil company workers were excellent hosts. As far as we knew the Arab oil embargo was still in effect, although we didn't know for certain. News was slow out there. There was no satellite radio or e mail and all we had were some radio news sheets and snail mail letters. If we were suddenly sent off to war we often joked that people back home would know about it long before we did. World affairs weren't high on the IC men's priority list. Sports yes, news, ahh, who cares?

We had a great adventure that Christmas season by participating in a tour to the ruins of Persepolis in an ancient Persian city known as Shiraz. We were flown there on an Iranian Air Force C-130 to an airport and then bused to a very amenable western style hotel. The hotel was interesting in that there were two bands playing in different lounges. One was a very talented group from a city in Poland. They played a western repertoire of songs like *It Never Rains in Southern California.* The Polish girl singing had a good measure of Eastern European accent in her lyrics, popping in that occasional v for a w, as if she were *Arnold Swarzenegger's* little sister.

There we were, a small gaggle of Yankees in an ancient Persian city listening to an Eastern Bloc band belt out American tunes. The band was actually quite good, I've heard far worse. In a different lounge was a local Iranian trio. That side was packed with people enjoying the much more popular local flavored tunes. *"Ching a ching ching.. Ya Ya ching a ching."* Sorry, no disrespect intended to Iranian music but it just wasn't working for me,

The era of the Pshaw was one of openness to American life styles. The women weren't covered in burkas, they dressed like American business ladies. The one thing you could not escape was the image of Rezi Pahlavi, the Pshaw. Money coins, billboards, and posters. If they could have figured a way to put his likeness into the sky to eclipse the sun with his silhouette he would have done that too. He must have been a swell guy. Boy, were these folks in for a rude awakening. Still, it's hard for me to accept that a group of people, especially their military would soon be so vehemently opposed to us because during our visit I can't recall a friendlier group of sailors, nor do I remember ever being treated better by another ship's crew.

The ruins were in fairly good shape for ruins. Rocks and structures as old as history itself were there to be photographed. Keesey went on this trip and loved it. The Keesey SLR camera was snapping away like a hungry hen pecking corn. *Snap, snap, snap.. snap.. snap…* Steve, to educate himself with a historical perspective of the site queried Keesey, "*Keesey, did you ever visit here when this place had people*?" Over all it was a good trip. I remember one final scene, we were on the bus heading back and we were traveling through some dusty desert terrain passing an occasional goat herder when whole bus broke out in Christmas carols; this being a typical *Navy tin can Christmas*.

We were underway again, steadfast in our well practiced routine of pounding holes in the water. Occasionally we managed to get on each other's nerves. Steve was pinching me one day. He was trying to gauge my pain thresh-hold I suppose. He found it and I about strangled him with a sound powered phone cord. Luckily I let go or I would be writing this from federal prison. Steve was unhappy with me for awhile and I felt despondent for a long time about that.

Now Steve and I had actually over purchased our personal supplies, especially the items of shaving cream and powder. One day Steve was sound asleep, his hand open as he nested peacefully in his rack. I could not resist. I filled his hand with shaving cream which he rubbed continuously all over his carcass for the next several hours, all while fast asleep. When Steve woke up he had a slight skin rash from the shaving cream. He was really whiny about what was a very minor prank. That evening as I hit my pit I felt the goo of the shaving cream filled pillow ooze through my fingers.

The gauntlet was thrown, war declared. It was a strategic conflict of epic proportion, yet the battles and sneak attacks were waged with reckless abandon. Toothpaste, pickle juice, and other sabotage materials were incorporated into the ensuing struggles for supremacy. Armageddon occurred early one evening as we broke into salvos of baby powder. Blasts erupted as I hit Steve with a white powder broadside. The retaliation was chaotic and effective as Steve manned two large canisters of Johnson and Johnson. We were covered with powder, as we emulated the abominable snowmen of the Himalayas. When the emotions of the battle subsided it was too late. The powder had formed a toxic cloud in the berthing compartment. The white fog was wafted on the gentle breeze of the compartment ventilation system. It centered gently over the center of the compartment where it hung pleasantly over the evening card game taking place among the senior gunner's mates. As they began to experience the cloud effects of the *Abominable IC Snow Men* or the *DGUTS Pillsbury Dough Boys*, we knew we were in the abyss of deep shit. The gunners followed the trail leading to the culprits.

The immolation of the battle was irremovable. After the verbal flaying, the cleanup began and continued hour after hour after tedious hour. Cleaning up a white residue of powder from an infinite number of cracks and crevasses is a tortuous exercise and I never engaged in baby powder wars again. Our berthing compartment had a test ban treaty now in effect. The treaty was put in effect by the senior gunner's mate. He effectively banned all chemical weaponry in perpetuity. Anyone violating the treaty would receive a size 13 in the ass without warning. This highly effective treaty remained unbroken for the remainder of our tours.

Just as thoughts occurred in dreams that we were dead participants in some *Twilight Zone* horror of a never ending patrol of the Persian Gulf, we commenced the beginning of the end. Out chop was a high light we all waited for. It was time to head home. The adventure was fun but it was time to move on back to the west and revisit the mother country, USA, complete with rock'n roll, muscle cars, McDonalds's, discos, and all that American potpourri we bitched about when there, yet we missed sincerely when gone. We were relieved by a ship, the name of which I haven't the foggiest. As out chop day began, the 1MC played Simon and Garfunkel's *Homeward Bound*. It was still going to take a month to get out of the Indian Ocean and around Africa, but at least we were heading in the right direction; south, west, north, west, Norfolk. Keesey's gyro was doing just fine. We were steaming at sixteen knots, steady and stable.

We did do a liberty port in Mombasa Kenya. Many of the crew went on a driven safari and had a blast. Sailors and rhinoceros, I could not venture to speculate on who got the best of that encounter. I wasn't able to experience that tour due to due to duty requirements. There were times when your number was up. That meant it was your turn to stand the watch and that was exactly what you were going to be doing. On a deployed DDG your number in port was every third day. What was amazing was that inside the ship everything was the same, as if we were in Norfolk. There was the work, the PMS schedule, and the cleaning assignments. What constantly shifted was the view on your back porch. Now it was certainly possible to stay home and go nowhere. Many Sailors did just that. They get underway and stay right there between the lifelines for six months. I have always found that commendable but I could personally never do that. But we are an organization that encompasses all types of personalities. For every party animal there is a matching reserved family man, doing his duty, and getting his job done. Those Sailors are content to stand their watches and get back home.

I had enlisted out of wanderlust. In my early years I was a student who held a great deal of interest in history and geography. I was driven to visit the places and scenes I had viewed on the printed pages of my text books and in the well worn copies of the library's *National Geographic.*

I was fulfilling my aspirations. Here you had to earn the right to visit somewhere exotic, like staying underway for two straight months, but this was a great vehicle for a nineteen year old without an expense account to gain an understanding of the world.

Mombasa Kenya offered all the unusual hand crafted purchases that the west coast of Africa offered at the beginning of the cruise. The crew loaded up on final purchases of all manners of wooden animals and other gifts of interest. The LAWRENCE was becoming a menagerie, so stowage became ever more critical.

What I found surprising about Mombasa was their pristine beaches. In my mind Kenya was all about wildlife and safaris. Someday I would also include great distance runners in that mental picture. It was a pleasant discovery to find it also offered excellent beaches. As for the

Kenyans they were an animated and colorful people who spoke fair English in a very engaging manner. It was impossible not to like them. Being reflective, I have to thank OPEC for the Arab Oil Embargo and for closing that Suez Canal because it made for a much more interesting Middle East deployment. I know that my fellow citizens had to endure gas pump lines and high inflation so we were the lucky ones in that regard. We missed most of that hoopla and by the time we returned again the lines were once more normal at the local Exxon station.

We departed Mombasa and headed back the way we came, retracing our route around Africa from months ago. This time there would be no port stops. It was nonstop to Bermuda. There we would take on fuel and have a liberty call prior to pulling into home port.

The final month was uneventful. We were an efficient IC Gang by then. We could fix any malfunction that placed a challenge to our skills. We were fueled by an oiler at sea on a regular schedule. The USNS oilers consisted of civilian crews that refueled and supplied Navy warships. They had a few active duty signalmen and ops types but they are primarily crewed by civilian government employees. They often stay at sea in a deployed status longer than our active duty personnel. They are scary good at what they do and everyone on a USNS ship is efficient, based normally on years of experience and an overflowing bank vault of sea time.

One thing of note on the return trip to Norfolk was the second Shellback initiation. On the first crossing, the ship boasted approximately forty Shellbacks and about two hundred and fifty Pollywogs. On the second go around those statistics were reversed. The thirty or so Pollywogs we had acquired over seas were in trouble. I decline detail, but to their credit they lived, and they prospered.

Bermuda and the town of Hamilton are so beautiful and picturesque that regardless of where you point a camera you create an instant personal post card. Bermuda is a unique island. It wasn't tropical as many perceive it, just pleasant. The city of Hamilton has the quaint British flavor and offered reasonable deals on English clothing. The adventurous LAWRENCE Sailors had their fun on the mopeds, the transportation method of choice on the island. We were passengers in carts or cabs for a half year and it was nice to control a motor even if it did require pedal assistance. The moped provided an excellent method to see the island and traversing the island one could view the large hotels on the beaches, the luxurious golf courses, and the cozy cottages nestled in the hills. Zooming around the island at about twenty-five miles per hour, I understood why people would choose to vacation here.

Every Yankee Sailor learns about the Royal Navy at some point. Sooner or later you will mingle with our British brethren. They are a very amiable group and you may well get away with a stereotype that says they all have a sense of humor. They also approve of us, and being liked is usually a good thing. One thing an American Sailor learns quickly is to never attempt to out party members of the Queen's Navy. It ain't happening. That's not stereotype, that's just fact. They have the party market cornered and we should respect that and take our place as a distant fifth, because if truth be told the Australians, Canadians, the Germans with their evil *Jeagermeister*, along with the champion RN, will all put the light beer drinking Yankees to shame. My advice is to acknowledge their eminence; allow them their victories; we can not be the champions of everything. Some of our guys, feeling festive at the conclusion of our cruise thought they could hang at the *Hog Penny Inn* with a group from an HMS frigate. The Brits got to singing, the Yanks got to singing, and the patrons observing were actually enjoying it. When the Brits began passing around knee high boots of beer, pulled off the raunchy foot of an RN machinist mate, the Yanks started falling out quickly. The boot was also being laced with gin, scotch, and other substances. The Brits sang on, the Americans defeated, left for cab rides back to the comfort of their pits. The Royal Navy had held serve, *God Save the Queen*.

As we were nearing our final hours in port one enterprising fellow did not have time to return his moped to the moped rental establishment. Apparently, the thoughtful young man solved his problem by driving it off the pier and into the harbor. It is impressively amazing how quickly some guys can solve problems. No moped, no problem, this gentleman was obviously thinking ahead. That was the only incident I can remember on that entire cruise that shed negative light on the LAWRENCE crew. With our cruise under our belts we all made it 1/8th of the way to our next subsequent good conduct medal, except for Mr. Moped of course. Whereas most were greeted by wives and sexy girlfriends upon arrival, Mr. Moped was visited by some stern looking officials of the law enforcement community. He was soon to become the proud purchaser of a brand new moped, which he donated to the friendly Bermuda rental dealer. They must love when Sailors do that.

Finally the day prior to homecoming arrived. We had a great channel fever night. Channel fever night was all about being too excited to sleep. The ice cream machine churned and spewed, while all remaining snacks were broke out. The movie projectors whirled throughout the night, nonstop with whatever female intensive flicks we had left, although by then they were already viewed several hundred times. That never mattered though because we were all happy. We were home.

Married guys like Rogers, or guys with girl friends like Ole Keesey were understandably ready to go home or to go on leave. My girl friend, an old Kawasaki 500 two stroke, that shot like a rocket and sounded like a broken banjo was hibernating in my Mom's garage in Pennsylvania so I took Roger's duty on the first day.

Pulling into the pier had a very Hollywood flair to it. Our officers were all wearing turbans, and we posted a large banner that said *LAWRENCE OF ARABIA* across our bridge wing. It was cool, it was festive, and a picture of a Navy ship's homecoming should one day be a caricature selection on the back cover of *Reader's Digest*; an excellent choice for their life in America page. It is pure red, white, and blue, a true apple pie moment. As family members poured aboard, tons of presents, popped out of secret spaces. Bundles of loot from afar were shouldered up and hauled off the brow.

The electricians rigged shore power, the HTs helped pull aboard the cables, and the engineman brought aboard steam and fresh water. The food service guys hauled mountains of trash to the dumpsters and the IC men established phone lines. It was back to an in port routine. If only for a little while, the high stress pace of war fighting preparation was placed on low speed. We had returned safely without incident. The LAWRENCE reputation had grown. We steamed for the entire deployment, never once losing power as the old plant answered the call, exactly in the manner the shipyard intended when they laid the keel back in 1957. The LAWRENCE was good to go and still had many miles remaining to be displayed on the odometer of her underwater log.

The IC Gang had morphed into a well run top notch group of talented technicians. We each became third class petty officers on time. I was merely one cycle ahead of the other guys so I was Keesey's second in command. I didn't get to adorn my pajamas with epaulettes or anything so ostentatious, but being an IC3 instead of an ICFN had merit. The standing joke was ICFN stood for *I can't fix nothing*. The hole snipes loved it and never grew tired of springing it on us. IC3 was welcome for more than just a paycheck increase.

I rode the Kawasaki south to Norfolk in April on a liberty weekend and although it was sixty degrees in the Pittsburgh area, it was lightly snowing in the mountains near Somerset, Pennsylvania. I wisely turned the bike around and nursed it home. I managed to get extended liberty from Keesey, and I attempted the trip again the next day. That time I crossed the Pennsylvania mountains and made it south. It didn't matter that I was colder than a polar bear's rectum, and wetter than a nasty high school principal in a dunk tank. When I stopped for gas I had to be peeled off the handle bars. Fortunately, I was able to stay erect long enough to get back to the ship, where I was promptly given a four hour sounding and security watch. When it's your turn, it's your turn. There are certain things you must do on a ship. Numero uno; relieve the watch on time. A watch stander rightfully expects to be relieved on time. Being late or making someone seek you out makes you a bad shipmate. I would rather get a root canal without Novocain or anesthetic than have Keesey get a report that I didn't relieve the watch on time. I was there on time and I stood the watch.

We soon completed the standard leave period and new people began to arrive and old people migrated on to further duty stations or to civilian life challenges. Almost all of the Vietnam era guys were on to their life's work. Twenty four pages had already been ripped from the Playboy calendars since the ship disengaged from the coast of Vietnam. I never heard from Schmidt, Knight, or Horgan again. The Navy is such a dynamic here and now organization, always focused on the road ahead that it is often tough to be reflective or nostalgic. Ship mates come and go and become legends but we rarely see them again.

The HTs added a wiry and curly haired guy named Ira Heavens in their shop. He was Missouri born, small in stature, and full of energy. He could weld pretty darn well, but he definitely wasn't your big gorilla HT type. If I had to compare Ira to a group I've seen it would be a NASCAR race driver. He had a mint condition 1968 GTO, and he loved going fast or talking about it. He was a true gear head and his idea of the ultimate good time was to be strapped into something that goes two hundred miles an hour and to drive around in circles with like minded individuals. He wasn't going to the NASCAR circuit anytime soon, so the streets of Norfolk in his GTO had to suffice. However, Ira, the welder and motor head also liked to party and have a good time. Although he didn't look like a night life kind of a guy, he had a leisure suit, and respectable disco abilities.

The seventies back in port were fun. Inflation was awful, but we weren't home owners either. We were still living for free on the good ole USS LAWRENCE. I passed the motorcycle safety school and had upgraded to a flashy purple Kawasaki 750 ring a ding two stroke engine motorcycle. The bike was universally disrespected by Harley riders the world over, but it was like getting shot out of a cannon. For sheer quarter mile speed it was unmatched. That two stroke engine would smoke, and then explode, loudly polluting the innocent Earth's atmosphere. I believe they are all illegal today because they polluted worse than a hillbilly clan having a tire fire.

My bike, despite being a rocket just wasn't the ideal form of transportation to the rage of the times, meaning the discos. So we had to tighten our seat belts, and hang on for dear life while we rode around with Ira in the GTO.

The base clubs were hopping back then, there were also clubs out in town that were quite a good time. We had leisure suits and other rather ugly attire. Even Steve found one in a thrift store.

There was a point of contention among Ira and Steve. They would mix it up every now and then about gas. The GTO had a big motor, 400 cubic inches. IRA drove it like a race car and it burned some fuel. As we all pitched in for gas, Steve would get irritated at Ira's lead foot method of vehicle operation. I would usually step in as peace maker. For whatever reason, I assumed that role, or so it seemed. Even Sailors on liberty can have drama.

As participants of the era we were disco Sailors for awhile. Some guy from the electric shop, a kid from Brooklyn, Walter Rogers who called himself the Dancer taught us a disco line dance he called *The Brookline Walk.* I suppose we mastered it because people responded and wanted to learn it. We spent our weekends as disco babies, listening to *Play That Funky Music White Boy* and other such songs of lyrical genius. For all the people who profess to despise disco music, those clubs were certainly packed full of polyester clad dancers. As everyone from that era states that they all hated disco music, I can only suppose that all those disco babies from the seventies are either lying or dead.

Perhaps it was the flattening of the seedy strip or maybe the end of Vietnam but whatever the reason, the Tidewater area became friendlier to the Navy. I did not see one sign there directing me to keep out or to stay off the grass. During my first year there I spent most of my free weekends going back to my parent's house. But after a couple of years Southeastern Virginia began to grow on me. There was a lot to do there. There was always something happening on the ship or on the base. Duty days were a pain but it was good to stay home once in a while. Your money lasted longer with duty days thrown in.

The other IC men began buying motorcycles. Steve, Bean, and some guys from the ET shop all started to ride. We used to throw a coin on the road map on a liberty weekend and wherever the coin landed that became the destination. One weekend we were miles away and we queried some country kids what there was to do there. He said we ought to head out east for about a hundred miles; we would get to Norfolk and Virginia Beach, "there were all kinds of *stuff* to do there."

These rides were kind of fun, but all good things must come to an end, often abruptly. That summer Steve broke his ankle in a parking lot broadside. Bean wiped out and was on crutches, and I had a spill on Atlantic Avenue while the midnight revelers and inebriated spectators cheered my misfortune in drunken glee. Fairly bruised and battered, I was still the least affected. The chief engineer was not a happy camper to see most of the IC Gang hobbling around like the survivors of a Civil War prison camp, all in varying states of disrepair. After that there was a slow transition to four wheeled vehicles or more often to no vehicles at all.

I had a personal dilemma to deal with. I was in my own personal conundrum, with my motorcycle. At the time I had insurance with a company that provided motorcycle coverage based on engine size. One's driving record was not a factor. That insurance was offered right at the bike dealer's shop. It was convenient and although expensive, it was affordable. The dilemma was that the Kawasaki did not contemplate how to go slow. I was a Pittsburgher of Czechoslovakian descent playing Kamikaze on a Kawasaki. Slowly but surely the Norfolk police, the Virginia Beach Police, and the State Police all got to write me expensive love letters at some roadside spot. I paid and I paid, until I could pay no more. Then one night my affliction culminated on Hampton Boulevard in Norfolk. I was at the foot of the bridge near Old Dominion University when a souped up Triumph Trident pulled alongside me at the traffic light and revved it up in a clear challenge. The *Kamikaze Kawasaki Kid* could not refuse the call to arms as the testosterone was in total control of my brain. Yes, I waxed the Triumph by a country mile. I was fast, I was a streak, I was an atom in an electron gun, and I was a super nova bursting through the universe. I was, as the cop stated to the judge later, the fastest thing he'd ever seen. And my reward was a summons to appear in court for reckless driving.

I knew my court date was fast approaching and I knew I needed money for what promised to be a fine of magnanimous proportions. Being the resourceful individual that I was, I went to the Atlantic Fleet Credit Union. Once there I talked to the old retired chief who was their loan officer. I informed the sage banker of my impending crises; his response was a smile and a wave bye- bye as he bid me best wishes in jail.

The Norfolk traffic judge was actually an important historic person in Norfolk, Virginia's legal history. He was famous for knowing every street sign, every traffic light, and every tree in Norfolk. The GPS satellite surveillance systems of today were no match for the memory of this most honorable judge.

He was known to go through cases quickly, and my reason for exceeding 90 on Hampton Boulevard was unimpressive to the wise litigator. I was remanded to jail with the nameless Triumph rider as my despondent companion.

I spent a day and a half in jail in rather disgusting squalor. I felt like a chicken in a coup. The place even smelled like, well. … a chicken coop. Actually I am insulting chicken coops nation -wide with my comparison. This was worse. I would not recommend the Norfolk jail holding pen of that era as a must visit vacation spot. There were about twenty of us in this cage. Most were in varying stages of sleeping it off. They did feed us some bologna and bread sandwiches. They must have let the bologna sit out and season for a week or so in order to match the ambiance of the environment where it would be consumed.

Back in those days you were permitted to attend court without your chief escorting you. Now they must attend, the reason is obvious. In case you are incarcerated the ship will know where you are. I was now in the can and the LAWRENCE did not know. I was sure Steve would let Keesey know, which he did. I was a hot commodity for the ship at this time but not for my charming personality.

We were about to have one of those acronym inspections called an NTPI or some set of initials like that, and I was the security system alarm technician designated for that particular inspection. I was the person who had to demonstrate to an inspector how I performed my job. I was in short, *a person of value.*

A jailor came up and said, "*Boy you know somebody in high places, cause there is somebody with a lot of gold about to get you out*!" The heroic LTJG Spencer had arrived in full uniform to get me out and back for that inspection. I had no idea who he talked to, or what he did, but he didn't like to lose. Spencer was a destroyer engineering officer, so losing wasn't in his acumen. I knew that he was taking me back to the ship. The JG was heroic. He had saved me from the putrid bologna sandwiches and the toilets that were unusable because someone always had his head inside the bowl engrossed in the process of close inspection. I suppose Mr. Spencer thought I had been through enough so he refrained from lecturing me about the incident. We passed the NTPI or whatever it was with flying colors. LAWRENCE was completely recertified to nuke whoever needed nuked.

The ship was going to go through a nine month overhaul period through the next winter and spring. Ira and I decided to reenlist; we were having a good time so why get out. It really was truly just that that simple. The captain was ecstatic because we were going to stay right there on the LAWRENCE. You were required to serve five years at sea before you earned a shore tour anyway; so why not stay put?

I did persuade Mr. Spencer to send me to electrical gyro compass C school in Great Lakes, Illinois over the winter. This fit the schedule as the ship was undergoing an overhaul in the Norfolk Navy Yard. I wanted the jewel of the IC rating, gyrocompass expertise. Keesey was a gyro man, and I wanted to be a gyro man. The equipment was thought provoking. The MK 19 Electrical Gyro had the biggest and thickest technical manual I ever saw. It contained a myriad of weird concepts such as period and dampening, and it even proclaimed to contain a start gyro within the gyro itself. The system control cabinet housed a host of resolvers and amplifiers that corrected for vertical and horizontal earth rates as the ship traveled over the world's oceans. I readily envisioned the idea of this contraption in a *Jules's Vern* novel, *Captain Nemo* using it to enhance some wild adventurous tale. To master MK 19 Gyro School you had to learn theories of rigidity, processional force, and gyroscope tendencies. They covered the operation and troubleshooting process of the entire system, including its standby power generator. It not only provided indications of ship's heading to end users, it provided roll and pitch information to the ship's weapons systems. In short, the gyrocompass was the one major system on the ship that made IC men critical. It was a challenge to go to that school as a third class and would not be easy.

Ira and I reenlisted on the bridge of the LAWRENCE, a little less than three years from the day Gary and I flew off to Great Lakes. We took the oath for six more years. Most of our peers thought we were nuts. Even our reenlisting officer, the gung ho, balls to the wall LTJG Spencer asked if we really wanted to do this. But the journey begun three years prior wasn't completed. Where it would eventually lead no one could say for certain. I had discovered enough about the world to know that the grass wasn't always greener on the other side. The LAWRENCE was a good ship, despite not winning any ribbons or awards during my tour. The *Working Your Ass Off Ribbon* still hasn't been invented, but maybe it should be for ships like the LAWRENCE. I enjoyed the work, and my friends. As for the ribbons, an old under-decorated master chief once said to me, "We can't all be *Audie Murphy*." On the LAWRENCE, snipes didn't get bogged down with award ceremonies.

The LAWRENCE Chief's Mess did know how to recognize talent. They put every effort in 73 to keep Knight in the fold. The pay and opportunities just could not compete with the civilian opportunities. One year later they made a tremendous push to reenlist a first class fire controlman named Mikulski. He was as sharp as a tack and an outstanding Sailor, highly regarded throughout the ship. They couldn't keep him either. The Navy was going to have to start winning the battles to keep these types of people or a huge talent shortage would predictably ensue. As the seventies surged ahead many Navy wide problems were looming, and changes were essential.

When I departed the LAWRENCE in route to Great Lakes Training Command in the fall of 1975, few if any of these big picture issues were anywhere near the zip codes of my thought processes. A few things had evolved over time. I went home to Pennsylvania a lot less. I was a confident technician on a ship I liked. I had good friends from many different places. I smoked too much, and I still loved to raise hell. Making a machismo statement, I upgraded my two wheel ride to a Kawasaki 900, four-cylinder. My reckless driving ticket penalized me six months suspension of driving privileges, and of course this prevented me from developing realistic thoughts about car insurance. On a glass half full note at least my driving record would improve over the months I would be in Great Lakes because the Kawasaki was securely stowed away in a storage facility, sleeping soundly.

I gathered my orders from LAWRENCE and once again I was TAD to school. That summer I had weathered a 400 hertz motor generator school in Norfolk. Now I was in route to the big IC prize, gyro school, well worth the sacrifice of the Great Lakes winter. When I arrived at O'Hare, I pressed on with my recovered sea bag, stepped outside to the bus stop and ran into a Sailor with the IC3 telephone on his crow. After initial salutations, we discovered that we were headed in exactly the same direction and ultimate destination.

Craig Wilkins was a Texan who had also lived in Louisiana. Or maybe he was from Louisiana and now lives in Texas. He has a bit of the drawl from somewhere on the Gulf Coast. At that age Craig was a dark haired slim guy. Today, thirty-five years later Craig is a dark haired slim guy. He had a slight stutter which he always thought was worse than it actually was. Truthfully it helped make his jokes funnier, and Craig's joke repertoire was infinite. To this day, I still receive an ample internet supply from the rangy Texan.

Craig and I hit it off immediately. When we arrived in Great lakes and checked in, we were assigned as room mates. A day later a local Chicago kid was added to our room. I only remember him as *The Crab,* aptly named as he brought his tiny friends to our room for a visit about two weeks later. This resulted in a trip to sick bay for the appropriate body wash treatment and eradication procedure.

Craig was onboard for closed circuit television school and he too would serve in Norfolk on an Adam's Class DDG, The RICHARD E BYRD. The closed circuit TV school was a tough curriculum, generally regarded as the most difficult one to get through in the entire IC rate, but Craig managed to do quite well in it. I never witnessed him stressed over a test the entire time I was there. He also earned his own nick-name, *Rip Van Wilkens*, bestowed for his unnatural ability to rest well for long periods of time, almost to the point of hibernation. Being from Texas or Louisiana he probably thought all Yankees hibernated for the winter. Personally, I had to struggle through gyro school to keep pace. We had an amazing instructor, a senior chief named Holsworth. He would stand in front of the class and trace circuit current through the control cabinet, without visual referral to the large schematic drawings behind him. He was big guy, but he off set his brawn with a large pair of BCs, or what we refer to as Navy issue birth control glasses, specifically designed to discourage second looks, or rather any looks from any living breathing female.

Senior Chief Holsworth had a gruff voice and would go through a very complicated and technical process on the schematic and then punctuate his instruction with a pointer slap to the print and his trademark phrase, "*No problem.*"

It was: "*Current flows to pin 6 of K808 operating the relay for the first time to the second position. This applies a voltage across the indicator lights illuminating DS1-DS6. Start amplifiers….*, "he would end this seventy second burst of stuff with a slap and, "no problem." He was the *Czar of Gyros*. Senior Chief turned the Mark 19 tech manual into a work of art. At approximately one foot-thick, it contained troubleshooting charts, parts lists, and schematic drawings. The *Sperry* people who thought this thing up probably were so smart that they in all likelihood never dated or matched a set of trousers with a shirt. There were many geeks participating in the work force prior to the proliferation of personal computers. Their numbers congregated in defense electronics.

I bumbled my way through the school, gyros by day, easy barracks living by night. It was cold in Great Lakes, so going out was a real chore. Steeler mania had hit all Pittsburghers in full force and we became the most obnoxious fans in the history of sports. Years later, in 1999 I heard a joke that said, "*How many Steeler fans does it take to change a light bulb?*" The answer, "*five. There is one to change the light bulb and four to tell you how great the Steelers were in the seventies.*"

That's how we were in that era of Steeler dominance. Just mentioning the Steelers evicted a loud STEEEEELLLEEEEERSSS!! From one's voice. Being a Steeler fan in the midst of other team's followers only enhanced our vocal ranting. Each week that the Steelers pummeled an opponent into submission elated us to the next level of fan exuberance. We felt as gladiators living vicariously through the performances of Swann,

Harris, Lambert, Green, Bradshaw, and Blount. We were they, and they represented us. After a lifetime of frustration and lovable ineptitude, the Steelers personified power. The mention of their name evicted an adrenaline rush as all those years of pent up frustration burst out of their fans lungs. Their leader, *Emperor Chas Noll* created a victorious group of warriors that became the best of all time. This team created a black and gold nation that lives to this day, and I was no exception to the throngs of black and gold followers. Watching a Steelers game in a lounge of varied fans allowed our Steeler contingency to gloat in superiority as the victim team's fans stomped out in anger and disappointment. My favorite line to the inferior was, "*You should be proud that your team scored three points against the awesome Steeler defense.*" This was usually said after a 27-3 whipping. Unfortunately, my heartfelt words of comfort failed to alleviate the pain of those vanquished unfortunate souls. They sulked, we gloated.

One memorable Sunday the Steelers were in a critical play off game, their opponent, forgettable, not worthy of remembrance. In our room we had the TV going full blast. The party was on with about ten guys in participation. It was a true Steeler "*Dude Fest*". The temperature was approximately six degrees that day in Great Lakes and the snow was coming hard. The snow was also flying in Pittsburgh at the site of the game. The menacing black uniforms in the blizzard were having their way with the unfortunate opponent. We wanted the effect of being at the game so our windows were wide open. The snow was about an inch deep on our room floor. We had our coats on and we created the desired effect as we shared brandy to fend off the cold. We were that day the forerunners to virtual reality television. We were there, in the game and it was great. STEEELLLLEERRSS!!

The senior chief was a very unique individual. The amount of knowledge he held in his head was absolutely dazzling. Granted the opportunity, I couldn't resist an impromptu moment at an attempt to emulate him. One splendid class morning senior chief was detained somewhere and there; leaning against the blackboard adjacent to the enlarged blue print was his personal sword, the famed wooden pointer.

It was perhaps the half way point of the class and we had bonded, as all Navy classes eventually do. In this environment I felt comfortable in grabbing the pointer and beginning a complete rendition of his teachings and mannerisms. I ended my electrical circuit training with the customary, "*No problem*," after each technical stage. Unknown to me was the appearance of senior chief in the door way behind me. My class mates were only too willing, allowing me to hang there as I continued my ranting.

The senior chief said, "*You missed K808 energizing for the third time to the sixth position. Other than that, no problem.*" Holsworth was the MK 19 Gyro. He was a part of the system, no less important than the eleven type one amplifiers or the gimble rings, or the start gyro. Without guys like Holsworth, there teaching, the trade equipment was just a big pile of expensive junk.

After a hard day of school, the hour or so just before chow was the hour of the day to let out your stress. The entire barracks would squeeze into the TV lounge for the 1630 showing of the black and white "*Three Stooges.*" One of the local channels ran the old classics every day and there we would gather, a large gaggle of comedy addicts, laughing until our sides hurt as we watched the shows that each of us had viewed dozens of times already. Having twenty, twenty- year olds all laughing together at 1930s slap stick comedy somehow made it all even funnier. Curley, running from a balloon stuck to his ass doesn't seem humorous, but somehow it worked for us.

A great big deal happened that winter in Great Lakes. Somehow, I made it to second class petty officer. I was now one of the Navy's most valuable commodities. Ask any chief what he would like more of and they will normally want a few more second class petty officers. The second class is usually a competent technician with enough experience to troubleshoot and repair systems independently of close supervision. Having that second chevron is a major step for any young Sailor. In the seventies it was difficult for the Navy to keep its second class petty officers enlisted for continued careers. The junior officer ranks were even worse, and it was an issue demanding attention in the near future. It wasn't cost effective to pay for schools and training just to have officers and petty officers wave goodbye and saunter off to *Hughes Aircraft, RCA, or Honeywell.* But indeed, that was the state of the Navy in 1975.

I departed Great Lakes and headed back to the Navy Yard and the LAWRENCE as a second class IC man with a gyro compass NEC. I had come a long way since I left Pennsylvania. I felt ready for an increased role. I still had many goals to address, but already, because of my reenlistment to remain onboard, I had been a DGUTS crew member longer than ninety-nine percent of the present Sailors assigned. The good news was that the core of the IC Gang remained intact throughout the yard period. The ship eventually pushed the yard period to completion in eight months instead of the allotted nine. Everyone was happy about that as yard periods have a tendency to wear on a Sailor after a time.

Surprisingly, the hard times commenced in earnest at the end of the overhaul. When a ship enters a yard period, thousands of events and processes take place. It truly is a time to say *shit happens.* In the IC room for example many pieces of equipment were removed to shops where they were refurbished, cleaned, calibrated, upgraded, and returned. Switchboards were invaded and new circuits were added in, often entire systems were added or deleted as technology demanded changes. For the IC men it was the addition of a cathodic protection system, a hull mounted device that supplied a low voltage charge controlled by a magnetic amplifier to slow down hull corrosion. Much of our overhaul though, involved refurbishing the equipment we already had. The problem is that often these systems have minds of their own. After not working for close to a year they become energized and the long dormant gremlins commence to wreck havoc, especially when voltages are applied to their lazy underused circuits. Fuses blow, wiring melts, and indicators oscillate in rebellion. The gremlins wage their war of disobedience resisting like dedicated guerillas. They fight viciously, unpredictably, always searching for the weak link. The little bastards will take advantage of any loose screw, moisture on a connection, or a potentiometer turned a quarter turn too far. Alarms that were set to ring at a certain tank level in the morning, will not work at night. As the war of the post ship yard shake down wages on, one answer was to take half days off. Yes we went to the luxury of half work days; 0600-1800 Monday through Monday. This became our new working hours, as we battled the pure evil of electrical gremlin chaos.

The heroic crew of LAWRENCE fought the ship yard gremlins with all that we had. The plant sputtered and started, stopped and stalled. Like a long awakening giant she was sputtering back to life, stiff and sore, like *Rip Van Winkle* after his twenty year nap. It was the hardest time I ever remember on LAWRENCE. The post yard was when everyone overcame the inertia and lurched into the swing of being an active fleet asset.

It was the gremlins, the mindset of the crew, the drills that had to be practiced, and seamanship skills required to be relearned. For this the Navy had the perfect answer, Guantanamo Bay Cuba, or better known as GITMO. For good reason the Navy held on to this piece of paradise, right in the backside of our good buddy, Fidel. GITMO was the ideal place for a gremlin infested, training depleted crew fresh out of the shipyard.

GITMO was filled with a group of brown juice- spitting sun tanned amberjack and snapper catching fisherman chief petty officer types who had one purpose in life; getting you and your ship ready for anything, anytime, anywhere. They really weren't concerned if you thought they were being too hard on you. You either completed satisfactorily every aspect of the training or you simply remained there forever. The best way to approach *Refresher Training* was to act as if there was no other place on earth that you would rather be. Yes, if you were to win a ten million dollar lottery, you would enlist for the LAWRENCE just to go to general quarters in the waters surrounding Guantanamo Bay Cuba. Properly setting material conditions of readiness and correctly stenciling compartment bulls eyes was your main reason for living. Having fun was being dressed out in a full fire fighter's ensemble, knocking down the imposed flames of a compartment class "A" fire in 100+ degree heat. If you learned, if you cooperated, and if you were enthusiastic, then you could possibly leave in about six weeks. Usually by the time a ship left GITMO, the gremlins were dead, maybe they were eaten by the protected but truly grotesque banana rats that populated the island. In addition, the seamanship skills and damage control prowess of the crew were reestablished better than ever.

The training teams were there on shore duty and didn't work on the weekends so a portion of Saturdays and Sundays were usually spent at ship's cookouts, soft ball games, and illegally diving off the rock cliffs until chased by the shore patrol. The fishermen amongst us found that the pier was all the further they had to travel to catch red snapper and many other species.

There was an open air walk in theater and a club that reminded you of an all male academy dining hall. At that time GITMO had one big shortage and that was women. The club, with plentiful beer and an overload of testosterone combined with beer effects often resulted in a shore patrol challenge as various crews ineffectively duked it out. For transportation, there was the famous *cattle car* of Guantanamo Bay. It was normally super humid, even at midnight as we herded into the cart for our trip back to the pier. Packed in like meat off to the market, my fellow nautical steers would begin to moo, stomp, and generally make their best cattle herd sounds. This activity occurred one hundred per cent of the time. I would wager a hefty sum that a Guantanamo Bay cattle cart never made a trip without a minimum number of worthy livestock imitations. These actions were often enhanced by a Sailor stomping one foot and using index fingers as imitation horns as the human steer rammed the side of the enclosure. The duty corpsman was often called to the quarterdeck as a substitute veterinarian to effect repairs on would be steers.

When a ship left GITMO the crew was usually ready for anything, especially a good port like Nassau or Fort Liquordale in South Florida. Port Everglades or Fort Lauderdale is a party town that Sailors love to visit. The lone exception perhaps was the commanding officer because a Sailor has unlimited opportunity to get into mischief in a good time port. Call it; the *Happy Hour Syndrome.* Future sociologists will someday ponder and debate the society that discouraged alcohol abuse yet enticed alcohol purchases by young people with the strange phenomenon once known as *Happy Hour.* The LAWRENCE, to her credit managed to survive the Florida beach scene with minimum damage. The crew fit right in with the revelers. We were all sporting two month old Caribbean tans and folks were looking lean after all the rigors of *Reftra*. The fact is, there was nothing note- worthy about that port visit. I may have been having too good of a time to reasonably recollect, but more likely it was just normal unmemorable fun.

After arriving back in Norfolk I noticed more Sailors traveling in personal cars than ever before. There were also a slew of new ships making their presence known and a capacious pier expansion project was in vigorous progress. Prior to that, city planners unceremoniously and probably with glee flattened the strip from D&S piers to the waterfront.

The steam driven destroyers were no longer the big bully on the block. The gas turbine destroyers beginning with the arrival of SPRUANCE were now the new tough guys of the Norfolk waterfront. The behemoths arrived and the rest of us were envious. The new *Spru Cans* seemed to demand patrician obeisance from their weary and weathered Adams class brethren. The BTs were indignant, knowing that the gas turbines included none of their greasy toed ilk in the make up of their ship's company. The very idea of seventy degree engine rooms made our hole snipes declare the gas turbine mechanics wimps. But the future had arrived and the new bad boys were staking out their turf.

For the DGUTS crew it was business as usual; inspections, underway, practices to hone gunfire support skills, and submarine chasing ASW exercises. Little time for pensive speculation there was always something happening or about to happen. The DGUTS crew, reverted back to the Cold War Navy routine, and functioned well as an operational unit, albeit a senior citizen among the pack of greyhounds now in her midst.

As is the nature of ships, people come and go. Some you meet again on other ships or establishments. Some shipmates who you hung out with every day for years leave and you never hear from them again. There is no time to commiserate the departure of a good friend. You never forget these folks. At times their names will escape you, but you never forget them because you grew to know them in the same manner you knew your family members. It has been stated by a wise man that God gives us family members in order to learn how to get along with people we wouldn't necessarily hang out with. The same applies to your shipmates. You can't stereotype the ninety- plus guys in your bedroom, too many diversified personalities for that. But you learn to coexist comfortably as long as you're mindful of your own small turf, keeping it squared away and microscopic insect free.

The day finally arrived when Keesey and LTJG Spencer received orders to move on to bigger and better things. I haven't mentioned the captains or the XOs by name, or even the chief engineers, because until that point in my career the leadership I received was primarily from Keesey and Mr. Spencer. Keesey, the old salt was known as our *Sea Daddy.* He was the shop. The way we worked, the tools we carried, our methods of troubleshooting, how we codified our job sequence log, and how our uniforms looked; were all Keesey's standards. We had a talented shop by then, and although he deserved a lot of accolades, Keesey never received them, nor did he expect them. He always felt like he was just doing his job. In truth, his indelible mark on LAWRENCE was us. I once asked Keesey why he wasn't a chief. He cracked me up in his bristly manner and said "*I have too many congressional letters of complaint*" Keesey may have or may not have made chief. I think he would have made a great chief. I hope he did in fact make it. When Mr. *Fixes Everything* walked off the LAWRENCE brow for the final time he was tracking west to shore duty in Memphis to an *easy street* job at an air station. To this day IC1 Keesey was the best interior communications electrician I ever knew. He was in my military career the single greatest influence on everything I was or was to become. When hoary old Keesey left, I never saw or heard from him again.

Mr. Spencer was a dynamic junior officer. He played the tough guy and had a strong personality. Anyone who ever met him would remember him. He had the energy that rivaled most thermonuclear devices. On the ship he was everywhere; his tall lanky frame negotiating passageways at the speed of light. He was charismatic, sarcastically funny; always pithy. He had no mercy for the lazy. Above all, he made training and the material condition of the ship his number one priority. His classically piqued "*Fix IT, Sooner*!" reverberated around the ship in memorable parody through the voices of those he tasked. Some folks might call it mocking; friendlier subordinates considered it contagious repartee, but Spencer, the pacesetter got the job done even if he had to drag you there and make you do it.

When you combined Spencer and Keesey it provided the DGUTS IC Gang with a truly memorable early chain of command. Those guys would fight it out verbally like a rooster and cat in a burlap bag sinking to a river bottom. There were classic confrontations ending with thespian Keesey's dramatic grip on the hammer replete with the threat of breaking his own knee cap and abruptly departing for an extended hospital stay. Spencer would usually end that round, trying very hard to be dudgeon; yet he was ineffective; failing to control his laughter at the old fart's grousing antics.

Together those guys got the job done and done right. And then Spencer left, transferred to bigger and better things. I would see the *Great Spencer* a couple of more times over the years as we traveled up and down the Norfolk piers and on through the ranks on various ships. At those briefest of encounters we would salute, give each other a few accolades, replete with smart ass remarks, and then move on for another, five or six years.

Chapter Five:

The LAWRENCE Continues

Keesey departed and by default I gravitated to the shop LPO for a temporary stint. That did not equate to *Least in the Pecking Order*, but rather leading petty officer. I had reenlisted for the LAWRENCE and the sixty month sea tour I opted for as a DGUTS Sailor still had time remaining to complete that particular obligation. I was now an important *Wahtuba* in the LAWRENCE engineering department, in our shop however; obeisance could never be expected from my peers, Steve or Rogers. The chief engineer and the other more senior officers began to know me. Historically it was Keesey and Mr. Spencer, now I was becoming more immersed as a participant in the oft assembled meetings of the minds.

Not that the multimeter disappeared out of my hands or anything that drastic, but after years onboard I knew something about the ship and its little quirks. We added a new ICFN to the shop, an Irish kid from Pittsburgh. Kevin McGill was total Pittsburgh. Steeler fan, *Iron City* drinking, cigarette chain-smoking tough Irish Catholic from the city. He cussed rather eloquently and steadfastly held the belief that the Pope was the closest human to God on earth. His primary fault was hideous flatuation. We hit it off immediately. I always maintained a special place for home boys, we banded together on the ship in our allegiance to the *Black and Gold,* to do otherwise would be heresy. Many may have thought us fair weather fans because the Steelers kept winning, pounding opponents and asserting their will every week of every season. But the truth was, how could one be judged as *fair weather*, when you never had a test of inclement elements for that assertion to be made?

McGill had an old beat up jalopy he used for point A to B transportation. Ira had transferred to a billet on a tender so the fast car era was reposed to history. McGill's car bellowed out great clouds of smoke as he drove through Ocean View, usually rolling obnoxiously slow in the fast lane. In the shop he tried hard to work things out and understand the DGUTS IC systems while he progressed through his acculturation. It suddenly dawned on me that he was anointing me *Keesey status*. Events would occur with equipment and I would know the problem just by the description of it on the phone call. I was right a very large percentage of the time. Abased at times, Kevin looked at me and asked, "*How do you know that stuff*?" I thought about that later and I knew then that it was probably the right time to move on to new challenges. Kevin meanwhile developed a problem at morning muster. He developed a wicked cough for a young guy, probably based on chain smoking *Kools*. Thus; the division created his nickname and dubbed him *Lung Cookie.* Surprisingly Lung Cookie actually liked the name. Nicknames were truly an aphorism with the DGUTS IC Gang. Rogers had developed the nickname *Combat* due to some type of 1MC test error he made. What was amazing was how the names adhered permanently to the individual. I was Zeke for the entire five years I served on LAWRENCE. Schmidt dubbed it and there it stuck for my entire tour. During my first shore tour someone renamed me Zack and that one stuck forever. The only one who escaped a nickname was Steve and that eventually changed in a most peculiar manner.

I was relating some youth nostalgia story one day in the shop. The ship was underway and I was discussing an old high school buddy named Ed Baird. Ed Baird may have been the fastest white kid to ever run in Western Pennsylvania. He would have dusted *Gump*, I guarantee it. Ed also talked fast and would often use his last name, and Gump-like he would refer to himself as Ed Baird. The kicker was if the engaging speedster liked you he would christen you with his last name and from that day forth you incurred forever the coveted title *Baird.* It was a great honor to be a *Baird.* My nickname as a kid was the *Hat.* By Ed Baird and our associates I was referred to as *Hat Baird.* It was much catchier than one would suspect.

Well Steve loved this semi-glossed over sea story and immediately began to refer to himself in the third person as *Stebaird.* He would say things such as "*Stebaird hungry*!" or "*Stebaird so friggin tired*!" *Stebaird* became the nautical version of Ed Baird, though not as fast. Ed Baird, due to his lightning sprints also had the added nomenclature of *Crazy Legs Baird*, but we only used that format during no equipment tackle football events.

It wasn't long before the whole shop referred to themselves as the "Bairds." Being a Baird was akin to being accepted into a group of cool beings. Being anointed a Baird by us, you were considered worthy in our group. You couldn't call us anything as sophisticated as a clique. To be one of us actually required you to be rather unsophisticated. Being worthy usually meant that you would chip in for beer, and your smell was tolerable. All other faults were normally overlooked. Our IC Gang was very powerful consisting of Frog Baird, Flash Baird, Lung Cookie (Baird just didn't go with his name), Combat Baird, Bean Baird, Stebaird, and Zeke Baird. We were no longer the IC Gang. We were simply, *The Bairds.*

A significant arrival to LAWRENCE was Mr. Spencer's relief. An ex-enlisted, Ensign Mike Ward was a hard- nosed officer; he was never really an ensign. I think he really started at about the lieutenant commander level. He had spent quite a few years as an enlisted man. He strung wire in the jungles of Nam or some similar tough guy job. He was always someone to stay on the good side of. If you were a performer he'd take on a rabid dog with his hands tied behind his back for you. If you were doing something he didn't like you knew about it first hand. Mr. Ward was a technician and he looked at your work with a technician's eye. He had a built in *bull shit detector* and he had that great talented ability to get to the bottom line. He appeared physically as a cerebral type but he soon proved that he could be Paul Bunyan with a sharp axe.

A grizzled old Propulsion Examining Board member once asked him why a screw was missing out of a junction box and the ensign told him, "*because of a quarter million screws there is only one missing*." What Mike Ward had quite frankly was, *balls.* There were few people I had worked for that were harder than Mike Ward, but probably even fewer, if any that I would rather work for. He didn't go around slinging accolades at you for everything you did, but he would reward you by trusting your input. For a petty officer growing into a leadership role, he was an ideal division officer.

After Ensign Ward's arrival, along came IC1 Johnny Ray Lyons. Johnny Ray Lyons hailed from Monroe, Louisiana. He had an easy going manner and a great voice. We found out that he had only one mood, calm, and only one way of operating, persistent. Johnny Ray was an African American from the Deep South who held no prejudices. He probably had more than a few reasons to feel differently, but I sincerely believe he held the whole shop in high regard. He was a lot more easy going than Keesey, but not as talented as a technician. In fairness to Johnny Ray, no one was Keesey. Keesey was a unique electromechanical magician. Keesey had a *Mr. Goodwrench-like* natural talent for fixing intricate items that employed gears, motors, springs, and coils. His gray countenance at work in the IC shop, bent over a disassembled wind indicator transmitter gave one the impression of a nautical Santa painstakingly manufacturing a worthy child's reward. It was a tough act to follow.

Johnny Ray was all about motivating the talent of the team to complete the job. He was patient, persistent, and polite. Both guys got the job done they just employed very different methods. Johnny Ray never had a problem motivating a shop full of white guys to work. He gave a limited allowance for bitching. You were permitted to bitch, but you still had to do the job. Johnny Ray wouldn't placate you. How Johnny Ray never lost his temper is beyond me. Although some of us were beginning to become short timers, with Johnny Ray's prodding and sincere encouragement we still managed to keep working away as required.

An occasional prank was still a vital and important element of the DGUTS IC Gang. In the engine room we tested the wiring on our salinity cells or salt sensing devices by using a deckade resistor box which served to provide a dummy resistive load on a selected cell. One would go to the location of the cell and open its corresponding terminal box. The procedure required the tech to clip the leads to the proper terminals in the junction box. When the tech turned the potentiometer on box, the meter in front of the throttleman station would deflect to either the right or left depending on which way one turned the knob; thus indicating adequate wire continuity.

The top watch was a second class MM with the nickname *Boo Boo*. Why he was called that was unknown to all but a few, but all knew him as that. That day he was to be an IC victim. Rogers and I teamed together to perpetrate our cabal on the unsuspecting *Boo Boo*. Combat Baird was on the lower level on cell number six. He could hear me and he had my visual by peering up and around a short vertical cableway. His presence was unknown to everyone but me. He had the resistor dialed in on the cell ready to act in accordance with our plan. I said, "*Hey Boo Boo did you know that the salinity panel can answer questions about you*?" "*Yeah right,*" replied Boo Boo. I received the predicted response. I finally convinced him to stand in front of the panel and I said, "*If my question's answer is yes then the pointer will go to the right. If my question's answer is no, then the pointer will go to the left.* I finally convinced him to pay attention. I then asked, "*Is Boo Boo a faggot*?" Combat Baird immediately deflected the resistor and the needle pegged hard to the right. By then the other hole snipes started to gather around. The magic salinity panel answered funny questions for the next ten minutes. All in attendance were declared weak, gay, senile, and lacking in penal endowment. The panel told all the MMs that the IC men were smart, handsome, and studly. Combat Baird left quietly through the escape scuttle in the lower level and I abandoned the engine room, freeing the MMs to ponder my *Kreskin- like* abilities.

Mr. Ward was tough enough, but our new chief engineer was like Jack Lambert on an empty stomach or Iron Mike Ditka with a jock itch. He was all business. One day the Cheng, the universal nickname for the chief engineer entered the IC room. The guy looked around our small space and asked, "*Petty Officer Zahratka, there isn't much space here is there?*" I replied, thankful that a senior officer was finally recognizing our crowded plight. "*Yes Sir, we are pretty tightly packed down here*" The Cheng replied rather matter of factly, "*then let's get rid of the chairs*." Then he walked out.

I do not believe he harbored a tender love for IC men, but then again being in a repair rate usually meant that you were often only remembered when something was broken. No one answered their telephone and said, "*Gee I'm so happy my phone works, those IC men are a great bunch of chaps*." No one wondered aloud when standing bridge watches, "*Wow these IC men are good. All the indicators for ship's speed, gyrocompass, and wind are working correctly*." However, let something not work and it would usually result in IC men being equated down there with whale shit. This was especially true with other engineering rates because they admittedly had more physically demanding and more uncomfortable environments to work in. Added to this was the fact that few engineers did work in combat information center or on the bridge. But the IC man, he is everywhere. Wherever a phone rings, a growler howls, or an alarm sounds, there you may find a need for the services of the much maligned, yet critically important IC man. Officers in engineering would call us *Prima donnas* and hole snipes called us *skates*. However, they all needed us, so we held the pat hand. As far as the relationship with the chief engineer was concerned, he expected Mr. Ward to keep him out of trouble with IC equipment. It paid big dividends to have a strong leader as a division officer. With Mr. Ward it started and stopped with him. The Cheng was his business. We IC men didn't have to worry. We were all about pulling cable and crimping wire. The less we had to deal with the upper echelon the better we liked it and with great stealth *we kept the chairs*.

Folks finally rotated off into the future. Bean migrated to Ohio. Steve Baird moved out of his North Carolina armory and made plans to relocate into the woods of Wisconsin to hunt wild game. Combat Rogers moved on to pursue big bucks in the tech world of Huntsville, Alabama. Flash went off to seek fortune as an entrepreneur in the Atlanta area. Frog leapt to New Jersey to sample fine restaurants. Lung Cookie, and Johnny Ray, stayed behind to sail the LAWRENCE on to further adventure. As the process goes Lung Cookie became me as I had become Keesey. We added a new little guy to the pack of pranksters, who Lung Cookie immediately named Ying Yang. He was not oriental and I can not explain the name. It just was.

Mr. Ward was still there and I would meet up with him again in another adventure. As for me I had been on board for sixty months. I had served under four commanding officers in that time frame, and who knows how many XOs? During a period of sagging morale, the captain called me to his stateroom for an opinion. He and the XO wanted to know my thoughts as a sixty month crew member on why morale was so low at the time. Reflecting today from a mature perspective I could have listed erosion of buying power, and lack of pay increases. But from my perspective then, I offered that the ship needed to go somewhere. Port visits, lands left to be discovered, were calling for the DGUTS presence. That is what I told the captain. "*If you are going to be on a ship you may as well be going somewhere.*" I think he liked my answer, after all, the seventies advertisement said" *it wasn't a job, it was an adventure.*"

Nothing could get the rumor mill going faster than a schedule change or port call. Schmidt used to catalyst the rumor mill just to hear how it sounded when it got back to his own ear. He would start something by saying we were hitting Halifax Nova Scotia, and by the time he heard it return, we were getting underway for a deployment as a NATO ship starting in England with the Brits, and we all had to get special hepatitis shots in the ass prior to departure.

As for myself, I finally negotiated orders and I was heading for a two year shore duty to the glamorous command of Inactive Ships Maintenance Facility. It was near the shipyard in Portsmouth, Virginia and was not a renowned vacation spot.

When I stepped on the LAWRENCE main deck it was January of 1973. When I left it was January 1978. Five years had passed. I spent the five years learning a trade and seeing first hand a vast tract of geography. The LAWRENCE wasn't the easiest tour but it was possible to learn something there. I arrived as an undesignated fireman apprentice and I left there as interior communications electrician second class or IC2. As an E-5 over four I still managed to be a two ribbon guy. Soon they would come up with a sea service ribbon that would earn me a third. But for now I was sporting one hash mark; a Good Conduct, and the National Defense, which I received in boot camp. The LAWRENCE won no awards in the years I was there. I knew she did after I left and she had earned many before I got there. But it wasn't my fault that the Navy hadn't produced a *Working your Ass Off Ribbon* because the Lawrence would have won that one with many bronze stars for multiple accolades. But it was what it was; and so it was for me. However, I was off to a new adventure, and after five years of arduous sea duty, it was about time.

Chapter Six:

Ghost Boats

Inactive Ships Maintenance Facility was overall my least favorite duty station. It wasn't that it was a bad place to work. It was actually kind of fun as far as the work itself was concerned, but it was remote and far removed from the main stream. One felt isolated from the rest of the fleet and the up tempo of fleet activity.

Our job was to maintain the *ghost fleet.* Our particular shop was tasked to wire dehumidifiers, install flooding alarm systems, and rig ships for towing with appropriate running lights operated with a battery power source. The interiors of the ships were normally dark and unlit and the flashlight was an indispensable part of our tool chest.

A dark abandoned ship can be a macabre place and it was possible to allow your imagination to run wild. This was especially true on a duty night. Duty consisted of living quarters in a small compartment of an old preserved destroyer tender. Receiving a remote pier alarm at the gate required you to jump on a bicycle and ride off to the appropriate pier and vessel to investigate possible flooding. Often you entered an abandoned ship at two o'clock in the morning in inclement weather. Once aboard you had to make your way through the dark environment until you reached the below deck bilge areas. Often times, when I was doing the investigation, *Dracula* or the *Were Wolf* would dart by and mock me with some sinister sound designed to give miniature coronaries and jettison disastrous amounts of stress chemicals into an already nicotine corrupted blood stream. The abandoned mine sweepers were lurid, with their creaky wooden hulls creating a cacophony of hellish sounds reverberating everywhere around you. Mental apparitions would often appear through the wavering light of my dimming flashlight. Wind and thunderstorms often provided added special effects, as the ships would gain a little bounce and swagger to enhance their sarcastic and haunting little dances.

Of course as a watch stander one had to be brave and maintain the mindset of the invincible sea warrior who feared no force living, or from the great beyond. Therefore; I was left to harbor my fears and anxieties every sixth day as duty days came and went.

Our shop consisted of an interesting mix of Sailors and a sprinkling of retired chiefs who worked along side us. Jerry, Raymond, and Big Lee were in actuality the guys with all the talent, our retired chiefs. It was a great learning experience to pick their brains, as they had forgotten more than most of us actually knew. They all were very different from each other, but they all held one thing in common, and that was a complete and utter dislike of our president, Jimmy Carter. Those guys would vent for hours on end about Jimmy. He was their own personal villain, and his broad smile never adorned the walls of our shops. It was actually my first real exposure to politics at any level. The LAWRENCE crew never seemed to care or demonstrate interest in any political conversations. We were too involved in personal issues as young people. During the Revolution, I faked it. I was only there for the *beer.* But these Navy retired vets were serious about their beliefs. When our embassy personnel were taken hostage in Iran it only served to dump gas on the fire as they viciously voiced their displeasure.

I was the only IC man in the group. The rest were electrician mates and for this I would occasionally take a ribbing from my EM peers. Our first class at the time was a guy from Western Pennsylvania but he wasn't a Steeler fan. To me that meant he was probably a Communist infiltrator or a closet supporter of the *Green Peace Movement.* Not that I disliked the guy or anything. He was just someone with whom I wouldn't hang out with by choice.

Later in my tour we got an IC man as our leading petty officer, and Shorty Sharp was an easy going LPO and a genuine leader who skillfully managed the shop without being pushy or omnipotent in any way. Most workers who feel good about their jobs want to go to work in the morning. I never understood why that was so hard for some leaders to comprehend. IC1 Shorty Sharp never pretended to be JFK. He was just genuine. His mantra was this is what needs to be done and I know you can do it. Thanks for doing a great job. Simple stuff and basic methods were all he used to get work done, without a lot of coerciveness involved, and never any backstabbing.

The shore tour at Inactive Ships granted the Sailor a chance to breathe a little bit from the fast pace of the ship. There was some opportunity there for recreation. Jerry gave a spirited attempt to teach me to golf. That was his passion and frankly he was quite adroit at it. After many tries and after many sessions of patient instruction I finally decided that there were certain things in life that one should not do. Golf was that thing for me. I can still recall my final 18 at Eagle Haven in Little Creek. After losing many balls attempting to tee off across an expanse of water, I got smart and finally threw my old second hand driver into the expanse of lake before me. To be free of this exasperating game was akin to being a hostage unchained. Never again would I excavate and pitch large plots of sod into the air in pursuit of fun, as other more skillful players looked on with empathetic pity. Many helpful golfers tried to provide me with sound advice as shots careened off into unpredictable trajectories. My typical eight putts would amaze those gathered around the green as my ball and the pin would repel each other like two magnets with like charged ends, futilely attempting to merge. Yes, my golf game ended right then and there, and I have not placed my hands on the shaft of a golf club since.

What my golf experience left me with is a great amount of respect for those who play the game with skill. In my estimation, Tiger Woods is the greatest athlete on the planet. He is the best athlete at the world's most difficult sport. To an inept golfer such as me, the drives and putts of the Tiger are wonders of the world. His skills are almost beyond my comprehension as I can only shake my head in bewildered respect and amazement at that man's prowess. I'm very thankful he is an American so I can root for him in tournaments.

Another activity that we got started at Inact Ships was our own bowling team. As a bunch of electrical types, we called ourselves the *Circuit Breakers*. I actually stunk at that too. But it was fun and at least I consistently broke a hundred. Team sports were usually an important part of most Navy commands but Inactships really didn't exude the passionate participation as did LAWRENCE. Ship crews also have a large pool of youngsters to draw players from, whereas the shore commands usually have a group of old salts with family commitments.

That started to change when a few Sailors such as Chief Ken Bean, EM2 Paul Angelicchio, and me arrived at the command. We had an old softball field with lights next to the facility. Using that field as a starting point, we smoothed out the long abandoned diamond by dragging it with a railroad tie. Then we quickly recruited a force of potential ball players and created a team. We now had a practice field and a team in place. We generated plenty of exhibition games because our field had working lights. The shipyard or even the Portsmouth police force would on occasion come over and beat up on us in practice, as they were more established with a much larger talent pool. But we improved our game by playing a truly better level of competition, so the whippings were justifiable.

The command was great for crabbing off the piers, but getting money for softball shirts and hats was a much more difficult task. The command had no means to generate money so the team raised the money itself. Thus was born the *ISMF Jokers,* our name of choice. We entered the Portsmouth Naval Hospital League, with the idea that if injured, we would be immediately administered to. Playing Orthopedics was having the ultimate opponent. Imagine sliding hard into second base and severely twisting your ankle. Quickly the second baseman calls for his medical kit as he expertly examines the joint in question. A qualified team of medical experts quickly assemble at second base to determine the next course of action for their opponent turned patient. That's better treatment than the major leaguers get for an injury occurring at Yankee Stadium. Where else is the opposing team comprised of qualified doctors and EMTs?

The Jokers did well in the Portsmouth Hospital League, although we probably smoked more than the medical personnel whom we played against. Our poor wind probably cost us in the long run. I believe we actually won a trophy that year, not a first place one but a runner up model, so the Jokers were a success and what we started actually evolved into a successful morale building enterprise. I believe we won because we chose black and gold shirts and having a black and gold uniform in 1979 was a symbol of power. Nineteen seventy- nine was a Pittsburgh sports fan's dream year. The *City of Champions* was rockin, being victorious in both baseball and football. Stargell and the Bucs coming back against the Orioles to the sounds of *We are family* was an epic story itself. It was heady times indeed to be a Pittsburgh fan. Bradshaw to Stallworth killed the hopes of twenty million Los Angelinos as the *Team of the Ages* won the Super Bowl for the fourth time in six years.

There were times at morning quarters when names were called out and the only word I could utter at 0700 when hearing my name was STEEEELERRRRS!!! By rights, no one city should have that much success it was almost unfair to the rest of the country. But then again, after forty years of humble losses, I thought it was quite justified to win the Super Bowl forty more times. After so much success, Pittsburghers thought it was a divine right to win all of them. The reality that sports dynasties do not last forever did not hit Pittsburgh fans until the eighties. By then we were all spoiled rotten. Regardless, the *Steeler Nation* was forged and thrives, multiplying like rats on *Viagra*, with millions of followers to this very day.

Inact Ships as a whole was a blip on the radar screen of a career. EM2 Paul Angelicchio, nuclear power electrician from the nuclear cruiser VIRGINIA was a good friend and ship mate. We got along from the beginning because he was from of all places, the same little town where I was hatched. We even knew many of the same people. Paul was a little younger than I was and he probably still is today. As a fellow Steeler fan he was worthy, and strength lies in numbers as together we touted the greatness of our sport's teams. I ended up running into Paul on occasion for the next twenty years or so. Both of us got to the top of the enlisted ranks, of course it was because we were Steeler fans. Once in a while, although not very often, a very opprobrious event would occur; the Steelers would actually lose a game. Our joyful ship mates would rejoice in unbridled ecstasy as they peppered Angel and me with insults about the Steeler's ineptness. They would cheerfully predict gloom and doom as they castigated us for our unshakable faith in future Steeler glory. The next week the men in black would right the ship and our large mouths would ring loud and clear, filled with vengeful glee as we caused near donnybrooks in haunts not hospitable to the fans of the confluence. Another victim fell as a predictable sacrifice in the *Temple of Doom* known as Three Rivers.

I enthusiastically volunteered for a road trip to Philadelphia on a late summer week, tasked with light preparation for a vessel making ready for towing. I traveled in style, taking Rip Van Wilken's motorcycle along, as I was caretaking it during his deployment on the RICHARD E BYRD. I completed the job uneventfully. I had all the tools in a truck that another petty officer took along for his end of the job. Wrapping up, I left on the bike and set out to explore Philadelphia. I was relieved to remember to keep the phone number of the other petty officer with the truck. I was going across the Walt Whitman Bridge that evening when I hit an oil slick. The huge four cylinders slid out from under me and the bike rode on its side for what seemed like a country mile. Now comes the very bizarre part and I swear on the name of John Paul Jones that this is the truth. I went off the back end of that huge machine and surfed in my street shoes for a minimum of fifty yards. I never hit the ground and remained standing as I traveled the slow lane surfing at 55 mile per hour. It would have been home video of the year. *Jackie Chan* would have begged for my autograph after that one. Unfortunately no one witnessed it. The bike was bumped and bruised but I remained unscathed. The soles of my shoes had a little wear, but that was the complete summation of my personal damage. It struck me as very strange that the accident occurred without any influence from another driver or from an error on my part. It was merely the element of the road surface and the oil. Shorty Sharp never tasked me with another road trip. I was the Banzai biker from then on- I vowed to get a car soon.

Two years of shore duty roll to a close very quickly and soon it was time to contact the detailer for orders once more. I recalled the way the SIERRA worked and I thought I'd like to try a repair ship. On a tender you were required to work on many different ships. I forgot that a tender actually had a ship's company that worked on the ship itself. There were two distinct groups and there was a method to this madness. The detailer informed me of the mission of the YELLOWSTONE class ships. They would be instrumental in keeping the Spruance destroyers, FFGS, and the new Aegis cruisers that were being built, in good working order. As I had no bargaining options, I accepted his offer to a billet on the YELLOWSTONE (AD-41), the first of the class. The ship was being built in San Diego California and would be commissioned in September of 1980.

At Inact Ships I was granted permission to participate in the first class petty officer examination. Rating exams happen all the way to chief petty officer and each test gets significantly harder than the one preceding it. The test was tough and I remember it being a strictly technical test. There were very few of what we called gimme questions on that exam. I suspect the Navy needed ocean going first class IC men at the time, because the results came back and I was a confirmed selection. I would soon be advanced to the rank of IC1. I guess I had to thank the *Russian Bear* or the *Big Red Menace* because those commies really helped keep the deep water Navy in business. For the entire length of my career it was always about the Soviets. Once in a while at sea you received an emphatic reminder. Perhaps by getting buzzed by a Bear bomber or pinging one of their subs. Always their little spy trawlers were lurking, watching our fleet, picking up our garbage, and generally I suspected being miserable with some political officer filling their heads with some kind of outdated political dogma and absolutely no rock'n roll. No wonder they downed the vodka by the water glass. Who wouldn't?

After finding out that you were selected for advancement the commanding officer had the opportunity and authority to frock you to the next pay grade if he chose to. Frocking meant that you were elevated to the next pay grade in all respects with the exception of pay. I had never been to a non judicial punishment hearing for any reason, and my evaluations weren't bad. I don't think at that point in my career that I was a candidate for a photo model in a recruiting poster, but overall I was an adept and competent journeyman IC man. For some unknown reason the commanding officer would not frock this good son of Western Pennsylvania. I believe his expressed reason was that he had no billet for an IC1; therefore he declined to advance me. Personally I came to my own conclusion. He must have been a closet *Cleveland Browns* fan and he must have heard that I was in fact *Mr. Steeler*. In my mind, he probably got me with a little jab. It hurt, certainly, but to tell you the truth I could not name that particular captain if I tried all day. I couldn't pick him out of a line up. Quite frankly, I can't remember ever seeing or meeting the gentleman at all.

When I left Inactive Ships I was quite ready to go to active ships. Personally, I think shore duty is somewhat overrated and I was anxious to help commission my new ship. I left Inactive Ships Maintenance Facility in December of 1979. I was about to become a first class petty officer aboard a brand new ship. The fact that the YELLOWSTONE was being built by National Steel in San Diego California didn't break my heart either. That's what I loved about this job. Just when something gets tiresome you're off to a new adventure.

Civilian acquaintances would ask late in my career, "*How could you take the military for all those years?*" The question I always had for them was, "*How could you take working in the same place for the same asshole all those years*?" A great selling point for the Navy is simply this, "*If you don't like your current boss just give it a year or two, one of the two of you will be gone and you'll get a brand new set of bars to salute. Just be careful of what you wish for, it may not be what you wanted*."

Up to this point, the most dynamic leaders I had were first class petty officers. I was about to become one, even if I had to wait on my advancement date. I had reached a point in my career where I would answer a great deal more often to chief petty officers and officers. Soon I would have to consider that eight or nine year point where a career decision had to be made. Once you served ten, you are usually there for at least twenty, so that 8-10 year decision is huge. It is also a number that can creep up on you very quickly. I still felt as if my future was back in Pennsylvania. The roots run very deep there. Although the job market often projected bleak opportunities, recruiters often related that Pittsburgh could be a tough place to recruit because so many people loved living there. I thought in the back of my mind that I too would be numbered among those returnees, but there was time enough to consider that. The PCU YELLOWSTONE was on the horizon and another new adventure was about to begin.

Chapter Seven:

The Wanderers

When I reported to the Electrical C Schools building (where pre-commissioning offices were located) on NOB Norfolk I did not expect the kind of sincere welcome that I received. It was the most affable group of people I had been around in a very long time. Pre- commissioning units are made up of people who are excited about being the first. Everyone is new. Everyone is trying to contribute something and the welcome you receive is very genuine. After a couple of years in a laid back out of the way maintenance facility, the energy I felt from the precom unit was exciting and I quickly realized that getting this assignment was a great privilege. When I met the administrative officer, a chief warrant, I queried him about being frocked to first class petty officer. This warrant, whom I had known for two minutes, made a bigger deal out of my selection than my previous command had. It took him about five minutes to make it all happen. That may be an exaggeration, but the warrant had me wearing that first class crow faster than Ricky Williams could get to second base, and I thought it looked and felt rather fitting.

Shipmates view you a little differently when you are a first class petty officer. Soon I was going to be Keesey to someone else. I was the one who was supposed to have all the answers ready to go. The first class LPO of a shop was the person leaned on to get things done every single day. The second class petty officer was often required to be a top notch technical troubleshooter, but the first class had to be a leader. It was a big leap. As a first class you were assumed to be a career man from that point on. Personally, those were heady days, and my advancement intensified my resolve to keep plugging away at the next challenge and see where it would lead.

I met the future B division officer soon thereafter, a pleasant young ensign named Kelsey. She was the first female officer I ever met in the Navy, and she delivered some good news, informing me that I was off to the ship's building site in San Diego. I was assigned to the electrical division of ship's company and I was leaving in a matter of days. It was going to be important to pick the brain of the ship yard workers who were putting YELLOWSTONE together. The next six to nine months would bring the ship to completion. We would then outfit her, train the crew, and ride her back to the East Coast. The agenda was packed, and would present many challenges in the months ahead.

I had a few days to get out to the West Coast and I wanted to do something different and eccentric. I always desired to drive across the country, so instead of hopping on a nice convenient aircraft, like a real adventurer, I opted for a cross country bus ticket. Given the choice, never do that folks. It was a nasty three days. Watching Texas roll by for about ten thousand miles or so was really no adventure. I can recall a tremendous redundancy of brown flat topography. The bus was cramped. People began to smell bad, and the pot smokers in the back grew exponentially more obnoxious with each hundred mile marker. This was not an ideal trip. From Virginia to New York it may be fine or at least tolerable. But Virginia to San Diego, big mistake, never again would I attempt that by bus unless it is similar to the one used by John Madden and I own it. Otherwise; it is a heinous experience at best. On a positive note, it did provide me an opportunity to contemplate things as the endless miles rolled by. I sat there and cogitated about the sheer pleasure it would give me to choke the hell out of the loud mouthed dope smokers in the back of the bus. To wrap my hands around his throat….. Anyway fly *American, Delta*, or whatever, just forget about the bus.

When I arrived in San Diego I saw that a great transformation was taking place. San Diego in 1980 was already a far cry from the 1973 version I recalled from A school. Being here as a twenty-five year old was also a far cry from being here at eighteen.

I somehow got from the bus to the shipyard where I met my new bosses, Senior Chief Gradine and Chief Worthy, both electrician chiefs. They both seemed like, well, chiefs, authoritative, competent, and ready to get you to work. I didn't know it right then and there but I was really going to like those guys. Now I wasn't sure when I met the E division officer, Warrant Officer Joe DeMaine, I knew it was close to the same time. But between Mr. DeMaine, Senior Chief Gradine, and Chief Worthy we had common sense leadership and most important, all three of our khakis had a sense of humor. Usually as long as a boss had that much going on, I was a happy subordinate.

Senior Chief Gradine provided a synopsis of the personnel he had available so far. He quickly informed me how he wanted training to go. We had a lot of young guys and they were to be my responsibility. He was talking to me like I was some kind of polished first class petty officer. Maybe he knew I was new, but it didn't matter because he kicked the ball in my court and challenged me to run with it.

I saw the ship for the first time that same day. I went aboard with a hard hat and a badge, and I was still in dress blues. I met six or seven guys that installed just about the entire suite of IC gear. The leader was a grizzled old guy named Smitty. Under Smitty were a retired senior chief IC man, and a retired master chief electrician. They were very intelligent and had a great time with my one red hash mark and three ribbons. They thought I must be a nuke and as one would expect they gave me crap on a regular basis, but they also provided me with a great deal of instructional knowledge about the ship and how it was put together. The ship was huge, absolutely dwarfing the SIERRA that I had known years earlier. Compared to my five years on the LAWRENCE this promised to be luxury living.

I met the group of IC men and electricians I would be working alongside with over the next year or two. They were a motley group at best, and I say that affectionately. I am unsure in what order they arrived. If they weren't already there they started appearing with regularity from the East Coast. Together we formed a group of trainees assigned to learn the ship by tracing systems and walking the spaces.

Chief Worthy helped me settle in a hotel room in National City. The ship had no place to live so they had to pay us an exorbitant housing and food allowance while the ship was being constructed. I could get used to this situation, Not only being in Southern California, but having money also, *Wow*!

The first people I met aside from the division officer and the chiefs was an EM2 named Mark Rothrock, IC1 Ron Rogers, the closed circuit television technician, a first class electrician named Bob Schmidt, and one our ICFNs named Tim Molnar. Pat Branch, Rocco Romanello, and Mike Holloway would report soon. I also met a few folks from the other shops, several BTs and MMs were among their numbers. The onsite pre-commissioning crew was mainly ship's company. The much larger repair department wouldn't form up for several months.

Ron Rogers was one of the smartest IC Men I ever met. He had one mode of operating and that was laid back. The big Alaskan Eskimo would often comment by just saying *HMMMFFFF*! Nothing riled Ron. He could pick up any schematic look at a circuit symptom and say, "*HMMMFFPPFF! That's simple.*" Without exception he was always right. We got along well and would be good allies during our tours on YELLOWSTONE. Ron was so easy going that he was always fun to have along on liberty because he never got on your nerves. He was very soft spoken; I can never remember him raising his voice once in all the time I knew him and professionally, I will say this; you would find it very difficult to locate an IC man that was more adept at figuring out a system's operating process than Ron Rogers. He was an incredible talent, and the YELLOWSTONE was lucky to have Ron assigned to the crew.

Another superstar talent was the tall electrician mate second class by the name of Mark Rothrock. Mark had done a previous tour on the sub tender USS HUNDLEY home ported in Scotland. He enjoyed his tour there and was looking forward to working on the YELLOWSTONE. Mark was one of those guys who did everything well. It didn't matter what he tried, he was successful. He was a tall physically fit type. His favorite word was, "*excellent.*" He had a girl friend named Debbie, a small blond with a cheerful demeanor and they went together like cake and icing. I would be quite surprised if they weren't still that way.

Mark, like Ron was a laid back guy. He was into flannel shirts, a jeep with the top down, and chewing tobacco. I was rather stunned to discover that he was actually a well-heeled child from a renowned Louisville, Kentucky medical family. His clear speaking voice and good manners were the only evidence that hinted at his background. He had none of the snootiness you would associate with a kid who drove a Bentley to his high school prom. He was a regular guy and a lot of fun to be around. It would be impossible to guess that Mark was or had ever been affluent. While Mark's background would support that he exhibit some type of supercilious behavior the complete opposite was in fact the truth. On top of his down to earth manner, he had a great sense of humor and he was genuinely friendly.

Without doubt Tim Molnar was one of my favorite and most memorable people of all time. Tim, although a fireman, was close to me in age having started his career a little later in life. We got along well from the start. Although short in height, Tim was a savvy California kid from the bay area. Tim had the looks, and the humor. So he was a short, funny, sarcastic guy, who had a lot on the ball. Tim was also a lot of fun to hang around with. He had worldly smarts and it would be a very rare occasion for someone to take advantage of him. Tim also had the great gift of instantaneous mockery. A chief or officer would leave our presence and Tim would have the voice and mannerisms down perfectly. He would even provide instant recall to every word stated verbatim. He was a California version of comedic sarcasm and parody, and he probably could have made a living on the comedy tour if he wished to pursue it.

These guys were a sampling of the initial cast of characters I was dealing with on the YELLOWSTONE and for certain they had some personality. More were to come soon, but of the group we had I was feeling as if this tour was a lucky choice.

I soon tired of my hotel room in National City, so I became involved in a four way rent split with some first classes from another part of the engineering department. They were basically good guy cowboy types and we got along well enough. We found a place in Coronado that we could have only dreamed about living in without four- way per diem. It was a waterfront community across the great Coronado Bridge. It had all the amenities. Large pool, tennis courts, Jacuzzi, indoor golf driving range, and a party room to borrow whenever. It was a huge step up from a small hotel room in National City and was California living as it advertised to the world. Primarily a geriatric community, it was filled with numerous senior citizens who implied affluent robust health. I do know that the boiler tech who provided our transportation to work had the only enlisted man's sticker in that parking lot. I believe we were nested in among an earlier era list of California *who's who.*

Not that our blue collar life status mattered, because the folks seemed to enjoy the energy that we brought to the place. Soon we were having Friday afternoon division rope yarns and the Sailors integrated well with the seniors. Mark and Debbie taught me how to play tennis and I actually started to enjoy that sport. It was much more amenable than the perils of the evil golf course.

Processes at the ship were progressing nicely and on schedule. The NASSCO IC group of yard workers was a helpful bunch and they went out of their way to provide a good product. We were the current generation of Sailors that they had once been, and they were intent on doing it right. They took no short cuts in what they did. San Diego was doing an outstanding job in bringing the ship to life. The tender was a ship that was made to last fifty years or more. It was a repair ship; solid, simple, sturdy, and capable. Unlike the LAWRENCE 1200 psi system, the YELLOWSTONE would operate on a 600 psi system with two large D type boilers. The evaporator system would gush two hundred thousand gallons of fresh water every day while underway. She would be able to generate power not only for herself, but for destroyers alongside. Her medical facility could house a hundred patients. Her 1200 strong repair department unfettered would be tasked to fix almost any casualty reported for everything but submarines. Submarines had their own tenders, and they had their own unique way of doing business.

As we continued to learn the ship and familiarize ourselves with the systems and equipment, there remained time to enjoy some of southern California. A piano bar within walking distance of our apartment served a macho sized margarita. It was made for a thirsty Hercules, but it was good. The heart burn it provided could get slightly overwhelming though, and on several occasions I was relieved that it was a short walk back.

I found an old car to borrow off a girl friend of one of our HTs. It was a smoky old Rambler with holes in the rear floor boards. It got us around slowly, but for ten dollars a week it was a ride. I would not trust it beyond a five mile radius though, much too risky.

Mark had a jeep and would occasionally take some of us out to explore the country side. There were about four of us out together one day and a new song came on the radio. The top was down and everyone started bouncing up and down on the seat laughing like hell. There was something about hearing the *Whippet* song for the very first time that shocked people. We had a good laugh over that one, but we must have looked silly as hell, with four grown men bouncing up and down to the beat of the *Whippet.*

Two new electricians swelled our ranks. One was a Mexican American named Pat Branch from Houston Texas, and the other was an Italian stallion from Connecticut named Rocco Romanello. We had a Rocco and a Rothrock but somehow Pat Branch ended up with the nickname Rocky, go figure.

To describe Rocky Branch, think in terms of loud and animated. Snuff rubbing, joke loving, good timer, he could be merciless if it meant getting in a good jab on you. As far as his mannerisms go, I would place him somewhere between *Moe of the Three Stooges* and *Yosemite Sam.* He would start a lot of sentences with "*I can't believe…*" then he would let you have it. Goofy people were attracted to him because he was funny, but more about that later.

Rocco Romanello was your classic Italian. He was a big guy with a vintage Southern Connecticut accent. To us he sounded Brooklyn. He looked Italian, he acted Italian, and he loved being Italian. He was kind though because he forgave us occasionally for not being Italian. I could easily envision him as one of those Mafioso guys running the neighborhood with a couple of other *good fellas* from the offices of the local bowling alley, which he probably now owns. Rocco was fairly quiet but he had a perpetual good mood and the best laugh on the East Coast, thus he would often spur on the antics of our funniest people, Tim and Rocky.

Tim and Rocky provided a witty a match for the ages. I call it *competitive smart asses.* They were constantly at each other, barbing, parrying, and matching wits of insult. Tim with his goading mannerisms would push buttons on Rocky based on his tobacco chewing red neck qualities, while Rocky would chastise Tim about his California clog wearing attire. As the neutral mediator I was also the sly instigator who would get them going at each other. Truthfully, little effort was required. I could never declare an out and out winner between the two, but there were several occasions when Rocky would get to laughing so hard he was unable to continue.

They loved pranks, especially Rocky and he pulled a tremendous coup one morning. Of course I quickly established my role as an obnoxious Steeler fan. Rocky of course was a Bum Phillips Houston Oiler's fan. He despised the Black and Gold for all the times they abruptly ended the Houston dream. Well every morning it was customary to fill my coffee cup and launch into Steeler smack. I suppose Rocky had enough. One morning I raised my freshly filled Steeler cup of coffee to my bragging lips and felt the hot warmth of the fluid as it drenched my freshly ironed chambray shirt. Rocky was contorted with the exhilarated pleasure of one who experiences the ultimate joy of retribution. He had gotten over on an obnoxious Steeler fan. Yes, his painstaking drilling of my Steeler mug was worth whatever penalty I would exact in revenge. But, I felt no need to act. The constant defeat of his Oilers in competition with the Steelers was punishment enough for the Houston hopeful. I allowed him his victory. Plus, it was a damn good joke.

Now Tim had a lot of LAWRENCE Steve in him as far as the issue of frugality was concerned. He knew how to survive on very limited funds. He wasn't a boozer at all and I can honestly say I never saw the man inebriated one time, even though he always had a drink in his hand. The drink was usually Perrier water with a slice of lime and he would sip on that one drink throughout the evening. I did see him drink once though and that was at a gambling establishment in the Caribbean and the drinks were free.

Tim was always looking ahead with a plan in mind. He was in total in control of himself, he insisted on maintaining his California life style. Wherever he is now, I suspect his house is very well furnished. I will wager that he probably lives well and in a fortuitous manner. He didn't believe in going out on rainy days, it wasn't a California thing to do. Navy showers were also for other people. Tim required an hour. Clogs and Hawaiian shirts worked in 1980 San Diego. They were a little odder in Norfolk Virginia. However they worked for Tim regardless of location. He could be persuasive and could usually get you to see things his way. He had a knack for making the world accept his point of view. Today, I could envision him as a mayor of a California coastal city, an upscale town of course.

As the YELLOWSTONE PCU marched through that San Diego summer of 1980, the day of moving aboard ship drew closer and closer.

Personally, I began to like San Diego, California more and more. In reality it's almost impossible not to love San Diego. The ship went on a sea trial event that lasted a few days. It was unlike any sea period I had previously experienced. The food was catered by gourmet chiefs. NASSCO, the building ship yard, wished to introduce the ship with style. The ship was built solid. Although it wasn't fancy, it predictably did all it was asked.

The YELLOWSTONE was going to be a good ship. It would have all the capability that you could imagine for a vessel of that type, and it could deliver support services anywhere in the world.

A sprinkling of Sailors rounded out the crew as the ship prepared to become an active fleet asset. After acceptance sea trials we would pull anchor and steam north on the West Coast to Vallejo, California. There we would load out; spending some weeks taking on all the necessary stores and equipment we required to fulfill our mission.

Prior to Vallejo, Big Goofy arrived. Now Big Goofy had problems and I believed they were psychological in nature. Once you got past the fact that he was a little bit off his rocker he was OK. He had a slight problem with the truth and he could manufacture the most capacious whoppers on earth. Tim used to try to get him going just to see if he had a limit. Once he got on a roll about high school wrestling. Before the conversation was over Big Goofy had concocted a story about how he was in the Olympics, wrestling for the United States Olympic Team. He had defeated the Pole, but he had lost to the Russian. Now that was good stuff. Big Goofy had taken himself all the way to the Olympics in one conversation. Now Rocky was a rather magnetic guy and Big Goofy kinda latched on to him. I don't think Rocky liked that too much, but whenever Big Goofy got going Rocky never had a problem telling him he was full of shit. Tim on the other hand would really get him rolling in order to test his limits of *BS*.

There was an occasion when Tim accompanied Big Goofy home for Thanksgiving dinner. It was all going very well until Tim interjected about how everyone must be proud of having an Olympic wrestler in the family. I think someone choked on a turkey bone on that one.

Personal challenges arose as I grew into the role of a young version of Keesey. We augmented our crew with a second class petty officer who was double my age with half my smarts. I only opine what I believe. Perhaps that sounds like so much braggadocio but many old salts will nod their heads to this. He resented working for a younger man and was quite annoying; consistently complaining about how he was the only one with experience. His experience was not impressive. The bottom line was that he could not repair the equipment and senior chief eventually put him in charge of mid-ship's main passageway maintenance. He and the passageway were a good fit, very attractive and quite glimmering deck tile were the results of a solid effort and under the observance of his watchful eye no Sailor dared to traverse the deck when shrouded with fresh wet wax. As for us, we managed to survive without his vast experience in the mix. Senior chief or chief did counsel me several times for doing too much manual labor, but I liked it and I believed they were secretly pleased that I was a pace setter.

Our Southern California lifestyle came to an end late that summer and with more than a little regret we prepared to abandon this fine city on the Pacific. Even then the real estate was getting expensive and it was understandable. The place is a jewel and I had a great time. Those who do not enjoy San Diego, California should get immediate mental health therapy. If someone dislikes San Diego then what they desire may have to wait until their afterlife.

We began moving out of our adopted geriatric community. I returned the remains of the Rambler having been guilty of pollution in the first degree. The Rambler was the worst polluter in California history. Even to this day I feel very guilty for the bag of beer bottles that fell through the floor board holes in the back seat. We spent twenty minutes picking them up at the bottom of a Pacific Beach hill. The car really had to go, the carbon monoxide started to become a problem, caused by the exhaust venting in through the floor board holes. We rode with our respiratory systems in jeopardy and luckily we survived to breathe in fresh sea air soon after.

We would return to San Diego to pick up cars prior to heading through the canal to the East Coast, but it would be a matter of days not weeks before we left this place for the final time. We departed San Diego looking forward to further adventure, but it was very difficult to leave this jewel of a port.

The ship was not commissioned when we set sail for Vallejo and we still had many shipyard workers aboard for the journey to the Northern California. I was looking forward to yet another place I hadn't visited. Back in my Revolution days San Francisco was a Mecca for me, but I had never made it to this sacred bastion of liberalism. In retrospect, that was probably a good thing.

When YELLOWSTONE tied up in Vallejo the weather was much cooler. Here in the wine country it was vastly different from San Diego. The only thing similar was the laid back California lifestyle. Even here in Northern California the folks were not as hustle bustle as they were on the East Coast. They were much more Tim-like which was reasonable considering that we were in Tim's back yard.

Tim spent most of his week ends home in San Francisco with his wife. As happens with many Navy families they had to endure long periods of separation. It would still be some time before Tim would move Julie to Virginia after the ship arrived on the East Coast.

Mark had to bid farewell to Deb also, as they too would be apart until the ship got back to Norfolk. This is the way of the sea service. The family separations are always on the horizon and the Navy is a force that demands families to be apart many times over a career. It is a much more family oriented service today. There was a time when an authority would tell you that you weren't issued a wife or husband in your seabag. But even back then the hierarchy was getting somewhat more sympathetic to the Navy family. With Navy Family Services, Navy Relief Society, and other similar organizations the Navy has an outstanding network of people ready to help. If someone stays in long enough the chances are good that at some point they will benefit from the efforts of one of these groups. I will always personally vouch for the *Navy and Marine Corps Relief Society*. They help Marine Corps and Navy families without large paid staffs. When you support them almost every dime goes to those in need.

In Vallejo it was all about stuff. It was getting parts and tools inventoried and stowed. Bringing a new ship to life was a huge undertaking and it required a tremendous effort. In addition to loading out, we prepared for our September commissioning ceremony. We had to look good and man the rail as we ceremoniously brought the ship to life and set the watch for the first time. A great admiral spoke at the event that day and I can clearly remember him saying that day that a tender was as valuable to the fleet as three destroyers. Statisticians probably came up with that, but the statement drew out some tender pride. We had no gun mounts, missile launchers, or other weapons of significance but we were to become the *Battle Tender.* I guess that meant we would not hesitate to go in harm's way given the chance. I could not figure out how else you could actually become a battle tender, so that must have been the true link.

While in Vallejo I took the opportunity to take one trip to Reno where I immediately lost all my money. I never had that much anyway. But I liked the town and I vowed to someday return. That was twenty- six years ago and I am still waiting for that chance. I need to get a move on that vow because I really don't want to wait until I'm between ninety and dead to make that trip. One thing I noticed about that town. If you didn't gamble everything else was cheap. Lodging and restaurants were actually reasonable. At least that was true in 1980.

This was also the time frame of *The Empire Strikes Back.* The movie was the topic of the day and the *Star Wars* sequel had people lined up around the block at every theatre. We made our first trip to San Francisco, traveling there by bus and my first glimpse of life in this city was the vision of two bearded gentlemen engaged in passionate lip locking at the bus station in broad daylight.

I didn't head back to the ship right then and there but I thought about it. We actually ended up having a real good time doing the tourist - type activities available there. Fisherman's Wharf, the street Mimes, the sidewalk performers, and the cable cars were all part of a fun day. I also took account of many sad folks on the street. It was as if they were still living in 1969 and never left that decade. Perhaps I brought my *Steeler karma* with me to this city by the bay, seeing that their 49ERs would soon be to the eighties what the Steelers were to the seventies. They were about to absolutely love football in San Francisco, with the help of an undersized kid from the Pittsburgh area named Montana.

The YELLOWSTONE was an official commissioned ship in September of 1980. We were all certified Plank Owners. With pride, and with the enthusiasm of being new, we stepped up the pace for our return sail to our homeport of Norfolk. There was a brief stop in San Diego to load cars and then it was on through the canal to our final residence in Norfolk. We would also do a port visit in Acapulco Mexico and that wasn't breaking anyone's heart.

In San Diego I bought a little old Toyota Corolla from Bob the electrician. The body looked great and I paid close to nothing for it. However that car never did run right, and I basically gave up on getting it operational after a while. I was stuck riding only motorcycles because I never had any luck with cars back then. I would sit behind the wheel of a perfectly good car and it would turn to junk just by virtue of my having sat in it. It went far beyond car buying strategy. It was as if I had a citrus fruit attraction. Some folks loved citrus fruit. With me, I was loved by the fruit and that fruit was the lemon. As Arnold Swarzeneggar would someday develop into the *Terminator,* I was the *Lemonator*, forever cursed to attract four-wheeled vehicles that did not run and would malfunction for no sane reason.

In San Diego goodbyes were said to friends that were made and YELLOWSTONE sailed off to fulfill her destiny as the Navy's newest asset. The West Coast was going to receive the third and fourth tenders of the class, so there would be no need for YELLOWSTONE to return to the California again. So goodbye to San Diego was in truth, goodbye.

Acapulco was as you would expect with a ship full of Sailors, a hell of a good time. The IC men went out and rented a sailboat. We were confident because Tim claimed to be an excellent sailor. Tim skillfully guided us into a surf battered rocky atoll in the middle of the harbor that almost ended this book right then and there. We finally managed to free ourselves from the dangerous situation but another pressing issue occurred. We were unable to get the boat back to the rental spot. Days passed thirst overwhelmed us, and we thought about eating…. Not really, but for those of us who were still addicted to the carcinogenic poisons of tobacco smoke it was time to get back to shore to continue the party and to burn a Marlboro. Finally that nautical genius, Tim, ran us aground somewhere on the Mexican Coast. It didn't matter because the boat rental people were right there when we landed. They probably experienced expert sailors such as us every day because they knew precisely where to find us.

We spent one of our days inviting all the people that passed by us on the beach to meet at the lobby of a popular hotel that evening for a party. We had no idea that they would all actually show up. So we had an impromptu first YELLOWSTONE outdoor party in Acapulco Mexico. They had a good band playing there and the hotel loved the business.

As required by all visitors we had to view the cliff divers. They are amazing children with great nerves and coordination. The diving itself was spectacular, but watching those kids scramble up the side of a cliff like *Spiderman* clones in *Speedo*s was equally amazing.

Soon we departed Acapulco, and headed for Panama and the famous canal. Our festive visit to Acapulco left us with a lesson. Don't drink the water. Hundreds of us needed the facility in the ensuing days. The trouble was we all needed it at the same time. Many of us were on watch when the great pay pack for festivities occurred, but fortunately by the time we reached the canal we were fine. No one died, many would remember. The remainder of the cruise to our home port was uneventful except for our appreciation of the canal while earning our *Order of the Ditch.*

When we arrived back in Norfolk, we were already *Plank Owners* and recipients of the *Order of the Ditch.* During our time in San Diego the precom crew had formed a tight bond. We weren't a missile shooter but we were proud of our mission. The YELLOWSTONE would always maintain the reputation of a hard working ship. That would continue through the ship's history, regardless of the crew or the occasional social scandal.

Our homecoming was interesting and as engineering we were the first people to man up the ship in San Diego. Soon all the members of the repair department augmented us with their much vaster numbers. I can remember some contracted psychology group coming aboard and giving us some education and briefings about the women who were going to arrive in significant numbers to work side by side as our shipmates. They provided some type of X's and O's analysis. Whoever bought that contract got taken to the cleaners. It was silly. The women came. They went to work. Some would lead. Some would follow. But c'mon, we have sisters, and mothers. Even at *McDonald's* in high school you work with women. I could see the X's and O's training if we were getting aliens from the planet *Zorbideux.* But we were getting corpsmen and electricians from Indiana and North Carolina. They were a novelty for about six hours, and then they were just Sailors like the rest of us.

The expected social nightmare never materialized. Occasional problems occurred, usually because someone ignored it. The best way to handle social issues is by enforcing professionalism in the work place. That's all. Unfortunately there is always an occasional exception and that is what gets the press. These incidents are often disgusting but keeping the women off the ships is definitely not the answer. Like it or not, and many old salts disagree, they have a right to serve and without question the women of the Navy have convincing proved they can do the job. They have contributed with the overall success of the Navy, making tremendous accomplishments while breaking down all the barriers and organizational stereotypes one by one.

For every *Tail Hook* type incident, there were a thousand others where the interaction was respectful and professional. In many ways Sailors may not seem like ordinary citizens but for the most part they are as ordinary as everyone else, the difference being that they are sometimes tasked to do extraordinary things.

Once back in Norfolk we forged into the swing of things as an active fleet asset. The shops started welding, the motor rewind business went into production and the print shop was active in manufacturing a wide range of documents or pamphlets needed by the fleet. Even our doctors and dentists were busy giving exams and physicals. The ship was a flurry of activity.

The IC men and electricians had several duty requirements. One requirement was manning an outside telephone line switchboard to patch telephone calls from the interior of the ship to the outside lines. The position was eliminated after several months because we were needed for more critical assignments. Although the watch while we were providing the service was rather easy, it soon became very annoying. Often we were faced with young lovers who felt an impulsive need to communicate every fifteen minutes or so. Then there were the lovers of *Dominoes Pizza* calling out for pizza deliveries every few minutes.

Often it was appropriate to patch these calls if a caller asked politely. It was when they called and demanded "*Get me Dominoes*!" the retaliation from E Division was forced to be swiftly enacted. A man named

Fred Domino was listed in the white pages of the phone directory. Although I must now apologize to Mr. Domino, we were forced to make him a pawn in our retaliation. Whenever a shipmate called the switchboard and said, "*Get me Dominoes*!" he was patched to the residence of Mr. Fred Domino. That would normally result in a call back to the switchboard. "*I wanted you dudes to call Dominoes Pizza and you called some dude named Domino, Man*!" The switchboard operator would then reply, "*Well if you had asked nicely to please place you a call to Dominoes Pizza then you would have been patched correctly. But if you say, gimme Dominoes then you get Fred.*" They learned that he who controls the phones and the movies is all powerful.

We eventually interrupted our daily routine to get underway for a jaunt to Florida and the Coco Beach area. We were dispatched to provide support for a space shot recovery or something meaningful. Our services ended up not being required. As good Sailors and Navy ambassadors we spread our good will throughout the local area. There's really nothing much to remember about that excursion, except that the small local taverns in Florida really treat the Navy well. Ships always appreciate the hospitality of the cities and citizens they visit, and Florida ports are always among the best hosts. I heard very few complaints from Sailors about Florida port visits over the years. We returned to Norfolk after traveling around the ocean for about a month, and then we prepared for that old friend where all ships had to go, Guantanamo Bay Cuba.

GITMO was a repeat of the old LAWRENCE visits except that tenders really throw some outstanding picnics. GITMO was also pleased to have a repair ship alongside the pier if for no other reason than we could do a lot of work for the other ships that were there. Repair ships didn't make for a pretty silhouette against the setting sun, but they sure as hell came in handy at the pier when someone needed a motor rewound or radar repaired. GITMO went off without a hitch and then we had a great weekend in Montego Bay Jamaica. I know that people usually say, "*I can't wait for liberty to get away from all these Sailors that surround me*." Then, when liberty call is passed those same people congregate in groups of one hundred or more. When Sailors say they don't enjoy hanging out with their ship mates they are of course, lying.

We managed to get out of GITMO in record time. The cattle car was still alive and well, and tender Sailors could *moo* as well as the *tin can* guys. I can't remember anyone getting in trouble at all, so outside of things like underway watch qualifications and general maintenance our attention turned to the first inaugural YELLOWSTONE at Sea Talent Show.

We had a fairly large mess deck area so the crowd promised to be a big one. Being a tender we also had a large Peavey PA system with a collection of high quality microphones which we had open purchased in San Francisco at a famous music store. It was called *Don Weir's House of Music* or an establishment close to that name. It was memorable because the day we went in to purchase it there were a couple of jamming musicians trying stuff out. Only they weren't amateurs. We found out later that they were actually from a very famous band. I can't tell you which one but there are apparently many of them in that area. Some things we'll just never know.

One important item a ship must have is good PA system. You need it for captain's calls, ship picnics, and an infinite number of events that always seem to pop up on the ship's calendar. I firmly believe that architects should create on every ship a small space near the flight deck or wherever the ship routinely gathers as a group. This small space should be designated as Interior Communications Sound Equipment Room. That would save a lot of wear and tear caused by dragging huge speakers around the ship and banging them constantly into hard metal objects. Because of the gyrocompass the IC Room is usually located in the center of the ship and below the waterline. YELLOWSTONE was no exception, so hauling around the PA system was one of those irritating tasks that occurred several times a day.

Our E Division talent show preparations were in their infancy with a week or two to prepare. Now no one ever says I'm talented so let's enter this thing. It usually starts as a joke or a dare and builds from there. After awhile you may get locked into being an idiot in front of about 400-600 people. Now that can be quite nerve wracking except for the fact that we had two good *Weird Al Yankovitch* types, namely Chris Shane and me, tasked to adapt lyrics to a nautical repertoire. In addition we had a young electrician named Kevin Breen. Breen was a high energy type. If I had to compare him to anyone it would be a young version of *Robin Williams*. He even looked similar to *Mork*, just a whole lot shorter. But just like Robin Williams, get Breen in front of a crowd and he could rock the house. I have no recollection about his skills as an electrician but he was a mama whale in Maui with a microphone in his hand.

We ended up developing a song or two. Then we practiced and it started to get funny. Practice was difficult, constantly interrupted by our own laughter. With that, the song list kept expanding and growing, until we created a repertoire, while also adding guests and props. We went on CCTV to advertise our entry in the upcoming event. This was going to be as swell as *Alfalfa* wooing *Darla* at the *Our Gang Garage*.

Mark was in for singing and harmonica. Breen was in. He was the star. I was in as a singer, and Shane our Electrician was the deep voiced anchor. Ron Rogers, Big Goofy in a fire fighters ensemble, Doc Holloway, our latest IC addition, and Rocky Branch were all support technicians. The show was starting to evolve into a huge production. The songs were set to old tunes but reworded as to apply to our business.

Our list was impressive as you may well have guessed. The absolute energy that we expended into this very extravagant event was in the highest keeping of ship at sea traditions.

OLD JOE NAVY (to Old Man River)
He's Old Joe Navy, That Old Joe Navy
He don't do nothing. He don't know nothing
He just keeps rolling. He just keeps strolling. Along...
That Old Joe, He don't do shit. We all work while Joe just sits.
We bust our balls to earn our pay. But that Old Joe drinks mud all day...
He's Old Joe Navy...

COME WATCH THE MOVIES PLAY (to Life is a Cabaret)
What good is lying alone in your rack, with nothing to do or say.
Come to the EDF Old Chum; Come watch the movies play.
We got great shows. Everyone goes.
It's the best in entertainment; it won't cost a cent in payment.
Refrain:
We got great shows. Everyone knows.
We've got top notch Bell and Howell projectors
So come watch, don't be a defector
What good......

IF I WERE AN ENSIGN (to If I Were A Rich Man)
If I were an Ensign Ya ba dab a dab dab a dee
All day long I'd Piddy paddy pum, didle dedle didle didle man.
I wouldn't have to work hard ya ba daba....
All day long I'd ....
I'd have a room sized rug with my own sink and shower, right in the middle of the ship.
I'd sport a fine wooden plaque engraved with Ensign, then my name.
I'd eat a gourmet breakfast every morning in the ward room
Eggs Benedict and prune juice.
For lunch I'd have roasted real stuffed goose.
And ....

IF I ONLY HAD A BRAIN (To the Wizard of OZ)
Oh my hair'd be long and wavy
And I wouldn't be in the Navy
If I only had a brain.
I'd wile away my hours picking stems and flowers.
If I only had a brain....

The SHIP'S STORE (To Stairway to Heaven)
As the ship's records show, the ship's store is always closed,
Cause their having a big inventory
There's a sign on the door, and it says we're secured
In three weeks you can get what you came for.
Ooo Ooo Oo, Ooo Oo OO Ooo
They are having a big inventory. ....

This repertoire of songs was practiced and discussed but due to constraints, a dress rehearsal was impossible. We had to communicate clearly and in intricate detail our top secret musical mission, with the sincere hope that responsible stakeholders would execute in a professional manner coupled with military precision. The success of the show depended on the execution of both the performers and the supporting cast.

Not to be slighted we adopted a name for our new found vocal group. We decided on stealing the *Saturday Night Live* name of *Not Ready for Prime Time Players,* and converting that into the *Not Ready for Prime Time Sailors.* The *Saturday Night Live* show was the most talked about show of the era so the handle was perfect.

The evening prior to entering port was show time. This was our *Channel Fever* night and folks were feeling somewhat festive after a few months of being absent. Most were anticipating pleasurable and romantic reunions of some nature. The night before entering port was a perfect choice for the event.

The mess deck was packed and several acts had taken place when we were introduced. We extinguished the lights, and then on cue the strategically placed Doc Holloway energized the movie projector to project a *Bugs Bunny* Cartoon on to the screen. When Bugs said his trademark "*that's all folks,*" a spot light then focused on us as we launched into "*Come to the EDF and Watch the Movies Play.*"

Joe Navy to the Rescue brought out Big Goofy in a silver fire fighter's ensemble designed for high heat. He had a strobotach trained on him in the otherwise blacked out mess decks, providing a flashing disco light as he danced like a grizzly with a tuna fish. The crowd went crazy.

Just as we launched into *If I Were an Ensign,* as if on cue, down the ladder to our starboard side came one of the ensigns out of the wardroom. They immediately shined the spotlight on the surprised scapegoat and made her the song recipient. Breen stole the show. He was a grass-hopper side-stepping a blowtorch; high energy and full of one- liners in between every song.

The applause was thunderous as we took our bows, Big Goofy included. By the time we got everything stowed the vote by crowd noise was chosen, and the winner was unanimous. I can't remember who it was, but it wasn't us. Then I had the midwatch, and our careers in show business were over. I have wondered over the years about Breen though. He would have made a great thespian or excelled in any career related to the theater.

As we settled into the Norfolk ship routine, a few car owners started to sprinkle in among us. Mark and Debbie settled into a cozy little beach bungalow over in Norfolk's Ocean View, and visiting them was always a pleasant respite from the rigors of living on the ship. Rocco drove down his 1971 green Plymouth Satellite, and it became the flagship vehicle for our group which consisted of Rocky Branch, Tim, Rocco of course, me, along with the newest arrival Dave Hales, a snuff rubbing Brown's fan from West Virginia. Dave was from the repair department and he was one of those really smart Ron Rogers types, who really knew stuff without trying exceedingly hard. He had a good brain, but bad taste in teams.

One of the movies the ship brought aboard was a big hit with us. It was about a bunch of New York kids from an earlier era. It had a great sound track of old tunes. *The Wanderers* soundtrack cassette tape was immediately purchased and we adopted the name for ourselves as we tooled around Tidewater in the vintage green Plymouth. We were similar to our earlier group, the *Bairds,* and like the *Bairds*, the *Wanderers* incorporated that one elixir of social behavior, fun. We just cruised around jamming to the oldies, listening to Rocky and Tim verbally filet each other. We'd travel to a few favorite watering holes. Tim latched onto Perrier and lime so we always had a sober driver. Eventually the days of the Wanderers as happens to all things Navy came to a conclusion. Tim brought his wife Julie out to Norfolk so he was gone. Dave married a tall girl from West Virginia and together they began having future volleyball stars. Rocky Branch fell for a Roanoke lady, and Rocco, I believe, went back to Connecticut where he in all likelihood still cruises to this day, thirty years later as an original Wanderer trapped in the story.

I continued on through my YELLOWSTONE tour thinking about a return to the Burgh. Maybe a good job on solid ground was where I should focus. I had some good leads on possibly getting into the phone company. Craig Wilkins had left the RICHARD E BYRD and was working with Honeywell down in Texas. There were options. I was close at this juncture in history to declaring myself free and heading off to CIVLANT. That's when several events occurred that were crucial to the continuation of my career. Senior Chief Gradine and Chief Worthy wanted to know why I was bailing out just when the going was about to get good.

There was a new king in our court, *Ronald Maximus Reagan* (and I must admit plagiarism in stealing that great middle name bequeathed to the president by the brilliant Rush Limbaugh). President Reagan was about to launch a continuing program of pride and professionalism that would span the decade. There was something else that was going to have a great effect on the Navy. It was a prolific change that would rid the ranks of a problem that had festered for many years. About to be enacted was the unglamorous and simple process of urinalysis. It proved a development that turned a drug tainted military around. As it evolved over the next several years into a program of zero tolerance, the entire Navy changed along with the new great vision that Ronald *Maximus* held for us. The hostages in Iran were freed, the Navy received its biggest pay raise in decades, and the chiefs were feeling empowered. It was to be a good decade for the Navy. The changes of Reagan would eventually bring down the *Red Menace* and all that went with that, but at that instance in time my thoughts were on the Burgh and a very real change of direction. Senior chief and Chief Worthy were convinced that I should stay. They attempted to sway me to continue my career, but I wasn't convinced and I started looking forward to CIVLANT. I was still under ten years and ten is the point of no return for most of us. So my departure from the sea to the rolling hills of Pennsylvania was certainly a very real possibility.

Chapter Eight:

IRIS & HOT SHOTS & SPAM

Enter Mike Ward. Mr. Ward my old division officer from the LAWRENCE years honored me with a special visit. The ex-enlisted tough guy from my DGUTS days was here on the YELLOWSTONE, and it was a recruiting mission. He knew a dynamic perspective commanding officer who was gathering a crew together for a brand new destroyer. The Ayatollah Khomeini, shattered American relations in such a manner that the lucky U S Navy was to receive a windfall of four highly capable DDGs that were originally slated for the pro-American Pshaw Pahlavi, former leader of Iran. Well, their loss, our gain. The Ayatollah was now their *Great Watubah,* and he needed new destroyers about as much as Nolan Ryan needed to add a knuckleball. He wasn't about to get the KIDD, SCOTT, CHANDLER, or the CALLAHAN. They were always meant to be American ships it just took the politicians awhile to realize it.

Mr. Ward was visiting YELLOWSTONE to recruit me for the SCOTT crew. I thought about going to that new ship, with a dynamic CO; returning to a *Man of War* was intriguing. It seemed so much more adventurous than the telephone company. I can't confirm this, but I believe Mr. Ward may have threatened bodily harm to the career counselor if I terminated at the end of my enlistment.

I told, now Lieutenant Ward that I'd think about it, but my mind was already churning, as I nostalgically remembered the LAWRENCE years. They say, once a *Tin Can Sailor,* always a *Tin Can Sailor*. The YELLOWSTONE was a great ship and I really enjoyed the environment of a tender, but the SCOTT was to be a *Hot Shot* and in the end the call to adventure on the SCOTT won out. Truthfully, it was probably time to move on at this point. All the *Wanderers* were settling down and the YELLOWSTONE had no impending deployment on the immediate horizon. IC men were once again in demand by Navy manning, so when I reenlisted I was given a little cash as a bonus. In a few months I would be on my way to a second precom unit, the USS SCOTT (DDG- 995). I bought a stereo and a car with the cash. Finally I was shifting from two wheels to four. It wasn't much of a car, an old Dodge with a 225 slant six engine. It was old and worn, but ran perfect. I had no idea what a superior American product that 225 six cylinder engine was. Over the next two years that car would be beat like the bass drums of the University of Southern California Marching Band, but it would continue to run anyway, gaining the impressive status of an icon and the widely renowned title of the *USS SCOTT Steamin Demon.*

I was committed now over the ten year mark. I would in all likelihood be a member of the world's greatest Navy for at least twenty. Everyone back in PA offered sage words of wisdom on my decision to reenlist for the second time. My mother said, "*Aint nothing here.*" My uncles all said, "*I wished I'd a stayed in.*" Some things are attractive because they are so predictable. PA was predictable, destroyers were always unpredictable. The only thing predictable about a United States Navy destroyer was its unpredictability. A destroyer Sailor gets used to being surprised. Most claim a longing for a simpler and less stressful life, and when they get that they get bored. Lucky for me, I realized that before I bailed out and fell into the routine of a *Universal Widget* employee.

When I arrived at the SCOTT Precom Unit, I was there long enough to update the page two in my service record, before they tasked a large contingency of us to proceed south to Charleston, South Carolina where we would observe first hand how gas turbine ships were operated in the fleet. We were going to be working guests of the USS NICHOLSON, a SPRUANCE class of the era. It was interesting to see how they were doing business, but like any crew they had a ton of their own woes to keep them engrossed. Most destroyers, even in port end up with a hundred pounds of *shit*;… err… I mean *marbles* that they try to stuff in a sock that holds fifty. In this case we were some of the excess that fell out. A positive development was of course, the predictable bonding that occurred between the mixes of engineers who were participants in the excursion.

I quickly ingratiated myself with my fellow first classes, and some of the troops that would form E division. This was a group of solid yet colorful characters and would be augmented by more as the next several months would pass by in preparation of the ship's commissioning. The ship was being built by Ingalls Shipbuilding Pascagoula, Mississippi. If you're not sure where Pascagoula is, it may help to know that it is about twenty-five miles south of Escatawba, Mississippi. That was where we would congregate the crew and that's where the ship was scheduled for commissioning.

The week spent in Charleston in that summer of 1981 had to be one of the hottest weeks on record. If you *googled* scorched earth it would probably hit on that particular week. It was serious heat. I could now understand why the population of the South didn't explode until after the invention and implementation of air conditioning. I now understood why Fort Sumter was fired upon in 1860. The local militia was probably cranky and in the middle of a heat wave.

The SCOTT Precom Unit maintained an air of military respectability by marching from the barracks to the brow of the NICHOLSON. As snipes we were not often applauded for our military bearing but we actually did quite well as a marching unit that week. I was introduced to a whole new breed of animal while in Charleston, the gas turbine technician. GSM1 Jim Bowens was my favorite. He was a common sense mechanic with an excellent sense of humor, but at the same time he knew how to get the job done. It was easy to understand how he made it to master chief in as short of a period as possible. He definitely had a leadership persona; the young engineers never questioned his direction. Although Jim and the other GSs were hole snipes, the gas turbine engine rooms were worlds removed from the fire rooms of the LAWRENCE. As we toured the NICHOLSON, I wondered "*Where's the heat?*" I saw Sailors exiting the engine room in foul weather jackets. This was strange and incredible. The engineering central control station or CCS had a Star Wars look to it. The space appeared more in sync with a combat systems suite, adorned with an impressive array of indicator lights, switches, and remote throttle controls. This space was night and day from the LAWRENCE throttle control in their Main Control or even the YELLOWSTONE engine room.

The NICHOLSON was a clean and impressive ship. Their IC rooms were mausoleums compared to what I had experienced on the LAWRENCE. Their equipment was understandably advanced by light years from the Adam's Class I was weaned on, or the simple efficient circuitry of a tender. The gas turbine destroyer promised to be an interesting platform from a technical perspective. I clearly remembered how impressive it was when the SPRUANCE first tied up to the pier in Norfolk. The gas turbines were commissioned with regularity in the late seventies and early eighties, and having them nested at the piers in numbers projected a formidable visual of a powerful force.

While in Charleston, the SCOTT Precom crew traveled by bus trip to a local lake for a little outdoor recreational activity. I was able to observe several of my young subordinates in social action and I made a mental note that a few potential behavior calibration projects were on display that day. One guy in particular had a persona that said, "*stop me before I self destruct.*" I knew I would have to deal with him soon. The rest of the crew was for the most part was typical fun loving Sailors. They were doing a good job of fitting in and getting acquainted. One of our guys even managed to find a girl friend down there, a robust Hawaiian girl with green teeth. He was very proud and became known as our lady's man, the *SCOTT Valentino.*

The Charleston trip in general accomplished two items. It provided a method for the crew to become familiar with each other. The precom group was now at ease with one another. That was a good start because the requirements that lay ahead would require crew cohesiveness and interdependability. Our other accomplishment was some outrageous sunburn from the Charleston heat. Like I said, the Low Country was cooking that week. The SCOTT Hot Shots were physically reddened to match their motto, with almost everyone displaying a torched epidermis.

It seemed like a mere fifteen minute wait back in Norfolk before I was packing up the Demon for a prolonged stay on the Gulf Coast of Mississippi. I had no idea if the Steamin Demon would make it that far. The 71 was already ten years old, and who knew how many had owned it before me? There was also the luck factor I seemed to have with vehicles. If I had pondered it deeply, taking the Demon would have been considered risky at best. I actually had a copilot for this trip, a gas turbine electrician first class named Hernandez. John was a Puerto Rican New Yorker who had some excellent methods of self-expression. He could provide litany of colorful cusswords in rapid staccatos that were quite impressive in their ethnic alliterations. The trip south was actually a pretty decent ride. No breakdowns, no catastrophes. There was one memorable lightning storm near Atlanta where some entity in the heavens was chucking one hundred thousand volt spears directly at the Demon, followed by thunderous laughter that scared the hell out of us. But the Steamin Demon refused to cave in to the mere force of Mother Nature. Defiantly, the heroic Demon rolled on through the torrential rains of Georgia, bent on delivering its cargo. I was relieved that the Demon knew the way, because we couldn't see shit… *errr anything,* for about two solid hours throughout that storm.

Personally, I harbored a fear of the Deep South. The fear was implanted from my Revolution days where it was passed around by the hitchhiking crowd who rumored that traversing through the Deep South would be unwise for ride begging Yankee types. I embraced and fully believed in the stereotype of the southern sheriff who would readily admonish the unfortunate hippie hitchhiker to the pea picking farm, never to be heard from again. There, for the remainder of days the lost idealist would be bent over in a hot field making amends for the defeat of Robert E. Lee in his native Pennsylvania. I was mentally convinced that southern gentlemen believed the War Between the States was an ongoing affair. I viewed an abundance of southern pickup trucks adorned with the Stars and Bars, not to mention the bumper stickers that stated, "*The South will rise again*."

With that in mind the Pittsburgh Yankee and the Puerto Rican New Yorker kept the Demon rolling smoothly but never too fast. I never had a problem in the past with Southerners, but I did wonder about our reception by the local population in Pascagoula. I wasn't about to press the buttons of any local law enforcement types by playing the part of a Yankee lead foot. It did not resonate as a winning proposition to get on the wrong side of an entrusted sheriff. Therefore; the Demon would obey all the traffic laws that the good state of Mississippi wished to place in effect.

We arrived on the Gulf Coast and cruised into Pascagoula, Mississippi on a high note. The Steamin Demon was rejuvenated by the long run. The old Dodge must have experienced a burst of endorphin flow because that old 225 was purring like a cat in heat. What the Demon truly desired, was force on the pedal and gas in the carburetor. On into Goula we rolled straight into the eventful summer of 1981.

What I first remembered about Pascagoula was the smell of nasty tennis shoes or a type of still to be identified cheese. Pascagoula built ships, but it also had a paper mill, and the early morning smell would help anyone trying to comply with the *Weight Watchers* diet regimen. We were not getting the big per diem deal we had from my YELLOWSTONE precom days. Here we were nested in a dormitory type location known as Lakeside Manor. Lakeside was several miles from the shipyard and it was one stop shopping complete with galley, rooms, and a night club. In this Nirvana, one never had to leave its friendly confines. It even had a lake and picnic area on the premises.

They still build ships in Pascagoula, but I could not tell you if Lakeside Manor is still in existence or not. It is one of those maybe yes, maybe no things. It would be a guess on my part to state that it still existed or that the US Navy still used it. I was assigned to a second deck room, and my new room mate RM1 Jim Rasmussen introduced himself. Jim looked young for a first class petty officer and today he looks young for a forty something retired Lieutenant Commander. Jim was from that square state to the west of blessed Pittsburgh, but thankfully he was a die hard Dallas Cowboy fan and not a Brown's fan. I couldn't imagine rooming with somebody cheering for the despicable Browns. It was bad enough putting up with my deluded cousins from Elyria at family reunions.

Jim or Raz as he was aptly dubbed informed me that our room air conditioning was out for the count. I was directed to the trouble desk where a cute little seaman was doing her duty by answering the phone and taking messages. Although I remember very little of what was later described to me as very obnoxious behavior, it was alleged that I instructed the young lady to get our AC fixed or she would be forced to face the wrath of the Great Spirit. It was noted, she was not impressed, and one young lady across the room observed my antics with extreme distaste. That lady's first impression of me was, *"oh what an Asshole!"*

Although I now believe that my misbehavior has been gleefully embellished over the years, perhaps I could have done better by exhibiting a kinder and more engaging deportment on that introductory day. Although I have not performed penance in a Ramadan like way for my indiscretion that day; I do realize the error of my grousing demeanor for that specific incident.

Although I doubt that my surliness caused the AC to get fixed, it soon was and I was ecstatic for that because Mississippi is unkind to those who forego the effects of Freon through a compressor. In Mississippi you must have food, clothing, shelter, and air conditioning to survive, although I fully embrace adding cold mud or mosquito repellent to that list of must have items.

Raz was a truly amazing petty officer. He knew everything about the shipyard, the ship, and the officers who would form the wardroom. He was a radioman, a communicator by trade and he was always the perfect go to guy when something needed to be done. He was one of the first to arrive in Goula, and he also knew the layout of the area. Raz was the guide book for clubs, restaurants, and other places to go.

He also knew the story of each of the girls of the Fleet Introduction Team. They were a group of attractive young ladies who were assigned to the shipyard to help outfit newly commissioned ships, and to help with a wide range of other duties unique to the environment. They were drivers, phone watches, administrative workers, and material outfitters. They had to be flexible to do whatever support task popped up unexpectedly. They were also hit on regularly with never ending barrages of pick up lines, from one passing crew after another. They heard the entire repertoire of nautical BS and they had their choice of Sailor if they wanted one. It didn't hurt that they were attractive. Jim, being a gentleman and genuine nice guy had one of these ladies as a girlfriend. Debbie was a soft-spoken attractive girl from Ohio. Jim and Debbie had the same home state in common and they were a perfect match. They are two excellent Americans who I have grudgingly forgiven for their Ohio roots.

The curious may wonder about my Cleveland negativity but all Steeler fans completely understand. One of the great rivalries on the planet Earth is the Cleveland Browns and the Pittsburgh Steelers. The two teams have been at each other like a pack of wolves fighting over a venison steak nonstop for about seventy five years. Both teams are well known for mud and blood football. Both teams have fans with bad breath and braided nose hair. The similarities are obvious and both cities inhabitants, because of their one hundred and twenty mile proximity usually have relatives in the respective enemy den. In reality it is the rivalry of the relatives that perpetuates the actual animosity. Plus as an NFL *Stiller fan* its pure euphoric joy to kick their asses.

I really did not dislike Jim and Debbie's Ohioness, but as any loyal Steeler fan would, I had to address it. Regardless Jim was granted a special exemption because he was a Cowboy fan and I harbored no great hatred for America's Team.

An important person who stepped into the picture at this junction was my new boss, EMCS Johnny Holub. Johnny was a soft talking Texan who was a great man to have on your side. He was also a person who you never wished to anger. If you did good things no human on Earth would toot your horn or sing your praises with more enthusiasm. It didn't hurt as I was to find out that the captain held Johnny's opinion in high regard. But on the other hand, get the senior chief irritated and he was like a piranha ending a hunger strike. You were going to lose an arm, leg, rear end, something. Health conscious I remained on his good side. It was much safer.

I already knew the first classes in engineering and now I could add Raz to that group. We added Smitty, the HT1 and a crazy boatswain's mate named Cora. He was loud and obnoxious but made up for it by being very funny. We had John Hernandez our GSE, and of course Jim Bowens the GSM1. Altogether this crew was shaping up as a good one; the first class mess would be strong. After a few trips over to the favorite watering hole, "*Roy*'s *Bar*," I started to meet some of the chiefs who would commission the SCOTT. They were a solid group and I knew I had made an excellent choice getting this assignment. Eventually I met the chief engineer, Lieutenant Bill Luebke who totally shattered the image I maintained of Chengs I had based on my experiences on LAWRENCE and YELLOWSTONE. Mr. Luebke was a tall handsome and articulate officer who maintained a non vulgar vocabulary. He had a great sense of humor and really seemed to enjoy people. He was always well mannered and polite. This was quite strange for an engineer. He didn't smoke or chew, and I would not have been surprised to discover that he also didn't drink. He was genuinely the type of person that parents wanted their daughters to bring home to dinner. If you were in the presence of Mr. Luebke he would always give you a sincere greeting. Captain or fireman apprentice, it didn't matter. If someone was in trouble or screwed up he was sincerely disappointed. Yes, he would make you accountable but one could easily discern that he didn't relish it.

Our division officer through commissioning was Senior Chief Holub; we didn't have an ensign just yet. We were informed it would be awhile before we got one. What we did have was a chief damage controlman. Our DCC, Chip Rowland was the czar of damage control. Bring on damage and Chip would find a way to get it fixed. Chip was a character, but a very predictable character once you got to know him.

Chip always had a big chew in his cheek. I'm not sure if he slept with a pinch or not, however it wouldn't surprise me if indeed it was a permanent fixture. He woke in the mornings and thought about conditions of readiness, namely the proper setting of fittings on the ship's door, hatches, and scuttles. I don't mean to sell Chip short at all. He had other matters he did care about such as the training of the in port and at sea fire parties and the training of the damage control repair locker teams. He was sincerely dedicated to operational repair lockers and the proper numbers and maintenance of fire fighting equipment. He was a veritable encyclopedia of damage control expertise, and he was fully committed to ensuring you, the crew member knew everything you needed to know to survive. Chip had no tolerance for loose ends. As the SCOTT progressed through its building phase, I believe that Chip never left the shipyard. I think he just slept there in a repair locker.

Chip transferred to Precom SCOTT from a damage control instructor billet in Guantanamo Bay. We were damn lucky to have him training us, and in all of the ship's damage control inspections we excelled, always.

I discovered at some point that Chip had a good family life, but down there in Pascagoula the only thing we knew about him outside of damage control was his love for fishing. Chip was the *Gaddabout Gaddis* of Navy anglers. At some future date, on another ship he became known as *Amberjack Rowland* because of the character he adopted for his home made damage control training films. It was also ironic that Chip was one of the very few Sailors I ever met who actually grew up in Norfolk, Virginia. Chip was to damage control what *Orville Redenbacher* was to popcorn. The captain, the XO, and the engineer were all mighty glad to have this guy on the team. It was almost as if he were a part of the equipment package. He was like a living and breathing 180 psi fire pump, spitting out knowledge, training, encouragement, or a motivational ass chewing when needed. The entire concept of Chip's damage control training was to get you so good that when the actual emergency struck you just went into auto pilot and did everything the way you were taught.

Raz, back at our room one evening was filling me in about a rumor I had heard back in Norfolk several months earlier. He had told me about the little night club they had here at Lakeside Manor. They called this place, our temporary home, the *Bufferillo Bar and Grill,* or BB&G for short. It would open each evening at around seven o'clock and would feature a band, or DJ. It was a good deal; if you drank you didn't have to drive. It did allow civilian patronage and the patrons as advertised were usually very large tough girls who desired a nautical friend. These large ladies were called *Buffs*. I thought it sounded condescending until I accurately discovered that they actually embraced this label; some even wore the T-shirt.

Each evening Jim and I would gather at our window for the evening adventure termed *The running of the Buffs.* They would arrive in a loud manner, cussin and hollerin. Sometimes later in the evening they might even provide a little fisticuff entertainment as they would mix it up over some Don Juan. I could understand why the place was famous on both the East and West Coasts. There could be only one BB&G; the planet could not have two of these places in operation. The energy expelled in two taverns like this may have caused the earth to tilt off its axis or to do something to cause a geophysical imbalance in nature.

The day to day business of learning the ship was much more tasking on Precom SCOTT than on Precom YELLOWSTONE. Because Johnny was the division officer, I became the division chief. Not in rank of course, but in terms of some assigned duties. As our Sailors began to arrive, I was tasked with integrating them into a cohesive unit, and the added chore of certifying all the electrical equipment on the ship worked properly and within quality assurance standards.

The process was such that after a system was installed then a test or measure was presented to a designated crew member for a completion signature. I was that crew member for electrical systems. The SCOTTS 1MC general announcing system was integrated with an external relay device to the ships dial telephone system. By dialing an access code number, one would tie his voice into the paging system. It was noisy all the time; O'Hare Airport had fewer announcements to make than Precom SCOTT. However, the process rendezvoused people where they were needed. My unusual Z name was butchered like Bambi at a Tennessee road kill, so my name after many different attempts at pronouncing the letter jumble evolved into plain old biblical Zachariah. It was only vaguely similar, but for several months I was called routinely to a thousand locations with pure muddy water colorful diction. This urged my compliance with a sense of responsiveness when called. "*Zachariah, Zachariah, I need Zachariah in the helo hangar right now; ya hear*?" "*Zachariah!*" I think the Ingall's workers just loved that name "*Zachariah.*" They would say it as many times as they possibly could insert it into each sentence. There was one unfortunate fellow who did get it a little bit worse than yours truly, Zachariah. Now Willie maintained every key to the ship. Because Willie Rau wasn't a Sailor; and because Willie was a company man; they could be a little more forceful with him than with yours truly, Zachariah. "*Willie Rau, Willie Rau, you need to get on up here to the helo hangar if you wanna keep that job. Hop to it now, Willie Rau.*" I think they were kidding, but I certainly could not ascertain that. I did know that Willie Rau didn't pay much mind to the pressure tactics. I believe he had a little Keesey in him. If they ever fired Willie he was assuaged in knowing his replacement would take a month to figure out the cryptic key ring. It was lucidly clear that he held the shipyard hostage in the *Willie Rau Grip as the Royal Keeper of the Keys."*

The leader of the ship's building process was a short powerful man, Mr. Bramston. Mr. Bramston was a guy no human wished to antagonize. The good news for the Navy was that he always got the job done and I believe on time. I remember an incidence took place where a senior officer became weary of the 1MC to telephone tie in and had it disconnected. Bramston immediately ceased work until somebody hooked that thing back up. Until it was delivered to the Navy the SCOTT was his ship and it was going to get built the way he knew how to build it. He made no compromises.

Ahead of the SCOTT in the production process was the first of the Ayatollah Class, the USS KIDD (DDG- 993). After that was the USS CALLAHAN (DDG- 994). We were the 995 and the CHANDLER was the newest level of construction as the 996. There was one final SPRUANCE class being built, the HAYLER. It was rumored that the HAYLER was created because of all the excess material remaining after a long line of ship construction was drawing to a close. Of the Ayatollahs, the CALLAHAN and CHANDLER were to be Left Coast ships, while the KIDD and SCOTT would be Norfolk home ported. There was more than a little professional competition between the crews in those days as the KIDD readied itself for departure.

The IC gear on the SCOTT was as expected vastly different from the LAWRENCE. Instead of a Mark 19 Gyro we received a Litton AN WSN 2 Inertial Measuring Unit. The WSN2 was much easier to work on than the older Mark 19 and it occupied only a fraction of the space. IC2 Curt Wiedrick had the NEC for the phone system and he was a wizardly tech. Lock Curt up in a room come back a little while later and he would have it fixed. Curt was an excellent technician and like most of the good ones slightly eccentric. We allowed for his eccentricities and he provided us with the expected genius. As the division LPO, I had to spend significant time with the electricians. They were a tougher group. An electrician known as Mac was our best fix it guy. He would work like a sled dog on an Alaskan Moose hunt. There was no quit in Mac. He was also very talented. Mac was unfortunately, more self destructive than Jim Morrison on a rock tour. He had an engaging personality, but he had a hard time cutting it off when partying. There was a lot of soul searching when Mac was killed in a tragic motorcycle accident several months after commissioning. I suppose we all thought about what we could have done differently back in Pascagoula months before the tragedy occurred.

One gift that Mac possessed was the uncanny knack for circulating slang vernacular from the past. He would take a 60's word and get in to the main stage of peoples conversation. One of Mac's catchy words was *gnarly* which soon matriculated through the Precom crew like a case of Tijuana crabs? Soon everything and everyone was; *gnarly*. Even when providing reports to the chief engineer we ended up getting the word gnarly in there somehow. The engineer would ask, "*Petty Officer Zahratka, how did the test go for the gyro repeaters today?*" My reply, "*This big gnarly dude brought up the test data and the process was right on the money with no oscillations. Sir.*" "*Gnarly*?" the Cheng would start to crack up. "*Yes Sir, very gnarly, Big time gnarly, Sir.*" I believe the Cheng came from a background where people spoke well. He had the voice of a professional broadcaster, quite close to *Joe Buck* actually. At any rate, I suppose he found the colorful expressiveness of his blue collar work force entertaining. There's never anything wrong with being appreciated by the boss, even if the subject is humor.

Our next arrival of note was Yac, formally Joseph Yacisen. A native New Yorker from New Rochelle, Yac was to be our poster boy IC man. Yac had great looks and a hard earned weight lifter's physique. He was the strongest kid on the ship and he worked hard at it. He was often gulping down huge quantities of egg protein shakes to support his nutrition requirements. Although he looked Italian he claimed to be of Czech descent, like myself. With his New York accent he was a taller and better looking version of Sylvester Stallone. I believe Yak's hero at the time was Arnold Schwartzenegger. He knew a great deal about nutrition and about producing muscle. Yac as we were to discover over time actually had a lot more brain than brawn. Right then though the brawn was very evident. Yac was a talented worker and he was destined to do many great things on the SCOTT. But like a lot of young guys he could get a little bit of *pistivity* going now and then. Things weren't always fair in the Navy and leaders weren't always perfect. *Justifiable Pistivity* occurs from time to time in the Navy, just as it does in all venues of labor. It's the handling of one's *justifi-*

able pistivity that marks maturity. Sometimes it takes a few lessons to live and fight another day. *Controlled pistivity* for a leader in a position of authority can often work as a tool. But it has to be utilized sparingly, as a catalyst for action. Therefore, the key to effective leadership is to turn *justifiable pistivity* into its more mature form, *controlled pistivity.* Good leaders can not run around in a constant state of being *pissed off.* We'd all hide from them if that were the case. Yac, at that time had an occasional temper burst, but he would learn as we all did. I think he had a hard time realizing that other folks just couldn't do things as well as he could. He was quite frankly one hell of an IC man. He had the rare blessing of intelligence in the brain that was transmitted to the hands. It's really too bad that he got out and went to school for eight years and become a renowned orthopedic surgeon. He would have made a great Chief IC man. OK, I'm kidding, everyone who knows Yac is proud of him. However; no one is surprised.

At some point prior to our first sea trial we were introduced to the XO and the captain. Commander Harry Maixner had more charisma than *John Wayne* in a WWII movie. It was easy to tell he loved the SCOTT and he sure as hell loved the snipes. He knew as the ship was fast approaching sea trials that the snipes would be tested early. He was an involved leader who loved not only the ship, but also his crew. We were *Harry's Boys* and he was gonna get the most out of us, but it would be very rewarding. Once the ship started to get underway after the yard relinquished control, we found out that the captain wasn't hesitant to kick this bad boy in the pants. Captain Maixner also looked the part of a sea captain; steely eyed, strong-jawed, the whole Hollywood persona was there. Someone else must have recognized the fit, because they utilized the SCOTT as a platform for a recruiting infomercial. He was the perfect choice and after watching that short film I would have been interested in the U S Navy officer program. He also liked our senior chief and it certainly didn't hurt the division to have a small measure of positive press with the skipper right out of the barn.

Lieutenant Commander Joe Lee Frank was our XO and he was memorable. To say the XO was tough was like calling titanium rather hard. He was a powerfully built man. He looked like a wrestler and when holding XO's Mast for NJP, I could imagine a young Sailor standing before him soiling his pants in mortal terror. But when the XO spoke he had a marvelous North Carolina drawl that made him sound like an influential southern senator. As a matter of fact his vocabulary was so well versed that junior officers would jot down words he used at officer's call in order to research their meaning later. A normal observation was a junior officer scribbling in his notepad as he whispered, *"How do you spell turpitude?"*

The XO was in charge of overall ship's cleanliness and I honestly can't recall a single dirty SCOTT day with Joe Lee Frank. We were as clean as the bedrooms on Donald Trump's yacht, especially the berthing compartments and heads. If you took the time to clean a space then Lieutenant Commander Frank was going to invest the required energy to meticulously inspect that space. Believe it or not there is a science to these inspections and he was the expert. Hiding things was only going to get you caught. Berthing compartment petty officers in charge quickly learned how to achieve the standards or life became unpleasant. What was positive and perhaps different about that ship was the unusual fact that people would get recognized for doing a good job on some very unglamorous tasks. It wasn't only super techs fixing equipment who received accolades. A fireman properly preparing a space for painting was just as likely to get some public atta boys or as the Navy says, *Bravo Zulus*. The SCOTT had a solid foundation of leadership and I do believe the majority of the crew was excited to be there.

Our influx of personnel continued and we received a few more Sailors in E division. Jake was a young jokester with a great Boston accent. Stokes was Yak's challenge to the biggest and strongest guy on the ship. Stokes was a towering 6 foot 5 inches tall. He resembled a Nubian warrior or perhaps a prototype NFL defensive end. His mere countenance was intimidating, an overwhelming attribute at first meeting. However; once Stokes spoke in his slick New York City vernacular and added in his refined sense of humor all feelings of apprehension immediately dissipated. Stokes was an enjoyable character. He entertained us with great stories about mugging joggers in Central Park, but personally I believed it was *bushwa*, that old Bronx gutter term for bull shit. He was overtly mellow; it was difficult to accept his claim of violent propensities.

Our newest IC man to add to the gang was Pierce. Bill Pierce from Detroit, Michigan, was our WSN2 gyro tech. Pierce, a short guy with the persona of the local garage mechanic; loved taking things apart and putting them back together. Often using a personal method of trial and error Bill eventually developed into a very adept and competent tech. He worried little about the occasional left over parts but that was Pierce. Yac and Pierce eventually became IC1 Wiedrick's (Curt soon made first class) two work horses. Further diversity, was impossible for those two. We had Yak, the *All American Boy*, and *Frumpy Pierce*, the inquisitive fix it man. Differences aside they held two common traits. They were both amusing in their unique individual manners, and they could both expertly repair IC equipment, or as we say; *fix stuff.*

Evenings in Pascagoula were normally carefree times at the *BB&G*, or on occasion at a rock'n roll bar called *Thunders*. Sporadically I'd pop in on the chiefs at *Roy's Bar*. Roy's was a little hole in the wall oasis that became a beacon to the chiefs. There was also a country place where people actually knew how to do all those country line dances. Locals in Mississippi actually knew how to dance country. In the Yankee world I migrated from they were always in a perpetual state of learning the steps. The local establishments in Mississippi served shrimp in the manner places up North served peanuts and popcorn. Mississippi claimed the label *Hospitality State,* and for the most part the people whose paths I crossed lived up to that motto. Sailors were well received by the local community, so all the fears I had about the South to this point were far-fetched. I had heard about a contingency of reveling Sailors who wondered into an out of the way tavern a respectable distance outside of Pascagoula. The story goes that they were running their mouths in that establishment and this particular squad of testosterone –filled peacocks had their feathers abruptly plucked. At least they made it back alive, which was a good thing.

I suppose that being a heterosexual male all my life that I eventually had to meet the right person. When Iris Sampson chose me I was totally helpless to say no. Iris first saw me on the day I arrived. It was she who observed my bristling at the innocent watch stander and thought "*what an Asshole!"* She never tires of telling that story. After twenty-six years my dear life-long partner can ring that one up like it was occurring as she speaks, embellished with each replication of course. Iris was eventually convinced by her good room mate Debbie and my good room mate Raz that I was actually a decent and humorous character with a positive upside. She eventually agreed to meet me, and I fell in love in about two seconds. She was gorgeous with olive skin that accompanied her Latina heritage. She had high cheek bones, and the most perfect lips I ever saw. But her best feature has always been her large wonderful smile. She'll probably read this and say,"*gag me with a spoon,*", but it was true then and it remains true to this day. Zman married way over his head, but I refuse to apologize for that.

After a missed communication; our first date did not occur as scheduled. I went to pick Iris up but she wouldn't answer the door (although she claims I didn't show up). After that we were inseparable. It's been said that when you fall in love your brain goes through some type of chemical change. Mine did. We danced, went to the beach, movies, and restaurants. *ET* hit the theaters and we loved it along with the rest of the planet. At times we were with Jim and Debbie, sometimes we were alone. Yak and the girl I chewed out in my now famous *AC is Broken episode* became a couple. She was an attractive girl and they were an amicable pair. At times they accompanied us on an excursion. We were becoming a close knit group down in this suddenly wonderful town of romance- Pascagoula, Mississippi.

Along came a small guitar packing guy from Pittsburgh named Matt Augustine and a small guitar packing guy from South Carolina named Charlie Houser. They arrived on the scene as newest members of the SCOTT Precom crew. Once they meshed with a few other musicians on the Precom, namely a Jim Croce voiced ET named Dan Strode; live entertainment reverberated on the lake by Lakeside. Those guys were excellent musicians and their services were often in demand to entertain the ship.

Before people conjecture thoughts that the Navy had the *Taj Mahal* of residences at Lakeside Manor Pascagoula, Mississippi please allow me to clarify what was meant by the word lake. That pond by the apartment units was one that swimmers dare not utilize. The lake served as a hatching facility for the state bird of Mississippi, the mosquito. The mosquitoes of Pascagoula were always raring for a nice raw meal and Sailors served as a delicious food source. For some reason mosquitoes to this day find the lovely Iris particularly tasty.

The lake at Lakeside was more flood drainage than lake. If anything it may have served as the film site for that Sailor mess decks classic, "*Spawn of the Slithis.*" A large mutant lizard type monster emerging from the depths of the murky lake would have been most appropriate. If such a beast were to appear, the SCOTT Precom Unit would have served it beer while Chief Rowland would have tried to get it hooked on a fishing line. The *Slithis* definitely would have been forced to party. Pierce may have kept it as a pet, while Yak would have surely wrestled it.

As Augie, (Matt's nickname), became known he blended into our ever growing group of *SCOTT Hot Shots*. He landed a date with another Navy girl named Denise and this lead to a group outing of four couples. It was quite natural and very Raz-like for the intrepid radioman to discover some obscure river in the middle of nowhere. Raz organized a canoe trip to the Wolf River. Upon arrival you parked and a bus hauled the paddlers approximately a thousand miles upriver and dropped unsuspecting revelers off somewhere in Iowa. (Slight exaggeration) but it was a quite credible distance. You were given a canoe for every two people, oars included. It was essentially a story of simple misfortune how yours truly became the darling of this particular adventure, but I can't make this up.

Our downstream excursion began in excellent fashion. Lots of laughter and carrying on was the theme for this trip. Rain had been scarce that summer and the Wolf River was quite lower than normal. With that there were a few incidents where the canoes scraped bottom but we were still able to make progress in the shallow river. Yak had to ease off a bit because his *Tarzan Strokes* powered his canoe with a noticeable overdrive effect. Eventually we came to an idyllic location where the river formed a pool at a sharp bend. There was a steep bank and an often used vine begging to be tested by a passing showoff.

Yours truly, the *Ape Man* could not resist. I clambered up the bank, grabbed the vine and proudly displayed my prowess, swinging out over the water. Yours truly, the stunt man of the Wolf River immediately slipped off the vine and plummeted into a dead tree hidden about two feet below the surface of the black water. Yak and others felt that my dive into pain warranted a score of laugh like hell. I stood my ground as a hero and did not scream or cry although truly I was in max pain. If alone, I would have cried like a baby with a diaper rash. I would have howled like a werewolf after a *Bufferillo*. Alas, I was in mixed company. Rather die than cry; I held back my tears and jitterbugged into a little encore slap stick performance. Yak produced a New York comment of high wit by saying something profound. I think it was- "*You dick!*" Speaking of that particular appendage, I glanced down and was thrilled to discover no damage in that area. I had a very nasty bruise on my thigh, indeed; it was a close call and I am quite appreciative not to be authoring this as an employed eunuch in some Moroccan sheik's harem.

After recuperating from my near death experience we were back to our task of rowing through the tame supine river. Enjoying the outdoor beauty, disaster struck again on *Z-Man's Black Sunday,* but first a little medical background. Actually, I was a real outdoors kid growing up in Pennsylvania. I was often called upon to perform chores for one of my many aunts in my home town. One day while mowing my Aunt Nancy's grass I rudely ran over a nest of honeybees. Their retaliation was swift and vigorous and I yelped like a puppy getting whipped with the Sunday paper. It was no big deal though. My aunt put some lotion on the stings but lo and behold my head swelled up like a medicine ball. Fifteen minutes after that bee attack I went from cute thirteen year old to sinister poster child of the *Chilly Billy Cardilly Show*. I was allergic and ugly, the ghastly head totally disproportionate with the rail thin physique. With no particular sense of urgency my sister *Karen the Sympathetic* drove me to the doctor taking great glee at my looks for the entire journey. The doctor fed me his magic potion and I quickly reverted back to the old me. For several years I faithfully carried around an emergency bee sting kit but over time as I developed into an indestructible teenager I permitted the episode to lapse away into a bizarre childhood memory; the kit archived in a dark drawer in Pennsylvania.

That was my last memory of a bee sting which brought me to that testy Mississippi afternoon. There I was in the middle of rural Mississippi, possibly a good thirty miles to the nearest medical anything. So of course, Mr. Bee calculated that it was an opportune moment to visit the Z Man. When he dove to the attack he must have smiled, the Kamikaze thrilled at bagging a Yankee. So there I was with the love of my life on a canoe trip. I was wounded from my slip off the vine- yes that was true, but I was still enjoying the moment. Now it was about to end. Iris was going to have to witness my transformation into the "*Creature from the Black Lagoon*" as my head would surely swell up to a magnanimous proportion totally out of whack with my small frame. I had not carried a personal bee sting kit on me for years- indeed eons. I could even croak and that wasn't currently on this one score and six year old's agenda.

Sailors are heroic if anything and our team went into action. I got into Yak's canoe and we started paddling down river like two trappers getting arrowed by some pissed off Apaches. After gaining about five miles on everyone, I noticed that absolutely nothing was happening. My head refused to swell. There was a tiny bump where Mr. Mississippi Bee had directly assaulted me, but that was it. I had no idea why my head wasn't already the size of the planet Pluto, transforming into the expected supernova of heads. All the commiseration was wasted. I remained plain old battered and bruised Zak, but that was from the *underwater evil tree from hell* and not from the *Pissed off Rebel Bee from Mississippi.* I believe the bee's DNA firmly held a conviction for the rebel cause. Had our killer bee discovered that Iris grew up in Jersey instead of Honduras most assuredly she would have joined me as a Yankee target.

As I now reflect on it, we were all very lucky that the entire swarm of southern bees did not attack because truthfully all parties on the Wolf that day were Yankees. I suppose that someone had to be the entertainment and perhaps that was my special day. I promise you this; every one of my fellow paddlers loved that day; as it is human nature to rejoice in another's angst and misfortune.

Jim Bowens, our worthy gas turbine mechanic actually brought a ski boat to Mississippi to play with during the precom period. This meant I was about to add a third sport to my list of no business engaging in activities. I already covered golf and bowling and after a day on the Mississippi black water I was sadly forced to add water skiing to my list of inept no business engaging in activities. At least I discovered a purpose; driving Jim around as he skied in the wake. He was a very adept water skier, a one ski guy; two was much too easy for Jim. Zak on the other hand, water skied about as well as a domestic turkey attempting to migrate south for the winter. I was thumbs down for walking on, skiing on, or most other water surface events. But I did in fact give it a go, and sometimes all one can do is roll the dice and take a chance; for that I will accept a minimal modest credit

Johnny our straight shooting senior chief, hit a mid life crises. He deservedly made senior chief and went out and bought himself a sports car, a gorgeous blue Camarro with a T-top and a white leather interior; a fitting vehicle for a successful man trying to hang on to his youth. It looked vastly different a few weeks later when it was totaled. I think Johnny ended his mid life crisis right there and he returned to his standard Texas pick up truck with an armadillo etched into the rear window glass. There is an unwritten law or perhaps a plain old stereotype that applies to who in the Navy drives what. The chiefs' parked vehicles are usually referred to as "*Redneck Row.*" Their vehicle of choice is usually the Dodge Ram Pickup, GMC Sierra, or Chevy Silverado. Of course the Ford F Series is the reigning king in *Redneck Row.* The Nissan Titan and Toyota T100 are probably now included without bias to the elite group in most *Redneck Rows.* The officers mainly support the Bavarian provinces of Germany through the junior officers' purchases of the Z-3, Porsche, or Mercedes sports flavor of the year. Married senior officers normally gravitate to the ultra safe and well constructed Volvo Wagons, although certain Acura and Infinity models have made recent inroads.

As the summer of 1981 drew to a close our commissioning date, as one would expect drew ever closer. We underwent sea trials and the ship performed flawlessly. This was certainly a crew with a swagger. There was all star talent there for development. The captain adopted *SCOTT'S a HOT SHOT* for our ship's mantra and bumper sticker. We were all convinced we were as we lived the label.

As it was always meant to be I sprung the question to Iris one night. In the beautiful enclave of Roy's bar she said yes. I should have chosen a more romantic environment but I had no control when it came to my feelings for that girl. I was just happy she said yes. If this is painting you a happy picture, then excellent, because it was about as good as it gets back in those Mississippi days. I was part of great command. I was in love with a beautiful girl, and the crew had both character and characters. It would have pleased me to no end to have remained in precom Pascagoula for another ten years.

There was one minor unfortunate incident though. One night during a visit to Biloxi the Steamin Demon was sabotaged in the *Hospitality*

State. Someone must have been annoyed by the Virginia license plate and he put a welcoming crow bar through the worthy Demon's windshield. However; no mere crowbar could stop the Demon, in defiance a sock, an old smelly sock at that, was placed in the windshield hole and the Demon continued on without missing a beat. I felt distraught about it, the Demon deserved better. But truth be told; actually the cracked windshield with the sock stuck in there added some salt and character; like a pirate peg-leg or an eye patch, the entire Demon persona was enhanced. The Demon was a warrior with wounds to display for its service. It was no flivver of a vehicle; it resembled a snipe's car and the Demon legend grew. Air Force personnel would never permit the Demon within the confines of their pristine base at Keesler. The Steamin Demon was purely nautical, a true Sailor ride, brine encrusted, sandy bottomed, and jury-rigged.

Eventually our stay in Pascagoula concluded. Commissioning boasted all the pomp and ceremony that the YELLOWSTONE had earlier in 1980. The crew looked spectacular; the ship was freshly painted and adorned in full dress with flags and bunting. SCOTT appeared formidable, worth every penny the taxpayers spent on her. The ship resembled a thoroughbred race horse in the starting gate, straining at the bit to sprint forward like a bat out of hell. And it did.

All the usual events lay ahead for the SCOTT. The engineering department personnel were adorned in red hot coveralls for the cohesive unity of the snipes. They looked good for awhile, but it was at last a failed gesture as they deteriorated into bright red greasy and wrinkled pajamas. The Hot Shot attire soon became the Hot Shots with black dots. The reds finally retired, passing to oblivion, replaced by the much more appropriate and practical navy blue sets. It was also much gentler on the eyes.

In the snipes early days Mr. Luebke was bombarded daily with flak from the XO about engineering berthing, home of the snipes. I finally grew weary of the mismanagement and the flow of executive poop to the first class snipes. I went to senior chief and the engineer and told them I volunteered to be in charge of the lackluster compartment. They were delighted to actually gain a volunteer for the thankless task. I got down there and found the people lollygagging with no plan. Each work center was tasked to provide a body to help clean. Leading petty officers sent the people they deemed unproductive. The identity of the problem began with that. The mission was to create a place of prestige using a group of underdogs as the work force. Hence we jokingly created the *Engineering Berthing Swarm Team, or* EBST Team. Once we had a catchy name the misfits began to fit. They fit so well that they would quickly evict non swarm team members from the compartment. They decorated their T shirts with the catchy

SWARM TEAM logo. They cleaned like the *Noah's Arc Prep Team*. They swarmed to the mission. Like an angry nest of unwanted insects they invaded every nook and cranny devouring dirt and creating order out of chaos. Soon the XO had to admit that the notoriously lugubrious space was a glowing gem of military symmetry. The best the XO could get from us was the rare pubic hair in the sink drain. We were locked in. The USS SCOTT Engineering Berthing Swarm Team should have been featured on *Comet* commercials. The catalyst that really promoted swarming was the rock'n roll on the ship's entertainment system. I was the head IC man so I controlled the ship's entertainment system. I allowed the Engineering Berthing Swarm team carte blank disc jockey privileges. They selected the music. Hearing their names come through the ship's entertainment system was a real ego booster and they rocked to their task. At times they would grab their swabs and use them as microphones during a kick ass rock tune, but our air bandoliers would return to their tasks with zeal and pride and we all lived if not happily ever after at least cleanly ever after.

At one point there came to pass a SCOTT underway talent show. The XO sang the *Keeper of the Eddy Stone Light* and he was justly pelted with hot dogs and disgracefully booed from the flight deck in total humiliation. He cried. However, the Engineering Berthing Swarm Team did an outstanding air band rendition of *Jethro Tull's, Aqua Lung*. Complete in their snorkel attire and frogman's fins they rocked the crew singing of *snot running down his nose*; and *greasy fingers smearing shabby clothes*; they completely stole the show.

As petty officer in charge of the ship's entertainment circuits I procured us a respectable and varied assortment of training films from the waterfront movie exchange in Norfolk. There was a vast selection of subjects from damage control which pleased Chip to no end, to medical education films, which pleased our Doc, Chief Raible. We also maintained an inventory of training films on the hazards of drunk driving and on technical systems. We showed them randomly at lunch to give the crew something to watch while they were eating, or when they took a noon break in berthing. One afternoon we were having the captain's favorite menu item, grilled tuna with cheese sandwiches. They were different, but a worthy minority of people enjoyed them. We slapped a film on and paid no mind to what it was we were showing. It happened to be an old black and white WWII era production about venereal disease. It was very graphic in the display, and the picture of the young man's bulbous and infected… did not mesh well with the grilled tuna and cheese. Many sandwiches were tossed and the XO's suggestion box was stuffed with complaints that threatened congressional action. They were anonymous of course. The XO, Commander Frank addressed this as the *Great Chancre at Lunch Episode* and he felt that if someone did contact their legislative representative that at least Congress would know we were holding training on the good ship SCOTT.

The ship was back in Norfolk and Iris and I had broken up. I wasn't being a Sailor, she broke up with me. Jim and Debbie were also apart. They were still together just not geographically. But soon Debbie would be transferring out of Pascagoula, her tour there was drawing to a close. Yak and the Debbie he dated broke up. She transferred to Hawaii. Yak got over that in about an hour or so and life moved on.

The SCOTT as the new kid in town was in dour need of major mileage. We would be going south for ops then off to GITMO and back to Pascagoula in early 82 for some final yard work. Then it was ramp up for a six month UNITAS, where once again the chance to circumnavigate South America presented itself.

At this juncture we were augmented with a new EM1 named Dave Owens. Dave was near my age and he sported a slight North Florida drawl. The blonde hair blue eyed Dave was one of the most amiable people I ever met. His arrival allowed me to relinquish the electricians to him, and I became an IC man again. No more laundry motors or flight deck lighting for a while. Dave had it. We would still give each other assistance when needed, but Dave was an excellent electrician and if truth be told he was probably the best EM I ever knew from both a technical and leadership standpoint. There was a Senior Chief, Bill Villanueva, who I would meet in the near future who was an equal to Dave as an electrical expert, but to say who was best is foolish. One could call it the classic Celtic question; who was better; Larry Bird or Bill Russell? They were both great and won championships; so who really cares?

Dave was one of those mild mannered types who you could talk to about anything. He was also one of those hard working mellow types who may get pissed off five or six times in a twenty year period, maybe in a lifetime. I wouldn't want to be around if and when it ever happened because it would probably be a volcanic eruption of magnanimous proportion; maybe a Dave St Helens. I say this because Dave stood as the calmest person I ever met. An action guy, he just worked, maintained that caring attitude with his shop, and he got outstanding results.

Yak's hero was *Arnold Schwarzenegger... duh,* this fact was supported by a vast collection of muscle magazines scattered around the shop effectively promoting the masculine inferiority of the rest of us. Someone provided me with a snap shot of Pierce, who Yak referred to as Gnarly Pierce, justifiably so. Personally, I believe Pierce attempted to live up to that adjective, it was a *persona of gnarliness*- Pierce embraced it. Gnarled, the root is after all, knotted, contorted, twisted, and bent, and those were the traits Pierce wished to project. I confiscated a great pose of Arnold flexing in a muscle magazine and carefully glued the cut out head of Pierce to the body of Arnold. I then posted the new enhanced Pierce on Yak's locker. We queried all who passed if they noticed the new and improved Pierce mounted proudly on Yak's locker? Even Pierce himself basked in admiration of his new found masculinity. When Yak saw it he almost cried as he blurted out in disbelief "*Oh No, You got Gnarly Pierce on Arnold's body, Oh No!*" This was like putting *Granny Clampett* in a Playboy Centerfold. We loved it.

Pierce and Yak both made third class and continued to improve their skills. Yak was particularly adept at any installation work. His cable installations were always meticulous and correctly fastened into existing cable runs. Whenever a circuit required installation in the wardroom areas, Yak was counted on to make it look better than the shipyard's work. Pierce was a good man for tinkering around with stuff until he got it working again. Prints and technical manuals were irritants to Pierce and he was apt to disassemble anything- he had confidence. IC1 Wiedrick was just your everyday electrical wizard. He had a great technical mind and once focused in he transcended to a personal zone. He was best at very challenging tasks. With these IC men in place the shop was a smooth running operation; an efficient enterprise; and we wished to maintain this method of doing business.

Senior chief was very fond of Dave and me and when something of a positive note happened in the division he ensured everyone knew it. We also had allies in the Chief's Mess from other areas of influence. Bob Capello, the senior chief master at arms was a big man with *most juice.* He knew who was working hard - as the ship's sheriff he routinely roved all areas of the ship; arriving unexpectedly at any time in any space on the ship. He also worked directly for the XO. The ship's corpsman, Doc Raible and certainly Chip were both ship wide leaders and they knew a great deal about was happening and what progress was being achieved in damage control training. Our newly reported command master chief, Frank Caron was one tough SOB as I would soon find out. He ran a very tight CPO Mess. Another addition to the ship's company surprised both of us. I had a second cousin from back home -Mike Ellis. As fifteen year olds we worked in a bowling alley setting duck pins up for 10 cents a game or line. We were the manual machines; termed pin boys. I knew Mike from working there. He was a big prankster and a real hoot to hang around with- a tall slim and curly haired guy who I knew to be a lot tougher than he looked. Now he was my shipmate on the SCOTT. We were quite surprised when we ran into each other.

Mike was a twidget. He was a smart guy, a fire control technician. They only let smart guys be fire control technicians. Their schools were much too demanding to wing it. He had made first class before me and he actually had a year or two on me as far as time in service. I wasn't entirely sure if the Navy could handle both of us together on the same ship. Time would tell about that.

The ship got underway on a trip to Fort Lauderdale, Florida where Debbie and Raz met up. Iris and I reconciled forever and we had a great time in Fort Lauderdale in the reconciliation process. It was a very romantic couple of days. Debbie and Iris received orders to Norfolk at SUBLANT and would depart Pascagoula about the time we would be getting underway to go back. It was funny how it worked that way at times. The SCOTT was a greyhound with an attitude and the Navy wasn't about to keep this beauty tied to the pier for any prolonged length of time. Soon we were back in Goula getting things added, readjusted, and tuned up prior to being turned loose to the fleet permanently.

The Ingalls workers were an amazing group. They were blue collar America at its best. I recall the summertime construction of off shore oil rigs they were creating. I observed in awe the welders forge together an immense rig in the hottest part of the Mississippi summer; the workers covered in full protective attire. They never missed a beat. Invite those folks in for a meal on the mess decks and they would act so honored that they would take you out on a shrimp boat for a day. These were seriously hard working and grateful people and there was nothing they couldn't or wouldn't do for a ship's crew. Our return trip to Pascagoula wasn't as much fun as our previous Lakeside manor stay. It was get in, get out, and get underway. While we were there we had one long weekend to make a Norfolk visit. Dave Owens had a dilapidated white and several earth tone colors pickup truck. Feeling adventurous; Bos'n Cora, Mike, Jim Bowens, and I traveled all the way to Norfolk in the back of that thing. It was a rough ride and absolutely crazy. The bos'n passed tremendous gas clouds throughout the trip. To reek at sixty miles an hour from the back of an open pickup was somewhat amazing. The bos'n was proud of his nauseous creations; his victims felt medical attention was warranted. At least I now know first hand how some migrant workers must feel getting trucked around to farm jobs across the country. We made it all the way to Norfolk nonstop except for running out of gas somewhere in rural North Carolina, the truck not the bos'n. I felt blessed when I was able to catch a military air lift flight back, but a one thousand mile drive for a weekend visit with Iris was a small price to pay and well worth the agony of the ride in that old rusted truck.

The SCOTT departed Pascagoula, Mississippi with an attitude; rooster tail churning the black water of the Gulf at full speed with 100 percent pitch- four engines on line, both shafts turning viciously, arrogantly defying the drag of the sea. Left behind was another great American machine of an earlier era, the Steamin Demon, a fallen victim to the pillagers of spare parts. The Demon served engineering department well in Pascagoula, having hauled around the gnarliest of the gnarly for many months. It left a legacy of supreme respect for the Mopar slant six 225 cubic inch engine. A twentieth century chariot for its American sea gladiators, all SCOTT snipes paid homage to the Demon engine with reverent respect. The Steamin Demon remained an important element of many HOT SHOT sea stories far into the future and its story lives on in the lively tales of the founding *Hot Shots.*

Now it was back to Norfolk, *Navytown USA*, and preparations for a wide assortment of acronym inspections that would boggle the mind. All would be well though because Iris was there and our marriage was in fact going to happen. We had decided that a simple justice of the peace ceremony was all we wanted. Iris' mother and father were there in attendance and on the 5th of March1982, the Honorable Rufus of the Norfolk Justice of the Peace Department pronounced us married as husband and wife. I believe that Luz and Tomas had many reservations about the cigarette smoking gringo as a new son-in-law, but those reservations would dissipate soon enough as they would learn over time that I indeed had the best of intentions.

A short time after our wedding we traveled to New Jersey where they threw us a huge party, a true authentic Latin festival. I embraced the culture completely and to this day I am a gringo in name and looks only.

Our first apartment was a cozy little two bedroom near Old Dominion University. It was about five or six miles from the base making the commute very convenient. We had a tiny kitchen with a table in the living room that actually folded down from the wall. Shortly after moving in, we invited Yak and another big guy from the electrician shop named Mason over for a spaghetti dinner. All went well except seating the 225 pound linebackers on our fold out bench didn't work well and they collapsed like a slap-stick scene on the *Dick Van Dyke Show.* At least we didn't spill the spaghetti, it was all good.

We had to get a car and I found a classic 1971 Chrysler New Yorker with a perfect body. It was one hundred and fifty miles long from the front to the rear bumper. It stretched, when parked from Norfolk to about the halfway mile marker to Salisbury, Maryland and it got about five and one half feet to a gallon of gas, about on par with the USS JOHN F KENNEDY. We lived within five miles of the base so gas wasn't a budget breaking issue yet. We did have a color TV with a 27 inch screen, but the vertical hold had behavior issues, possibly ADD, and it would roll about every four to six seconds. If two or more people jumped up and down like the Baltimore Ravens doing their pre-game warm-up routine it would usually quit for several minutes. Other than that we had each other and it was a wonderful time.

As if 1982 wasn't already treating me well by being a newly wed with a gorgeous wife; Raz, who always knew everything before everyone else, appeared in the first class mess and excitedly announced that I was on the CPO list as a chief selectee. At first I thought Raz was BS'n me; that irritated the worthy radioman and he presented me with the list, and there, correctly inked, last name, comma, first name, selectee, appeared my name. The first idea that popped into mind was to let Iris know and she was even more ecstatic than I was, genuinely thrilled. It just feels good to make chief. For those fortunate enough to be selected, it matches up well on the list of life's great accomplishments. It is a true life highlight to become a United States Navy Chief Petty Officer. As happy as I was to be on that list, I was just as happy to see Dave Owens, Jim Bowens, Smitty the HT, my cousin Mike, Tom Brady from the ET shop, and Fred from Supply Department. This was truly a great group to go through initiation with.

The initiation process (now called induction) for chief petty officers is a comprehensive and long lasting traditional process that incorporates deserving first class petty officers into the realm of a very exclusive group; the Chief Petty Officers of the United States Navy. Becoming a chief is a tremendous accomplishment. As many are aware there is an initiation process that is both tasking and arduous and many outsiders have wondered inquisitively about what exactly occurs during a CPO initiation. I will explain and reveal to you as much as I dare about the chief petty officer initiation process in the following pages:

Go to Next Page

Go to Next Page

...and then we stood there, our wives and sponsors pinned us with our anchors. The captain and the command master chief presented us with our covers and we recited the *Chief's Creed.* We all shed tears of joy; including the captain and all the chiefs. Any chief who informed you that he or she didn't cry, quite frankly lied. This is true in all cases one hundred percent of the time. We were *Chief Petty Officers.* If you wish to know more about this very sacred process, then you should enlist in the Navy at a fairly young age, maintain sustained superior performance, primarily at sea for normally ten years or sometimes much longer, and you may earn the rare privilege of being a part of the greatest organization in the history of the planet.

It was a long process following life's direction from Western Pennsylvania to the deck of the Navy's newest destroyer as a chief petty officer. I had attained it in just under ten years. Everything I had accomplished to this point was directly attributed to someone along the way taking the time to calibrate in a measured way this Sailor in need. It was Worshick back in boot camp. It was Mr. Spencer as a high energy division officer. It was Lieutenant Mike Ward going the extra mile and Senior Chief Gradine tasking me to lead. It was IC1 Schmidt granting me an opportunity. It was Horgan and Knight patiently teaching and explaining what they knew. It was the encouragement of Johnny Ray Lyons showing me how to keep my cool in any given situation. It was the support of Senior Chief Johnny Holub ensuring recognition when quiet accomplishments were made. It was the support of peers like Dave Owens, Jim Bowens, and Raz. I owed much to my subordinates who always did their best; Sailors like Yak and Bill Pierce. Before them it was Lung Cookie on my first ship and the first group of peers I was with; Stebare, Combat, and the Bean. It was the support, love, and happiness I received from my new wife Iris. I owed a lot to the wardrooms of various commands and to outstanding role models like LT Ward, CDR Luebke, CDR Frank, and Captain Maixner.

But the single greatest influence on getting me to the rank of chief petty officer was without a doubt the training and calibration I received at the hands of Don W Keesey on the USS LAWRENCE. Keesey was the task master I needed to learn a trade, but that only scratched the surface of all that I learned from him. Keesey was the reason that fathers and mothers send their sons and daughters to the Navy. Keesey and others like him are the reason those sons and daughters come home trained and confident, ready for life's challenges. Keesey was a true Sailor's Sailor. When admirals address enlisted crews and refer to the back bone of the Navy, they are referring to those Keesey types. I don't know if Keesey ever made chief petty officer. I sincerely hope he did. I do know that he was the reason I was selected, and for all that he did and for all that he was I shall be forever in his debt. As I was about to venture out to a vast new set of challenges as a new chief in a very different role, one that would provide a greater circle of influence, I would always remember what a shop run by Keesey was like. That was always the ideal and model I attempted to emulate, the Keesey model of effectiveness.

PART II:

KHAKI

Chapter One:

HOT SHOT CHIEFS

People view you from an entirely new perspective when you make chief. Being in khaki people expect you to know things. I'm not talking about ordinary rating expertise but about all subjects known to mankind. Not only are you expected to know how to change out an engine in a 62 Chevrolet, but you should also be well versed in *Maslowe's* hierarchy of needs. If a chief doesn't know the answer to something he may be confronted with genuine grief, shock, and total disbelief. An appropriate answer to an "I have no clue question" is to reply "*Just do what I tell you now and we'll get to the philosophy shit later.*" Then you quickly get informed and impress that Sailor a short time later by saying "*I gave your question some thought and the opinions of Nietzsche seem much to far-fetched in today's world of equal treatment.*" This will impress the Sailor who asked the question and legend of the chief will continue to spread like an algae bloom in the Everglades until you, the chief, *Sea Faring Oracle of Delphi,* will be granted the label "*Most Juice.*"

Juice can be a very mystic thing. The juice concept originates in what the chief can accomplish within the mess. Gaining juice is about working things out in the mess for the overall good of the crew. Ideally all chiefs will have juice, because with the cooperation of their peers they will accomplish what often seems to be overwhelming and daunting tasks. Officers may call this *synergy* but it has been with us much longer in the chief's mess as *juice.* It's not that the chief himself has all the answers or solutions to each and every problem; it's primarily about what is shared, suggested, and then agreed upon behind the door of the esteemed *Goat Locker.*

To state that the SCOTT commissioning crew had a good chiefs' mess was like saying the 1976 Steelers could tackle. The SCOTT Mess was loaded with talent. Many of the chiefs in this mess would rise to master chiefs, limited duty officers, and warrant officers. There was a tremendous amount of talent there; precoms are often manned in such a method as to get a new investment off to a great start. It also didn't hurt having very strong leadership at the top with Harry Maixner and his XO Joe Lee Frank.

In our mess, the style of our new command master chief, Frank Caron was to do things right because you were always under scrutiny. After a port visit in St Thomas we discovered what he meant. By *we*, I mean Cousin Mike and I. We were on our way back to the SCOTT in the liberty boat and struck up an impromptu tune that was rather catchy. The twenty or so revelers were howling at the lyrics. The diddy had something to do with herpes and other venereal diseases, all set to a popular sixties tune *I've Got Rhythm*. Of course rather than the word rhythm we interjected the appropriate STD.

We all chuckled; quite pleased with our wittiness and impromptu pithy lyrics. We climbed the brow and hit our pits until we were soon roused by a junkyard dog with a fierce Texas drawl. It wasn't *Cujo* in a nightmare. No, it was Master Chief Frank Caron; much more intimidating than a mere rabid dog. Mike and I bunked across from each other, so at least Frank didn't have to do this calibration exercise twice. When he was done saying his one way transmission, my comment was; "*no problem, Frank.*" I never required Frank's counseling again. I really didn't care to experience Frank's direct method anytime soon. Too graphic, too personal, and such an encounter did not provide a warm fuzzy feeling of being loved.

Not that all my entertainment was bad. I was mildly famous as a first class in the precom for my blues rendition of the lunch product *Spam*. If *Hormel* ever saw this impromptu blues song they would have hired me on the spot for advertisement commercials. The beauty of the Spam blues song was that I could never remember the words from one rendition to the next, so I would have to improvise an entirely new song with each attempt. The concept was born from an ancient episode of *Monty Python* where Spam was added to someone's restaurant order whether they wanted it or not. I just adopted it to a blues theme about greasy red meat. Its popularity grew to the point where Auggie would start strumming the blues and Kelly from the celebrated Swarm Team would start on the harp and the gathering would chant, "*Spam, Spam, Spam.*" I would never attempt a rendition without at least three nectars of the Gods served very cold in bottles or cans.

After I attained chief status I had to tone down those types of behaviors for the foreseeable future. It would have been inappropriate humor and I don't think Frank would have been a huge fan of the Spam song. If he didn't like the herpes song, he most assuredly would not have enjoyed *Spam*.

Not only is making chief an adjustment for the new chief. The crew may also be shocked for a day or two. The first day after initiation, Pierce said, "*damn Zak do you look different!*" Senior chief jumped right down his throat and that ended the old Zak persona right there on the pier. There was another moment about a week or two later when I was traveling down the pier and ran into the tallest guy in the D&S piers zip code. It was none other than the great Mr. Spencer, now a department head on one of the ships. When he recognized me on the pier after the customary salute, he said, "*What are you doing Zak? Do you have on your Dad's uniform?*" That was quite Spencer like. I was glad to see he was also on his way up.

I enjoyed a good prank as do most Sailors. I realized I had a real tough guy division. So I pulled this one on them. As a part of morning quarters I would read the highlights of the Plan of the Day to the division where they stood mustered on the fantail. This would occur promptly after officer's call. I would also include all the pertinent information that wasn't found in the POD itself.

I created a make believe message that sounded convincingly official. Reading my home made message as seriously as I could manage, I watched for the reaction to my words. It stated: "*Effective immediately all E7 and above personnel are granted the authority to inflict corporal punishment upon E3 and below personnel in lieu of non judicial punishment. This authority is being granted in an attempt to eliminate minor mast cases from the agenda. Up to three strokes with a 1 inch fire hose cut into lengths of no longer than 27 inches will be utilized. A certified independent corpsman will be in attendance for all pending sessions.*" That was about all I could get out. Yak knew me too well and was chuckling. Everyone else was getting pissed to the max. I heard a lot of "*aint no moth... fu.... gonna touch me! I'll knock the ....!*" I couldn't hold it back any longer before I said "*Gotcha!*" They told me they would get me back, but alas, they were much too ineffective at retaliatory treachery to present a serious challenge.

The E Division guys were making rate right on time but one ole guy really let that crow get to him. Overall he was quite effective, but he did have a little issue with power. I won't mention his name but the story goes that he had big Stokes our Nubian warrior in for a few hours of extra duty for some minor infraction. Truthfully he was working poor Stokes like a delivery horse on a muddy 18th century, New York City street. Stokes finally had it and approached me to complain about the Gestapo tactics. In height, the perpetrator came up to approximately Stoke's ribs. I counseled them, "*Sometimes we come to these disagreements and there is just one thing to do. We have to work things out physically in order to establish authority.*" Now Stokes eyes lit up like an Aztec witch doctor getting ready for a Saturday night sacrifice because he thought he was about to be turned loose, freed to give an authorized ass whipping. I said, "*Stokes, what we have here is a lack of training. So I want you to do some observing on how to do the job properly, so it will be a less burdening task.*" The petty officer in question had no recourse except to pitch in, so instead of a managed laborer we now had two participants and the dirty job was quickly finished. The guy toned it down after that. He was no longer *Ivan the Terrible,* just that good guy *Mr. Helpful* from the *House of Courteous.*

The SCOTT did so many underway jaunts that summer that I can barely remember it all. It was a whirlwind of activity. We accomplished a deperming event at Lambert's Point in Norfolk. Dave was the prime mover in this time consuming process. The event is done to create a smaller magnetic signature making the ship less attractive to mines. No Sailor desires a date with Ms. Mine. We wrapped the ship in cables and pulsed current through the hull, thereby reducing the natural magnetic field of the ship. Dave was on it and his competence was evident throughout the detailed choreograph of the process. The ship's responsibility went off without a hitch.

SCOTT spent a great deal of time in the Caribbean. GITMO was like a second home by now. Going to GITMO with Chip was like bringing *Eric Clapton* to a guitar test, predictably we had no problems in Cuba. Chip was much tougher on us than a mere GITMO Fleet Training Group.

On one excursion, the SCOTT traversed the Panama Canal making that my second personal trip through the Ditch. We did a little drug chasing that time. To say we were busy was like saying *Eddie Murphy* had a sense of humor. I knew that my new wife wasn't happy at my always being gone. Poor Iris stepped on a nail in a rain storm and really hurt her foot. As is usual with destroyer Sailors I wasn't there and like many Navy wives Iris had to mend on her own, and she still had the responsibilities of her Navy job at SUBLANT.

SCOTT received a new engineer along with a new XO and a new captain. The engineer was really an old acquaintance; LT Mike Ward. Mr.Luebke had moved onward and upward to bigger things, he was a super individual and a leader whom I would never forget. The evaluation he wrote for me was surely a very important reason I was selected to chief petty officer. Leaders who take the time and make the effort to write effectively really can do a tremendous amount of good for their people. I will forever maintain the highest regard and utmost respect for Bill Luebke, an excellent Cheng and a first class human being.

The first thing LT Ward did with E Division was take a long tour with Dave and me over every inch of our equipment and spaces. With a trained eye he asked all the probing questions. He hadn't changed. He just became more adept. He was an engineer who left no stone unturned. We found that out about six AM one morning when he wanted to know why the cathodic protection reading wasn't taken. Lesson learned.

The second thing LT Ward did was save me from being transferred to an Adams Class DDG. I felt that five years on the LAWRENCE was enough, and to be quite honest going from a brand new Ayatollah to an Adams Class was like trading in your Ferrari for a Plymouth Volare. Ferrari-Volare; *hellooo...* I did not want to go. Adams Class destroyers were extremely taxing and I was getting to be an old chief now. I had turned twenty- seven that summer and I wished to maintain my youthfulness. After all, I had a young wife at home. Mr. Ward worked some magic and I remained a *Hot Shot*.

Speaking of home, Iris and I stepped up in the world and rid ourselves of the temperamental Arc. The old New Yorker gave us more trouble than Huck Finn in a military school. It was a beautiful car from a cosmetic standpoint, built for comfort and cheap fuel. But mechanically it had more quirks than Dr. Frankenstein on an acid trip. It had to go. I saw the car many months later at the new D&S piers. It was broken down and some young Sailors with tools were swarming on it like beetles on a …. Well, never mind. At any rate with all the tremendous problems presented by the Arc they were apt to learn a great amount of seventies auto technology and mechanical procedures.

We turned to the Japanese for our transportation by purchasing a Toyota diesel pickup truck. I only fueled it with gasoline twice in the several years we owned it. The truck performed well and despite the irritating noise of a diesel engine at least it didn't break down every other day.

The final days passed prior to our departure on UNITAS and Mike, his wife, Iris, and I were out for a late celebration prior to our departure. We attempted a street crossing at an intersection when we were nearly run down by a passing car. Mike yelled something colorful at the driver. The car screeched and out came a *Troglodyte.* Now I have nothing against gay cavemen, I even have *Geico* insurance, but *Og of the Hairy People* wasn't impressed. Og decided that I needed a good round house to the head. I dropped like a punctured blow up Santa and he left the scene gruffly and without an apology. I recovered fine except for some ear pain. The following day, less than forty eight hours from sailing off to UNITAS I had a short operation and a patch was placed on my freshly ruptured ear drum.

Chapter Two:

FIX SHIPS

I was medically transferred faster than Willie Parker racing a pit bull. My SCOTT tour was over, more abruptly than the ending of *Fahrenheit 500.* The SCOTT was a great ship and being a *Plank Owner* and an original *Hot Shot* was a true privilege, but if truth be told, the IC Gang with Curt Wiedrick there really didn't need me. The SCOTT I left behind had great talent and Dave was as strong a chief as the division needed. Dave and I really had conterminous positions in regards to our ship responsibilities and to keep us both was overkill and not the best use of Navy assets.

I was sent to Portsmouth Hospital where I underwent surgery and continued routine visits afterwards. My hearing ended up being fine, although today Iris contends I am partially deaf; her diagnosis offers that I suffer from selective hearing loss. I was actually surprised that they granted me so much time off, including six months of limited duty. I had received a hernia operation over at the Portsmouth Naval Hospital in the early seventies and after I was released from the hospital I was granted three hours to get back to the ship. I'm not kidding about that. I think the doctor was irritated with me because he asked me a question about stool color and I told him the Cheng made us deep six our chairs. The other meaning the doctor had in mind wasn't a recognizable vocabulary word in my blue collar Pennsylvania lexicon.

With the ear operation, I received more down time than a grizzly in a January sleep in. That was fine because Iris and I purchased a new construction Virginia Beach townhouse. Furnishing our new home was an exiting time for us. I was engrossed in the moment when orders arrived. I received a temporary assignment to Electrical "C" Schools in Norfolk, a training command, while I remained under medical scrutiny. It was a good deal. I could learn something valuable and revisit the technical side of my rate prior to gaining a billet on another ship. This was a much better assignment than pursuing uniform violators at the Navy Exchange or some other under the radar task usually provided to a limited duty person.

I arrived at Electrical "C" Schools where I was assigned to assist two other IC men. AL Hall was a quiet low key guy from a country western Virginia town known as Bluefield. They didn't come any more affable than AL Hall. Al's forte was patience and an easy going manner that aided him as an instructor. Al's partner was IC1 Arnie Pon. Arnie was and is a unique individual. Arnie is big guy. His mother was German, and his father was Chinese. At about six feet five inches Arnie was the tallest Oriental I ever saw until someone invented Yau Ming. Arnie didn't appear overly Oriental but you could identify the trace. Germans and Orientals always get stereotyped for their technical prowess and Arnie did nothing to dismiss those analogies. He was a very talented IC man and it was obvious that he was going places in the Navy.

But what I liked best about Arnie Pon wasn't that he was a super technician and instructor. What I thoroughly enjoyed was his sharp Brooklyn wit. Many folks confess to a personal dislike of New Yorkers. Personally, there's nothing more entertaining than a New Yorker's pithy sense of humor. Arnie had that great gift of wittiness that seemed to ooze out of the *Big Apple*. You sometimes had to grab the home made words that he used and analyze the implied meaning to really appreciate what he was saying. Arnie used interesting words such as *"Bluke"* to mean the sex act. I know not whether it was a Brooklyn derivative or just an improvisation on the fly. He was well versed on a capacious range of subjects and he was never boring. Of all the instructors I observed at Electrical C School I could think of none who were more talented than Arnie Pon.

Arnie and Al were the team that taught the Navy courses for two different plotting systems. They were pieces of gear that assisted combat information personnel in tracking and quarantining submarines. The newer Mark 10 Dead Reckoning Analyzer Indicator was much less complicated to work on and teach than the older generation Mark 9 DRAI. It was engineered with repetitive electronic circuitry which made it much easier to troubleshoot and repair.

Because there were still numerous Mark 9 machines in the fleet, there was still a viable need for technicians to repair them. The Mark 9 was a much more thought provoking device than the Mark 10. The Mark nine was an electromechanical marvel of gears, motors, and synchros. Arnie, tasked to rewrite the entire course of instruction for the complicated system, zestfully attacked the challenge. The khakis at that command must have realized what they had in Arnie because he was more thorough than a young mother getting her kindergartner ready for his first day of school. Every comma and every sentence he wrote was carefully scrutinized. I provided Arnie with some assistance during my brief stay there and we got locked into more than one debate about semi- colon versus comma. When he completed that course it was a work of art and a model manuscript for many others. Within the six months I was there, I witnessed Arnie Pon get an officer's commission and continue on with a meteoric rise and a stellar career.

As a student in Arnie and Al's classes I had a very enjoyable time. Arnie would plan intriguing statements such as "*Kircshoff* was a *beer guzzling wino* who *said, at every node , the sum of all current entering must equal zero, while the current entering is the negative of the current leaving*." He would bring this out in a loud deep voice with a little Brooklyn thrown in for effectiveness. He was an engrossingly good lecturer.

Al was very adept as the laboratory rat. He would toss a few problems in the equipment and have the students rack their brains trying to figure out the bug. Al was not parsimonious with what he knew; he was actually quite generous in his instruction. But like most good teachers students were forced to wrestle with the symptoms and come up with solutions. That Al could be amused at a technicians discomfort… well that's another story, but suffice it to say Al possessed a slight touch of technical sadism. Realistically it was guys like Al and Arnie who produced very outstanding technicians in the Navy. When someone graduated from a Navy school, he or she wasn't just a fix it tech. You actually had to learn the theory behind the engineering of the device. Many Navy technical classes would often begin with a full review of basic electronic and electrical theory because the Navy desired proficient techs that could think on their feet and repair technically challenging equipment when a ship was four thousand miles away from a service station. Navy technical instructors were often iconic teachers and the legend of their abilities often spread through the ships on the waterfront. The common expression usually verbalized among Sailors as "*…so and so really knows his shit.*"

Working regular hours and being around a contingent of dynamic people, well, one could get very used to this lifestyle. Arnie's wife, Lucy and Iris bonded as friends, both having common Latin ancestry and we spent some enjoyable Sundays together. This was in spite of the demise of the *Pittsburgh Steelers*; as I had to endure Arnie's New York Giants begin their rise to prominence.

As it was, Al and Arnie personified the Navy instructor. They were very dedicated professionals, but they were also real Sailors who had the unique Navy sense of humor. I believe Al retired as a Chief. Arnie, as an officer rose through the ranks to become one of those inspector types. He was one of those engineering guys that couldn't be fooled about anything on a ship. They should have a term for people like him. They should be called *Shiptologists* or *Nautical Oracles.* They are a breed apart in the scope and breadth of their knowledge of shipboard engineering systems and weapons platforms. The only thing that I believe kept Arnie apart from this group was that he never developed that characteristic southern drawl and he didn't spit brown juice.

Just as I was really getting used to having a regular job, change occurred. When I first joined the Navy I was unaware that there even was such a thing as shore duty. Usually a Navy shore tour is remarkably similar to a regular civilian job. There is routine, traffic, things to do at home, life with the wife. It was often cozy and comfortable. For an IC man it was also guaranteed to be temporary. There were certain Navy ratings that have a sea shore rotation attached to them that said for five years sea time, you get a two year reward of shore duty. At times that could be stretched to three. For instance, if you agreed to a family accompanied duty assignment overseas then it was probable you would get a three year shore tour. But you always knew as an IC man you were sooner, rather than later going to be haze gray and underway.

Within six months of my departure from the SCOTT, my hearing intact and freshly educated from a few months at Electrical C Schools I was in receipt of orders. Whenever you come off of limited duty for medical reasons you are sent where the detailer needs you. You actually have no negotiating power. That was the orthodoxy of a system designed to be fair. In all likelihood, what saved me from traveling was the fact that Iris was also in the Navy. The IC detailer was rather benevolent, keeping me in Norfolk for my new assignment. Ironically, my new ship wasn't new at all. The IC detailer provided me one choice in Norfolk and that was back to the good, but not so old USS YELLOWSTONE AD41. As an ICC on the YELLOWSTONE I would serve a tour in repair department's electrical division this time. This division on a tender was known as R3 and it had quite an array of capable repair shops. My shop was 51G, the gyro repair shop, but we would fix all ship system IC equipment problems. No work request would ever be turned down by R3 division.

In addition to the IC shop, the YELLOWSTONE R3 Division had an outside electrical repair shop, a motor rewind facility, and a motor balancing shop. All of those shops stayed very busy in the manner repair ships are accustomed to. They are always a flurry of activity; whereas a carrier flight deck simulates an ant colony in its well coordinated choreography, a tender is like a beehive with its flurry of activity. YELLOWSTONE in its five years of fixing ships had gained a reputation as a real working ship. Maybe it was not the prettiest, now that a newer one, the SHENANDOAH was alongside in Norfolk, but nonetheless YELLOWSTONE was highly regarded as a ship that could get things done, and that is always the preferred label for a repair ship.

When I stepped aboard the ship it was four and a half years after commissioning and anachronistically there was still a minute sprinkling of Sailors serving from the commissioning crew. Those Sailors who stay on a ship in excess of four years are quite rare. Dave Simms, the Brown University graduate was still in E Division. All the IC men had departed. Ron Rogers had made chief and left for greener pastures. Tim got out and returned to the Left Coast.

Most notable of the holdovers to me personally was Dave Hales, who was one of my top petty officers in R3 Division. I felt good about that, because Dave was a very sharp technician and an excellent fix it guy. I still felt some pity for him as a Brown's fan, although in those dark days of football, the despicable Browns, lead by the unorthodox Bernie Kosar were outperforming the struggling Steelers. That was extremely tough to take, but I was hopeful that the Steeler woes were short term and that we would once again be back on top of the heap. When I reported aboard, Dave was off to Mark 19 Gyro School and he would be in Great Lakes for a few months. I found another very unusual cast of characters in this shop, just as I had in all the others. I now believed that peculiar and abnormal character flaws were in all likelihood a preponderant and universal trait in all Navy IC men, worldwide. We all displayed whacked out eccentricities that mainstream Americans would judge as strange. I'm sure most Sailors throughout the Navy would concur with this assessment of IC men as I have this vision of shipboard Sailors world-wide reading the proceeding sentences as they nod their heads up and down in synchronized agreement. We didn't seem to attract normal people in this rate. There aren't a lot of us and that may be a part of the attraction of the rate to unconventional personalities. Regardless of the psychology and anecdotal theory of IC men abnormalities, once again, here I was with a fresh group of characters that could easily fit in for a prime time sitcom casting call.

IC1 Mike Demers was a jolly good natured first class who made do with an amenable personality and a good sense of humor. He wasn't a forceful or tough guy type, but he could get people to work by using a personable approach. Alan was good old country boy who was small in stature and very opinionated. He had brazened opinions on everything and it usually aligned with the train of thought that felt the South was going to rise again and relegate all Yankees to second class citizenship. Countering Alan was the low key Tracey Mayfield, a lower Alabama kid who was always respectful and worked harder than a Pittsburgh brick layer. Narvy, a good natured yet laconic African American said three sentences in two years.

Larry Williams was a fun loving garrulous guy from Georgia who could do great Eddie Murphy imitations. He went by the logo of *Cool Breeze.* Larry was a hard worker and I would rely on him often to complete the hard jobs.

Jerry was a big jock from Kentucky. The former high school tight end was just your basic good ole boy. He enjoyed a good joke and he stood as a dedicated audience listener whenever Larry got on a roll.

Neil Mossbrugger was a big affable teddy bear type. He was your basic *do gooder* and all around nice guy. Obviously, his nickname Moose fit him well. One of life's great pleasures is the sight of a lady, graceful, lithe, and fluid in dance; conversely, one of life's great displeasures is viewing the spastic gyrations of the Caucasian male attempting to dance. White males dancing in high voltage pained contortions fully support the case for suspending use of the electric chair as a tool against capital crime. Moose however; shattered that opinion for me. He had a very noteworthy talent. The two hundred and change Moose was a true *Fred Astaire* type dancer. Country or ballroom, he was a master technician of both. To watch a guy his size move like that was actually quite amazing. He was more than willing to provide in shop demonstrations of the *Moose is loose* as he prepared for his routine rituals at one of the local country honkytonks. We often stepped into the shop in the early morning hours to catch the Moose two-stepping gracefully with the shop push broom.

In my opinion Kelsey Storr was one of our most interesting characters. Kelsey as our African American Republican marched to his own drum beat. He was very articulate and enjoyable to communicate with. He was ambitious and forcefully engaged in a plan to get to the top. Although I don't know if he ever made it, I thought he would make a good officer someday. I would not be surprised if in fact he did. Other than Dave, who I already knew was the smartest guy in West Virginia; Kelsey in my opinion probably had the greatest potential to rise through the ranks. He had sincere ambition, and he would soak up information like a "*ShamWOW*" sponge.

As for my chain of command, I couldn't have found a better duo than Senior Chief Bill Villanueva and CWO4 Jack Lake, our division officer. They were both true leaders and had the undivided respect of the entire ship. Bill Villanueva was a big guy, very tall for a Filipino. He was over six feet in height and he had a commanding presence. He knew what it takes to be successful and when he gave you advice, you could take it to the bank. I cannot recall anything he ever stated as being inaccurate. He also had the insider's scoop on everything that was occurring on the ship. Not only R3 Division Chiefs, but most of the chiefs on the ship sought his counsel. That group of chiefs was the true catalyst of accomplishment on

YELLOWSTONE. Bill Villanueva had you guessed it, *most juice.* He was effective and respected and got things done. It made life a lot better in the chief's mess being in the same division as Bill.

On tenders, division officers' billets in the repair department are often filled by salty dog warrant officers who spent many years in the enlisted ranks where they excelled, rising to the top to become warrant officers. They are leaders who balance budgets, manage repairs and assets, and keep the fleet in a high state of readiness. They are normally bottom line leaders who need no supervision from the top. The repair officer gets information and status reports from a repair department warrant or from a ship superintendent and its credible one hundred per cent of the time. They don't get easily side- tracked; they stay focused on the mission, while they gauge success by direct results. They are usually competitive with other divisions and they enjoy finishing second to each other or anyone else as much as the Yankees enjoy losing to the Red Socks. Maybe you could claim that I am stereotyping once again about a group of people, *oh well, what is, is.*

CWO4 Jack Lake was all that and a lot more. He had a rugged demeanor as did most of the warrants that I knew. Jack Lake got results without argument and without yelling. He would tell us what he expected and it would get done. Every morning he would go through our entire computerized print out of jobs to be worked and those in progress. One by one we would update our entire repair package. It was in your best interest to be up to date and accurate with answers or standby for discomforting poignant questioning.

Senior chief acted forceful when required but we had quite a few senior people in R3 and although we had our fair share of hot jobs there were none that required any whip cracking. The chief who was in charge of the electrical repair shop and I got along fine because Smitty was a former LAWRENCE Sailor. He was on LAWRENCE quite a few years after I had left and I knew he understood the tough life having spent a long tour on an Adam's Class.

The motor rewind shop had a very polite and knowledgeable LPO, EM1 Sharon Lee. Sharon Lee was as nice as a little kid's Sunday school teacher until she had to get forceful. It could get scary then. She could get the unmotivated motivated quicker than a spoiled teenager could get daddy's last dollar. After her group became suddenly energized she would immediately revert back to her former refined quiescent self as if nothing had been said.

We had an enterprising young man who fulfilled the role of the division yeoman. EM2 Clendenon was hot stuff because he had a state of the art *Trash 80* computer from Radio Shack. It was one of the first ones to show up on the ship and he made good use of it by printing up lists and documents and generally keeping Mr. Lake well informed with statistics and printouts.

When I look at how computers have churned into conflagrations of check lists I find it amazing. Entire careers can now be spent in front of a PC making lists and checking lists and documenting lists of lists. Today no work may occur without the security blanket of a well-developed and many times refined check list. I have a seventy year old neighbor named Bob. He is a retired lawyer and he is in great health, and he hasn't the foggiest idea of how to use a PC. And he doesn't want to. I know that leaders have taken action to get people out from in front of their PCs and out into the spaces so I believe there is a movement afoot out there, but for awhile the PC addiction was a problem needing therapy.

This was the historical moment that Ronald *Maximus* Reagan brought back the *Dreadnaughts.* Everyone on the YELLOWSTONE wanted to go work a job on the IOWA. Those battleships just oozed out testosterone. They sent the message overseas that we as U S Sailors always wanted to send. When a battleship aligned itself pier side in a foreign port you always wanted the locals to think "*Those Americans are really nice people, but I'd sure as hell hate to piss them off.*" If you could do that then you succeeded in executing a successful foreign policy. That was the message sent by the four mammoths of the New Jersey class.

The Navy under Ronald Reagan was booming. The Aegis cruisers started to filter in with the TICONDEROGA and the YORKTOWN arriving from Pascagoula. These were real *Star Wars* ships with an Aegis Radar capability that must have kept them awake at night in the Kremlin. From the YELLOWSTONE perspective, in R3 Division we approached every thing with the Jack Lake simple motto; *fix ships.* That's what we did and we did it well. We had an excellent mix of technicians and enough experienced folks to be on top of almost any job. When a group of techs arrived from YELLOWSTONE to help out some overworked under manned frigate crew, they appreciated us. It was always a good feeling to get things up and running for those guys. I believe frigates or FFG crews had the heaviest burdens along with the men of the remaining Adam's Class destroyers; still hanging tough as they approached senior citizenship. The manpower on an FFG is small and if something had to be done you usually found that somebody on your name tag. If a tender could give them a little maintenance and repair help then they gained kudo entries in the *Book of Life*.

The old Adam's Class destroyers such as LAWRENCE became increasingly difficult to procure parts for as time went on. Tube technology became archaic; the AEGIS era was here and now. However, the Adams Class destroyer had a guided missile system so they were kept in service; a viable mission even during the Ronald *Maximus* era.

YELLOWSTONE was an amenable group and for the most part we had a steady stream of work. We rarely ran into a situation that required frenetic action. Six section duty wasn't too bad and quarterdeck watches were for four hours. If you only had to do that once every six days there was no justifiable reason to complain.

The chief's mess on YELLOWSTONE was about five times the size of the SCOTT's. It was a closed mess, meaning that there was a mess caterer and that gentleman provided a different menu from what crew was served. Some ships were rumored to be parsimonious in their crew portions to stay within budgets. The YELLOWSTONE CPO Mess was the polar opposite, providing generous portions to a fault. On duty nights you could sign up for steak of choice, Alaskan king crab, or fried shrimp. Sliders were always an offered option. There were always candy bars, ice cream, (complete with all available goops), and an assortment of chips and snacks. In other words it was very possible to blossom into a large figure in no time whatsoever. One could arrive on the YELLOWSTONE as a lean mean chief petty officer, svelte and macho in photographs and within two months you could transform directly into the *Tapioca Tundra.* It was justifiably presumptive to believe the crew's mess also served healthy portions. At lunch they had full course meals or the quicker speed line for burgers and fries. However; when the late *Clara Peller* was in vogue with her famous line of *"Where's the beef?"* all speed line customers reiterated that famous quote for months. At first it was innocuous to the speed line server until the monotonous repetition drove the burger man caterwauling over the edge with annoyance and rage.

The chief's mess president and command master chief was an HTCM named Jack Lewis. Jack was somewhat eccentric but he was a very capable administrator. He could get things done because he possessed very adept organizational skills. Jack was also a goal setter and he seldom allowed anything to interfere with his intentions. If he told you he was going to get something accomplished then he would in fact do exactly that. He had some quirks and two great and identifiable passions, running and beer. While I was on the YELLOWSTONE the material handling passageway often served as a track, about six laps to a mile. Jack, purblind to distraction when in the runner's zone could easily spend a few hours in that circle. He was identified by a unique pronation and a steady beep he used with a state of the art pedometer that echoed its pulse to set his pace. You always knew if Jack was coming around the corner. You just listened for the beep. Jack was a New Englander from Massachusetts; he projected his voice well with some serious volume. As far as we were concerned the mess seemed to work on autopilot. Jack as the CMC had a tremendous amount of energy and he kept pace by executing programs, dotting the i's and crossing the t's. His neuron bundles were decidedly well developed from all that exercise because he was definitely energetically involved, having great blood flow to the brain.

Most tenders understandably spend a great deal of time in port. Their primary mission is to fix other ships so they have to spend abundant time pier side. If you observe the hull of a destroyer tied to a pier it screams at you, *"I gotta move on*!" A tender on the other hand, projects a picture of moored although active contentment, with its conveyers hauling stores and parts, or its cranes in action recovering large cargo. A tender has shore power cables hanging by the dozens, strange powerful dreadlocks, connected to satisfy her incessant thirst for the power to run a hundred plus whirling, pressing, grinding, spinning, or cutting, machines; all of which are extremely dangerous to the non professional. Some captains have dressed up the brows of their tenders with canvass proclaiming their ship as a *Battle Tender*. The motivation is there but I'm not convinced that the *Battle Tender* self proclamation is seriously received by the DDG and CG crews who share the pier space with the local Battle Tender.

The YELLOWSTONE was about to break the mold of that content pier side tender concept. No longer would *Tin Can Sailors* refer to us as *Bodacious Building 41*. We were soon off to a winter time North Atlantic trip. There was an amphibious operation going on in the fiords of Norway and we were invited to tag along in support of the Marines who were participating in the event. We had a huge sick bay and if frost bite became a medical problem, well there we were, ready and able to fix those Marines' frozen feet.

We got underway and the repair department went to work on the transit, helping engineering department fix anything and everything that displayed the slightest symptom of malfunction or being out of calibration. After about a week the entire ship was in pristine condition, totally void of all gremlins.

Our shop did a tremendous amount of training. I was glad I had brought the entire DRAI MK 9 course because we taught the whole thing during the time we were gone. We had a repair department manned by hundreds of people and there weren't any broken ships to be found in the fiords of Norway. We arrived there and the scenery was spectacular. It was a winter wonderland of snowy mountains and rustic fishing trawlers that sailed close by as we sat there swinging on the hook. We anchored there in our beautiful rustic surroundings and waited, and we waited, and we waited.

Our evenings were spent in *Trivial Pursuit* matches. Dave Hales had returned from gyro school and we played teams each night. In time we memorized the entire box of questions, even the despicable literature questions in the awful and hideously challenging brown category. We ceased play due to lack of opposition once we finished an entire game without missing a question. We had attained that great level of *Masters of Useless Bullshit or MUBS.* In a brief amount of time we had managed to strain out most useful knowledge and replace it with tidbits of mental dung.

It is a very difficult task to maintain discipline when you have a ship full of folks with little to do. There came a time when I had to act like a *Jerry Springer security guard* pulling a few guys apart who had grated each other's nerves once too often. It quickly smoothed out and regardless, it wasn't as if those guys would be going to Disney World together. Toleration was the most to be hoped for at times. A break came about half way through our anchorage when a British frigate pulled alongside. We opened our doors to welcome their crew over. It was good just to chat with humans other than our everyday shipmates. Brits are always quite the jocund conversationalists. Quite a few of our crew members were invited to their ship and they returned in a rosy mood probably close to the .08 BAC. It was gossiped that the master at arms force was busy. There was a bombinating suspicion of increased incidents of hanky panky, but I didn't see anything so I can't personally attest to misbehavior that I did not witness. At that time we had no women assigned to shop 51G.

Back to the chief's mess food issue; the caterer ordered an abundantly rich diet. We ran out of all the mundane food and we were left with only the King's fare. Did you ever experience people tire of T-bones, crab legs, or lobster? We did. We would have welcomed a plain stew. Our evening ice cream bar was as good as any drive through in America and with that being one of my chief weaknesses I could feel myself expanding by the day at the midsection. All my life I had been thin and weight had never been an issue. This was to change for the worse. No longer did I possess the metabolism to indulge in vast mountains of rich chocolate chip ice cream, coupled with a huge dose of physical inactivity and expect to remain a svelte size. At boot camp graduation I was a diminutive 115 pounds. As a Chief aboard YELLOWSTONE eleven years later, I was expanding my waistline faster than the Federal deficit. I was nearing the unthinkable, two hundred pounds, no muscle, all flab, *oooo Yuk.*

The eating and flatuating in the fiords finally finished and we raised our anchor and headed for the rewarding portion of the trip. We touched base in Hamburg Germany, Portsmouth England, and finally on to

Amsterdam in the Netherlands. Amsterdam is one of those party towns where you should never stay longer than just a couple of days. Anything beyond that and you either become very broke or very hung-over. It is still a great place to visit and full of European culture. But if you are not ready for it, it may be a little shocking.

Germany is a place that functions smoothly. All the public amenities are reliable and efficient; phones, traffic lights, buses, and trains. They all work with admirable and efficacious precision. Their taverns are always spotless and almost everyone speaks English. I had an easier time understanding a German bar owner than I did understanding the British comedian we watched in Portsmouth England. Not that I like the Germans better. I love the drolleries of the British. However, from what I have witnessed that entire credence of German efficiency seems to actually be true.

Portsmouth was hospitable, as only the British can be. The RN (Royal Navy) was still feeling good about the way they acquitted themselves in the Falklands. They had high morale, and deservedly so. Having a few pints with the Brits was always a memorable good time. You just had to make sure it was only a few; few being the difficult element in beer consumption.

After our Northern European reward, we cast off the lines and made turns for 37 degrees N latitude at a heading of 270 degrees at 16 knots. We really weren't needed for much on that trip and perhaps that was a good thing because it meant that no Marines were injured in the fiords of Norway. The Marines did well and YELLOWSTONE acquitted herself likewise on a Northern European vacation.

We were scheduled for a couple of months in the yard at Metro in Norfolk, and then the schedule had us off to the Med on a new tender deployment cycle. The PUGET SOUND was home ported in Gaeta Italy but she would be heading stateside for overhaul and the YELLOWSTONE was going to be the Mediterranean repair ship for a six month deployment cycle. It would be YELLOWSTONE'S first major deployment and with a rotation in effect all the tenders were about to get a little deep sea water run through their evaporators.

I was glad to be home with Iris for Christmas. She had our first child in the oven and he would be here in June of 85. We were both very excited and it promised to be a great holiday. She was a petty officer second class now and receiving great evaluations for her outstanding performance at SUBLANT.

Metro shipyard in January was a ghastly place. The doleful shipyard grounds were not paved and the mud on a wet January morning had an easy time making its way into the interior of the ship. Executive officers really dislike dirty ships, even fat ones are kept clean. I'm certain our XO wasn't overly enthralled with the shipyard period. There are times when ship alterations have to be installed, and that's what we had to do. We still fixed ships moored at D&S piers. If it meant driving to the Norfolk waterfront from down town Norfolk, a ten mile jaunt, then that's what we did. Shipyards aren't the most pleasant environments, especially if you continue to live on the ship but there are worse things than being home with the family for awhile.

The time passed quickly with uneventful convention as we continued with our routine work. Finally, after a few months of clogging through the mud of Metro it was time leave the yard and shake out the bugs and gremlins. Regardless of eminence, from the captain to the most junior seaman, leaving the yards is a high note and YELLOWSTONE was no exception. We would be going on a short sea trial to ensure all systems were in acceptable working order. Mr. Lake was on a high note because the captain had recently given a personnel inspection to R3 Division. Then he announced on the 1MC to the entire ship that he was impressed with R3 Division and the fact that the entire division was one hundred per cent outstanding in military appearance. CWO4 Lake was elated and walking tall after that accolade.

The exact date we departed for that sea trial escapes me. I can only attest it was memorable. We had a chief in our 51G shop that week; I believe he was from one of our supporting reserve units, faithfully contributing his two weeks of active duty training. We had many yard workers onboard who were embarked to test the work that had been completed over the last several months.

There was a regular schedule of events as we traveled out of the channel. I can't recall a lot of detail about when it happened. I know it was daylight and the weather was good. The bridge announced stand by for heavy rolls, or at least I believe they did. I know we took a hard roll to starboard. We continued to go over on our fulcrum until the movie *POSEIDON Adventure* started feeling very familiar. I was seated in the office with Senior Chief and Clendenon. The first thing that happened was all the welded bookcases broke loose. The filing cabinets were next. We were temporarily stranded in a starboard side lump of debris struggling to gain the crest of the hill of books we were under. The ship came back slightly but not entirely to an even keel. Senior chief, the first to recover said in alarm, "*the rewind shop!*" We struggled into the rewind and balance shop to find a large bearing locker had broken loose from its welds and carried itself and our EM1 right through the starboard bulkhead. He was badly hurt with severe lower body injuries. The 1MC was steady repeating medical emergencies and giving compartment number locations. Our corpsmen and doctors were heroic that day.

After the initial shock, those who were unharmed sprung into adrenaline laced action, helping victims and clearing debris. Our EM1 was the most severely injured. We later learned that he had ruptured his spleen and that he had severe leg injuries. One yard worker in the fire room had suffered a broken leg. Mr. Lake was assaulted by a popcorn machine in the wardroom. There were many injuries throughout the ship, the neat symmetry of the spaces immolated. It was amazing that the cranes hadn't fallen off the starboard side. We may have been close to the precipice of losing them. We headed immediately back to port where we docked at Craney Island; the opposite side of the harbor from D&S piers, and when we closed the pier, 13 *News,* a local channel, was standing by with cameras. I spotted a few solicitous wives on the pier, one was crying in terror. The entire scene was intense, and we all felt absolutely awful about our EM1 and the others.

The ocean will always demand its due you if you ignore its rules. You have to play by the book. You can't guess on any issue that involves sea worthiness. Great Sailors and officers make errors at times. However; there is no margin for the mistakes of omission. The rhetorical age old lesson of the sea as unforgiving for those who short cut was once again reinforced the hard way, and a very popular captain who made the crew feel good about being Sailors had to move on. It was sad, but a certain Friday afternoon fatefully came and the chief of staff from the squadron surreptitiously assumed the duties of commanding officer.

Weeks later Sailors purchased T-shirts proclaiming membership on the *Rolling Stone* or *I survived the Roll of 85.* Those T shirt alliterations and memories will always be with those of us who were there. To the rest it was soon forgotten, the exception being the lesson of underway preparation. For any disaster the Navy experiences, there is a documented lessons learned to improve upon its methods and performance. With that, at least our mistakes can be fused into the training of the future so hopefully history won't be repeated. Even in a lighthearted script such as this, preparation for safety at sea is an interminable repeat lesson that remains steadfast for all seafarers and generations of ship's to come.

The new commanding officer was not sure if he was going to be our permanent CO or not. He wanted to stay on full term as the commanding officer; immutably most senior officers relish command at sea, but he would have to wait for the verdict on that. He was a stickler for two things that became readily apparent. One was proper procedures, especially the activity on the Quarterdeck. The other was work ethic. If a watch stander screwed up on the 1MC he had to stand the next watch also. Mistakes in passing the word were brutal. Four hours on the Quarterdeck could be tough. Eight hours of standing was grueling.

The new skipper had a very colorful manner of holding captain's mast. He invited the crew to watch and I guess some people enjoyed viewing other's misery. When a large gathering arrived for his session the canny skipper looked at everyone and said "*I have no problem with you all being here for this proceeding, but this is time away from the job, so whatever time you spend at this mast will be added to your work day*." The crew scattered like cockroaches under a flood light.

His justice was indeed swift. If he thought an accused was lying he wasn't beyond getting a half an inch from someone's face and stridently scolding him with a hundred decibel, "*HORSE SHIT!*" In response to an obvious false denial or fabrication, it worked for him and it was extremely effective. Anyone attending or witnessing that captain's mast never wished for a return visit, ever. That was the intention and the purpose of the invitations of course.

In Norfolk, while ramping up preparations for the Mediterranean deployment, myself, Mr. Chunky, decided on a diet and exercise plan before I actually burst the small metal latch of my rather new work khaki pants. The point of no return was looming on the horizon, the abyss of obesity within close proximity to several more banana splits with goop. Yes, I still smoked but I was addicted to the heathen devil weed nicotine and I remained unsuccessful in ridding myself of its rancid poisonous effects. For the fat fight, I found a book lying around the ship titled the *Quick Teenage Weight Loss Diet.* I figured if a kid could do it, so could I. It was basically portion control, no bread or fried and all the fruit and veggies you could stand. I also started playing basketball at lunch. The entire shop began playing and we actually became a competent squad. Dave was an animal underneath the hoop. Cool Breeze had moves, and I developed a hook shot from the left side that was effective in waterfront competition. We counted coup on quite a few make-shift foursomes from other waterfront ships. As a shop we bonded over those B-ball days. The weight poured off of me like the *Blob* under a blow torch and I was soon svelte again in the 160s. I owed it all to the *Teenage Quick Weight Loss Diet* and *the U S Navy Sailor Hackers half Court Basketball Lunch League.*

Meanwhile, back at home Iris was distressed. She felt she had been pregnant for about eighteen months. She honestly thought she was having an elephant, but on June 30th she had our son Andrew in the ancient maternity section of Portsmouth Naval Hospital. He was perfect. He looked nothing like the elephant we suspected and we were ecstatic about his favorable resemblance to actual newborn Homo sapiens. We were as happy together as a family could be. Then I promptly left for the Mediterranean on a six month deployment. Andrew was only a few weeks old. The silver lining was that I would once again be up for shore duty when the cruise concluded. I had discussed some manning issues with the IC detailer in the past and I suppose I spoke with intelligence on that subject matter because he offered me a shore duty job in DC having something to do with manpower issues.

Now stupid me; thinking Iris could get a job as a Navy yeoman in Washington DC. Why in the world would the Navy want a second class petty officer and administrator in the DC area? What was I thinking? But as we said our goodbyes, that's how we were planning. I would get this cruise over and we would do career enhancing shore tours in Washington DC. This would all work out perfectly.

Senior chief departed for San Diego, California leaving behind a legend of eminence in YELLOWSTONE lore and ICC Calvin Jones joined Mr. Lake and I in the R3 office. Two IC men under the warrant, this would work out well. Chief Smith of former LAWRENCE lineage also departed for another assignment.

Cal Jones and I hit it off from the beginning. Not only did we get along very well, but strangely enough we also resembled each other in our physical appearance. People would often get us confused and of course we would play that mimicry for all it was worth. People would arrive at the office and began talking to one as if he was the other and we would routinely let it continue until the end. It was mildly interesting to witness the embarrassment of the duped and disconcerted communicator.

Cal was raised as a Navy brat and had spent sufficient child hood years in Germany. In fact, he was actually fluent in the language. He was primarily a *Tin Can Sailor* having served on the small boys such as frigates and destroyers. Our backgrounds obtuse only because Cal was truly a West Coast Sailor and my roots were the East Coast. From Cal's perspective, Norfolk was a temporary experience prior to a return to California someday. We all eventually develop preferences for certain locations or duty assignments. I knew that Ron Rogers was in his comfort zone as the chief engineer for the television studio in Naples and we would actually visit him there during this deployment. Ron was always the TV tech and that was the area of expertise he had down pat and felt most at ease with. I always felt most comfortable on a destroyer type ship. As much as I knew the YELLOWSTONE was a good assignment, I always felt more in sync on the LAWRENCE and the SCOTT than I did on the much larger tender.

Prior to the Mediterranean deployment Dave Hales, talented gyro tech and cataclysmic rebounder at half court waterfront b- ball moved on to a new assignment. He would change rates to fire controlman, making a departure from the IC rating. It was a lateral move that would increase his upward mobility plus provide a platitude of technical schooling opportunities. It made sense and it obviously worked because Dave made chief soon after that. With the *Trivia Pursuit* box fully memorized Dave needed further cerebral challenge; missile fire control electronics was a wise choice over a run as a *Jeopardy* candidate.

When the ship commenced her Med deployment she cruised across the Atlantic like the reliable steamer she was designed to be. While she maintained her sixteen knot pace, YELLOWSTONE wasn't glamorous, but she never broke down while living up to her nickname *Old Faithful* as her shaft rotated in mulish stubbornness. She proved a great asset to the ships in the Med. If you were on a small boy with a bunch of broken stuff that fat ship tied up along side could look awful gorgeous right about then.

Our first port on that journey was Gaeta Italy where we did a turn over with PUGET SOUND. We weren't there long before we pulled anchor for Naples Italy. Napoli became our home away from home for the next six months and by the time we left there we were more familiar with lira than dollars. We also developed a liking for *Peroni beer*, and nearly all hands became addicted to cappuccino. Through trial and error we gained adept skill at dodging the mopeds that routinely borrowed the sidewalks. Naples is a city of traffic, and traffic signals meant green for go, amber for go, and red meant really go like hell before someone else goes first. My first experience on that deployment with a Napoli cabbie was a trip to the Navy Base Exchange retail store, or NEX, about a ten plus mile ride. Four of us climbed into the cab, negotiated the price as we catapulted off in his ancient Fiat. The cabbie addressed me directly prior to blast off and stated in a very engaging Italian form of English, *"Mario Andretti number two; me number one."* With that began the most harrowing half hour of our lives. The story nearly dead-ended here, but with certain divine intervention, we avoided the streetcar t-bone by a whisker. I'd also like to credit the Italians for how clean they kept Napoli, but why embellish this story with total fiction? Perhaps that random thought crept in here because of the many unidentified objects we avoided on that trip.

Our stay was for one major purpose, to *fix ships*. That was the plan, and we executed the plan. We found a routine and clicked along at a steady pace, knocking off the jobs in steady numbers. A great deal of planning went into this deployment and the YELLOWSTONE carried a tremendous amount of material and spare parts for our customers. The Boy Scout motto, *Be prepared,* paid off exponentially because having parts available that ships needed to get back to their missions at sea was a key element in our excellent accomplishment rate. With all the old salt warrants and salty dog chiefs we had in the repair divisions, being prepared wasn't an option, it was merely business as usual.

The evenings were spent cavorting around Naples. It was different being in port on a tender than on a destroyer. Because we were here for so long one actually became known by restaurant workers and tavern owners. Many residents spoke a few words of English, but most did not. They did get to see enough of us to be at ease in our presence. Sitting pier side in Naples we also had American TV transmitted from the naval base there. The crew was treated to live football games and American TV shows every evening. This was as one would suspect a huge morale booster.

Eventually we were required to visit France. Toulon France was home of the French fleet, and the smashed sandwich. It was fall, the weather was cooling off, but the waterfront restaurants were in full swing. I know that Toulon had an area of town where there were a lot of bars operating but for some reason the bars minimally attracted the YELLOWSTONE crew. The French were not as engaging as the Italians and when a Sailor doesn't feel the warmth of his hosts, he refuses to spend his money in that spot. The YELLOWSTONE crew found a more suitable method of entertainment and gamboling about. We bought large bottles of beer; big green bottles that we drank in the alleys out of paper bags. I know it sounds like the Navy was becoming the overseas Bowery but why bemire fun had with frugality? This started with one or two folks. Then some wooden crates appeared for seats. Then more folks appeared. A guitar playing Sailor found an eager audience for his renditions. Here he could be Dylan or Croce. Fan appreciation for a musician is an aphrodisiac to the psyche of an amateur guitar player. A rendition of the theme to *Gilligan's Island* started, and then there was another song, maybe the theme from *The Brady Bunch.* Soon we had the alley transformed into a 60's style American block party. The outdoor street vendor who sold the smashed ham and cheese sandwiches sold scores of the tasty morsels while the remunerative grocery store next to the alley sold big green beers as fast as they could stock them. *Dick Clark* could have done a lively version of *American Bandstand* right there in the cold Toulon France alleyway. We saw it as exporting American culture. After all, when our Sailors tried to go to one of the nicer French establishments, they were told, *"preevitt"*

The Yankees demonstrated to our French allies that the one thing you can't deny a Sailor is fun. They will have fun. One of our Sailors while visiting a French city some distance away as part of a sponsored tour found himself in conversation with a well-heeled French citizen. The Frenchman upon discovering that his conversation partner was a U S Navy Sailor said" *Oh yes, you are one of those people who sit in street drinking large bottles of beer, yes?"* Honestly, the most fun anyone had in Toulon France was sitting in an alley drinking large bottles of warm beer in paper bags doing karaoke, without benefit of a karaoke machine.

I had a very interesting conversation while in Toulon. At a corner café near the edge of town was the bus pickup spot for our return ride to the base. While walking there I was approached by a very young couple who looked like models from *GQ* or *Cosmopolitan.* Unlike many of the French they were inquisitive and attempted to engage in conversation. The young man about twenty-five with big blue eyes, blonde hair, and perfect teeth spoke; while his female partner, a *Jessica Simpson* clone looked on smiling. "*What is your name?*" He asked. I said, "*Terry Bradshaw*," wondering where this was going. "*Oh, you had a sore arm while playing the football. Are you from the American ship*?" he asked in close to perfect English. "*Oh yes*," I replied, inner red flag rising while the sickle and the hammer alarm commenced an internal warning beep. Next, he asked a barrage of questions about how many people we had on board, where we were going, how long we would be staying. To all queries he received bodacious whoppers. I can never prove it, but I certainly believed I was talking to some information gathering disciples of the *KGB.* I let the YELLOWSTONE Sheriff know about this when I returned to the ship. I must say that he and his accomplice were the friendliest people I met in France, although the grocery store guy who sold the mass quantities of green beers in bags was a close second.

We left Toulon and I can tell you it ranks right up there with Turtle Crick, Pennsylvania as a great place to visit. I hoped someday to return to relive the Detroit style alley way harmonizing, but unfortunately Toulon wasn't slated for a return visit on this cruise. We wannabe *Miracles,* and *Spinners* would have to discover a new venue. But the ambiance of the cold Toulon alleys drew out our artistic talents in a way that no other location probably could. There were far too many distractions in other ports; too many places to go, too many ships to fix.

We were back in Naples. Back at it, fixing ships, swarming like bees with a mission statement; *Royal jelly from the YELLOWSTONE*. The USS AUSTIN had a terrible helicopter accident on her decks and the YELLOWSTONE went into a blur of activity to get her repaired. Times like that are when powerful fleet planners feel justified in creating big fat repair ships, instead of an additional and more glamorous and sleek Man of War.

A hot car without good grease monkeys will soon become just something to look at. YELLOWSTONE was the fleet grease monkey.

After our return to Naples and sandwiched in between all the hard work R3 Division accomplished they experienced a mild run of misfortune. First, one of our second class petty officers, who happened to be our current *Sailor of the Quarter,* engaged in a slight altercation with our duty shore patrol. I suppose he got to feeling a little froggy in a local tavern and thought he was the new *Joe Frazier," Down goes Frazier!"* He lost his bout in one round.

Soon thereafter, we had a command picnic for a Sunday rest and relaxation excursion to Carney Park, the Navy's outstanding recreation facility. Carney Park is located in a long dormant volcanic crater outside of Naples. It was a perfect day, with softball, beer, soda, and burgers. Everyone had an excellent time and a lot of needed exercise. On the return trip there were two buses. The executive officer, who exhibited little external humor, was in the front seat of the second bus, while several of R3 division's electricians were seated in the rear of the lead bus.

Our brilliant electricians thought that mooning the second bus with bare cheeks pressed firmly against the rear glass was an excellent idea. The XO, the ships executive disciplinarian received a full moon in a dual formatted live presentation. Our EM's were proud, our EMs got hammered. The XO had no choice and he was not amused at the gesture. It was mixed company. Pants were required to remain in the up position while in public. It wasn't as if they were contributing beneficially to national security as Steve and I had many years earlier in the *KIEV Mooning of 73.* No, the *YELLOWSTONE XO Mooning of 85* only resulted in one really pissed off warrant officer who only responded amenably to basking in the warm and blissful glow of accolades for his division's activity, negative attention was an irritant worse than a steroid induced itch in the crotch. For the perpetrators, I correctly predicted...*an uncomfortable near future.*

Unfortunately that still wasn't the culmination of misfortune for R3. We were to have further leprous events. Often we were tasked to dispatch our technicians to remote Mediterranean ports to fix ships. The command provided the funds and tools required for completing casualty repairs and they launched on what we termed *Fly Away Teams.* Two of our IC techs, Jerry and Moose were tasked with an underwater log repair job in Triest, an Italian port. They were required to travel by train carrying with them a piece of test equipment called an *elvs box,* or electromagnetic voltage simulator, a special piece of test equipment used for making calibration settings on a ship's speed indication equipment. They were provided with an ample amount of cash for the trip.

The pair boarded the train with no problems, rightfully expecting a short routine trip. On the train they met up with a very engaging Italian fellow who must have been quite the conversationalist. Moose, the friendly master of the *Texas Two Step*, offered him some ship store purchased junk food. Accepting, he countered their generosity with his own incantations and a personal contribution of fine Italian chocolate.

We received a message from the US embassy shortly thereafter. Jerry and Moose were in the hospital recovering from their sedation. They still had the elvs box, but the cash was gone, their allotted trip money now being spent on *Mr. Congeniality's* cappuccinos and Napoleons. Mr. Lake was an unhappy camper, his *Winston 100s* burned in fury. The ship, that was in Trieste awaiting repairs; weighed anchor with a broken underwater log.

Those were the ignominious lows of the cruise and we recovered. At least the incidents were ephemeral, here and gone. Sailors have to get past things. Fortunately we recovered and reestablished our reputation and no one held a grudge. Cal Jones and I had short memories. If someone screwed up, they could make amends.

I received a mountain of letters and pictures from home of Iris and Andrew. They were doing fine. I bought an awesome tea set and mailed it home as a gift. It arrived in Virginia Beach in pieces. Iris glued the entire set back together, a time consuming and very painstaking process, but her patient artisan craftsmanship applied to my mailing error made it very presentable, and the set displayed proudly in a wall unit for many years after.

One day I was looking through a letter from Iris and there was a picture of Andrew in a *Cleveland Brown's* shirt giving the touchdown sign! Dave Hales had slithered over to my house and struck a blow that was despicable in all respects. There was nothing I could do to retaliate or to assuage the dudgeon pain of such a heinous act. I had to sit there and merely view the horror of my son attired in the colors of all Steeler fans mortal enemy, the despicable Cleveland Browns. I felt helpless but I vowed to someday repay Dave Hales in triplicate for his devious victory. It was bad enough that Bradshaw was gone and we were going through quarterbacks like *Smithfield* goes through pigs. Times were hard in the Steel City, as the *Golden Age of the Steelers* had ended with the Bradshaw rotator cuff, the Lambert turf toe, and the aging of the greats. All the fan carping in the world could not recreate what was, and we *Stiller fans* suffered through the rebuilding process with love for what was and pain for what we now had. Quite frankly we were spoiled and had to be weaned from winning. It was sad but few gave us pity for now we were but a faded bully, at times thrashing out and gaining victory but more often being thrashed by local boys who made good; talented and good looking Western Pennsylvania kids with names like Montana, Marino, and Kelly. Not that the *Stillers* were without talent with the likes of Tunch, Wolfley, Woodruff, and Lipps. They were scrappers, but it wasn't enough against the elite arms of the Western PA gunslingers.

We were off to Palma Majorca when I received a message from Iris that stated quite bluntly that I could go to Washington DC and she could go to Greece. Or we could both go to the Navy Communications Station in Nea Makri Greece. For me, it was a clear choice. I was going to Greece with Iris and Andrew. Thinking about it; I don't know why I assumed that the brilliant idea of us both going to DC would work out. It seemed too sensible. If I had denuded the rules and guidelines I suppose I should have known that we would not be in DC on shore tours together simultaneously. It was clear enough. I was afflicted with brazen tunnel vision, caught up in the abundance of jobs available there for YN2s. Regardless of yeoman employment opportunities in the District, however, we were going to sunny Greece. We were scheduled for departure shortly after YELLOWSTONE'S arrival in Norfolk. I liked souvlaki so obviously I thought Greece would be interesting. I could not fathom what an IC chief would do there and I already felt underemployed just thinking about it; even though it was several months before we would arrive.

Before we headed back to the Med to take up residence, I first had to complete our deployment in the Med on the good ship YELLOWSTONE. Palma Majorca is a picturesque little island. There are beautiful beaches, bars, restaurants, and all the standard vacationer glitz that make it a magnetic getaway for colder climate Europeans. It's great place to go if you're single and even better if you're with your wife. If you're married and your wife is home then have a cappuccino or a few pastries soak up some sunshine and get some rest. Palma was our liberty port and in the off season it can be very pleasant and laid back. The ship's visit was uneventful. The YELLOWSTONE crew was very good at enjoying themselves in a mature manner and by then all who were troublesome were weeded into a tiny group of distinction known as *liberty risks*.

Soon we were in route to Haifa Israel. Cal Jones had to travel home on an unexpected emergency, so my traveling buddy was going to abandon ship for a week or two. Haifa is a jewel of a city with a pleasant waterfront area known as Bat Golem. It makes one wonder how a place so idyllic could have such undeserved strife. It was a scenic place to visit and tours were plentiful. I believe everyone viewed it as a nice break from our beloved Napoli. We spent very little time underway on YELLOWSTONE. We traveled to Israel, moored; then returned to Naples, always in pursuit, not of the enemy, but of *work packages*. That is the nature of a tender. Their primary mission is in port. My mind, now in overdrive as transfer beckoned was already planning ahead to my next great adventure, shore duty in Greece. Attempting to plan ahead, I obtained a tourist passport in Naples in preparation for my transfer to Nea Makri. When we departed the Med for our return to Norfolk, my incandescent thought was "*I'll be right back.*"

Chapter Three:

YASU, TIKANIS? AND KELLY FROM GREECE

Navy homecoming is always a joyous occasion replete with celebration of loved ones safely returned to their glorious nests. It is one of the great pleasures of Navy life; a scene that a Sailor never finds cloying. Andrew was a blast. He was near double his original size. He must have eaten *Miracle Grow* and been watered daily. As I saw he was a perfect example of the well nourished American baby. Iris and I were in a big hurry; the sweat pumps of life were going full pressure. We were required to settle some time consuming issues before heading overseas to Greece.

Moving in the military is a way of life. That doesn't mean it is fun. On the fun meter it ranks right on par with a colonoscopy. Renting out your home and finding suitable renters is also quite joyous. That process gives you the pleasure and satisfaction of an IRS audit. Alas, everything eventually falls in place for no other reason than it simply has to. Even Andrew had a passport at seven months old. The movers arrived, packed our stuff, and drove away. It would be a few months before we had the use of that stuff. We had traded in our last car, a vintage Toyota Supra for a new Renault Alliance. I will have a lot to say about that car later. But *George C Scott* was on television urging me to buy this great car and to my way of thinking; if *Patton* thought it was a good car then it was truly an outstanding selection. With Patton's televised encouragement we selected an attractive little two tone and shipped it off to Greece via the Norfolk terminal.

We eventually rented out our town house to an attractive couple. They were a clean cut pair who seemed the perfect caretakers, a true *Ken and Barbie* couple; more about *Chucky and the Bride of Chucky* in three years. After an endless number of items to take care of, we were finally as prepared as we were going to be, ready to fly off to the east on our trek to Ancient Greece. Once again my wanderlust was being fulfilled by a new great adventure. Iris was somewhat apprehensive. Little Andrew, I can honestly say, was ambivalent as long as he received his regular feeding.

Back tracking ever so slightly, several months prior to departure we received a very nice letter from ETC John Pugliese letting us know that he and his wife Claire were our sponsors and they intended to meet us at the airport in Athens. Hellenikon Air Force Base actually shared the runways with the city of Athens. Just saying the name Athens evoked all these past memories of tenth grade English and the study of Greek Mythology. I was starting to get very excited about this tour. I knew I would miss Cal Jones and Mr. Lake but as it was the way of the Navy, we would be meeting new people and expanding our circle of friends with each and every duty station.

Our tiny trio departed in route to Philadelphia via the Norfolk Regional Airport. We had only enough suit cases and uniforms packed to last us until our express shipment arrived in a few weeks. It would be several months until we got our Alliance there from the States. At the time, because we were military travelers, we were required to be attired in dress uniforms for the overseas trip to Greece. Andrew was allowed to be in his civilian pajamas, footies and a zip up front were authorized attire for traveling rug rats.

We landed in Philadelphia uneventfully and had several hours layover while waiting for the chartered overseas flight to Rota Spain. There we would change planes and fly into Frankfurt Germany and eventually on to Athens. Iris's Mom and Dad trekked down to Philly from New Jersey, along with her brother Tom and his wife to say goodbye and to see us off. Iris's Mom was a worrier and you could hear it through her Spanish. Iris was also apprehensive but hid it from her mother. It would be a long time until we were back again and I knew it was an emotional moment. Andrew's needs were keeping Iris fairly occupied, that was a good thing to alleviate the tension.

The time finally arrived. The tearful goodbyes were said and we boarded a very large airliner for the transatlantic crossing. Win, lose, or draw my family and I were off to another great unknown adventure.

There are always little disconcerting quirks in military life that only those of us who have lived it can identify with. They are not all the same, obviously, yet often they have a common thread. There is usually some rule that an authority puts in place for a valid reason. There is often someone victimized by that rule later. Often that rule wasn't put in place to victimize that person, but nonetheless it happens, often via the avenue of strict interpretation.

Our plane landed in Rota Spain, and we needed soy formula for Andrew. However, our dilemma was that we had no ration card to make a purchase during our layover. People making purchases on U S military bases overseas were required to have a ration card. Iris became irritated with the situation. She was determined to get some formula or someone was gonna get hurt. Luckily Iris met up with a sympathetic person who held one of those coveted ration cards. The Good Samaritan made the purchase for us and we were very grateful for that gesture. I'm sure that ration card rule was not put into effect to keep young active duty moms from buying baby formula, but often common sense is not authorized.

Soon we were airborne again. This time not on a capacious airliner, but on a C130 cargo plane equipped with a few rows of seats. Keeping ear plugs in Andrew's ears was as easy as making Jane Fonda sponsor campaign commercials for Reagan. It just wasn't happening. We were doing a little dozing on and off when Andrew let out a good burp with a heavy load of soy formula dousing our dress blues in an attractive off white. We wore Andrew's first meal on foreign soil. I don't know if Iris made that a footnote in his baby book or not. Regardless of the question of annotation we had to remain in those uniforms for about twenty-four hours as we were to discover.

We landed in Frankfurt Germany looking a little ragged and beleaguered, not to mention a feeling of crankiness. Andrew was doing OK for the most part, but he wasn't in dress uniform with a film of soy vomit, I'm sure that contributed. We departed the plane for refueling, a military passenger safety precaution. It would require a few more hours in the air to reach Athens from Germany. When we were seated for the final leg of the journey, we sat there, and we sat there. I was reminded of driving through the Hampton Roads Tunnel in Tidewater, Virginia on a Friday afternoon. There too you sit and contemplate things such as the quality of life, and how you would like to campaign against all incumbent representatives, wondering why none of your tax dollars ever cures the traffic congestion problems. Similar thoughts crossed through my mind as we sat on that runway for three hours while they worked on a gyro problem. Eventually we were removed from the plane and they transported us to a room on base. An airman informed us that we would be gathered up when the plane was fixed. Relaxation was a blessing for all of us. We were exhausted and it was nice to be off the disabled aircraft, if only to stretch out.

The knock came too soon, and we were airborne again, Andrew punctuated his feelings about the trip with a solid upheaval of soy that once again whitened our blues and I entertained myself with cruel thoughts about what I'd like to do to the *Great Watubah* who made the uniform must be worn rule for MAC flights traveling all the way from Philadelphia to remote world-wide locations while transporting small children.

When we landed in Athens we resembled ship wreck survivors. We were a scary family. The Puglieses would probably run like hell when they finally met the disheveled vagrants.

We passed through customs and I observed that Greek writing on the signs was very unusual. The Greeks, nice people that they were, had English versions of the Greek writing accompanying each message. I thought that was quite amenable. Modern days in the states we seem to be doing the same thing with Spanish in certain places. Because of all the dual language requirements, I supposed the printed sign business in Greece was booming.

We passed through customs without a hitch, a very efficient and not too painful process. The Pugliese's, John, and his wife Claire, were right there to greet us. They gave us a warm welcome, and they were thrilled with Andrew. Best of all, they didn't scream and run for cover when confronted with our haggard appearance.

It was late at night or early in the morning, I'm not sure which, when we arrived at Steve's Astoria in down town Nea Makri Greece. It was a small room, but cozy enough to be comfortable. Much too exhausted for anything else, we slept. We had arrived in one piece, in chic stylish military fashion. All worries could be addressed later.

The early spring weather in Greece wasn't bitter cold but in marble structures it could get rather chilly. At sea level on the Aegean Coast we were swept with a steady wind blowing across the Steppes of Western Asia. It was bearable but required a jacket to be comfortable.

Iris and I did our check in on the base together and we were introduced to the folks we would be working with for the next several years. There was a certified day care on the base and Andrew would actually be located about halfway between my shop and the administration building, where Iris would be employed, perhaps a quarter of a mile distance. There was an indoctrination class for new arrivals and it was rather odd going through Indoc with my wife, but it was still nice being together. Indoc overseas was much more in depth; obviously a requirement was to learn about your host country's unique rules and regulations.

Iris had a normal yeoman position on the base. In admin she would be doing regular admin work. There was another couple working in administration, Chief Personnelman George Patterson and his wife Linda, a first class yeoman. They were great people and we felt an immediate kinship with both of them. The other couple, who we really loved, was John and Clair Pugliese. They were incredible sponsors, the best anyone could ever imagine and of course they are a part of almost all the stories and experiences we had in that wonderful exotic country.

My own job was going to be rather strange for a sea going IC chief. For all practical purposes I was to be a part of the Nea Makri Telephone Company. This was a big departure from destroyer and cruiser IC gear. Personally I thought the job would be rather low key. Sometimes things happen and you have to find a way to make wine out of sour grapes. This would be the big challenge here. I met my new boss and I was pleased to discover he was a warrant officer 4. Warrant Officer Terry Metz was a great Sailor. Being entirely old school he would have been best friends with Mr. Lake. Mr. Lake was an electrical repair expert. Mr. Metz was a communications expert. Mr. Lake smoked *Winstons*. Mr. Metz smoked *Pall Mall* straights. Both guys spent a tremendous amount of time on the job. Mr. Metz in all likelihood knew the ins and outs of the communications world better than anyone else alive; John Pugliese, a close second.

Both of those guys had worked a credible number of years in the field and any question I ever had was answered. John was as patient as an elephant and he would go to any length to ensure you understood a fact or a point he was trying to make. He knew better than anyone how to interface with Greeks both technically and personally. His wife Claire was Greek and he had done quite a few tours in this country. He knew how to get things done here and trust me it was a very different process from our American methods. There were layers of bureaucracies in Greece that you had to work your way through if you wanted to accomplish some on base project. John knew better than anyone how to work through those issues. More importantly, he also knew when you were spinning your wheels on something unworkable.

John and Claire were our constant companions and very close friends for the years we stayed in this beautiful country. It was very educational to learn about Greece from a native and one who had spent so many years here. The customs made sense when taught from a true Greek like Claire. She was high energy and loved to teach you about Greek life. It made everything you were looking at or observing much more real. As teachers they were a wealth of knowledge.

Mr. Metz, the Great Communicator, had a ton of charisma. He was a tall lanky guy with light colored hair. Mr. Metz had a medical issue with his leg that would cause him some problems. It was obvious because he would often have to stop and get the circulation going while walking. I do not know what was wrong and Mr. Metz never verbalized anything about his pain. I did not ask, and knowing Mr. Metz, he would have said nothing was wrong anyway.

The warrant, as with all good Div Os knew his people well. He gave me the rundown on the telephone shop which I would be supervising.

He described what seemed like a typical group of young people. They were willing to work, and eager to be challenged. They were an intelligent group and I would have to keep them in a growth spiral of expanding their knowledge. This was fine. The construction electrician first class was near retirement and he was leaving the country within days. He was the resident expert and his loss was significant. We did have an IC1 named Moore who was somewhat of an enigma. By what Mr. Metz did not say about Moore, it was hidden that there may have been a strained relationship there.

I found out that the two of them meaning Mr. Metz and Beebe Moore were fairly close neighbors in town. Mr. Metz would observe Beebe at times and his behavior would rouse the suspicion of the observant warrant. Beebe Moore I found to be totally likeable. He was a large black man with a great sense of style, humor, and charisma. His real hang up was that he was a professional entertainer trapped in a technician's job. His enthusiasm was all directed at the morale, welfare, and recreation activities that he volunteered for. When introduced, the first thing he stated to me was that his primary goal in life was to be in show business. As a chief when your first class tells you that upon introduction, your first immediate thought is,*"oh shit."* I guess that sums it up in an adequate two word expression.

Even with Beebe Moore not an incarnate personification of the ideal technician, I still found him to be a good hearted amiable shipmate who just needed a little searching to find his niche. He was smart, he got along great with people, and he actually could sing like *Lou Rawls*. He rode around on a bicycle with large dark sun glasses, a white captain's yachting hat adorning his head, while he puffed on a *Douglas MacArthur* corn cob pipe for special effects. As he peddled down our one main street, his giant six five frame atop that bicycle he took the time to acknowledge all his ship mates as he passed by in an amiable roll. How could you not like someone like that? He was far too much fun to dislike even slightly.

For a second class petty officer I had a great technician, J. J. Hurley. Unspoiled, oldest of eleven, she was a straight laced freckle faced Minnesota girl whose biggest fault was too much compassion. Hurley was the ultimate good ship mate. She would work as if the telephones of Nea Makri were being used by Ronald *Maximus* himself. She was very good at what she did. An adroit technician she took great pride in her work and the only regret I ever had with Hurley was my failure to get her re-enlisted. She would have been a great chief petty officer. She was a doer and sitting around doing nothing was never an option on her list. Aside from being an excellent technician, she was a solid natural leader, probably indicative of being the oldest of eleven and ethical as well. I'm sure she was used to being looked up to and depended on.

J. J. had a multitude of good human qualities, not just her work ethic and technical skills. I hate to call her a mother hen, so I'll just call her a super good sheep dog guarding the flock. She was very protective and safeguarded those who worked for her.

Our shop also consisted of five telephone operators. Our operators were four women and one man, all civilians. Our Sailors were two females who worked on the switchboard electronics, Donna and Alison. Later we would add another Michelle. Our outside crew consisted of Kevin, a big farm boy type from Kansas, J. J., of course, and three females Marcie, Carol, and Jennifer. This group, primarily women would end up as one of the best and most efficient work centers I had ever been part of. In the telephone switchboard section, where the central office telephone gear was located, Allison, Donna, and Michelle demonstrated a great deal of pride in keeping the old equipment up and running. Donna and Michelle were both tough girls from Philly and they would work like hell without complaint. Allison was a tiny lady, but extremely bright and very proud of her ability to keep the equipment functioning. Allison was the leader of the group and as long as she kept the equipment operating and within tolerance we found no benefit in stymieing her efforts. J. J was the leader and I gave her the authority she needed to get the job done. If I had a need to motivate the central office technicians, I would have directed J. J. Hurley to enforce an agenda, but the women, although very young, approached their jobs with sincere dedication and enthusiasm. For the most part they were left alone to carry on without a great deal of interference or micromanagement, the most abused term in Navy diction.

The cast of characters under J. J. were actually quite interesting and distinct characters. Marcie was an outspoken Florida girl who was extremely loud. She often revealed more than one wished to know. Carol was a soft spoken girl from Tennessee. Jennifer was young girl from Puerto Rico. The best thing about this group in their diverse personalities was the common thread that they shared; none of them minded working. Kevin, our lone male worked about the way you would expect a Kansas farm boy to toil. He was an athlete, he worked hard and he played sports. That pretty much described Kevin. Whatever whining I heard was never about the work they were doing. Maybe a social issue would irritate them, but about fixing phones, they were on it, and that is about all you could ask.

We had some very unusual requirements over there. Our cabling throughout the facility consisted of significant footage of underground cable. Consequently there were times when digging a trench was a requirement. We had a few public works dozers and I can think of no better example of Sailor flexibility than watching some shipboard IC man run a back hoe to bury cable. The Greek government was very apprehensive about anything taking place on the base that would give the impression of expansion, so we had to be very careful in not doing expanded cable size or anything of that nature uhm… uhm. To get permission to do an improvement normally required many meetings over a great number of years until the project became lost in a black hole referred to as the *Commission.*

While Iris, Andrew, and I lived at Steve's Astoria we looked out over the Platea, or town square on one of our very first evenings in country. There was a political rally of some nature going on and we deciphered several statements about Reagan and Baker. The signs had a few sickles and hammers and Iris's first major experience in Greece was a local rally by the *KKE*, the dying Greek Communist Party. An identity of this organization was that as its population and numbers dwindled, they became inversely louder in their death throes. It was upsetting at the time to visualize how absolutely unpopular Americans were to some segments of the population. The vociferous ranting in the platea that evening sent a clear message to us. We really were in a different place and it was evidently going to take some getting used to.

John and Claire were awesome. There was no better pair to teach us about this ancient beautiful country. The political party of communists, the KKE it was explained had very little influence overall. They were an irritation at best. The actual politics was a bifurcated system divided between the Blues and the Greens, similar to our Democrats and Republicans. The Greeks were subservient to the Turks for many years so they took their politics and personal freedom very seriously. They actually condoned political differences. They appreciated freedom having experienced many years without it. However, belief in a Democracy did not mean that a citizen was above beating the government in the area of taxation. Indeed, beating the tax man was considered an honorable action.

A Greek family did not pay a government tax on their home until the construction was totally complete. A true Greek therefore, never finished building his house. This was condoned by a government who already imposed a 100% value added tax on any imported product purchased in the country. Based on their savvy business sense, I believe the Greeks probably benefited significantly from the European Union and the Euro that was to follow in the next century.

As military residents we received the best of both worlds. We could shop at the exchange and Air Force base commissary, and we could purchase gasoline on base for a comparable US price. We could eat out at numerous Greek restaurants and taverns for less money than it cost to buy groceries. Each day we discovered more nuances and subtleties about our host country. The Greeks loved Andrew. Boy children could do no wrong and often Andrew would act up in a restaurant and the owners would provide baby sitting services. A typical response by a Greek woman to an Andrew temper tantrum was "*It's all right, he's boy*." They would all rub his head. That was good luck. It would drive the toddler crazy and he would swing at them in spirited annoyance. The Greeks really loved to witness that feistiness first hand.

We were chauffeured around on house hunting trips. The lady in charge of house hunting and liaison with the landlords was an American married to a Greek. At one point she had been an active duty Sailor in country. She had great jokes, most of which could have caused her trouble. She got away with it. I doubt if I could. She had a gift for finding people homes and after several trips and steadily increasing stress levels we found an idyllic place in the nearby town of Rafina. As an added benefit, the house location made us near neighbors to the Pattersons, whom we liked immensely.

The house was actually a triple unit with the landlord Jorgo, his wife, and two sons living on the top floor. A quiet French couple lived on the second floor while we were on the first floor above a small sheltered parking area, its roof being the floor of our apartment. The structure was a staggered unit. Ours was offset to the side of the French couples. The winding staircase, in the center of the complex, led to the top floor. The landlord's house covered the entire top floor. Stained glass encompassed the perimeter of the flagship apartment and a dumb waiter assisted them with moving items to the top.

The structure sat on a few acres with olive and lemon trees covering the premises. As with most Greeks there was a garden of respectable size for growing fresh vegetables. A detailed stone driveway led to the parking area and we had one flight of stairs to climb to our apartment. Each of the dwellings had an excellent line of sight with a marble porch surrounding two thirds of the perimeter. Perched on a slight slope we could look down from our balcony across a scenic rural view.

The floors inside were all marble, the facilities were all new. We shouldn't have shipped dressers, because the closets were all recessed into the bedroom walls. They had a top level and an eye level. It was constructed so the seasonal attire would be at eye level and the off season apparel stored high. It was very thoughtful and user friendly, and the craftsmanship was superb. One would find no particle board or synthetic material of any nature in this home. We were the first people to live here. Because it was spring, the heating system installation was still a future event but Jorgo promised to install ours prior to cold weather setting in. If

I were to place this structure in the Sandbridge area of Virginia Beach, I would ask one to two million at a minimum. We were going to pay the prodigious sum of four hundred dollars per month rent. I was really starting to like this place.

Along with the ancient antiquity of the Athens area came countless other amenities to experience; the great food, the islands, and the beaches. Our Aegean world was full of sun worshipping tourists in the summer; while in winter the crowds were gone; our only delay the occasional crossing goat herds.

It was most certainly a slower paced lifestyle there. Much of it I loved. The cell phone explosion had not yet occurred and land lines were installed usually off of a three year waiting list process, or if you were a good friend of an OTE (Greek telephone company) representative. We had a new place, no well connected OTE associates, so we were without phone services for the entire three years. If the base wanted to communicate to us they would have to drive in a duty vehicle to Rafina. That was such a sad inconvenience, *uhmm...uhmmm.* The lack of a phone was actually quite palatable to me. No television other than VCR tapes was a little less palatable. Our TV sets did not have the same frequency as European ones and Greek TV was, well, Greek to us. So we didn't bother.

Our main form of entertainment was Greek restaurants, tavernas, and getting together with friends in the platea. The accommodating restaurant owners would set up a table in the square and people would just show up. It wasn't unusual to have a dozen or so people sitting out sipping retsina until late in the evening. There was another reason for this. Most Greek houses did not have air conditioning and if you were fortunate enough to have it, you dare not run it. Utility bills were one of the areas where you paid dearly. One newly arrived chief, it was rumored preferred a cool apartment and he ended up with a three thousand dollar electric bill. Deciphering his Greek electric bill was an epiphany moment for him and he became a taverna regular forever after.

Young people occasionally found themselves in trouble with long distance phone calls to the states. The calls of lonely lovers, captured in a long distance hormonal vise could wreck financial havoc on a Sailor's budget. Despite intense initial counseling on this subject many fell into the phone trap. Receiving a phone bill written in Greek with a large heart stopping sum at the bottom was very stressful, but the only way out was to pay.

Our car and furniture eventually arrived and we moved in. The Greek movers were very careful and adept; and thankfully, they respected our things. We were pleased with how well everything was going. We were issued Greek license plates for our Renault. They had ceased issuing the military ones as the terrorist issues gained greater focus. It seemed as if every year a high ranking military officer was assassinated by a group such as *November 17th*. An airline flight out of the Athens airport was also victimized by highjackers resulting in the death of one of our Seabees, Petty Officer Robert Stetham who was killed for no reason other than being an American Sailor. As friendly as the Greeks overwhelmingly were, we were advised to keep our heads on a swivel over here. That was the reality of it. This was a new, more dangerous world that now incorporated terror.

Greece, being the open and welcoming country that it was to all people, presented a launching pad for activities aimed at Westerners. We were instructed not to openly display our Americanism in public places. One could be a great impersonator. One could perfectly mimic the voice, language and mannerisms of a citizen of another country, and the Greek you were trying to fool would ask, "*What part of the States are you from*?" The entire idea of being a hidden Yankee was rather ridiculous. They know us well over there. I just hope it is not our smell that gives us away. If I had to guess anything I would say sneakers with white socks, and chewing gum with your mouth open, always clear indicators of being a Yank.

The Greeks even seemed to identify our Renault Alliance as an American car. I could be parked alongside thirty or forty cars, all of us lined up end to end on a no parking street and ours would be the one with a ticket. Tickets over there were quite vexatious. You could not mail them in, and they were about as expensive as a scalper ticket to a Stones concert. At least I received mine outside of Athens. In the city, they would clamp the *iron boot* over your wheel. That action was designed to cost you a king's ransom, along with the exasperating and distressing inconvenience.

As friendly as the Greeks were in conversation, they were aggressive behind the wheel. Their roads weren't up to American standards, (well maybe Pennsylvania pot -hole standards), and they could be rough. The shoulder of the road morphed into an add-on lane during times of dense traffic. We were alerted to the challenge of driving in Greece when security department informed us that we would get an award, if we made it through our tour accident free. They wouldn't say if you get into an accident, but the words were a disconcerting "*When you get into an accident...*" Perhaps I am grousing a little much because the roads never slowed us down from going anywhere in Greece.

As we settled into our jobs and established a routine we met all the people on the base and found them for the most part to be social and personable folks. Iris enjoyed working for George Patterson. The tall sandy haired PNC was probably the most knowledgeable personnelman in the Med, maybe in the entire Navy. He was one of those rare people with a brain so good it was anomalous. George was a veritable oracle of military correspondence; a *Tile 64 Computer Chip,* operating in a *Trash 80* world. Iris always respected competent people and she was learning a lot in her job from the perspicacious George.

Across from the telephone building was the calibration lab and there was our resident cal tech, Electronics Technician First Class, Marty Gaff. Marty was a smart ET, (almost all ETs have smarts), with a super sense of humor and we never tired of political debate. He was a totally committed left wing liberal. He made Alan Combs seem like a Pat Buchanan conservative. Marty's personal hero was Jimmy Carter, mine was Ronald *Maximus* Reagan; naturally our debates raged with both of us always declaring victory and righteousness.

Politics aside, Marty was an easy going intellectual and he loved beer, as did I. We got along well. John had an excellent group of ETs working for him. Jenny Hill was a very smart and ambitious young lady who always gave the impression that she was going places someday; and indeed she is highly successful today as a company president. Her husband Eric also an ET was an easy going guy and a Steeler fan so that automatically gave him high esteem and an enhanced rating of all around great man.

Randy Cappus our ET2 was one of those super star types you really wanted to keep in the Navy. He was talented with excellent leadership qualities. He was an *All American* type, a great athlete, polite, and a hard worker. Paul Koons and his wife Nancy were a young couple who bonded with Iris and me. They were a friendly pair from Maine and we loved having them over. Paul was as smart as they come and I thought that he would go a long way in the Navy if he stayed in. A very knowledgeable sports fan, Paul was an authority on the Red Sox, Patriots, and Celtics, a true New Englander. Paul also possessed an uncanny ability to take a mental snapshot of a room; therefore, if you moved any item in any way he would immediately notice it on his next subsequent visit. Discovering this trait I would often relocate pictures on the refrigerator or move a vase as a test to his prowess. He never failed to detect the disturbance. He would have made an excellent crime scene detective. Iris also has that same talent, but her focus is usually on things that I do to distort a room from its ordered symmetry.

A young couple arrived from the states. They were both from Texas; Kirk, a first class petty officer and a Seabee, and his wife Deb. They had a little girl about Andrew's age. We really liked them for their easy going southern manners, and Deb became Andrew's baby sitter for the duration of our tour in Greece. Kirk Kelton, like Randy Kappus, was another one of those super star Sailors who you just knew was going to do great things in the Navy. In fact, for a small base, Nea Makri had more than its fair share of outstanding petty officers.

The chief's mess had a cast of characters who made for great comrades. Scott Fields, one of our young radioman chiefs was an energetic guy with an interesting resume. He was a martial arts expert in Judo. I was amazed that his work out consisted of 1000 inverted sit-ups. Could you imagine? He was a small guy, but a coordinated athletic type just the same. As a young chief he added some needed energy to the laid back Nea Makri CPO Mess.

Jimmy Finks, our tall senior chief radioman was from Meadville, Pennsylvania and as expected, a Steeler fan. He also enjoyed a good time. He had commanding presence with his tall stature and a clear deep voice. Jimmy, like John had a Greek wife, and he also spoke the language quite fluently.

People came and went as with all military bases but over there in isolation there were certain things that people would avidly participate in. Kid's birthdays were huge. If you had an MWR birthday party, then people showed up in force. Andrew's #1 was a big hit, fully attended by a multitude of toddlers. The kids Halloween trick or treat parties at the day care center were also festive events. We found Andrew a professional kid's clown suit in town and he won 1st place for that costume. In addition, the small base newspaper also caught a snapshot of Andrew and Mary Beth Kelton, Kirk and Deb's daughter, in their costumes having a first kiss. Andrew's first kiss was a newspaper shot, and he was too young to remember. Oh, that's life for a military brat.

Often Iris and I would arrive home from work and at our doorstep would be a basket of fruit and vegetables from the landlord, complements of the day's gathering. We could not speak to Jorgo directly because he spoke no English so we communicated through his oldest son, who was a student of English. Jorgo was a talented guy. He was in fact, a builder by trade and the gorgeous structure we were living in, he built with his own two hands. With my own talent and skills I would never in this lifetime get to experience that same sense of accomplishment that accompanies the completion of a building project. Jorgo, to his credit was avoiding the home tax. Our unit had some dead end electrical cables hanging there as it readied itself for a few yet to be installed features.

The Greeks were unusually security conscious. I question why because crime in our area was basically nonexistent. They had very good door locks and tight window locks. Many even had bars in the windows. Everyone had a big junk yard dog. Jorgo's dog was Russ, a large German Sheppard who lived at the top of the driveway. He loved Andrew and tolerated Iris and I. He was also a reason people from the base did not seek us out. A petty officer from security came to our house during a recall drill and when greeted by Russ in the pitch black darkness he beat a hasty retreat. The rumors quickly spread about the *barr* (Texas word for bear) that lived in the Z's driveway. No one ever came by our place for duty related reasons again unless they drew the short straw.

We often held festive CPO functions at different restaurants. Dining out was a much practiced event and one of the chief's favorites was the Argentine Restaurant at a location called Mountain Road. There they had an outdoor charcoal grill and they would serve food in large quantities on huge stone platters. It was nothing fancy, just delicious and healthy. In cold weather they would have a great fire going in their large fireplace that created a very rustic and homey ambiance. You had to be careful with the wine though, the retsina was potent.

Retsina was the signature home made wine of the Greeks. I would describe it as what the imagination would conjure up as the taste of fingernail polish remover. But the wine, given a few chances would grow on you, just as the Greek food would. I must say that I never acquired a taste for their Ouzo, the clear liquid alcohol that the Greeks drank in moderate servings. I never messed with it. Many of the behavior incidents we had on the base were related to Americans misjudging the potency of the substance. It was probably a good thing that the majority of the young folks on base had no vehicle transportation. Whenever someone new arrived they were always warned about the surreptitious effects of the lucid Ouzo.

Our young Sailors actually had rather ostentatious barracks rooms on the base. The furniture was attractive, well above and beyond functional. They also had air conditioning which was something those of us living off base lacked. A summer heat wave occurred one year that had us seated next to the beach almost every night in order to keep from roasting. The heat was atrocious and many Athenians died that summer. Added to the heat was the problem of mosquitoes. These babies must have been first cousins to their relatives from Pascagoula, Mississippi because their feeding was like getting drilled with a 1/8th inch bit. They were indeed quite painful, like tiny winged dentists, flying around drilling you when you least expected it.

The Greeks did have a counter battery defensive plan to their dreaded assault skeeters. They had plug in devices that used a special pellet that emitted a chemical and the skeeters scattered like the Saddam's Air Force facing the *Blue Blasters of VFA 34*. Those pellets really worked. I've never seen them for sale stateside, so, I assume they probably cause tumors or some rare form of flesh rotting disease.

As we became more familiar with the area we began to venture out and see the country more often. We traveled the hairpin 26 mile run to the town of Kiffisia, the Greek version of Rodeo Drive. There, it was fun to order large ice cream sundaes with sparklers stuck in them. Actually it was rather exciting to have your ice cream on fire, although at times it was difficult to extinguish the burning ember. Andrew really thought it was cool. He watched the sparkler and wore the ice cream.

John and Claire who accompanied us on most of our outings provided colorful detail to what we were seeing in Greece. They also had two teenage kids, John and Elizabeth who were quite agreeable in their dispositions. American teenagers in Greece were in general allowed to be more independent than their stateside counterparts. It was safer I have to say. Because the crime rate was so low, kids were permitted to stay out later and they rarely got in trouble. The DOD (Department of Defense) school they went to offered a great international education and It wasn't unusual for an American teenager to attend a house party in Kaffisia at the residence of a Saudi Prince. They were learning foreign languages at the beginning of grade school while a field trip for their class was often to Rome or to the Pyramids of Egypt. Athletes could look forward to competing in Germany. Those kids gained an understanding of the world that the public schools in the States could never compete with. The DOD educated military kids developed a much clearer picture and scope of the world than their stateside peers.

During one extended summer weekend, Iris, Andrew, and I set out to explore the country. We drove to the North and visited Thessaloniki, toured the country side, and earned an expensive parking ticket. We stayed at a cozy beach side resort where I had a spirited sword fight with a talented yet vicious centipede in the bathroom. When confronted I wielded the toilet brush like *Zorro* as I rose to battle in the unexpected engagement. The centipede parried back with skill, sliding, thrusting, and charging in wounded rage. I almost retreated in defeat, but fearing a counterattack later, I moved in fighting against my inbred desire for survival. Finally, I wielded the crushing blow that sent the thousand- legger off to bug hell. We were saved. *Zorro* had prevailed. I thought about taking the corpse to a taxidermist but I had brutalized the carcass too severely, my exploits will have to remain only here, in the context of this story; just one more Spartan warrior to be glorified in the annals of Hellenic glory.

We also took an MWR bus tour on a trip to the monasteries of Meteora. This place was magnificently impressive. One really had to respect the Monks who built sanctuaries in these hard granite cliffs. Truly a marvel to witness, these people did not create these residences in a few years.

Instead they were life long projects at a minimum, made to last through eternity. It was very spectacular from every aspect and a sight I know I'll always remember, etched forever in my mind as the monks etched their existence into that granite.

Sports were very important at Nea Makri. We kept in shape playing basketball at lunch; and we participated in a very competitive softball league after working hours. Public works and Comm were especially competitive with each other and, particularly against the current Seabee detachment. The chiefs had a very weak team made up of old farts and a few teenage sons to help us out. Once we were actually winning a game. We were proud as we were crushing the women's team prior to a few ill timed errors in the final inning that cost us the contest. Oh well, it was exercise.

The Seabee detachments were a very unique group of young people. Our building projects served as their sea duty assignments. They would swoop in; stay for a few months completing their projects, then pack up for Gulfport or Port Hueneme, with the cycle repeating itself. They were tough outdoorsmen types usually, and they worked hard and played hard. At times they could get a little rowdy and break a few things. After a brief conversation with their chief the following morning, the damage would get repaired and a few improvements thrown in for good will. Using this method we developed a very attractive beachfront recreational facility.

Our base was female intensive and I believe the women significantly outnumbered the men. Whenever a Seabee detachment arrived, the Club Zeus would be packed, our normally T- shirt and jeans attired female Sailors would be dolled up in fashionable glory that would have impressed *Jackie O* herself. Soon attachments were made. Sailors fell in love and our base career counselor, Sam Beasley would play hell trying to get newlywed Seabees and radiomen to the same geographic locations. They just didn't need many radiomen in Gulfport, Mississippi. This was a problem that was often not considered before the need arose, love being all powerful -overwhelmingly chemical and all.

Our little base actually had its own fire truck and we doubled as the community's fire fighting force. There was one particular blaze that lasted for days before they got that one calmed down. In addition to fire fighting services our medical personnel often had to provide middle of the night emergency medical care to the community. Some of the traffic accident victims they attended to were particularly intense.

The local community reacted favorably to the base. We provided services and rented their homes providing incomes, particularly important in the off season when the tourists were long gone. Most of the protests we endured were from leftist organizations out of Athens.

Mr. Metz transferred to Spain which was his retirement country of choice. He was no doubt the most knowledgeable communicator in the Med. His very capable relief, an LDO lieutenant named Rich Rodriguez streamed right into place without missing a beat. John was still in country and there wasn't anything he didn't have a handle on making it an excellent situation and easy transition for the LT.

LT Rodriguez was a very personable caring officer who was much more than a manager. He really knew the division beyond the scope of work and he took the time to recognize the individual and their families. Coming up through the ranks he understood Sailors. He was a good leader who knew when to step in when to let someone run with it. He was a good fit in Nea Makri and he did a great deal to keep morale high. It is always a good thing to get a good boss. You are extremely lucky when you get a few in a row.

Our IC men were skillful at fixing telephones. They could troubleshoot a shore based telephone switchboard, they could splice cable, and they could terminate outdoor telephone cans. Hell, they could even run dozers and backhoes. Some of them drove fire trucks around town saving lives and property. But all IC men in order to get advanced in pay grade had to pass rating exams. The IC rating was based on LAWRENCE, SCOTT, and YELLOWSTONE type of IC equipment. IC men had to know about salinity systems, gyros, alarm systems, and synchros. Our shop in Nea Makri was disadvantaged. Most of our folks had never seen this equipment except for a brief look in A school. A dead reckoning analyzer may just as well have been a *flux capacitor* out of *Back to the Future.*

With a clear objective we set up a small schoolhouse in the telephone building. Through teaching, films, and basically grilling them mercilessly we ended up with an outstanding advancement rate. There was one very disappointing moment when J.J. missed first class by 1/100 of a point. Despite an intense search of her service record we could not find a way to get that 1/100 point. The next exam she advanced no problem, but it cost another test and a further six month wait. Truthfully that 1/100 was really tough for all of us to accept.

Iris made first class yeoman on her very first try with a score that was almost perfect. She had quietly made rate every exam on the first try. If she decided to stay in she would surely pass me by. On that I would bet money. She was going up the ladder faster than Jack was coming down the beanstalk with that Giant on his head.

One of the young guys, Brian in the teletype repair shop was about to marry a local Greek girl. Greek girls are not promiscuous and usually, if you date one, you are most assuredly going to marry her. Iris and I went to their wedding which was a very beautiful ceremony. I was impressed that they did not waste a moment throwing rice at the newly united couple. They did it right there inside the church. The Greek Orthodox wedding is a very traditional sententious and moving experience. I know that their marriage worked out well. We didn't see them again until long after we left Nea Makri. Twenty plus years passed until we went to a Nea Makri reunion, where we found them still happy together and still very young looking after all those years.

BeBe Moore had moved on to the States transferring to the YELLOWSTONE. He had made his mark with our training program helping his shipmates advance in rate. I thought he would do well in the repair department. I saw him once again several years later. He had married a Sailor that worked for me in R3 back when I was *Stoner* and they were happy with a number of kids. It seemed like everything worked out for him, but I do think he was born a few years too early because if ever a person fit the incarnate idea for the television show *American Idol* it was BeBE Moore.

BeBe's relief was a CE1 (construction electrician) named Mickey Simmons. Mickey was a Texan who was transferred in to the command from a rustic place called Coos Bay, Oregon. He loved that place and he wanted to return to that particular paradise as a retirement destination. Mickey had close to enough years to get to retirement and I thought Nea Makri was would be his final duty station. His wife was a hard working Greek lady named Maria who Iris liked very much. Mickey had done tours in Crete before and he had a great appreciation of red Cretan wine. In fact he would often strike up a home made ditty about *red red Cretan wine*, the subject always transformed to an immediate smile on Mickey's face.

Greece was one of those countries where it was easy to get attached. The slower pace and low crime rates combined with reasonable prices made it attractive. There was also the culture and the climate. The sheer beauty of the country made it often look like a post card regardless of where you took the picture. For Sailors marrying Greeks it often became a retirement destination. A few would stay on and take up residence. Personally I have been over much of the planet and I would call the world "*Pittsburgh and the surrounding area.*" In fact, I placed a large banner over the huge map of the world in the Comm Center that proclaimed the whole Earth to be just that "*Pittsburgh and the surrounding area.*" But I could understand the love people felt for Greece, particularly if they hadn't visited the *The Steel City.*

Under Mr. Rodriguez the division engaged in a credible amount of extra social activity. It was incongruous to Mr. Rodriguez to have his

Sailors sitting around in this beautiful country doing nothing. We would often take the MWR bus and go to restaurant outings as a group. This was nice because many of the folks had no vehicles to drive over there and Mr. Rodriguez was trying to make things better for everyone. One excursion found us at a Japanese restaurant in Athens. It was reported as a top notch establishment but we all became ill from the food. It went down OK, but it came back up faster than a blue marlin on a deep sea line. It was a tough ride home that evening. Many had breath issues from the rancid fare and more than one rode home looking rather sallow. Needless to say, that place was crossed off the must visit list. Morale of the story; when in Greece eat Greek.

We went to many different places with John and Claire as our companions. On occasion an American entertainer would venture into Athens. *Chuck Berry,* ended up in Athens for a concert. It was held at one of those plentiful ancient coliseum type structures with some added amenities, like seats. The old rock'n'roll legend and his daughter were great, but it was strange watching the large number of youthful Greeks attempting to storm the stage. There was quite a convoluted battle keeping Chuck safe from the frenzied crowd.

It was humorous to hear the citizens sing the words to *Johnny B Good* in very accented English. They loved Chuck Berry. Could you imagine how enamored they would be for a more modern band such as *Herman's Hermits?*

The Greek hunting season was short but very intense. I don't think there were many laws about distance from the house and discharging a weapon because they were directly in front of ours shooting down small birds with shot guns. I knew there was a certain Greek dish using small birds because I had viewed the tiny beaks popping through the pie crust in the delis. I had never tried the dish, it truly transcended my scale of edible considerations, but I often observed it in restaurant display cases and wondered who would eat that.

At work I made my mark by volunteering for every collateral duty that came up. I was the watch bill coordinator, the rights and responsibilities instructor, and anything else that developed. The time in Greece was really fantastic for family life and cultural growth, but professionally it wasn't the SCOTT.

When Andrew started walking it was an epic event. The landlord Jorgo saw him while looking down from his porch. There were cheers and clapping erupted all over. The landlord's wife came running down excited to witness the walking toddler. After all, as they say over there, *he was boy.*

Our home was in a rural area. There were critters. One visitor arrived from *Disney World*. I don't know when *Mickey Mouse* arrived, possibly on a Disney Cruise ship but small shreds of evidence began to show up in various locations throughout the house. Speaker wire eaten, the wood on the landlord's closets was frequently chewed. We knew we had an uninvited guest.

One day I caught him in the spare bedroom. I had cornered him in a drawer. My quickly contrived yet ingenious plan called for me to yank the drawer out and toss it out the open room door. It would be instantaneous Mickey eviction. I'd get him out in the open field where Mickey could continue his Greek vacation in peace. With the heroic Iris standing by as my brave assistant, I touched the drawer. I could hear Mickey in there, counting my spare change, probably getting together train fare for the *Montistriaki Express*. I yanked on the drawer and flung it. It sailed out the door but the nimble Mickey declined to go with it. Instead he bolted down the hall to the wall unit and dove underneath. He was probably petrified because of the heroic Iris and her battle cry caterwauling scream when he made his leap out of the drawer of captivity.

But now I had him cornered and his demise was imminent. Our non rent paying guest was about to answer for his misanthropic transgressions. I buried all the deep-rooted fears I harbored from the movie *Willard* and moved in for the attack. I had to defend the house from the enemy rogue rodent. Iris stood by, fearful yet brave. I shoved the wall unit sections apart carefully. Mickey bolted, the heroic Iris screamed, and so did I. My scream was not in true terror like that of the heroic Iris. No, my scream was more of a warrior's whoop, indicative of an Appaloosa riding Apache on the warpath.

Mickey was in retreat, now finding sanctuary in the vicinity of the refrigerator. As the battle ensued a new strategy developed in my military mind. I was a chief petty officer in the United States Navy, trained to think in stressful situations. I surveyed the terrain of my battle ground and laid my plan.

I opened the kitchen sliding glass door, slowly pulling them apart in such a deliberate manner as to not force my adversary into a Banzai suicide assault. I would have taken on the dangerous rodent with a direct assault, yet the stress it would cause the heroic Iris and Andrew could not be risked. It would be best to have Mickey experience his Waterloo outside the skin of our ship. It was imperative to force the evil intruder to our weather deck. As in any battle, chaos occurs. One must always expect the unexpected. As I slid the refrigerator I was looking down, expecting Mickey to be near the base of the unit. I was stunned to discover that Mickey had gone aerial. He leapt at eye level from the top of the refrigerator.

At that moment I realized my enemy's identity was in error. I was not conducting a war with the amiable *Disney World Mickey*. Nooo!!! The mendacity of my belief was now clear. I was in an escalated conflict with his super charged steroid created cousin, *Mighty*. Yes, mighty as in the ability to fly. *Mighty Mouse*, pumped full of MGH(*mouse growth hormone)* flew over my head in one leap, completely through the opened door and easily covered the six feet to the second floor railing. After the shock of an airborne super mouse subsided I felt the exhilaration of my victory. I danced through the house with my mouse war club. The imagined tom tom beat of the warrior providing me with rhythm as I celebrated in elation. Our dudgeon ended; our tee pee was defended, the intruder expelled; life was in equilibrium. Once again in the proudest traditions of chief petty officers, I had prevailed in the defense of the homeland. I knew then that I was senior chief ready.

It was a great Nea Makri day indeed when they opened the video rental store. The room was about 35 feet by 10 feet and the entire base was packed into the room like sardines in the can. Flicks flew out of that place quicker than *Cabbage Patch* dolls on an after Thanksgiving *Black Friday*. American movies for all of our formerly useless televisions and VCRs that we brought from the States were a major morale booster. That little store was the most popular building on the base for a long time after.

Our Seabee detachments were constantly making improvements to the base. In the short three years we were there I believe every building over there was either newly constructed or refurbished. Even the streets were freshly paved. There was nothing those Seabees couldn't do.

A few of them were serious body builders and they lifted cinder block by day and a ton of weights in the evenings. One guy was built like a tank, routinely lifting bar bells the weight of Volkswagens and eating a dozen eggs on most mornings, usually without the shells, I speculate. As you might expect, the young builder had a well earned reputation for great strength. Jimmy Finks knew of a fabled old Greek fisherman who had spent a lifetime casting nets and hauling in line. Jimmy said he had gnarled hands bigger than a catcher's mitt. The fisherman was rumored to be a descendent of Hercules and it was apparent that he possessed super human strength. Because Jimmy spoke Greek he was privy to an impressive array of local legends and the accompanying lore referred to stateside as *bull shit*.

The debate about who would win in an arm wrestling match went on for quite awhile. Most of the chiefs were going for the old Greek fisherman. It wasn't an American issue, but we had a natural affinity for the senior citizen. I don't know how Jimmy set it up but it took place in the Platea with a host of onlookers.

Unfortunately for us geriatric fans, our Greek Hercules didn't stand up to the young Seabee. That kid was strong. It was rumored that when the guy rolled back to Gulfport that Nea Makri's egg consumption dropped 27%. This is what amazed us in Greece. We were living lives similar to the American 50's. People were forced to communicate with each other. It was a great experience to actually go back in time to a simpler age. We were forced to be our own entertainment often enough. The DK Chief, Bert arrived with a Karaoke machine. It was an early model without videos but it had microphones and song books. We had a good time with that thing in the CPO club. We held a particularly entertaining bash one night engaging enthusiastically in some air band routines. Scott Fields and I did some *Blues Brothers* imitations. Neither of us was likely to replace *Belushi* or *Akroyd,* but Scott, the martial arts expert could do all those flips and splits. It worked out well; while the normally quiet John was a musical madman on a make believe key board doing *Jeremiah Was a Bull Frog,* by the *Three Dog Night.* The normally stoic George Patterson also projected some entertaining moves, his long legs pumping like Jack Lambert preparing for a blitz. We also had the added benefit of a chief corpsman who was an adept pianist. An occasional piano sing along was a good time for all.

Those Greek winters could be cold and it required flokati rugs and wool sweaters to keep warm. Many children were born in early autumn there. You do the math. We were no exception and Kelly Rachael came in October of our last year there 1988. Iris had an easy pregnancy with Kelly, except her belly seemed to dance non stop. The child was sure to have rhythm in excess.

Kelly was born October 3rd, 1988 in Lito Hospital, delivered by Dr. Zurvidakis. She was issued a birth certificate written in Greek and recognized by the US Sate Department as a natural citizen. Kids born to American military members at overseas locations are still eligible to become President of the United States. It remains to be determined whether our daughter wishes to follow up on that possibility or not. She may yet use the Arnold or Ronald *Maximus* approach, acting first, politics later.

As always, the base continued the ongoing process of people coming and going. The Pattersons left for Jacksonville. John and Claire departed to retire from the military in Virginia or Cleveland. Mr.Rodriguez, as a bachelor only did a two year tour. Kevin and Carol were going to sea. J.J. and Marci were getting out. Jennifer married a Seabee and had a baby; and I ended up by default as the electronic material officer or EMO at the Comm Station.

This was a weird assignment for an IC man. I would have to hold down the fort for the foreseeable future and luckily for me, I had a few good blue shirts to keep me out of trouble. ET1 Harold Barnes (nicknamed Barney of course) was my saving grace. He kept me informed and up to speed so at least I didn't sound too idiotic. It was quite an experience and gave me a deep sense of admiration for the work done by the technicians of other rates. Everyone brings skills to the show. Without these young competent technicians that vital communication link would have ceased operating very quickly. Their systems required a great deal of maintenance. I'm not singling out senior citizens either. ET1 Barnes may have been thirty but all the rest, the Hills, Barney's wife Linda, Skip Durbin, Paul Morris, Walt Meir, and Randy Cappus were all twenty something and all of them were smart and talented. It always amazes civilians when they visit Navy ships or facilities and realize how much responsibility ends up on these young people. Yet they rarely fail to perform. That's one two hundred year old tradition that thankfully remains unmarred by progress.

When in Greece it wasn't unusual for stateside relatives to take advantage of visiting. Iris's mom and her brother Oscar along with his young son Adam made it over for a visit. Adam and Andrew had a great time visiting Greece and getting their heads rubbed by the Greeks. It's just too bad that neither one of them was old enough to remember any of it later. Oscar admired our house as did Momma Luz. Oscar as a man who knew construction appreciated Jorgo's work. He saw it through the prism of someone much more professionally attuned in construction than me. Even though we all had a great time Iris hated seeing her Mom leave. The whole visit reminded Iris of her family and the magnetic attraction of the good old USA.

My Uncle Andrew and his wife Kate showed up for a two week visit during our second year there. They were two free spirits, ready for adventure and a good time. Uncle Andrew was a department English teacher from Pittsburgh and an authority on Greek mythology and indeed this place was very special to him. Kate and he hadn't been married for too many years and they carried a carefree fun loving attitude around wherever they went. Their good mood was infectious. We also had the added benefit of it being summer and the weather was picture perfect every single day. It was small wonder that civilization rooted there early, it was such a copious country, alive and beautiful.

Iris and I took some leave and along with Andrew and Kate, the five of us went on an adventure each day. Visiting these locations with my uncle gave us a new found appreciation for Greek culture, as he lectured the myths to us with expected enthusiasm, honed from a background laced with the academic knowledge of a scholar. I thought I had *Aristotle* himself standing in front of me, imparting wisdom in a pair of *Dockers* and sunglasses. I could understand it all. All those years of teaching these literary masterful tales in the class room environment and now here he was doing it at the actual venues. We were his avid pupils soaking it all up. In retrospect, we should have worn togas

We found ourselves at the *Oracle of Delphi, the Parthenon on the Acropolis*, and many other locations of Antiquity. We shopped in the winding streets of the *Montistriaki* in the ancient portion of Athens. We sampled a score of Greek restaurants. We took a tour to the great annual *Greek Wine Festival at Daphne*. The Greeks had an excellent method of trying all their seasonal wines at this event.

At the gate of the park you were required to pay a small entrance fee. From a large selection you then purchased your wine glass for the evening. The glasses ran the gamut from intricate to simple and the choice was your own. Entering the park we discovered various locations throughout the aesthetically pleasing area that housed barrels of wine for you to sample at will. There were also performances of folk dances in the Greek culture and custom.

My Aunt and Uncle loved it. As we strolled from one adventure to the next all my uncle kept saying was *"Why don't we have this in Pittsburgh*?" It was a magical event for someone to see the Greek folk dancers in their fancy white attire moving in a century's old pattern, while sipping some of the finest wines of Europe. Fortunately, we had a bus ride home, no driving required.

Speaking of driving, I had to go to the store one morning and Kate spoke up "*Oh can I drive there, I know the way?"* I thought about it relented and said "*Sure why not?"* About a half hour later Kate returned with the package. She was all excited about how friendly the other Greek drivers were to her. She said "*They all waved hi, holding their hands up to me.*" I thought about it and asked "*do you mean like this?"* I held up my palm facing her straight up. She said "*Exactly.*" Then I explained,"*Kate, you just received a number of evil curses very similar in nature to the United States of America middle finger salute."* She took the age old castigation in stride, giving the gestures no further thought.

The Greeks didn't cuss nearly as nasty as we Americans, at least not to my knowledge. The only Greek cuss word I ever heard was *Malaka.* I am not sure exactly what malaka means but someone calling you a malaka ain't inviting you to dinner. If you ever hear that word from a Greek, leave quickly! It was a humorous surprise for me a year or two later as I was driving up *Indian River Road* in Virginia Beach and there in front of me was a personalized license plate that read, you guessed it, *malaka.*

We culminated our in country vacation with an island adventure to the island of Andros. It was decided that Andros was the best choice we had of the alternatives, Tinos, or Mykonos, because Andros had the true flavor of the local Greeks. It proved to be a great choice.

Yes we were typical dumb Americans, dullards maybe; going on an adventure with no hotel reservations. In excited haste we climbed on the ferry boat and made a quick trip across the water, a fairly short distance to Andros. As always we were loaded down with diapers and all the Andrew necessities required for travel. After debarking off the ship's brow we did a little surveillance to get our bearings. There was very little to resemble a tourist-like atmosphere. It was as if we were dropped off in a very picturesque serene set; a perfect spot for a Hollywood movie shoot. We were soon approached by a very friendly cab driver who spoke a little English. Actually he spoke a lot better English than we had a right to expect. He was an old man, an ancient mariner type as all the islanders have a special relationship with the sea. I intuitively knew this man was no exception. When I said, "*American Marina*," he seemed to respect that. But as with all ancient Greeks the apple of his eye was the curly haired Andrew. After all, *he's boy."* The cabbie, or *Poseidon 's* long lost twin brother herded us into his cab and informed us that there were very few hotel rooms, if any, available at this time of the year. He said we would have to search for a place. He inherited us as his newly adopted family and he was unquestionably in charge. He drove with confidence around some spectacular hairpin roads until he stopped the car at a particular mountain spring. He informed us that the water coming from that spring was the best in the world. That water was the antecedent to the longevity of the Andros natives.

We drank a lot of it; I would never argue with someone as wise as that ancient mariner. The water was spectacular and indeed, I concurred with Poseidon it was the best in the world. The driver never lost his patience as he searched throughout the island for a place for us to lodge.

He was our appointed guardian angel. Maybe if it was just the four of us it would be different, although I doubt it. But with Andrew there was no possible chance he would leave us unsheltered, even for a respite moment. We were subservient to the Andros cab driver and glad for his rescue.

It was long after dusk and Iris was feeling a little nervous about our situation. Our patient leader was nursing his cab to the top of a mountain. The night time panorama of the harbor was spectacular, but a lack of a place to stay was beginning to make me feel as if we had taken too much for granted on this excursion. To Andrew and Kate's credit they were loving life and willing to roll with every punch.

Our cabbie stopped at a residence with a stairway leading to what must have been the island's highest elevation. The stairway disappeared from our sight in the moonlit evening, a spiral straight to the heavens. He told us to wait, that he would return shortly. He returned and gestured for us to follow him. We trudged the steps following him on the long upward trek.

There at the crest were two very gorgeous mountain top cottages with our names on them. Kate and Andrew were ecstatic with the Greek paradise we had been gifted. Iris and I were relieved that everything was working out despite the fact that we were just winging it.

In addition to an excellent apartment there was an ethnic Greek restaurant a short distance away. Our cab driver was just being a typical Greek, the perfect host. The apartment price was ridiculously low. The cozy sanctuary was complete with all the amenities, including some very fragrant fresh cut flowers.

The restaurant across the street was appropriately called the *Romantica.* It was carved into the side of a mountain and the side of the structure facing the harbor below was full glass with a breath taking view. I can't remember what we ate but I am quite sure it too was perfect; places like that usually were. Andrew and Kate loved this place and Iris and I felt happy that they were having an excellent time. Young Andrew had behaved the entire day. We were an old fashioned pair, Iris and I. When we went places we always packed up Andrew and hauled him along with us. He was seldom placed with a babysitter. The *Romantica* was aptly named and I'm quite sure my uncle and aunt thought so also.

I believe we all had a memorable and enjoyable stay on Andros. I kind of feel bad for Andrew today though, the poor man has been to some of the most gorgeous places on earth and he can't remember any of them. By the time he was three he had traveled the world. He did get to see some great pictures though. In first grade he was able to do a show and tell representing the letter A for a class project. He brought in an album of Andrew in Athens in August on the Acropolis. *How cool is that*?

In the morning our guardian cab driver was there before us, no different than if we were *Aladdins* who summoned our powerful genie by rubbing a magic lamp. He deposited us at the ferry and put us safely on the boat, rubbing the top of Andrew's head for good luck; it was the Greek way.

All too soon Kate and Andrew were gone and we were left to finish out our tours. A great and near catastrophic political event occurred there during that era. Greece and Turkey almost went to war over an issue of which to this day I am unclear of. The Greeks and Turks aren't crazy about each other. The Turks ruled Greece for a long time and I don't believe the Greeks were ever fond of being administrated by someone else. Today in Greece the expression *beat the Turk* is a tag of accomplishment that signifies that one got the better end of a business deal.

The *KKE*, the small in numbers, loud in sound Commies stirred up trouble by making a statement that we Americans were giving away Greek military secrets to the Turks. Trouble was stirring for our little communications station. As a destroyer warrior I thought I would be recalled to the base. PNC George Patterson thought the same. When the duty driver arrived he came to pick up the heroic Iris and the heroic Linda Patterson. The two yeomen were recalled while George and I were left with the kids. Iris and Linda went off to the crisis to type messages and to be key players in the unfolding event. George and I drank beer and watched the kids. That night the situation cooled and an understanding was reached, thanks to Jimmy Finks and his ability to communicate in Greek. The people about ready to tear down the base were convinced and satisfied that we were not enemy perpetrators. Peace prevailed and the crisis abated. Iris and Linda had helped save Nea Makri.

In our third year in Greece when Iris got pregnant, she knew it wasn't in her to leave little ones behind while she went to sea. Some women can do that and I decline to judge them for that decision. It just wasn't Iris's way. She also wasn't about to try and avoid sea duty for the next twelve years. With all that, and it is a dilemma that many military couples must contend with, Iris decided not to reenlist and to become a civilian mom for a while.

As Kelly tried every day to samba her way out of that belly, we drew ever closer to leaving the country. We played a lot of music in our marble house and old rock'n roll had precedence. Iris's belly would get to jamming at times, as if she had ingested a handful of jumping beans. When Kelly was a young teenager she had an unusual liking for the oldies and she made my well worn LPs an integral part of her teenage locked in the bedroom routine. I do wonder if that affinity was incurred from those summer months in Greece in 1988. Perhaps the rumbling vibrations in the marble enclave affected her in the womb. She does sing quite well today, sounding similar in voice to the late great Mama Cass Elliot,

When Kelly was born it was October 3, 1988. We left soon after in time for a stateside Christmas. I had to return in order to finish up my three year obligation, keeping everything on hold until I returned in March. Iris and the kids would live with her folks in Jersey until I arrived stateside in the spring.

Everyone gets trauma of some type in life and ours was little Kelly's health. Kelly during her first six months of life had some awful problems with reflux, asthma, and finally a respiratory viral infection. She was in and out of doctor's offices and emergency rooms quite often. To say something like that was worrisome was the ultimate understatement. When I arrived back from Greece we headed down to Norfolk. We had no idea at that time that Kelly would end up in a life threatening struggle. Much of her diagnosis to this point was incorrect. It wasn't until she went to the *Children's Hospital of the King's Daughter* in Norfolk that she was accurately diagnosed, treated, and quickly recovered. If not for the competence of that fantastic facility I fear the worst may have occurred.

Today Kelly is a freshman at Virginia Commonwealth University. She has no symptoms or lingering effects of asthma and she grew up very healthy, being one of those children who noticed no difference between winter and summer and refused apparel such as a coat. She seldom gets sick. Perhaps as you read this chapter she may well be in renowned Master Hei Long's Kung Fu class in Richmond, enthusiastically smashing a stout piece of plywood with impressive impact. Observing Kelly today it is difficult to imagine that as an infant she was one very sick girl. I know quite personally that many are not as lucky and we are very thankful and indebted that Kelly was spared and allowed to live.

I flew back to Greece after Christmas 1988 on an uneventful *Olympic Airlines* flight out of New York. The only thing I really remember was that the food was a lot better than US carriers and when we landed on the Athens runway many of the Greek passengers were doing some animated acts of celebration and prayer. It made sense to me as a witness of that thankfulness. Flying an airplane meant traveling in an aluminum tube at four hundred miles per hour not knowing the mechanical history of the device, and having never met the operator of the flying tube. That is a significant number of unknowns. They tell us the pilots are competent and the aircraft is safe, but my question is always, "*Who are they?*" I am not a skeptic by nature, but I'm always worried by "*they say.*" Therefore, I believe the Greeks demonstrate great wisdom when they thank "*The Supreme Being*" for their safe arrival, very appropriate.

It was about this time in my life, approaching my mid thirties that I began to develop my theory of evolution as it concerns the subject of baldness. When I was child I was taken as a matter of routine and without say to a local barber who wisely told me "*With the thickness of your hair, you'll never have to worry about going bald.*" Now about twenty- five years later I discovered that *Simmie* the barber had lied.

Now I could act like a hysterical left winger and scream nonstop as they do about George W. Bush and our failure to find weapons of mass destruction in Iraq. I suppose I could go back to Irwin, Pennsylvania, stand on Simmie's grave and scream, "*Simmie lied! Simmie lied!, Look at me, my hair is gone, Simmie lied!"* But Simmie's ghost just ain't gonna care, so I really evaluated this complete phenomenon of baldness and I discovered in an inspirational moment that it's all related to evolution. When I think this theory through it all makes perfect sense.

As you are probably well aware *Neanderthal Man* and those upright primates preceding him were much hairier than his following evolutionary partner, *Cro Magnon Man.* As *Cro Magnon* man developed through the eons into our present day form, he seemed to have less and less hair. This makes perfect sense to me. Two cerebral heroes that I most admire, *Dr. Wayne Dyer* and *Dr. Stephen Covey* have no hair. The reason is evolution. These folks and others like them, who have no sprouts of dead protein extending out of their scalps, are more highly evolved. So in effect, baldness really means that one is in a much more advanced state of development in the evolutionary process. Embrace it and be proud. I understand the theory won't sit well with certain hairy-backed men or ladies with mustache issues but the evolutionary facts are there to examine. Anthropologists probably recognize this already, but if they have a boss with a John Kerry, Jimmy Johnson, or even Mel Kiper hair display, how could they forward their theories without threat of repercussion? Bald men everywhere may take a measure of satisfaction in the realization that, although hair crowned men are more attractive to women; these same men are often placed on a pedestal based on the glory of a thick mane; when they are in fact less developed on the evolutionary track of male Homo sapiens. To those of us with a smooth crown, they are but *Troglodytes.* I say" To hell with the flowing tangled mane of *Stiller Pro Bowler Troy Polomalu*; better to emulate the smooth perfection of the *Hall of Fame, Brunswick-like* crown displayed by the great *Stiller Champion, Mel Blount."*

As for myself I have to maintain a slight amount of hair on the back of my head in order to disguise a large goose egg that never went away from my LAWRENCE days.

One day in my firemanhood I was flying up the lower level ladder on the LAWRENCE engine room when I smashed my head against a support beam. Not only did I see stars and alter my brain wave activity for life, but I have a lump back there that remains to this day. I have named the odd protrusion, *the Knuckle of Knowledge.* With a title my abnormality rendered me Shaman-like and only added to my personal reverent power. Because of the deformity I can't quite go the route of *Yul Brenner* or *Telly*

Savalas, but I keep it short, courtesy of that great barber Iris and her trusty skill with a Kirby vacuum hair cutting attachment. With all that I do apologize for being random with the firing of that particularly out of whack neuron.

As a geographical bachelor in Nea Makri, I moved into a small barracks room and wintered out my remaining months there. The big event of was the arrival of our new XO, the colorful A6 jet pilot, Commander Bubba Martin. Commander Martin was as charismatic as a *Hogan's Heroes* guest star. The chiefs loved him immediately and he often showed at the chief's club for our Wednesday meeting brought back often by popular demand. He was probably a little much for our stuffy little communication station wardroom but as a good old boy from Georgia, the former *Yellow Jacket* linebacker had a ton of common sense.

He wrote a unifying article in the base paper about a subject that would often get abused in conversation among peers. That subject was sea duty. Certain smugness would often get thrown in someone's face about lack of sea duty. Commander Martin wrote about how he often had to play the *bad guy* as a pilot in training missions, but it was still crucial to the mission. It was a well written piece on how we are *one Navy* and the sniping about folk's lack of sea time and other issues was the wrong way to treat your shipmates. It was a very effective piece and I wish I had kept a copy of that article. The sniping stopped.

It was XO Martin's idea for an officer versus chiefs volleyball game. The chiefs prepared for this event in grand fashion. There were haughty predictions and a lot of talk, mostly by the chiefs about how much butt we were going to kick. We should have learned our lesson from our nugatory softball season, but arm chair athletes have short memories and we chiefs were sure we could intimidate the youthful female intensive group of officers. We borrowed the base ambulance and with siren wailing away we marched slowly and purposefully towards the volleyball court adorned in outrageous piratical attire. We came as a united group of warriors preparing for battle. We predicted a slaughter and it was. They slaughtered us. It was utter humiliation and abasement. We felt like *Custer* at the *Little Big Horn*. We were mowed down by the more athletic nonsmoking JGs and ensigns. They completely kicked our asses. Good losers that we were we loudly groused that the referee cheated and was bought and paid for by the more affluent officers.

Without fanfare my tour in Greece came to a close. New competent khaki had arrived, an ETC named Joan and a warrant officer who smiled a lot and had the IC men transferred to public works department. Most of my original friends had moved on and my family was awaiting my return. The division threw me a great farewell dinner, which I humbly appreciated. I really liked these people. I had negotiated orders through my old running mate, Cal Jones, now a master chief and my detailer in Washington. He was sending me off to a new ship the ARLEIGH BURKE, the first of its class. It was to be the first of a long line of highly capable destroyers built to withstand battle damage and capable to deliver a knockout punch. This ship was a highly advertised technological leap and getting on the first one as a *Plank Owner* would be a great honor.

Cal Jones called me back soon after I said yes to tell me the perspective CO said no, that he had his own IC chief in mind. Cal informed me that the billet was still mine if I wanted. I gave his words some pensive thought. Did I want to force the issue and arrive with their new CO irritated from day one having me forced upon him? I would be as redolent to that skipper as a brontosaurus fart. It made good sense to grant that skipper obeisance to his will and accept another set of orders. When Cal informed me that the Aegis cruiser YORKTOWN (CG-48) was available I immediately said OK. I knew enough about CG-48 to know she had a reputation and a nose for getting in harm's way. I was returning to sea, but a little side trip to AN WSN5 Gyro School was part of the route. I would report to the ship in June of 1989.

NAVCOMMSTA Nea Makri closed within a few short years. The Seabees had entirely rebuilt almost every building on the base. The small commissary was brand new and the roads newly paved. The underground telephone cable was also new; despite the Greek's permission…. well never mind. Nea Makri was a great and memorable tour. The hospitality of the Greek people will endure me to them forever. Their work ethic and their sincere respect for their neighbors' opinions were traits to emulate forever. But now vacation was over, it was time to go to sea.

Chapter Four:

Back to the Lakes

I flew in to Philadelphia in March. Iris, the kids, and I were planning to transit back to Norfolk immediately. We planned to move back into our little town house for awhile prior to moving to a larger house. We departed that home three years earlier in pristine condition. When we returned to the now empty structure it was appalling to discover how much damage could be done in such little time. Viewing how bad it was for us; it was understandable why our former Greek landlord Jorgo loved us so much for the good care we gave to his place. We had actually approved the tenants prior to our departure to Greece. They were a young couple, well dressed and neat. They seemed perfect.

On return we found our once tidy little home in ruins. We were forced to call in the assistance of my dexterous brother-in-laws Oscar and Carlos to help us make this place habitable again. The carpet was so drenched in animal urine that we had to run in holding our noses, grab a hunk of carpet and then run out. We tore every shred of carpet from that place then fumigated the bare wood flooring. The stove had to be chiseled clean. Behind the washer was three years worth of discarded items. A leak in the wall near the fireplace had destroyed that wall entirely. It had to be torn out and replaced. The sliding glass door was no longer transparent having suffered from a large dog's consistent scratching over time. All of our back yard grass was gone. My once green back yard was now parched hardened clay. The kitchen linoleum was scuffed and torn as if Greek glass dancing was an evening ritual. The walls had holes. Not merely nail holes from picture frame mounts, but holes like the ones *George Foreman* could make with his fist if he ever got pissed off at fiber board. The bathroom counter tops had cigarette burns, ashtrays must have been too tasking to provide. The kitchen window was broken; it had served as an extra entrance. The wood around the exterior was rotted it would not have matched the remainder of the hovel had it not been rotted.

Other than that the place was in perfect condition. It took awhile but we eventually made the place habitable again. I know that many Navy families can well relate to this story. Many of my military friends have equivalent tales of evil renters, gremlins in disguise, poised to eat through properties like human termites, wrecking havoc on house items you would least suspect of being abused. They present themselves to the military landlord who is only too relieved not to be stuck with a mortgage, as the family is shipped off to exotic world locations. It may prove difficult to discern these sinister simians in well groomed human attire when they sign the lease. They are difficult to detect, and it is illegal to exterminate them, so just beware, and if you rent your home, *shaka*.

We thought the people we rented to were *Ken and Barbie*. We had no idea we were getting *Foghorn and Leghorn* in full fledged battle. When we first returned the town house resembled Dresden Germany in 1945. With the help of Oscar and Carlos it was resurrected as if the Amish were having a picnic barn- raising. With their skill and energy we were under roof in no time, back to the comforts of a charming little home. Without them we would have been in therapy.

It was really a good thing that Iris wasn't working at that time because when I flew off to Great Lakes for AN/WSN 5 gyro school, it was the beginning of a number of years where life was haze gray and underway. As happens with many Navy families, the stay at home parent becomes both Mom and Dad. Never underestimate how exacerbating and difficult a task that actually is. I don't think I could do it. But the heroic Iris is the stronger of the two of us even though she cheats without conscience when filling our wine glasses. If one of the two of us had to play Mom and Dad, she was clearly the best choice.

We said our goodbyes and I was off to Great Lakes, Illinois for a month and a half. It was spring and I would be back in June. Our shelter was secure. The townhouse was fine and the Renault alliance was well… *George C. Scott, Patton…lied*! I had an alternator replaced in Greece at 45,000 miles, shortly before we shipped it home. By the time that car had 50,000 miles on it, I had renamed it *Christine* after *Stephen King's* book about an evil car. I believe the French gave us the Renault Alliance because they dislike Americans. No one could make a car that bad unless they did it on purpose. At fifty thousand miles that car didn't need repairs, it needed psychotherapy. I started to put *Wellbutrin* in the gas tank but it didn't help. Everything went wrong: emergency brake cable, ignition switch, axles, radiator, and heater. Repair facilities loved the Renault Alliance. Most Alliance mechanics had villas in Cannes funded by the money they earned from me and others like me.

I kept fixing that car because it wasn't that old and the body and interior looked great. For six months I did this until the Alliance and I reached our personal show down at the *OK Corral.* But for now Christine was working and I was off to Great lakes for further training. The old training base hadn't changed much since I was last there in 1975. As a chief, I received my own room and it actually had a telephone so I was moving up in the world, gaining perks.

The WSN5 gyro was vastly different from the old Mark 19 Sperry gyros. The system was very well thought out and was actually much easier to comprehend than the old Mark 19. It was extremely accurate, utilizing satellite updates for precision. Internally the main component was an inertial measuring unit. Ships actually had an allowance for a spare one to carry as a supply part. That was a huge step up for technology. The WSN5 took up a small amount of space in comparison to the earlier generation Mark 19. The school was challenging, but it was well taught by some young chiefs who knew what they were talking about. In all honesty it was good to be back into shipboard IC gear again. Three years of telephones and underground cables was enough. Ship's cable runs were right there in the overhead, fully exposed for quick repair in case of battle damage. The only problem is that there are sometimes hundreds of them packed together up there, with hard enamel paint often covering their tag numbers. Cable tracing can be a time consuming task, even exposed cables on a Navy ship. However, at least they aren't three feet deep under clay.

One of my classmates was a chief IC man coming off a recruiter tour in Pittsburgh. He was a tall guy, very funny and certainly being a Pittsburgher, quite worthy. He was headed to a West Coast ship after school. He was a good guy, and like many Navy acquaintances; he would move on, leaving me to occasionally wonder how his future turned out.

Having left Greece I was completely addicted to Greek food. When I discovered a Greek restaurant that delivered to the base I jumped on orders of souvlaki and ti zi ki sauce. I can't spell it, I know but it sounds like tza zee kee. I believe the English spelling of that is some weird arrangement beginning with the letter T. The sauce tastes great but it is heavy in garlic and the leftovers of the meal created a harsh garlic stench that permeated the pea green paint of the room's walls. That room smelled like tsi zi ki for weeks. I decided on no further take out food from that establishment.

I know I went out about twice while I was in Great Lakes. Once with the big chief, from Pittsburgh, I believe his name was Smitty, it could have been Jones, but for literary expediency we'll call him Big Smitty. We ended up at a Cubs versus Reds game at historic Wrigley Field. Picking up some standing room only tickets from a scalper, we slid into some unoccupied box seats, where the rightful owners thanked us for warming them up. We repeated this process three times, at last safe for the duration.

I can't tell you who won or lost that day but we had a lot of beers that afternoon. After the game we ended up at a place across the street called the *Cubbie Bear* where sophisticated Chicago North Siders made fun of my Steeler sweatshirt with snide comments. It wasn't like the 85 Bears happened yesterday. They were also four years removed from their glory, but the Steelers were a 6-10 team, and the brunt of has been jokes. Little did they know that respectability was just around the corner with *Cowher Power* on the horizon.

Well Big Smitty liked the Cubby Bear and we probably stayed much too long displaying our skill on their pitching machine. I ended up dragging that guy back that evening and I confirmed that Big Smitty was in fact very big. Not defensive tackle big, but tight end big was a reasonable comparison. That Monday morning in class his first words to me were "*I hate you!*" I guess he had a head ache.

The other time I went out was with Ron Rogers. Same old Ron from the YELLOWSTONE years was now in the Training and Administration of Reserves Program acronymic as TAR. He was out of the Naples broadcast studio and at a repair facility in Philadelphia. He still talked exactly like the Ron Rogers I always knew. Somehow, I would have loved hearing Ron, the big Inuit spewing out a little South Philly diction. But Ron didn't seem influenced by the unique Philly dialect; he was still Ron, complete with the *hmmmfff...* and *that's simple.*

Ron was in Great Lakes for the same reason I had been there in 1975, the Mark 19 gyro. The older ships with missile launchers were still around and the SPRUANCE destroyers also had a backup Mark 19 Gyro, so it was still a very relevant piece of equipment for the fleet IC men.

The school that I had found so mentally challenging in 1975 was also presenting a huge challenge to Ron Rogers. No not the curriculum, but the distinction of being the best student in the class. It seems that there was a Greek Navy student in Ron's class and he was presenting Ron with a spirited contest of who could finish first with the highest average. Not that this would motivate Ron to actually study or anything that zealous, but it was just something that was mildly irritating him, an annoyance that brought out Ron's dormant competitiveness.

Foreign navy students often go to our military schools. We had one young Australian in our WSN5 class. It was from him that I discovered in numerous declarations that everything in Australia is the best in the world. I halfway believed the guy from all that I've heard about that particular continent and someday I would actually like to find out about all that best in the world stuff. But until then I'll just have to take his word for it and settle for the food at *Outback Steak House in Virginia Beach.* That's as close as Iris and I are getting to Australia anytime soon.

Ron and I went out to an Illinois cowboy place one night in early June. We weren't heading anywhere special, but we ended up there after the blizzard started coming down. June snow in Great Lakes, why would anyone want to live… never mind, we can't all love Hawaii. Actually it was a great time hanging out with Ron, the cerebral Inuit, while stuck in a June blizzard with Illinois cowboys.

Good news, Ron didn't need to worry; his near concern was unfounded as he predictably ended up number one in his class. Even I managed to achieve that in my class for a change. That was because these schools are supposed to get a little bit easier when you are a chief. The Navy in the shipboard arena particularly is a very young group of people. It is one of the few organizations in the world where you can be a thirty-two year old chief and the crew members will think of you as somewhere between eighty-six and senile. The belief permeates that once you are in khakis your ready for the *Geritol bottle.* It is kind of strange when a Sailor retires at the age of forty and finds out that he/she isn't necessarily the oldest person on Earth.

Personally, and I know this will be argued; I theorize that being around all these young folks actually helps to keep you young. So my advice is to simply stay in for as long as you can and avoid the *Geritol, Carter's Liver Pills,* and all the other items advertised on *Lawrence Welk* reruns.

Ron and I parted ways again. He was off to Philadelphia. If anyone in Philly meets up with a large Alaskan native man of quiet demeanor and great intelligence tell Ron I said hello. I am sure that someday I will run into Ron again. That's a funny thing about Sailors. We part ways and we won't see each other again, often for many years. After fifteen or twenty minutes together it's as if you had never been away. Everything falls back into place. Capabilities and intellect will change, personality doesn't.

Chapter Five:

Best Ever

In the Revolutionary War *General George Washington* led a ragtag army of farmers and regular citizens against the greatest army the world had ever known in the history of the world. The Colonials with the assistance of the French Navy of the era managed with ingenious tactics and a steadfast sense of purpose to defeat the British general *Cornwallis*. It was a battle of monumental importance in the history of the fledging republic. It was the *Battle of Yorktown* and that epic battle created a slogan adopted by a great ship in the modern era that also bore the name of that monumental event. USS YORKTOWN (CG- 48), *Victory is Our Tradition* was the logo of this Aegis cruiser. When I reported there, the still youthful ship had already been a key player in the ACHILLE LAURO hijack rescue. They were involved in directing aircraft into Libya in the attack on *Quadaffi,* and they had stood their ground against the bullying of the Soviet fleet, getting rammed in the Black Sea. Wherever trouble chose to rear its head there was the YORKTOWN prepared to answer back with force. The ship stood as a polar opposite magnet for attracting the *World's Assholes.*

This was the real Navy in my frame of reference; a sleek warship ready to go where the cautious do not dare. Walking up that pier for the first time and seeing that 48 on the hull I wondered what this adventure would bring. Just looking at the ship straining against those mooring lines told me that this was an unnatural position being tied up to a pier. This was a ship that screamed at you "*Get me outta here*!" *I need to be moving.* A cruiser pier side was like keeping a decathlete in shackles and handcuffs. I had a feeling I wouldn't be spending a lot of time in the comfort of my very attractive family. I was correct. The USS YORKTOWN was a national investment. Aegis cruisers with their incredible Aegis radar systems and gas turbine power plants were very expensive. Navy brass was going to get their money's worth from these ships and that meant haze gray and underway, in search of those plentiful *World Assholes*.

That June day in 1989 I first stepped aboard the ship and within an hour I was back in my element. I know it's a dorky cliché but nonetheless it's true; "*Once a destroyer Sailor, always a destroyer Sailor.*" That's who I was. I never felt like a communicator, a title earned by pros like the incomparable Mr. Metz. Nor was I a repair expert, like the great Mr. Lake. No, this was my comfort zone. It was imbued in me from the LAWRENCE days of Keesey, memories of nooners taken next to the warm 50 volt DC rectifiers in the IC Room and getting splashed in the chow line on the port side of the main deck. This was exactly where I was supposed to be.

I checked in with the ship's office. I met my division officer. I met the chief engineer and went down to the forward IC room at the beginning of a CSQTT visit. I can't recall today what a CSQTT was except that it was a combat systems related visit from some technical professionals. There was a chief IC man down there with my new shop personnel. I introduced myself and helped as much as I could with limited background. It seemed to help. We ended up doing quite well and that was the beginning of my first day. It didn't slow down for the next three years.

There were so many outstanding leaders and shipmates on YORKTOWN during those years that it is really difficult to find a starting point so I'll start with the one person onboard whom I already knew, DCCM Chip Rowland. There he was, the *zen* master of damage control, unchanged from his SCOTT years, except for his second star. Everything about Chip was the same. He was still torturing crew members one by one until they could cut shoring, set fire boundaries, don an OBA, or handle a fire hose in their sleep. He remained epigrammatic, but if I had told him he was epigrammatic he would have smacked me. After five minutes of catching up and cutting up with pithy repartees he assigned me as chief in charge of Repair Locker # Three. When my meeting with Chip concluded I may have been changed from my reporting Dress Blues to working khakis. I can't be certain, but at least I had my general quarters station.

Now this may sound like a boring Grammy exception speech, but my chain of command consisted of a young ensign named Chris Peterschmidt, the E division officer, Lieutenant Commander Michael Robinson, the Cheng, Commander P.H. Daly, the XO, and the commanding officer, Captain Pete O'Connor. I can easily remember those names because this was a cast of ringers, all important leaders who demand mention.

Ensign Peterschmidt was the ship's best athlete. He was a gymnast during his college days from Marquette University. He wasn't a very large man, but an elite athlete. He was a soft spoken and polite officer and he had an excellent habit of giving you his undivided attention when you were speaking to him.

LCDR Robinson, the Cheng was a friendly affable officer who had an incredible knack for getting you to do what he wanted. One could never underestimate how much they could accomplish at Mr. Robinson's request. He would assign the most irritating and mundane tasks imaginable and you would smile about doing it, only because he made it imperatively important. He was quite impossible to get irked with, because he, like Ensign Peterschmidt was a genuinely great character guy and you always felt like he sincerely liked you.

The executive officer, Commander P.H. Daly was the incarnate XO, the Vince Lombardi, Paul Brown, or my favorite Chuck Noll of XOs. He was a tough Chicago guy and had one standard and that was the perfect standard. He was one of those long suffering *Cub Fans* and I could imagine how it was at his house when that fan snagged the ball in the NLCS with the Marlins years later. XO Daly had a lot to do with the appearance and cleanliness of the YORKTOWN. Before he was there, and early on, the YORKTOWN was a clean ship, but with him as the XO it stepped up to become a *Smithsonian Ship*. The YORKTOWN became spectacular. No other American fleet asset could possibly have looked as good as the YORKTOWN. There, I said it, and I believe it. *The USS YORKTOWN was in fact, the cleanest ship in the Navy.* You can confirm that as fact and make it a *Trivia Pursuit Question*. I believe the most instrumental person in making that fact a reality was Commander Daly.

Our commanding officer when I arrived was Captain Pete O'Connor. It took awhile to meet him because of my immediate thrust into the ship's routine. I was crawling out from under a motor in the ship's laundry room when we met. I instantly liked the captain. He loved the ship and it showed. He was charismatic and I never tired of a Captain O'Connor Captain's Call. He would gather us in the helo hangar or on the flight deck and talk about what a special place this ship was. I could remember very few people who could get you excited about some acronym inspection but he had that gift. He was also a sports fan, Redskins I believe, but a sports fan is a sports fan so we had that in common.

I had a strong chain of command going up the line. I had the electricians and the IC men working for me. On YORKTOWN I did not have a Dave Owens to split the bill like on SCOTT. I had E Division for the next three years, but it all worked out well thanks to some extra hard working and talented blue shirts. Now to perceive our electricians or IC men as a normal and smooth functioning group of savvy professionals was like saying the cast of *Animal House* would do well in the *Vienna Boys Choir*. We were going to get the job done in E division but we definitely had imperfections too great to mask. We spent enormous tracts of time together so we were like a family after a while, and like any nearly normal family we certainly had occasional issues. In that manner we were normal, but our disagreements were infrequent and expected.

Jesse the *Bull* Santero was our first class electrician. Jesse was a good natured Filipino American who had a perpetual smile on his face. The only time I ever saw him not smile was when he was sitting in front of the EPPC Console on watch. He was usually asleep there as he tended to appear much more serious when in his sleeping state.

Our first class IC man was Warren West, a South Side Chicago guy who was coming into the IC men rating the hard way. It was possible for a petty officer of one rate to change to a more critical rating provided they added some schooling and met the ASVAB test requirements. IC1 West had transferred to the IC rate from the bos'n mate rating as a second class petty officer. To become a first class petty officer technician on a technically challenging Aegis cruiser showed immense drive and determination. West had a great sense of humor and a powerful laugh. However; when overwhelmed his eyes would blink very quickly, possibly at 7-8 hertz frequency, revealing his jovial or stressed condition. We had a cadre of merciless characters in the division who would prey on a ship mate's quirks, and extrapolate on them ruthlessly in parody or jest. E division boasted two very funny, actually belly laugh funny people in Fireman Electrician Lenny Singleton and IC3 Mike Castro; both certifiable nut cases who gave reasonable cause for incarceration due to rare mental disorders.

The backbone of our electric shop in the beginning was a tall gangly electrician second class with a laid back disposition. He was a less refined Mark Rothrock, that good guy known from my early YELLOWSTONE tour. His name was Lou Persinger and I called him Liquid Lou, for no good reason other than it sounded rather cool in its lilt. He had skills as a blue collar psychologist and he clearly understood the concept of *juice.* The IC men had worthy core performers also and these two young men were termed the H factors. Our H factor component boasted two second class petty officers who could fix anything and had great creativity. IC2 Chris Halliday and IC2 Kip Hunsinger were solid performers who thrived on the most perplexing and convoluted problems. They both came from tenders in previous duty assignments and I've always held the conviction that tenders produce great technicians. These two were the real deal and fully supported my conviction.

One particular character that we had in the electric shop was a young guy. Big Wingo was like a Teddy Bear. He was very innocent but like most bear cubs he could get in trouble on occasion. It was never anything he did with malicious intent. Stuff just seemed to happen to Wingo.

That was our main core of characters in the division. Major additions and transfers would come to pass but when I arrived this was our primary group of warriors, for better or worse.

The chief's mess on the YORKTOWN was a strong one. Most of the plank owners were getting short and would be rolling on soon to other assignments. YORKTOWN had been in commission for about four years when I reported and the group of chiefs we had was about as close knit a group as I had seen.

Leading us was a big tough master at arms named Hank Davis. The rating command master chief had not been put into effect yet, so a command master chief still kept his rate in tact. Hank was serious about physical fitness, his and yours. He kept things tight in the mess. Projecting a deep voice Hank looked like a command master chief. No one doubted or challenged Hank's authority and no one liked us more than Hank. He did have an issue with the obese chief stereotype. He told us point blank "*Stay in shape or I'll run your fat ass out of the Navy.*" That was Hank's effective method of sensitive communication that catapulted many off the couch and into jogging attire.

Larry was the master chief in charge of engineering. Most of what I was to learn about the gas turbine power plant and engine rooms came from Larry Burkette. He was one of the old salts, a common sense type. He never sugar coated a sentence to anyone about anything. So with Larry you always knew exactly where he was coming from. There was more chance of Larry Bird missing a foul shot than to have Larry Burkette get caught up in politics or gossip. He was all about turbines and never cared for bullshit.

R Division had Chip and A Gang, the enginemen, had Pete. Pete was a true engineman in every sense of the word. Pete would have made a great engineman on the LAWRENCE. On the SCOTT he would have been called gnarly, (in a complementary way of course). He worked about as hard as humanly possible. Pete was big and strong. He wasn't that muscular body building strong but that old farm boy strong. He could chew out his guys with more colorful metaphors than Shakespeare getting pick pocketed, but he also protected and took care of them. Pete had a hard time controlling his cussing. It was confounding for him to control his language so at some point he quit wasting his energy on trying. He wasn't attempting to be scurrilous or vituperative; Pete just said "*fuck,*" and he said it a lot. Coming from Pete you almost expected it. Messing with fellow chief petty officers who visited the ship for business, I often introduced Pete as RPC (religious petty officer chief) Pederson, whereas Pete would say "*How the fuck are ya*?" I think Pete tried to control his vocabulary somewhat around the Cheng because Mr. Robinson was a religious man, but I am not at all sure that Pete was very successful in that endeavor. Perhaps Cheng overlooked it with Pete because he worked so hard and put in about twelve to fourteen hours a day. That may be true. Personally I think Pete just used the word *fuck* the way teens use the word *like* or as some say *ah.* I believe it was only pause filler, nothing more. I mean with Pete even valve oil ring gaskets were "*my fuckin o rings*," so I believe it was in fact totally innocent use of the well abused vulgarity. Pete was my best friend on the YORKTOWN for the entire three years I was on the ship. With Pete, you never had to act special and he never spent time carping about anything off the ship. He saved all his frustration for the job itself. When he walked off the brow he was always speaking good things about his guys. He may have routinely threatened their lives with colorful shtick but he would let no one else mess with them. After awhile Pete's guys deciphered him; and his cussing and threats to their immediate well being were actually encouraged, as they took great glee in hearing what colorful metaphor he could label them with in his next sentence. In short, they just plain loved old Pete. Pete had a temper until he stepped off the brow of the ship. Then he was calmer than your Grandpa with a remote control in a soft lazy boy after a Thanksgiving dinner.

Our chief's mess had its own gadget guy; a senior chief sonar man and *MacGyver* type named Ernie Ladd. Ernie was inventive and he could ingeniously figure out methods to make all man made items work. As computers were finally entering our world, Ernie had the inside track on them. He was a natural fit for the world of computers and if you were going to label anyone as a future computer geek, it was Ernie. But don't allow me to sell Ernie short, anything that was technology oriented was right up his alley and he would enthusiastically utilize any gadget on the market in order to pull a prank on you; unwaveringly and without remorse. Ernie was apt to do you in with electric shock hand buzzers, remote control farting machines, or any man made item that would give you a burst of minor pain through a technological source. Ernie was at his best when you asked the question, "*Hey Ernie how could we .....?*" It didn't matter what the direct object was to your request, it was the cognitive process that counted.

Our torpedo man, Chief Macteer and the mess specialist Cedrick Davis were a little younger than the average chiefs in the mess; they were also a lot of fun to hang out with. Cedrick developed into our theme song soloist and theYORKTOWN chiefs adopted *You've Lost That Lovin Feeling* as our Chief's Mess theme song. Cedrick was actually right on par with the *Righteous Brothers.* Macteer's claim to fame was that he was the guy who could get you to go out when ya just didn't feel like it. Mac always made it seem like you would miss something great if you stayed on the ship.

Ron Flag, our signalman, I know, a signalman named Flag, go figure. He was also Mr. MWR. He always had the social agenda in full swing with high energy. Big Ted Uchiek, our gas turbine electrical expert was someone whom you would never wish to anger. It wouldn't be in the best interest of your health as he was an imposing man and probably the only mess member who could get away unquestioned with wearing a pink polo. Tom Smith, Smitty of course, was our gunner's mate technical chief, a typical crazy gunner's mate and a lot of fun.

This chief's mess still had many yet to come. Cecil Rumbo was the senior chief ET and the command physical fitness guru. Jim Fennell was a big sonarman chief who worked non-stop, a topside version of Pete the engineman. Mike Longo was the gas turbine mechanic chief; every chief's mess needed a Jersey guy in there to give the entire group an unbiased hard time on all subjects of interest.

Big Ski the supply chief from Pittsburgh would be coming later on, as would Jeff Montgomery, the ship's serviceman and Mark Dimmock, the launcher chief. Tim Slaegle was the YORKTOWN sheriff and a character fit for a guest spot on any Hollywood sitcom. All the eccentric personalities thrown together in this chief's mess made it the best I had ever been part of. I had been in a few by then. The SCOTT'S chief mess was outstanding, but this 1989 USS YORKTOWN group was really special. It definitely wasn't for those who were thinned skinned or couldn't take a joke. The onion skins of personal facades were quickly peeled by the razor wits of the YORKTOWN chiefs. At times all seriousness was set aside as these men were quite pensive about the art of high humor. I received my first inclination about how this tour was to be during a ship's Christmas party in August of 1989. Yes, that's right. We were leaving for a six month deployment that fall. It was going to be a return to the Med where I had just left. So in defiance we were having our Christmas party in August. It made perfect sense. The chiefs and officers were in choker whites. The wives were all decked out. They had a professional portrait photographer there and the ship was quite successful in creating the desired effect of Christmas. Iris looked spectacular and I took oodles of crap about why I brought my daughter. The chiefs immediately evicted the lead singer of the band off the stage and they took over the microphones. This chief's mess promised to be fun.

The chief engineer liked me; I believe because I gave him answers. Keesey's training paid off again. I memorized the JSN (job sequence log) log to both shops and kept hard at the status of every task pending. Preparing for a deployment meant material and working equipment. Whatever effort was needed to get everything fixed and working prior to deployment was the goal. There was to be no broke stuff.

Mr. Robinson informed me he would like me to stand engineering officer of the watch or EOOW. Because I was an IC man and not a Gas Turbine guy, he earnestly stated that he would refrain from using me as a participant in the Propulsion Examining Board inspection or any similar stressful agenda. When I qualified as an EOOW my very first watch after the captain's qualification board was under the scrutiny of the OPPE board. In my entire naval career, I was always one of the inspected, never was I blessed to be the inspector. It would have been a pleasant change of pace to be on the giving rather than the receiving end, but it wasn't meant to be. When *Mick Jagger* wrote *You Can't Always Get What You Want,* I knew exactly what he was referring to.

About two weeks prior to our deployment *Christine*, the French Renault struck. I was driving to duty on a beautiful Saturday morning on Interstate 564 heading towards the naval base. For no reason other than having to get up early on a Saturday morning Christine had a temper tantrum and exploded her heater into the interior of the car. It was a wonderful moment of bonding between man and machine. At 55 miles per hour the Renault was instantly filled with steam. I had to apply the brakes as I traveled blindly down the fast lane, the windshield view glassed over in the condensing steam. Miraculously and without crashing I managed to stop the vehicle. Two Sailors observed the clouds of steam coming out of the car and they rushed in quickly to assist. They pushed the car to the shoulder of the interstate and wasted no time. I was thankful because by then I was doing a painful Irish jig as my steam baked ankles swelled with intense pain. There I was on the side of the interstate acting like a leprechaun who just lost his pot of gold or Terrell Owens in the end zone after a touchdown catch. I got a ride with my rescuers to the base medical clinic where they did stuff to make it at least bearable. Iris rescued me a short while later.

When Iris and I said our goodbyes less than ten days later I came up the ship's brow in bedroom slippers. Huge water blisters remained on my ankles. I probably could have gotten out of leaving with the ship if I tried, but I really liked this ship, so I was allowed the luxury of going to general quarters in bedroom slippers for about ten more days.

Christine won, the little French tart ended up with a new radiator and heater because we couldn't yet afford a new car. Iris didn't have a problem with that car for the next six months. It was as if Christine was abiding her time like a venomous pit viper in hibernation. She had fed, now she awaited my return from sea, dreaming of the time she could unhinge her jaws and swallow whole the Sailor she had marked for extinction. She lived to strike again.

The YORKTOWN underway was quite different than the LAWRENCE at sea. There was space to rat-hole things. Shopping was a little easier. The ship did a standard Mediterranean cruise, visiting all the routine ports. Winter in the Med is, as one would expect a much slower paced environment. The ship fell into a routine of whirlwind activity when at sea, but there was a little time for fun here and there. We created a small market NFL talk show on our closed circuit television. There were three of us who would get together, discuss games, and make predictions. Our normal process was to invite a guest to help pick winners. One evening we had the chief engineer on as our invited guest. Shortly after the on air discussion began, the captain called CCTV and said "*Get him off of there, he doesn't know what he's talking about.*" So we had to evict the embarrassed Cheng. I felt bad, although it was all in jest. The captain was right though. Mike Robinson was no *John Madden*, and not to envy the captain but wouldn't it be great to only make a phone call and evict someone from the screen of your television; small wonder command at sea is so personally gratifying to those privileged to sample the intoxicating elixir of that great power.

We became the test platform for the INMARSAT satellite radio system, the forerunner for the satellite entertainment that ships at sea receive today. We were the first ship on the East Coast to have live sports and news feeds at sea. Television would come much later, but this was a monumental occasion to have news as it happened. The captain loved it. At times reception could get crazy and unreliable, this was especially true in port. There was a Redskin's game on, the captain's team, when we lost reception and it wasn't pretty. I think he told the XO "*If it was Pittsburgh the chief would have had that thing working, even if his IC men had to turn the dish by hand in a squall!*"

Somehow the word got out to the rest of the deployed battle group that we had this thing. After that, sad disconsolate IC men would visit us in different ports explaining to us that they were ordered to find a way to get one for their ship. I felt for the beleaguered IC Gangs on their *mission impossibles*, but there was only one of those things at the time and the YORKTOWN held the grail; lock, stock, and dish.

Our cruise was fairly uneventful other than the fact that we did everything perfectly. It wasn't a very glamorous cruise; no catastrophic world events occurred that required us going into action. It was a very calm and overall routine deployment.

One port of interest was Dubrovnik Yugoslavia. Our port visit occurred at a time when the country was still under the influence of some type of Communist control. We visited their old city there. Dress uniforms were a requirement but the people were very hospitable. I noticed that Eastern countries usually exchanged you huge piles of their money for American dollars. A few years later that certainly would change. With western freedoms on their horizon prices would go up soon enough for Dubrovnik. We found the people very hospitable, even though they could be intimidating at times with their great height. With a scenic old city and engaging citizens Dubrovnik would soon be an excellent vacation choice in Europe.

When I arrived on YORKTOWN I had spent the three previous years playing some serious lunch time basketball. I still smoked of course but at the same time I was a normal weight. When I was doing pushups for Worshick in 1972 I was a whopping 120 pounds of nothing but skin and bones. Now the pendulum had swung again. It was a similar situation to what I had experienced on the YELLOWSTONE in the North Atlantic several years earlier.

One day out at sea I was in the electric shop after imbibing one of Cedric's power lunches and Lenny Singleton took a look at my tight khaki belt and said, "*Gee Chief, when is it due*?" I was one of those big in the gut and nowhere else types, the curse of the dreaded *Chief's Syndrome.* Chief's syndrome must have some relative trick to it. If you examine the Hollywood stereotypes of a Chief, who do you get? Why *Don Rickles* of course. If you stereotype a sea captain or an XO who do you get? Why *Kirk Douglas, John Wayne, or Denzel Washington*, who else? We luck out once in a while with Hollywood. But that will only happen if you're on a SEAL team in their picture. Today's Navy is trying to get weight under control. There are still many pockets of chunky people out there that are slipping through the cracks, but hopefully they at least have to be stealthy about it. Physical readiness training is supposed to be a big part of the Navy today. I do hope it continues. Heart disease and diabetes being as rampant as they are in our well fed society. I have my own ideas that I may or not share with you on how I would enforce the physical readiness standards. It is one of those *"if only I owned the world daydreams"* and I'm still mulling over whether I wish to pontificate my take on the subject.

It was about two months until our cruise was over and I really didn't wish to have Iris on the pier observing me waddling down the brow, besides, Hank Davis was quite clear about a fat chief's mess. I don't mean to make Hank sound like a mean guy in any way; after all how mean and malevolent could a guy be who had the words *"Your Name"* tattooed on his derriere? Our CMC Hank did indeed have that and he won a whole lot of free drinks betting folks in bars that he had *Your Name* tattooed on his ass.

The bottom line was that I had stretched out the capacity of my mid section to a point that was going to require exercise and diet at sea, two months of bear type hibernation, or an exorcism to cast out the demons of hunger that occurred relentlessly in my belly. Unfortunately the first was my only choice, although hibernation seemed like the easiest route to a svelte appearance.

Mike Longo didn't have a big gut like me. His Achilles heel was the derriere extraordinaire. We had a couch in the chief's mess and if Mike needed a seat he would crash down into the narrowest of gaps. It was a known as *Longoing In.* Mike Longo'd in so often that we all adopted that as our term for gaining a seat. *"Mind if I Longo in?"* displaced the less colorful standard of "*May I sit down*?" or Pete's personal, "*Move the fuck over.*"

Mike started it and said "*Zak, we gotta start running.*" I said, "*OK, Why not*?" I knew he was right. The Aegis cruiser had a main deck that if you went around its maximum distance then you went a mile in six and half laps. On the flight deck, one level higher, the much smaller deck took about 28 laps to the mile. We started with about a half mile on the flight deck that day in February 1990 and I've been running ever since. The YORKTOWN had a way of getting someone to do things that would cause you to improve yourself or others. Whether you chose to hold the gains, who knows? But Captain O'Connor used to say with conviction, "*This is a special place.*" It really was.

When we pulled in I had lost ample gut. Basically my mid section twenty pound bowling bowl had been used up, burned in the energy I expended running in circles around that flight deck for six weeks. I told anyone who commented that they were imagining things. I had always been svelte and athletic.

Iris and the kids were great. The best thing about deployments, were always the homecomings. Iris had made friends with our next door neighbor, another young Navy wife named Karen. Karen and her kids were to become lifelong friends. At that time I don't believe her kids had yet arrived. Maybe Shanster, but I am sure Jonathan was still on the way. They were both destined to become amazing young adults, extremely bright and in possession of the rarest of gifts bestowed upon children, excellent and respectful manners. They became perfect tributes to a strict mother's upbringing.

Life went back to normal for a short duration. The YORKTOWN was overwhelmed with people coming to help. Every acronym on earth arrived and with each acronym we engraved in granite our motto, "*Best Ever.*" That was in accordance with the inspection out- briefs that the captain would routinely receive. It was because of our entire preparation process. Prepare like your life depended on it, then the actual inspection was a cinch. XO Daley never tired of preaching this approach. Hence many inspection teams would give the Captain the "*best ever*" label. Captains love to hear that phrase. In the chief's mess it became part of the informal lingo at lunch. A good meal may well be called, "*best ever*." Anything was fair game. We would often go jogging now as an armada, led by Hank. Often our runs would be called, that's right, *Best Ever*."

The YORKTOWN was a beautiful ship. We developed a lighting improvement project, increasing the number of fluorescents installed, and we painted all of our spaces a bright white. The color actually got renamed, "*YORKTOWN White.*" Before anyone painted a space XO Daley checked over its preparation. It received the Chicago once over, every space, every time, every detail, highest standard; that was the YORKTOWN way. Having a ship of extraordinary beauty, I am convinced gave us a psychological advantage with the legions of folks coming to help. I think the mind set leans a certain way when you step aboard a meticulously pristine vessel.

In E division we added a transfer in named Ed. Ed was a very slim guy and he smoked like a chimney. Talking to Ed I eventually learned that he passed up a track scholarship from a New York City college to join the Navy. The way Ed smoked and drank coffee it was hard to believe he could run at all. His coffee cup was the size of his thigh. I had to witness it with my own eyes to believe it, Ed's running, not his coffee cup. I saw Ed do a little practice run up on the flight deck and I knew we had our very own YORKTOWN version of *Gump.* He was an Ed, like the one I had known in my youth; at least as far as running was concerned. Ed was blazing fast, actually a freak of nature based on the fact that he smoked and never trained.

The command physical readiness test or PRT was approaching and the entire ship knew that now *LTJG* Peterschmidt was going to smoke us all, as usual. On our crew, LTJG Peterschmidt was the only one of us who consistently broke the 8 minute mark for a mile and a half. Being the instigator that I was I let everyone know that Mr. Peterschmidt now had a challenge in Fast Ed. Fast Ed was our running version of *Slim Willie McCoy.* When the run started it was Mr. Peterschmidt and Ed, with everyone else predictably far behind. They were in a class of their own. It was like watching the Kenyans on *Wide World of Sports.* They both broke 8 minutes. They were both as fast as lightning. They were blazing, as if they were shot right out of the gun mount. They were bullets flying out of the PHALANX. The trouble with the story is that I can't remember for the life of me who won. If you retell this story to someone, just pick one. It would be hard to root against either one. We had Ed, the underdog and we had Mr. Peterschmidt, the *All American* guy who was never obnoxious or arrogant. I recommend

Ed for enlisted storytellers and Mr. Peterschmidt for officers who wish to recant this tale.

In the central control station or CCS, we did have the infamous plumbing waste drain pipe. As the engineering officer of the watch, or EOOW, a big responsibility was the management of the electrical tagout log. People presenting you with improperly filled out tags had to be punished. Hence, the *plumbing waste drain pipe,* strategically located next to the EOOW's chair, served the secondary purpose of retribution pull up bar. Improperly filled out tags could cost you pull ups on the pipe. On the purple pipe, Mr. Peterschmidt was in a class of his own. The former gymnast could easily knock out thirty without trying. Lenny Singleton was the best I ever saw other than the JG, and he did about eighteen.

IC1 West and EM1 Santero were turning out to be excellent first classes. I insisted Santero study on watch. When he left the YORKTOWN he made chief right away at his next duty station. He just needed to get a little higher test score, his record was already excellent. IC1 West did well. He eventually made it as the YORKTOWN Sailor of the Quarter. That's not insignificant considering he crossed over from an entirely different rate. That is always a great selling point for the Navy. If you are a performer you can overcome obstacles like English as a second language, or completely changing your field of work. The opportunities are there and these two guys were jumping the hoops to get somewhere.

During one underway period I discovered a bunch of old tapes we had of missile shoots and footage of crew members actively engaged in the process. I got together with my two prodigies, Hunsinger and Halliday and asked if they could put something together as a ship's music video. We picked Pat *Benatar's Hit Me With Your Best Shot,* then the two mad scientists went to work splicing different film segments together to get it all to fit in perfectly. They worked for days underway on this project until they presented a professional tape that any *Right Winger* would be proud of. The song and the tape created a huge stir with its synchronized explosions. The captain loved ordinance on target and he loved that tape and the wardroom would present it to every distinguished guest that came aboard. The IC men stayed busy making copies of that tape for months. My biggest regret about that tape is that I can't find my own personal copy.

Hunsinger and Halliday were an inventive and talented duo. They were at their best if you gave them something difficult to deal with. You never wanted to be too specific with those two because you could usually get something special in a project if you gave them some artistic leeway.

The electrician side of the house had a problem that drove us crazy for a long time. We would stand watch in CCS and the electrical plant control console, or EPCC would intermittently show a 440 Volt ground on its panel meter. This could present a dangerous situation if left unattended. Our problem was just as we would start stripping loads from the switchboard load centers in an attempt to isolate it; it would suddenly disappear and vanish. It was most assuredly haunted.

This went on for days. What we finally discovered was a power panel with a loose connection. It wouldn't ground against the metal box unless the ship rolled a certain number of degrees to starboard. Things like that could actually cause hair loss. This may be worth launching a social investigation as to why electrical workers have less hair than those in other vocations. This may be anecdotal, but it is an observation I feel strongly about having noticed a preponderance of shiny heads in the electrical professions.

Now that I was exercising, I was tenacious in my resolve to kick the evil habit of nicotine ingestion. I would arrive to relieve the watch in the morning determined that I had had my last cigarette. By 1000 that morning I would be screaming for a watch relief. The heathen nicotine had an intense grip on me but as a good addicted smoker; one totally devoted to the destruction of my respiratory system, I would upon gaining a momentary watch relief fire up a smoke and inhale deeply in defeat.

Smoking and running go together like chocolate ice cream and green beans. Despite knowing that it was only a matter of time before it got me good, I kept on doing it. It was going to be that way for awhile. Cigarettes were winning all the battles; the outcome of my personal war on smoking was still very bleak. It was to be a long war with many battles and skirmishes. Cigarette smoke was a powerful enemy, enticing its opponent with a learned appreciation for its aromatic and addictive carcinogens until it owned its user, who was enslaved thereafter bowing to partake of its calming effect about once every fifteen minutes.

The YORKTOWN was rewarded shortly after the Med cruise with law enforcement operations or LEO Ops in the Caribbean. We chased drug runners, stalking them and trying our best to make the big bust. We did not get the bad guys on that trip, but we did get to go to Miami Florida for the Fourth of July.

Miami was jumping as one would expect. A local news crew visited the ship. By then we had a new captain and he was really into clean. He had a philosophy that he stated to the news crew: *"The ship belongs to you, the American people. We, the crew, are its caretakers, and we do in fact take very good care of it for you."* The ship amazed the Miami news crew with its impeccable pristine appearance, and that evening the female reporters were talking on local television about how they wanted to take home the crew members. Not for their romantic company of course, but to clean their houses.

The USS YORKTOWN was dirt's worst enemy. Any spec that invaded our sterile environment was swiftly destroyed. Some people suggested that we should remove our shoes at the Quarterdeck but Sailors walking around in socks could lead to a whole different set of problems with accompanying smell issues along with breakouts of Athlete's Foot conditions. Our great master at arms chief on board Tim Slaegle was like me, always trying to quit smoking. His method was to quit buying them. No one ever seemed to mind though. Tim wasn't your ordinary serious policeman type. He was actually a lot of fun to be around. Maybe it was because he was more highly evolved like me. Tim actually looked like a famous person. The guy on the bottle of soap or disinfectant known for years as *Mr. Clean* looked exactly like Tim or perhaps Tim looked like *Mr. Clean* as *Mr. Clean* may have come into existence prior to Tim. Regardless, Tim was justly dubbed Mr. Clean. It fit well because MAs are always by nature of their jobs the most squared away individuals on the ship, and in that regard Tim fit the stereotype.

Tim regaled in the antiseptic smell of cleanliness and he had a problem with bad smells. Big Pete had a foot issue. Even in chief's berthing we were sardines in a can and Tim would cry and whine about the contumacious aroma of Pete's feet. I don't know if Tim adapted nose clips or if Pete invested in foot powder but the issue seemed to die out after a while. Listening to Tim bitch about the olfactory sensation caused by Pete's feet or listening to Pete say nothing as if he were being addressed by an irritating flea made for an entertaining moment or two. The trouble with Tim was that he was fine on the ship. When you put him on liberty in an out of town port he became an instant cop, always suspicious and ever watchful for lurking danger. Maybe it was that whole cop thing, an internal relay that energized the proper mode and bearing, providing Tim with an innate ability to get a Sailor out of trouble before he got into any, and honestly you can't do better than that. Tim would exact any payment due the next day by getting a free cigarette from those he salvaged. I used to keep my own smokes, but I would have a few I would keep just for Tim. I would bum little short filterless smokes from someone; one of those ones that were so full of tar, it was like dipping a brush in it and rolling out your lung. You could call it a full effect cigarette. Some would call it full bodied taste. I loved to witness the disdain on Tim's face when you gave him one of those. The contortion of displeasure was well worth the effort.

During one of our underway periods XO Daly wished to generate a little fun with the crew. He approached me about an idea because as the

CCTV guy I had evolved into the role of the ship's MC. We thought about a talent show but XO Daly decided that the crew would probably be too shy to participate. He decided on one of our underway holidays to hold a *Hat Day.* The crew would compete making the strangest and most meaningful hats possible. The crew could wear whatever type of hat they wanted to around the ship on *Hat Day.* Those who wished to enter the competition would sit in as a guest on CCTV and be interviewed about their particular hat. The response was excellent. Ron Flagg came down with something called a *Sun Blaster 2000;* this was a straw concoction with strings and various attachments that dangled off of it such as sun glasses, beer cans, sun block, and other items that were there for the grabbing convenience. It was a very ingenious invention and certainly should have been patented. The fire controlmen showed up with some Viking Helmut that wasn't very creative, but it was reverent head gear and had a very meaningful and touching story line with it that I can't remember shit about. XO Daly was very unique when he showed up with this bear's head perched on the top of his imposing head. Why our XO would even have this thing out at sea with him is beyond my wildest guess. I have seen Sailors bring strange things with them to sea but never had I seen a senior officer bring along taxidermy trophies or animal pelts. Our XO, the *Master of Clean*, the inventor of *YORKTOWN White,* the *Scrutinizer of painting preps*, was standing there in CCTV being interviewed about the historical misery and pain borne among Cub fans the world over. It was a great hat but it wasn't quite up there with the one Lenny Singleton wore on the air, the *IVCS Wona Ponga Ping Pong Helmut Phone.* The cost of Lenny's phone hat was a mere 287,000 dollars; a normal price tag for an IVCS Aegis cruiser telephone. He had the IVCS phone bolted to the top of his battle helmet and was receiving calls from the captain on it. Lenny, always the performer, stole the show and was dubbed the winner by a unanimous decision. The crew loved *Hat Day.* The XO gave us a thumb's up. Months later, I showed some relatives a tape of our at sea *Hat Day* celebration. I thought it was hilarious but they didn't get it. I suppose one could surmise that in some instances Sailors are easily amused. Perhaps we lack the sophisticated intellect that requires a high priced cutting edge entertainer to make us laugh; because truthfully, Sailors love to laugh, and it really doesn't take much.

A real home grown honest to gosh Steeler fan checked in as our new supply chief. We called him Jed or Ski. Ski because that was the name that came after Jed with the letters *low* in between, was the complete Steeler fan. I think his first name was Ron but nobody called Ski, Ron, if it was in fact Ron. Did you all get that? He was Ski. A true Steeler fan, he was die-hard and totally obnoxious to fans of other teams. It was good to have an ally on Sundays. Ski would also volunteer to serve lunch to the rest of the chiefs at the serving line. In order to be served properly by big Ski one had to state his portion preference. You were granted one of three options, *manly, semi- manly, or non- manly.* Whenever we had visiting guests, it was probably bizarre for them to hear a line of grown men passing through the chow line stating, "manly, non- manly, semi- manly… etc," in a repetitive way.

Our food was good, calorie intensive for certain, but you could also get plenty of weeds if you wished. Cedric's night baker used to make the morning, *YORKTOWN Sinkers.* These were the largest cinnamon buns ever created in the history of mankind. If you had the morning watch in CCS, the 0400-0800 shift primarily then it was really torturous. CCS was located directly below the ovens in the galley. The batch of YORKTOWN Sinkers would be baking away and the smell would drive the entire watch team to ravenous insanity. Usually a few sinkers would end up in CCS to appease the hounds. I would estimate one of those things at about 1500 calories, but they were sinfully delicious.

Jesse Santero made it off to shore duty and we received his replacement, EM1 Don Miller. At first EM1 Miller seemed like a well mannered petty officer, a somewhat quiescent Sailor, but the longer you got to know EM1 the more you appreciated his skill and leadership ability. He was actually a pretty tough guy with very high standards. Not prone to tongue lash EM1 never yelled or a screamed but he kept his shop motivated and problem free. He made it quietly clear to his guys that until standards were met there would *be* no liberty, there would *be* no leave, and there would only *be* the job at hand. Thus our new chief engineer Lieutenant John Sims christened Don Miller with the name *Beno* and it stuck as EM1 thus became, Beno Miller.

While Mr. Robinson was still attached to the ship as the Cheng our captain grew a fondness for cappuccino. On our first Med we open purchased several Lapavoni cappuccino machines. The Lapavonis were the Ferraris of cappuccino machines. They were brilliant performers. Working correctly they steamed milk and swirled the fizzled sludge into an addictive drink that rivaled the premier Napoli street cafés. But like the Ferrari they required maintenance and fine tuning. We discovered a company in California that sold parts for the finicky machines and we planned well by stocking up on elements and an impressive collection of other gadgets that went with the Italian wonders.

After the captain's affinity to cappuccinos was honed it was imperative to keep the Lapavonis steaming. The main engines, the ship's generators, and the Lapavonis; these were the most critical systems of the YORKTOWN'S engineers.

All major systems in engineering have a process for reacting to and restoring from equipment casualties. The practice at sea takes place every, and I mean every night. The drills are called BECCES, basic casualty control exercises. The idea is to do these things so often that all the correct responses become as automatic as *Jackie Chan* doing a jump kick with a turnaround head slap. It works very well. Because the Lapavoni was now one of our most important engineering systems, we, meaning my watch team comprised of the Michigan born comedian Chris Head, the PAC Operator, Liquid Lou Persinger, our EPPC watch, and myself developed the Lapavoni basic engineering casualty control response exercise. The procedure started the drill as follows: *Central Control, CCS: Bridge, We have a loss of cappuccino machine in the wardroom in compartment 2-297-01-L. Away the Duty A gang, Away the duty Electrician. Provide from Repair Locker # Five*. Bell, ring, ring.... *Central Control, Repair Locker Five, Power secured to cappuccino machine in compartment 2-297-01-L.. CCS, Aye. Central Control, Repair 5, duty A gang on scene in Compartment 2-297-*01*-L. Central Control, Repair Five, Cover plate removed from the Mod LPZ 0021. Troubleshooting in progress in compartment 2-297-01-L. CCS Aye. Central Control Repair 5; Troubleshooting complete on LPZ2001; cause of casualty burnt element; estimated time of* repair 1 hour 45 minutes. *Cause of casualty burnt element; estimated time of repair; 1 hour and forty five minutes, CCS aye.*

It was hard to stay awake at times during a midnight watch. Once our damage control console operator fell asleep and Chief Uchiek painted his fingernails red with magic marker. He still wasn't very attractive, even with his freshly done nails.

We got on a *Saturday Night Live* parody kick by doing midwatch Samurai communications procedures. Using our best *Belushi* imitations we made our reports over the amplified utilizing the ancient Japanese warrior dialect. Each report ended with a punctuating *Haii!* For a time we became angelic and biblical in the nature of our reports by using the word *hark* prior to each verbal report. For example: "*Hark, Aux 1, CCS. Report status of dump valve on sixth stage salinity on NR 1 Evap., Hark.*" "*Hark, CCS, Aux 1. Sixth stage salinity on number one evap in dump mode.*" "*Hark, Aux 1, CCS. Hark, sixth stage in dump mode aye.*"

On one particular boring midwatch in the middle of some ocean we were engaged in our Samurai process. The Cheng had a bout of insomnia and was up at 0200 stirring around in one of the auxiliary spaces, hidden from view. When he heard the Samurai broadcast, he wasn't very amused.

We immediately went into the cease and desist mode of operation. Our *SNL* days were abruptly ended.

One of Pete's engineman was as pure as fresh mountain snow. The soft spoken Jim Hahn was as kind to his fellow ship mates as was humanly possible. He never cussed. He never raised his voice. *Mother Teresa* would have given him smiley stickers every day. He was appreciative to a fault. He was the humblest living person on the planet Earth. He was also at a stretched out 5 foot 9 inches, the strongest man on Earth. I once asked him how he got so strong and his reply in his soft spoken Tennessee dialect said, "*I'm not really very strong. My brother is a lot stronger than I am. He worked out a lot more than I ever did.*" "*Oh really,*" *What did he do for a work out routine,*" I asked? "*Well he just hooked himself up in a harness and pulled his car up the hill mostly. It worked real good that way.*" We would call on Jim whenever we needed something heavy and awkward put in place. A scullery garbage grinder motor had to be held up and set in place for a minute or two to get the bolts started. Call in Hahn. Some hot griddles in the crew's mess serving line needed changed. Call in Hahn. Built unlike a body builder Jim was a block of granite, a human chain fall, but kinder than *Paula Abdul* after a top ten contestant cut.

I used to love to mess with Jim on watch. I would buy him a soda and hand it to him. Jim would go into a long dissertation about how much he appreciated my generosity but he would appeal to me to instead give the soda to one of his fellow ship mates who probably didn't have any money. I would say, "*But Hahn I want you to have it.*" This would frustrate Jim to no end. He never wanted to feel an advantage over a fellow ship mate. Jim just reeked of goodness and oozed humble generosity. Everyone loved that guy. Even when YORKTOWN made overseas port calls people in other countries would sense Jim's genuine goodness and notice right away that he was someone to trust. The halo of kindness emanated from the powerful Tennessee country boy right into the souls of those he passed by. For the rest of us gum smacking Nike wearing Yankees, they kept one eye open, a brow of suspicion raised as they looked us over with warranted distrust.

To say the ship was underway a lot was akin to saying the Poconos had a duck poop problem. Duck poop was everywhere in the Poconos and the YORKTOWN was always making turns. This time it was a summer Med. Hank had transferred from the CMC into retirement. And who appeared in Hank's relief, none other than an old timer from the YELLOWSTONE years, the running man himself, Jack Lewis; there to assume the duty as the command master chief. Jack wasn't that macho persona guy that Hank Davis was. He was a doer though, with bolts and kilowatts of high energy. Jack was a little eccentric and those eccentricities gave him an identity that YORKTOWN chiefs could exploit with zeal. Jack loved running and he could do about 16 miles a day without trying. He never ran out of gas at anything he was doing. I suppose all that aerobic conditioning made him the Navy *Energizer Bunny* with a resting pulse of about forty. Jack ran the YORKTOWN loop with a loud pace beeper. He also still had his natural pronation in his stride that gave him his trademark running style. He would lap around the deck beeping away for up to two hours at times.

A fan of high fiber, Jack insisted that *Bran Flakes* was a miracle cure for all ills. Once he got severe pain in his side which ended up being acute appendicitis. Jack had to get his appendix out but he didn't go to the Doc for diagnosis until it was almost too late. He was convinced the root of his discomfort stemmed from the ship running out of *Bran Flakes* at an inappropriate moment. Luckily they were able to save Jack in time. Hopefully, the hospital had *Bran Flakes*.

Jack also loved beer. He would run many miles to earn beer points. Jack also knew how to find the cheapest beer in any port. It could be a horse corral with straw on the floor but if it was the cheapest beer then that's where Jack would be. Jack once told Pete and me why he reenlisted for the first time. He was in the Vietnam theater of operations and by reenlisting he would get $10,000 tax free. That was a huge sum back in the seventies. Actually it still is, but Jack looked at this amount from the perspective of beer. At that time you could get a draft beer in Subic Bay Philippines for the cost of 25 cents. Jack did the math and figured he would get forty thousand beers for his reenlistment. There we were in St Thomas Virgin Islands, close to thirty years later at Jack's final liberty port where he let us know that he drank all forty thousand of those beers over time. We all believed him, of that; we harbored no doubt.

Whatever Jack wasn't, more importantly there were things he was. Jack was a great admin guy. He got things done. He would take on the really unpopular programs and get them working correctly. One of these pains in the rear programs was the food service attendants or FSAs. Jack was the one who ensured people in the proper numbers were sent to the mess decks in an orderly and fair manner. Because Jack kept a tight track on the program no one argued with him and they cooperated. Jack tracked the quality of the crew's training very closely and he had an excellent grasp of all those programs that had to be completed in accordance with a strict timeline. He was highly involved in the areas in which others tried to avoid, and that is why he was totally effective. He was great at straightening up convoluted messes. In short, Jack earned every one of those forty thousand beers.

In the chief's mess we had certain favorite movie tapes we would put on the VCR at lunch times or in the early evenings. On the YELLOWSTONE we had paid homage and yielded to the *Terminator* and on the YORKTOWN our heroic chiefs' epic was *Road House.* In the same manner that *You've Lost That Lovin' Feeling* was our CPO theme song, *Road House* was our movie of choice. We loved every part of that flick and after Hank left we made a movie and sent it to him at his house in Virginia Beach. It was a tape of all of the chiefs doing *Road House* things and saying *Road House* phrases. We saw that movie so many times that we could just shut off the sound and mimic the dialogue unfettered and with uncanny accuracy. In our film for Hank we assumed the roles of underway *Road House* thespians, stitching fake wounds covered in ketchup and shit like that.

The YORKTOWN left for a summer Med this time. Iris and the kids were once again left to fend for themselves. This time she had had a power of attorney. We actually sold our town house and found an agent and a builder to construct for us a new home. Everything was progressing without a hitch. We rented a town house off of one of our good guy Lieutenants, Bill Nault. He was heading off to graduate school and we were going to vacuum in to his place while ours was under construction. Iris and the kids would move into the new home before school started in September. What a great plan. Everything fit perfect. The Naults had to go so we would be paying them rent while they were gone. Their home was conveniently located in a nice neighborhood. Our realtor, Ms. Dee Maltese was motivated and genuinely worked in our best interest. The entire process appeared slam dunk simple.

Andrew loved the Nault's townhouse. It was located adjacent to the number one fairway of the Kempsville Greens Golf Course. Every day he was delighted to receive a fresh new collection of golf balls in the tiny back yard. The draw back was the dented siding of the townhouses lining the fairways. I suppose the planners of this community thought all the patrons would just shoot their tee shots straight down the fairways. Little did they know or perhaps they forgot to factor in that within every foursome was a potential duffer just like me, waiting to unload a slicing missile into the inviting townhouses. The people of *Kempsville Greens* knew bombardment. They lived it every day, victims of friendly fire. I'm surprised that the crime rate wasn't much higher there. I would have guessed that the bunkered residents would have psychologically suffered and that the accompanying stress would have manifested in ill behaviors. But just as Hitler underestimated the resolve of the English in the *Battle of Britain*, so too did the errant golfers underestimate the resolve of the fairway residents who were continuously victimized by the careening *Titelists* of *Kempsville Greens*. Iris, Andrew, and Kelly found themselves in a battle zone and I was off to a summer Med where I would help the ship struggle through port visit after port visit, exhausting myself on demanding tours, fighting off the caloric influences of vast quantities of European dining delights, and full bodied beers. It was hard, but somebody had to do it.

In CCS under Cheng John Sims we continued our cappuccino machine maintenance but we discontinued our Samurai watch team antics. Instead we adapted a new style. Along with Chris Head, the Michigan madman and a damage controlman Harley rider named Bill we became the *Louds.* This was fun and extremely simple. We just made all of our verbal reports as loud as possible.

This humorous communication methodology spread to the chief's mess where the mess became bicameral and divided. We developed into the *Shoppers* and the *Louds.* Jack, our CMC was naturally loud so he required no adaptation. We added four or five new young chiefs to the mess from the previous September initiation and they were full of life and brought renewed energy. Mark, the good natured missile tech, Jeff Montgomery, the workaholic ship's serviceman, the reliable and trustworthy EWC Dave Jenkins, and a young fire controlman we nicknamed *McFly,* who was an absolute hoot to hang with. These guys were all fully vested *Louds.*

The *Shoppers* were those chiefs who spent their import time at various bizarres and flea markets looking for good deals on stuff. The *Louds* would go out usually in groups of ten to twenty. The two groups were not antagonistic to each other at all. *Shoppers* would often cross over and do a temporary outing with the *Louds.* Only rarely did the *Louds* cross over to a serious shopping trek. Bargains had to be found and that usually meant covering a lot of ground. There was little time for beer, food, or relaxation. Time was of the essence as the *Shoppers* rarely stayed out past dusk.

Pete and I maintained our running habit through the entire Med. Jack, the ship's most accomplished runner went with us and together we logged some serious mileage on that cruise. Jack beeped his way all over the Mediterranean and Black Sea. We probably ran at least a thousand miles through Italy, Israel, Spain, France, Greece, Croatia, Turkey, Romania, and Bulgaria.

It was in Marseille France in the summer of 1991 when I commenced my boycott of France. I was already unhappy with the French because of our car Christine and I was reminded of that association by the burn scars on my ankles. In the city we had discovered a nice little hole in the wall called *LeBox* where the owner and his wife spoke English and played nonstop *Beatle music.* This was a very amiable place and it became the impromptu CPO club for the week we were there. The Heinekens were reasonably priced so it was a comfortable hang out.

One day four of us decided to get adventurous so we headed out to the beach area of Marseille. Sitting there on the French coast soaking in the sunshine was a very pleasant experience at the little outdoor café where we had parked ourselves. It took a while to place our drink order from the supercilious waiter and I clearly remember the order, two six ounce bottles of Coke and two draft beers. It was an outdoor table, no dancing girls, no headlining entertainers. I'm not sure if we even had an umbrella. The total tab for this particular French experience was the French Franc equivalent of 56 dollars in US greenbacks. I love *Bill O'Reilly*, and I supported his gesture to boycott France in 2005, but I started a personal boycott in 1991. It was never my intention to pay off their national debt at the café on that day. So began a personal boycott that continues to the present. Their establishments are way to rich for my blood. They truly fail to realize that *Pittsburgh* is the *Center of the Universe*, not Paris or Marseille. Fifty -six dollars in Pittsburgh would get you into *Kennywood Park* for a day with enough left over for a *Wendy's Number Six*. Now that's a place to put on a pedestal.

Our latest division officer was a tough Texas kid named Kevin something. E Division ran through division officers. We had more idealistic young leaders pass through our shops than there were state police cars on the Pennsylvania Turnpike. These junior officers in order to receive a wide scope of training would often get switched to new jobs fairly often in order to understand the big picture of how a ship coordinated its efforts in the various departments.

One of the YORKTOWN specialties was our decorative up and over lights. We always took this process one step further and that was not only to go up and over, but to go all the way around the exterior of the main deck. Rigging lights was a process and Beno and IC1 Warren West nailed it down to about a two hour installation process through practice. They were good and they made a big job as easy as possible. Often during the course of a port visit, sections would have to be dropped and reinstalled if radar required maintenance or if some similar action was required. At best it was a tedious and time consuming process. Each day the strings also had to be checked for burn outs and replacement bulbs installed.

The captain for evening colors insisted that all light strings energize simultaneously. This was a project in and of itself because all those light strings were controlled by different breakers in some remotely located lighting panels. The method we employed to solve this was through the use of *wifcom radios*. Wifcoms were the damage control portable radios that worked in the interior of the ship. We would station senior members of each duty section at the appropriate lighting control panel. When the key controlling person gave the word, usually at the evening colors whistle, all the breakers would switch on in unison and the ship would glow like Vegas on a clear summer night. It wasn't a good thing for a duty section to misjudge their timing when energizing those lights. Our division officer Kevin from a hilltop hotel in Haifa once had to explain why the ship in the harbor below failed to energize its forward most light string on cue. Kevin resigned shortly thereafter. It was too bad, I liked that guy and I thought he had great potential.

We had a serious switchboard fire on that cruise. Our number two main electrical switchboard had erupted into a smoking Class C fire in the main engineroom. Our watch team isolated the board and managed to restore power via alternative means, but regardless, serious damage had occurred. I bring this up because the stalwart Beno Miller shined brightly in effecting repairs to this casualty. Although this was not the actions of a hero in battle or courage under fire, it was the type of selfless accomplishment that routinely made the YORKTOWN great. Beno Miller was one of the most uncomplaining and nose to the grindstone types I had ever seen. It took quite a while but the valorous Beno Miller beat the odds and restored the board to full operation. He was definitely chief's material.

Another hard working electrician we had along on the cruise was a young West Virginia kid named Vest. Michael Vest had developed a hard worker reputation before we left for the Med. He was the *Kowalski of Voyage to the Bottom of the Sea.* Tenaciously energetic, he was everywhere and could fix everything. I believed Vest could nail *Jello to the wall* if the need arose. He was quite a bit older than he looked, which isn't saying much considering he looked to be about twelve. I helped him out one time with some wheels. He went to the parking lot on base and found his well maintained car sitting on its wheel cylinders. Some friendly neighbor on one of the other ships had decided that Vest's expensive rims were just what he needed for his car. So this wonderful character helped himself to the objects of his desire.

We took care of the immediate problem by picking up some cheap tires and wheels so Vest could get his ride going. Within a few weeks lo and behold, a blessing- as luck would have it, Vest spotted his *one of a kind rim*s on that *sticky fingered purloiner's* car, proudly displayed for admiration and vanity purposes. A quick phone call to the youth's command master chief made life very good for Vest. His rims looked perfect back on his car. For young *Sticky Fingers*, life was about to become a real challenge with the commencement of his payback time and restricted status. It was indeed gratifying to have justice prevail and needless to say a smile crosses my face just to reminisce about the justice exacted from so many years ago against the profligate swine. Universally there is nothing more debauched to a Sailor than a thief. Stealing from a fellow shipmate is the ultimate evil act and to catch one is the ultimate coup d'etat.

The veritable ship YORKTOWN continued on, receiving accolades of *Best Evers* wherever we went and whatever we tried. Jack was still beeping all over the Med., running like the European version of *Gump.* Vest was fixing stuff at the speed of the *Roadrunner.* All that was missing was the signature *Beep Beep.* The chiefs were doing karaoke across the Med and becoming self described legends. We nearly won the singing contest in Rhoades Greece with Cedric leading the way on *You've Lost That Lovn' Feeling.* The *Shoppers* were shopping, and the *Louds* were, well… they were loud. This was a good deployment and analogous to all of the years I was on the YORKTOWN a very good time. A lot of work to be managed, but a fun ship all the same.

We were in another port and waiting for a late liberty boat at an unremembered place on the pier. There were probably twenty people there. A certain engineman chief had a unique gift. He had a bladder that could hold the Dead Sea. Come to think of it this incident may well have occurred in Israel. At the end of the evening the Dead Sea finally required draining. Moving off into the shadows so as to achieve a minimal portion of privacy our *Amstel* laden holding tank engineman began to pump bilges. A moment later due to his somewhat elevated position a many fingered stream of surprising volume deluged the weary liberty party. The accompanying screams as they were washed upon by the unsolicited sulfur like nastiness created a chaotic scene as many panic stricken Sailors scrambled to safety and higher ground. We all knew who did it. There could be only one.

On the home front I received communication that everything that could possibly go wrong with our well laid plans had, in fact gone wrong. The house was not going to be finished on time, the builder was delayed indefinitely. The Nault house was being sold and Iris and the kids had to skedaddle. My family was forced into nomadic gypsy status. Iris was tough though. She siced a lawyer on the evasive and excuse laden builder. Meanwhile she met some good friends, Christina and Andy Eccheviria; two staunch and trustworthy people who became friends for life. Andy of Military Sealift cargo master fame and his wife Christina who watched Kelly at day care insisted that they stay with them. So at least shelter was granted to the nomadic trio.

The builder, after the lawyer's formal urging finally got with the program, overcame his inertia, and gave Iris a choice lot in a more upscale neighborhood. The house was built and when I got home that late fall after a hard summer of Mediterranean port visits our beautiful new house was a home, along with a little instant equity.

Spouses have it so easy when their Sailors go off to protect their country. Nothing to do except move three times, supervise a house being built, enroll kids in schools in an area yet to be moved into, place all personal effects in storage, get a lawyer to pressure your home builder to produce the product as promised, then close on the house, move in, and put everything in its proper place. I was really upset that the *Heroic Iris* didn't manage to get the lawn going by the time I got back. I am just kidding of course. She was a pillar of strength and proved herself the wrong person to ignore.

We received a new XO for that cruise and Commander Vitale often got out there and did the main deck loop with us. I never set it up, but he was fast and I think he would have dusted Jack. Maybe not distance, but speed wise the XO was rather quick. Years later when I saw him on TV as an admiral flipping the coin for the NFL Pro Bowl I was hoping he would race some of those football All Stars across the field I wished to see if he still had the speed in him.

That was a very good trait about the YORKTOWN, somebody up there in people land just kept sending us very good ones. The YORKTOWN always had a cast of talented workers. Eccentric, outlandish, weird, physical deformities rampant, absolutely; but from top to bottom it was always a great crew and it never seemed to have that rise and fall that some ships have in their crew talent levels.

When the ship was in the Black Sea, the port of Constanta Romania was very new to the concept of freedom. They were very poor, their inflation was just crazy, about a hundred bucks to a shoebox full, and thus there were multitudes of destitute people roaming the streets. The country had recently dumped a real tyrant who made Adolph Hitler look like an Eagle Scout, so they were just getting started at many levels. They were great people for sure, but their dexterous pick pockets were quite remarkable. Jack had a touch of frugality in him. There was a reason he could find the cheapest beer. We were trying to exchange some money in the lobby of a reputable hotel. Although we were warned about the deftness of the local pick pockets, Jack decided to let a guy there exchange a few dollars for a stack of their stuff. The guy swapped out the greenbacks and exchanged them with blank pieces of paper in a nanosecond. He was then gone, disappeared without leaving even the slightest vapor trail. It was worth Jack's five dollar loss. Not to Jack, but to us. That guy was the *Houdini of Romania* and we were all entertained off of Jack's five bucks. But in Romania that was five beers and Jack wasn't real happy. But I have to give it up to that Romanian. He was quick.

One of the best kept secrets in the Mediterranean is the country of Turkey. Compared to most of Europe it is not as expensive. The food is excellent in their restaurants. The shoppers can do some serious power buying there. Their rugs, gold, and leather are very high quality, and it is almost impossible not to find a good bargain on something. I think everyone on the ship bought something in Antalya. The Turks themselves were very hospitable. The only demand they had was that you respect the national symbol of their great leader Attaturk. From what I have been told, Attaturk is like George Washington, Abe Lincoln, and Teddy Roosevelt all combined into one transcendent hero. His memory holds the most reverent of power. It was rumored to us that a few Sailors disrespected a statue to the great Turkish leader and they nearly paid with their lives. The moral of this story is quite simple. Respect Turkish national symbols. If you do that, the people love you.

In the down town area the Louds ran into a very small but hospitable man who spoke accented but decent English. He was so genuinely friendly that we immediately adopted him. He informed us that he made his living bringing English speaking customers to certain stores and by teaching English to his fellow citizens. Where he learned the language I had no idea. Without thinking about it McFly christened him as the Professor. The Professor loved his name and we quickly encompassed him into our inner circle. He escorted us to stores that actually did have high quality products and reasonable prices. At the time we supposed he would expect a tip for showing us around and we could understand that. He was a great tour guide. We had the Professor meet up with us on a second day and we all chanced adventure taking off to a coastal city which was picturesque and boasted better prices than any other comparable resort we visited in the entire Med. The Professor in a heartfelt moment confessed to us that he admired his American Sailor friends because we knew how to *"live our lives."* Coming from him in his genuine manner of speaking it sounded extremely wise and profound.

The Professor rounded us up and got us back to Antalya after a day of touring the town, beaches, and sight seeing with no problems. When we made an attempt to pay him he refused to accept a dime. He told us that with the YORKTOWN chiefs he had the best time of his entire life and he could not take payment for that. It was a rather teary eyed goodbye to the Professor. He was a great little man with an inimitable soul and I am unerringly certain that all the Louds who attended that excursion remember the Professor well.

We returned to America near Christmas. As always, the welcome home was the *best ever.* The YORKTOWN would have kid's Christmas parties, and even those were *the best ever.* The kids always received very nice stuff. No cheap breakable toys for YORKTOWN kids, we're talking *Barbies* and *Tonka*s; the YORKTOWN had class in all events foreign or domestic.

At some point in time after that second Med cruise in the spring of 1992 we prepared like crazy for the upcoming change of command on the YORKTOWN. Our captain had us clean up the cleanest ship in the Navy to a new standard of cleanliness that had never before been achieved in the world history of clean things. The YORKTOWN was in Norfolk where it rains frequently, particularly in the spring and our senior chief boatswain mate was getting a little perturbed with painting in the rain. The Louds made a catchy song out of that to the old tune *Singing in the Rain,* calling it *Painting in the Rain.* The creativity put into that song failed to make the senior chief feel any better though, and the Louds conservatively pulled the plug on that particular ditty.

In preparation for the change of command the YORKTOWN began to make the ships around us look comparatively ragged. We removed all traces of running rust. We smoothed out all unnecessary blemishes that could cause rust. Mounting brackets with rust were cut off like a laser treatment for unwanted zits and replacements were welded into place with new brackets of freshly manufactured steel. The work on the skin of the ship was like providing a giant *Terminator* with a metal facelift. Our captain in his quest for perfection in the appearance of the ship had created a vessel that despite a majority of its life at sea actually looked better than it did on its commissioning day. If I had to place that captain in a retirement occupation after his naval career, I would have made him a museum curator; his attention to detail was that amazing and his love for the symmetrical beauty of the YORKTOWN knew no limitations.

The day of the YORKTOWN change of command finally came. We would pay respects to the departing CO and the new captain would say a few remarks. To the Chiefs we were just happy to be in port. Personally, I was in a non stop state of euphoria. At seventeen years I had finally achieved the star of a senior chief on the YORKTOWN. It was a long time coming and I would forever be grateful to this great ship. Advancement lists are powerful things that cause both great jubilation and severe heartache. I had been through many depression cycles and finally I felt the gratification. Having waited a significant length of time for this promotion I am quite sympathetic to those who do not advance. If a feeling of depression is all encompassing then realize worthy shipmates that it is wholly justified. Too often mental health experts think we have to be in a constant state of happiness and it just ain't so. I have even been told that doctors now prescribe under new technology a rectal medication to improve on symptoms of depression. That's just wrong. Being pissed off for not being selected for advancement is a totally appropriate feeling. *A happy pill in your ass* ain't the way to go.

When the change of command ceremony started the old captain came out and thanked the crew, the Navy band played, and the ship looked spectacular. It was fully dressed with red white and blue bunting around the main deck. The up and over flags were flying proudly in the breeze. The new captain's family arrived in suits at the beginning of the ceremony. Encompassed in the new captain's entourage were a number of very suave and cool looking people in sun glasses. I had heard the new skipper was from California. The folks he brought had the California flair.

When the new captain stepped up to the podium I was about ready to stand easy as I attempted to stifle a yawn. Then this new guy started speaking and I could not resist listening. Great speakers come around very rarely. I loved listening to anything Ronald *Maximus* Reagan had to say. Here I was on the flight deck of the YORKTOWN and I was getting the same feeling. I can't recant exactly what Captain Mike Mullen said that day, but listening to this mesmerizing man got me very excited about being on the YORKTOWN. And I was a person who had already been here for close to three years. There was clear invigorating energy he brought in that very first day. He had a commanding presence and a way of communicating that made us all feel as if he were speaking directly to each of us. Maybe it's a California gift but Mike Mullen is in my humble opinion *Reaganesque.*

Just as IC1 Don W. Keesey was the most influential petty officer I ever worked for. Captain Mike Mullen was the most motivating leader I ever knew. On that very first day in that very first speech you knew you didn't just have a job. The cliché was back. The YORKTOWN Navy was an adventure once again. There was a genuine feeling that we were destined to do great things in the months ahead. This charismatic captain laid it all out in that first address to the crew and his guests. We were going to make turns on four engines with both shafts at full pitch. In harm's way would be the YORKTOWN way.

As Captain Mullen arrived Jack departed off into the civilian world. After forty thousand beers Jack still had more energy than a plutonium bomb and he could run a marathon for fun. He was going to do just fine.

Jack's departure ushered in Curt Cook as our new CMC and Curt was more of your standard command master chief. He had a tall commanding presence. He had an aura that said when I talk you listen. He had the Massachusetts accent going for him and that added to his nautical persona. I must say that Curt was a natural leader. Above all, I always felt that Curt was looking out for the crew and that included the chief's mess. When you combined Captain Mullen with Curt Cook you couldn't get a better one two punch than that.

Shortly after taking over the reins the captain was traveling up the pier early one drizzling morning. There was the bos'n supervising a crew doing some paint work over the sides. Puzzled the captain asked "*Senior what's going on*? " The Bos'n said " *Painting Sir*." "*In the rain*?" "*Yes Sir, we paint in the rain here*." "*Not any more you don't*." We liked the changes we were seeing.

Soon the ship was tasked with a trip to points south. It may have been for a gun shoot or law enforcement operations. Those memories seem to weave together over time, probably attributable to a natural decay process of brain matter on my part. We did in fact enter St Thomas for a port visit. The day before arrival Captain Mullen was in the chief's mess for lunch; invited often because he was a magnetic person and people had a natural inclination to be around him. The subject of crew's liberty came up after lunch when it was normal for the captain to question the chiefs. In the past whenever we pulled into a port there were strict times that crew members had to return aboard. It was always curfew by pay grade. The captain looked at us and said "*If they have liberty, then they have liberty until they have to be back to work*." He believed the crew should be given adult status. He didn't see it any other way. We on the other hand were very amazed. This was different.

Captain Mullen was one who encouraged ideas for improvement. When someone had a good idea he was listened to. Having your ideas heard and knowing you had access was a very big morale booster. I knew that that not knowing the personal history and any of the problems that a subordinate had going on was a huge negative with Mike Mullen. You were expected to know your people, and this went far beyond technician abilities.

When he spoke to a chief you knew he valued what you had to say. Captain Mullen was an involved leader. I saw him in that very first port we were in; there in St Thomas leading a procession of junior officers around.

It looked like Plato and his disciples. He was the leader, dynamic, instructive, never aloof. You always felt like a family member with the captain. You never felt like a tool in the kit, only there to serve a defined purpose.

Underway the crew would be out on deck in the late afternoon doing some PT and there he was, running around with the rest of us. We had captain's calls routinely and he would often explain to us what was going on in the big picture. Captain Mullen took over the 1MC, and when he had news to offer he never made us wait. The crew wasn't left to drum up rumors or to do much sea speculating. The YORKTOWN crew was well informed. If perhaps I sound like some type of Mike Mullen groupie it is only because I am in fact a true Mullen partisan. Fortunately the Navy got it right when he became the Chief of Naval Operations, and fortunately the military got it right when he became the Chairman of the Joint Chiefs. Admiral Mullen has been great for the military and I do care to opine that he truly is a great American.

Upon return to Norfolk I had to negotiate orders. My three years of sea duty had encompassed a great deal of the Earth's surface, and I was looking forward to having a job at home for awhile. On the flip side, the YORKTOWN was a great ship and being a part of that crew was memorable. I had met an unforgettable cast of characters on that ship. They were good people, the best. Were they normal, hell no!! They were in all likelihood hand selected from cities and towns around the world. Only the goofiest and most eccentric need apply. If they had a weird habit, an absurd superstition, or a third eyeball then they would fit in with us. Normal people, could not continue on as we had and still remain, *best ever*.

My final cruise on YORKTOWN was memorable. It was possibly a reward because our captain was great, our ship was *Smithsonian clean*, and we maintained a track record of *best evers* in all inspections and assist visits. We were going to Russia. We were departing on a goodwill mission to hold a Fourth of July picnic right in the town square of the Russian Northern Fleet at Severmorsk.

The YORKTOWN would be traveling far north of the Arctic Circle. We had scheduled port visits in Kiel Germany, Stockholm Sweden, Norway, and on to Severmorsk Russia. On the return we would visit Edinburgh Scotland for a few days. This cruise was a jewel of an itinerary and we hastened to make turns from Norfolk quickly because every other ship on the waterfront was turning green with barnacles, fertilized with pure envy.

There was a tremendous amount of planning incorporated into this adventure. We were going to have major press and *Great Watubahs* everywhere on the ship during the Russian visit. I had a brand spanking new ensign to play with, … err I mean train. I had been spoiled because for the several previous months our division officer was an LDO named Lefty Lefebvre, who as a former chief IC man obviously didn't need training at all. E division was usually a place for a youngster to go learn the ropes of being a division officer. It was an excellent starting place because although you maintained a vast amount of equipment, you didn't have a lot of people to deal with. Lefty was soon shifted to the main propulsion assistant, or MPA, and that was always a much more prestigious and demanding position for an officer on a cruiser. I inherited the brand new ensign.

My guy was a typical new ensign. He was fresh out of the University of Notre Dame and the *Fighting Irishman* was straining at the bit to conquer the world. He had mass quantities of book learning and the energy level of a rat on mega doses of L-Carnitine, and ALPHA Lipoic Acid. He was out to achieve the rank of captain by his 23rd birthday.

He was one of those very intelligent high energy ensigns who only needed to absorb everything with a little more patience. We needed a portable generator for the deployment. I was on a few days leave and while I was gone the ensign had tried everywhere to find one. When I returned he was in a panic over the generator issue, his sweat pumps in full bore. I didn't say anything, I just called a Seabee buddy of mine and he gave me a loaner for the trip. I loved the expression on the ensign's face when I drove up the pier towing that generator behind the duty vehicle. He was going to be just fine. Truthfully, I have always secretly admired the raw intelligence of junior officers aboard ship. They go through a serious learning curve from the time they hit the deck plates of their first ship until they depart for department head school or to a master's program if they are fortunate. While on their first tour they must qualify on engineering watches, CIC watches, underway bridge watches as OOD, plus they have to know all the answers to what's going on in their divisions. In addition, they get a tremendous number of collateral duties that may include anything from voting officer, to a religious lay officer, to morale welfare and recreation officer, or public affairs officer. They are never given a choice about these. The XO just lets them have it. Their immediate boss, the department head also lays it on them pretty heavy. The non empathetic department head usually harbors little sympathy for their young charges for they have walked in those shoes. I believe they want to see who rises to the top and the ones who do end up being pretty good officers. They are the ones who listen and learn. Their world is not for the weak or timid even if they can afford a nice car at a rather young age.

I had been through a score of these folks by this point in my career. And it was always a good feeling to see your guy get his surface warfare officer or SWO pin as he moves up the ladder of success. Chiefs are teachers above all else and young officers are often your star pupils. Often a junior officer, most often referred to as a JO is so smart that he can memorize the operating process of the steering gear unit after reading a propulsion plant manual. He can often draw you the waste heat boiler steam cycle after staring at the print for an hour. Trust me; at that point they still don't know *shit!* The first time they sit in as an engineering officer of the watch under instruction and do their very first basic engineering casualty control exercise they find that out. Once they gain a little humility they are then qualified to learn something. After that, they are fine. The ship's XO usually works their training plan in such a manner that they are in a constant state of tired, or at least they consistently make that claim. I theorize that the XOs and department heads keep them so busy that they are unable to do any serious damage. After a few years of this they are apt to hatch from their cocoons and go from squiggly wiggly irritants to competent lieutenants that everyone respects and looks up to. After that they sell their Z3s, get married, and purchase big Volvo station wagons.

Chiefs are vastly different characters. They usually stick with their pickup trucks. It's the whole macho thing. The bigger the truck, the better they like it. Chief's parking often gets a label such as *Redneck Row or Damnation Alley.* After all we are the people who thought *Road House* should have won the *Academy Award* for *Best Picture of the Year*.

Tim Slaegle our outstanding master at arms and shipmate of highest regard had moved on to the rank of chief warrant officer. His first duty assignment was as the sheriff of the large Second Fleet flag ship MOUNT WHITNEY, stationed with us at the Norfolk piers. One day upon returning from sea we tied up directly across the pier from MOUNT WHITNEY. One of our IC men dragged the phone cable down on our side of the pier where he discovered that some rogue ship had utilized all the terminals for the telephone connections. Now the MOUNT WHITNEY as one might suspect had a large staff of *Super Novas* who all required their own phones. Consequently, they were assigned extra lines which passed under the pier and tied in on the opposite side where we were. When our guy disconnected the Second Fleet from the pier he was not happy with us as you may well suspect. I am not sure if our IC man cut him off from the Chief of Naval Operations or not, but personally, even if he was cut off from *Domino's Pizza* it was neither a good move nor a happy moment when the ensuing poop storm arrived.

On the plus side I found out from Tim that the XO on the Mount Whitney wanted to see me, that he was an old friend. How could I refuse that? Once aboard there he was. A couple of pounds heavier with a very slight touch of gray, but the personality was 100 per cent in tact. Commander Spencer and I reminisced for awhile about the good old days on the LAWRENCE. We patted each other on the back, extolling the virtues of being hard working Adam's class Sailors. He asked me if I ever told anyone about him bailing me out of jail for the weapons inspection. My reply; "*Hell no Sir*!" I then countered and asked him if he ever told anyone about the sound powered phone generator fire. His immediate reply; "*Fuck no, are you Crazy?*!" After twenty years it took ten minutes to get back to where we left off. Commander Spencer was a great man, a true Sailor.

We acquired an awesome character as a transfer Sailor from another country. Max was a senior chief quartermaster from the German submarine force. He was assigned as a regular YORKTOWN crew member for a few years as part of the personnel exchange program or PEP. By our standards he was young for a senior chief, but Max had a great sense of humor and he was eccentric enough to be very interesting. The bridge personnel said that he really knew his business as a quartermaster. Max was a perfect fit in our chief's mess and he was undeniably a Loud. The Louds were now international in our entourage and when Max referred to the Louds he stated it in a distinct European pronunciation that actually made the term sound swank and fashionable. Being a Loud was now rather cool. We immediately affixed the name *Mad Max* to our Deutsch ally, and in accordance with all nicknames on YORKTOWN he bore it for the duration.

When we departed Norfolk we made a bee-line for Kiel Germany. In my mind this was my final trip on the YORKTOWN. I also thought it would be the last sea period of my career. I planned on enjoying this final chapter of my YORKTOWN tour. Prior to entering a new port it is customary for a JO to give a CCTV port brief to the crew about what there is to do for activities and tours. This is also where you are informed about off limits areas or unique customs different from our own. A little history of the region was often included. Because Max was certainly a German; and from Kiel; the port brief was naturally passed on to him. To assist Max we put a little spin on it for entertainment value. I thought that doing it with my help would help put him at ease. Could you imagine having to go on television and give a spiel to a bunch of people in their language? That would be an antacid moment for anyone. I put on Max's uniform and he put on mine. I of course was Max, and Max of course was me. He became an interviewer and I was the interviewer's subject. Max would ask me a question in German. I would answer in senseless German words and he would give me credit for my answers in English to the crew. I had no idea what I was actually saying. I knew some German words and would say them as if I knew what I was talking about and as if they were actually answering

Max's question. Max, posing as me, would then interpret my German over the TV in English as if he was translating for me, Max the German. Of course at that point he gave proper and accurate information. Max pulled it off well. He was after all, a *German Loud.*

At the Naval base in Kiel where we tied up, we observed that the Sailors lived in pier side apartments. They were happy and satisfied with their Navy. They had a pristine conditioned Adam's class called the LUETGENS and I spoke with a few of their machinists mates, one of whom had been a LUETGENS crew member for eight years. I would wager that German hole snipe could fix anything in that engineroom. He probably said *"Guten morgen"* every day to all the pumps, valves and turbines he had known so well and for so long.

The city of Kiel was clean, German clean. Those people must have a *Hazel fetish* or something and I am sure that *Martha Stewart* books sell well there. Kiel was pleasant organized, and modern. Many residents of forty and older looked very physically fit. They were obviously doing their fair share of aerobic exercise, because their beer, although fantastic, was doubtfully low calorie. The Louds had their share of that beer. Germany and beer are justifiably linked and the Louds were there to discover this first hand. The German beer was granted the *Louds Seal of Approval* and major discussions did take place about which beers were the best. Pete said nothing; he just punctuated the final arguments with a belch. That was the *Pete seal of approval.* Pete was easy though, he approved of both kinds of beer, cold and warm.

The ship departed the pristine port of Kiel and headed to Stockholm Sweden. When God made the world he called it *Pittsburgh and the Surrounding Area.* Stockholm was definitely an honorable mention though. This was a beautiful city, and regardless of the high prices and cool weather, a highly recommended destination for all who reside on the good planet Earth.

We dropped anchor in Stockholm at the same time the European soccer championships were going on in full force there in the city. Sweden was in the semis along with the powerful German team and a few other countries. The Brits had just been sent home packing prior to our arrival and although the remaining fans were rowdy, the over the top Brits had departed in defeat. We found our way to the to the soccer tents in search of cheap beer, but the crowd was weird and bizarre, even for the Louds. Walking around the soccer tents I felt as if I were cast in a follow-up episode of *Mad Max the Road Warrior,* not that our Mad Max favored Mel Gibson but the environment there seemed eerily similar.

This was where Max came in very handy. As a quartermaster he knew how to navigate. I was glad that particular skill extended to the urban navigation of European cities. Max knew this city and he was very comfortable with the subways and getting us to the places where the locals frequented, and not the expensive tourist traps. The Swedes spoke English better than many of us do as Americans so language there is never an issue. They were in a festive mood nation wide as we viewed the soccer championships for a few nights leading up to the finals when the powerful Germans went at it against the underdog Swedes.

The Swedes were absolutely nuts over their team's performance. Max, to his credit kept his pro German team feelings under wraps. He was elated at times during the final though, and I caught him a few times applauding under the table in muzzled joy. He was being politically correct in our host nation's environment, and besides, Swedes are big people and irritating them, particularly on their home turf could prove unwise. One of the teams won as you would expect. I can't remember who though, if that gives you an idea about my level of interest in the contest. I do recall a German player taking a hard kick in the crotch though, and since that day I've forever granted soccer the status of a tough guy sport.

One night I had duty and I knew Pete was out with his division. A small contingency of Sailors missed the last liberty boat and unfortunately they had to wait it out on the beach. When I viewed the shore from a distance that cool late June evening I spotted a camp fire and I knew Pete was there. Firewood was probably not available but rumor had it that a significant portion of a nearby civilian's fence was missing. Pete didn't like to be cold.

Our main focus was centered in the preparations for our historic port visit to Severmorsk. We would cross the Arctic Circle in route, but the captain elected to do the *Blue Nose Ceremony* on the return journey because of the number of embarked personnel and the preparations taking place on the front end of the trip.

There were a number of planned events. We would spend the entire visit in Dress Blue uniforms because of the formal and historic nature of the visit. Besides, most of us wore T shirts and jeans as civilian attire and I don't think our government wanted an ambassador of goodwill running amuck with a T Shirt advertising the benefits of *Jack Daniels Whiskey* or a message spelling out *PSYCHO WARD*.

Captain Mullen came on the 1MC shortly before our arrival and presented the game plan. I absolutely admired the direct way he informed the crew about what was going to occur and how we fit in with the overall mission. This was leadership at its best and with everyone knowing their role we were about to put an exclamation point on the phrase *"The end of the Cold War!"* The captain recommended that we record in writing the entire experience of the port visit. He understood the significance of what was to occur and he knew it was history in the making.

We had gained some insight into what the communist lifestyle was like the year before in Romania. The government store concept lingered in my memory. It was a place where all the clothes were cheap, yet ugly, where quantity trumped quality. Communism leads to low quality and complacency. If you want good products and good service you must have competition. Karl Marx was out to lunch on his theory. It didn't work for the seventy years the Bolsheviks were in power and it never will work. I will never fathom why people just don't understand that. U S Sailors always knew this, but seeing it first hand in Severmorsk really brought it up close and personal. What a week that was, the first week of July 1992. I did write that letter as the captain recommended, and I sent it home to Iris and she always kept it. It is now many years old, but here it is, the way I saw it then.

July 1st 1992

We were all manning the rail outside as we pulled in to Severmorsk. It was very cold and windy and I remember wishing I had on a pea coat. We entered the harbor and there it was; the whole northern Fleet of Russia, just sitting there. They got us tied to the pier and they had their band out there playing away. There were people out at the gate looking in; standing there on the hillsides in the cold, gazing down at us. The ships looked impressive sitting there, but we weren't viewing them up close. They were large and had a lot of weapons on them. The buildings, on the other hand looked like slums out of a third world country. It looked at first glance as if all the money went to the military and not too much for these people's lives.

They had a ceremony on the pier; honor guards, etc. Our Ambassador to Russia, Robert Strauss came aboard along with bunches of other "Big Shots." Finally, after freezing for 2 ? hours they let us secure from manning the rails. Pete, Rob Volpe, Mad Max, our PEP Program German, and I left the ship that afternoon. We walked through the gate but there weren't a lot of people. The ones we saw just looked at us and we just looked at them, and it was as if neither of us could believe the other was here. It was cold, like one of those windy January days in Norfolk. It was going to turn out to be one of the warmest days we ever had.

We walked through the gate where they had a huge statue there of a Sailor with a rifle. I think it was called the Defender of the North. It was a huge thing. There was a Russian Officer standing there and he asked us in very bad English if we wanted to go to his house. We went. His name was Vladimir. We got to his house, and he broke out the vodka, cognac, and tried for awhile to pump us with alcohol. We found out over the next few days that drinking is the national past time here. Well, we were there sitting in that room with this Russian Naval Officer and a civilian guy entered. The apartment was very small, but much nicer than I expected. He also had a nice TV and VCR. It was a FISHER. I know they are pretty good. Anyway, this civilian guy shows up and then we find out why we're here. This guy wants to sell us a bunch of stuff we don't want to buy. So we tell Vlad we gotta go. He is very insistent that we go with him. We get into his car and go to JACK Rabbit Storage, or their version. There were hundreds of painted sheds that fronted along this dirt road with big ditches. Oh, previously while we were at this guy's house, at one point he reaches in his pocket and pulls out a wad of cash about 6 inches high. It was all 1000 ruble bills. I know these people don't have money so an alarm says; OK this guy is into the Black market. Anyway, when he drove us to the shed, a four striper (they wear their uniforms most of the time) pulls out a can of gasoline and fills up the car. I figure this guy must be someone special, just because he has a car to begin with. We find out that the four stripes with the gas can is one of the COs of one of their frigates. I'm just guessing, but I think this guy Vlad is the XO. After we leave the guy drops us off at the submarine museum and tells us he'll be back. Before he dropped us off we have to stop at another place, which is different from the first house. I believe this is his actual home. There we meet his wife and say hello. There on his shelf is a ball cap that says USS KLAKRING FF something. So we now know that he was a part of the visit to Jacksonville Florida that they made. At the submarine museum we go in and take a tour. It's a boat from the 1930's and fought in WWII. It was real interesting; their alphabet reminded me of the Greeks. You can't figure out their writing at all.

They had this one interesting poster of a Russian, a giant Russian, butting Adolph Hitler, a little Adolph Hitler, in the head with a rifle stock. We left there after an hour of crawling around. This guy was supposed to pick us up but he didn't show. I had left a bag of junk in his car; just trinkets for kids on the street. We were told that is the thing to do. Buttons, pins, and stuff they gave us. The ship spent big bucks on this trip. We walked back to the ship and had dinner. Then the Russian shows up with my bag of junk. So we insisted he have dinner with us. I think they love our food. He left and then we did also. We went out to try and find a beer. We weren't sure if they even had beer. We walked into town and we were starting to get mobbed. The reason that there wasn't many people out earlier was because all their lives they have been told that Americans walk the streets with machine guns shooting people. They were afraid that we were going to be shooting them. Can you believe it? Well, by the time we left the ship after dinner, they must have realized that we weren't going to shoot them or anything so we were mobbed. They wanted autographs or anything else we had. The kids would say "Change." That meant they wanted to trade for something. We heard a lot of "Change" over the next four days. I said when we left the ship that we went to town, but it really wasn't a town. It was like a park or a main street, but nothing I would call a town with stores or anything. It reminded me of a camp.

We got to a vendor alongside the street and I had some of the worst beer I ever had in my life. It was "Terrible!" But Pete liked it. Then again Pete liked anything. We stood there getting mobbed for awhile. Talking to people that didn't understand us. Like Pete said, "It was like being Clint Eastwood," Signing autographs for everyone. People were giving us things. For all I know this may have been the biggest event in their entire lives. I don't think most of them ever met a foreigner, let alone an American. People were really excited about us being there. Russian naval Officers were coming by and inviting us to their houses. But I figured that hey probably wanted to do business after that first visit we made. So we declined about 25 invitations. These folks do have a hard time accepting no. We made it back to the ship before eleven which was when liberty expired. We were already tired. That was about it for 1 July. Oh, there were snow flurries on and off that afternoon. And it never gets dark, daylight twenty hours a day.

July 2

This was a busy day on the ship. There were tours from hell and they were lined up to get on the ship. Thousands of people, and that was just the military base. The people from Murmansk weren't allowed onboard. It was colder this day. Some of our Sailors went to their ship for dinner and some of them came here for lunch. They don't have Chiefs. They have Mishmen. These guys are Warrant Officers or equivalent. Their enlisted men are conscripts and

I don't think they get treated very well at all. All of their repair work is done by Mishmen or Officers. They came to the ship and had a good tour. They scarfed up the groceries. They loved bug juice. So we gave them a whole case of the poison. They couldn't believe what a clean ship the YORKTOWN was. The computer stuff really blew them away. So did non skid on the deck. They have smooth decks with no non skid on it. They were all amazed at the ATM machine and the Coke Machine. Can you imagine, they have never seen a Coke machine? We were to find out later that Polaroid pictures were amazing to them also.

When our guys went over to their ship that night they were given a good time with a lot of food. They tried to get them all drunk. After a day of tours we got off the ship around four o'clock and headed up to the park. There was a restaurant at that end so we bought some food and sat around. I had a glass of this green stuff. It was awful. The beers were OK. They were cheap, just pennies.

There was a Russian Officer in there who asked us to go to his house for awhile. There wasn't anything else to do so we relented and went with the guy. His name was Sasha. There was Pete, Dave Balance, Mark Dimmock, and me. We had to climb this mountain to get up to the house or apartment. It was cold, as usual. I borrowed a raincoat off Mark so it wasn't too bad. Well we got to Sasha's and the guy was so thrilled we were there. He called his neighbors and soon there were him, his wife, his friend, and others. The table was filled with food. At one point he broke out Champaign, vodka, beer, and Cognac. After about 100 toasts we were getting pretty toasted. The guy said "Russian Officer" took a whole 6 or 7 ounce glass of Vodka on the back of his hand and downed it bottoms up. I believe that if I tried something like that it would have killed me. Their apartment was nice but small. He was embarrassed because he sat down on one of his chairs and the leg broke. We knew that he just wanted us to visit because he didn't offer to trade anything. Everyone wanted to know everything about us. I didn't bring any pictures because I don't carry my wallet with me on the beach in these ports. We finally got out of there after a lot of eating, drinking, and toasting. I think we were able to communicate OK. I invited them to the ship for dinner on the third of July. They were all thrilled about it. They gave us medals and presents. We gave buttons, stickers, and cigarettes, stuff like that.

We were able to get back on time. We got back to the ship and listened to everyone else's stories. A real good one was about the Sheriff and Bos'n mates' trip to see the jail. Their Chief of Police could have passed for our

Sheriff's brother. Both were big and poker faced. The whole base pops tall for this guy. The Sheriff and the Police chief got along great with each other. They took a tour of the police station. They had three sections of security, the Sailor section, the drunk tank, and the bad guy section. They weren't allowed in the Bad guy section. The other two parts were four walls, no furniture, and a piss pot. The funny part is that the Police Chief brought out all of their weapons and offered them to the Sheriff and the Bos'n as gifts. They could have come back to the ship with machine guns, sniper's rifles, etc. They had to decline. The Bos'n asked if there were any restaurants in town. Instead of answering he sent he sent a guy out who came back with full course meals. That's about how it was with everyone out there. By now most of the Sailors were walking around the ship covered with Russian medals. It looks hilarious. This ended the second day.

July 3rd

This was without doubt my busiest day. I had duty. But I think I got to CCS twice all day and that was for tours. I was put in charge the day before we got here to organize a school kid's tour for the day. I had no idea how many or how old. I called for volunteers to help with this thing and I had about a dozen or so people show up. We ended up using all of them and a lot more. Early in the morning I found out there would be about fifty kids and that they would get there about 1000 AM. One thing I found out about these people, when they say they are coming, they are coming. We made up about seventy five candy bags and buttons and stickers, buttons and Slinkeys from Hand Clasp. It was good that we had a lot. I had a guy with a Polaroid camera on the Mess Decks (they never saw one before) to take pictures. We set up the PA system with mikes and I had a guy playing the guitar. When they got here there were about seventy plus a lot of adults. We took them around the ship, then into the crew's mess decks for cookies , ice cream, and the little candy bags . They loved that ice cream. It was a good time for us as well as for them. We found out they were orphans instead of the privileged. The fun part was teaching them Old McDonald Had a Farm. It always worked for our kids; I figured they'd like it too. We got them to sing the EIEI O part and I know they had a good time. They loved getting a Polaroid picture to take home with them. About a minute before it was over, the CMC comes up to me and says we now have a second kid's' tour. There are another sixty waiting on the pier. We hustled the first party off the ship, then we went to the ship's store and bought out their whole candy supply and we did the whole party all over again. It went just as well as the first one did. We all got a lot of atta boys, but these kids have nothing at all, not even warm weather. It was probably the most rewarding part of the whole port visit.

That afternoon Sasha, his wife, and a few other couples came by for dinner. It must have been a real big deal for them because many Captains only got topside down tour of the ship. They were all dressed up in suits and were thrilled to be here They loved our food, especially our ice cream. They went nuts over our Breyers ice cream. It was easier to talk to them because we had an Air Force Master Sergeant named Bill onboard who was interpreting for us. He was stationed in the embassy with the DAO, whatever that is. He was a real good guy. Anyway, they loved the food and we took them on about a two hour tour of the ship. Mark Dimmock loaded the missile launcher and spun around the blue birds. I could see by the looks on those Navy Officers faces that our stuff works a lot better than theirs does. They saw CCS, the bridge, YORKTOWN Square, but not CIC or the AEGIS Computer room. I think they were real impressed with what they saw. Anyway, they thanked us over and over, gave us more presents and off they went. That was about it for July 3rd.

July 4th

This is the picnic day. I didn't get to play DJ. We had to use the PA system up in the helo hangar for a VIP reception that night. At about twelve o'clock we headed over there to the picnic area. It was between 25 and 30 degrees and the wind was blowing at about 30 miles per hour. I had on sweat pants we were permitted to wear civilian clothes to this. I had on sweat pants, blue jeans, T-shirt, long sleeve T-shirt, gloves, and a yellow coat. My head was cold because all I had was a ball cap on. We had a tent set up at the soccer field. There were hundreds of people there. We had Hand Clasp toys to give out and they were being guarded. Then it began, a full five minutes of ice and hail. It was hilarious. A bunch of US Sailors cooking burgers for Russians near the North Pole in an ice storm. There was only one bathroom and the line quickly grew into a most uncomfortable situation. The soda and beer was gone in about two hours. There was thousands of each. A lot of people stocked up quickly. They took whole cases if they could. We had to stop some of them. They even grabbed the ketchup and the mustard bottles. At first it seemed funny, but then it's sad. I think that some of the Sailors who went to their houses as invited dinner guests were treated with everything they must have had. I didn't see many people who were overfed up there.

The picnic finally got to the point of handing out the kids gifts. We had hundreds, but there were thousands of them. We almost got crushed. It was real scary for a minute. The Police Chief showed up and the crowd saw him and backed away some. I offered him a Bud. He said no. I told him pocket, so he took it. We started handing these things out. We were trying to give them directly to the kids. Every time I needed d to get something the Police Chief lifted me over the crowd by one arm like I was a feather.

Good guy to have on your side I would say. I'm sure he must have twisted a few arms in his day down at the Gulag. We finally got the picnic over with. The Russian Navy and the Charleston Navy Band played for a little while. The DJ thing would not have worked anyway because it was so wet out there.

On the way back to the ship (everything was within walking distance) there was a guy on a flat bed truck selling liquors and singing YELLOW SUBMARINE with a Russian accent. So we helped him out. The next thing I know we do an impromptu concert and about a 100 people show up. The whole time Pete's signing autographs. They loved the singing. It was the whole Russian thing but I had to do, "If I Were a Rich Man." I guess it was a big relief finding out we didn't walk around with machine guns shooting people or each other. Anyway, that ended the Fourth of July picnic in an ice storm. The whole trip was fascinating beyond belief. The next morning on the 5th we left with one Russian ship that could barely make steam. It was a joint exercise that made a historic symbol, jointly operating with the Russian Navy for the first time in seventy years. We did a lot of Hip Hip Hoorays. The Russian Navy Band was on the pier and the US Navy Band was on the O'BANNON who was with us on this trip. The Charleston Navy Band played some great stuff. Then we were gone. Everyone died of exhaustion for the next 48 hours. All n all; I thought of it as a fitting end to sea duty. As long as I had been in, since 1972 they were the enemy and in the end we sat down with them and they found out we weren't so bad after all. That was the good part. It made my twenty years seem very worthwhile. Well, that's about it. I am looking forward to getting home to you and getting our lives back to normal as a family again. It's something I've been looking forward to for a long time.

I love you all very Much
Daddy

Our success in the Russian port visit for me personally was the transformation that occurred from the tepid reception that greeted us until we were embraced as celebrities as the visit continued. To survive under the ridiculous distribution methods of their failed system, we found the Russians to be master traders, entrepreneurs, and sales opportunists. They were masters of the deal and we were carriers of scarce goods. Anything American was in demand and as their shyness dissipated like the coolest of a desert night turned day, we became the equivalent of the *Beatles on Ed Sullivan in* 1961. I reflect back on those four days of fame and all the hundreds of signatures I signed and it makes me smile. I was Terry Bradshaw, and at times Franco Harris; it was ridiculous and at the same time oodles of fun. I experienced how fame can be seductive and addictive.

Another thing that amazed me is the Russian reputation for drinking vodka is well founded. The Brits, as renowned as they are at imbibing, would stand no chance against the Russian Vodkateers. Shaka, who I described in my 1992 letter, was actually a journalist who carried a video camera around on his shoulder. He knocked down about three of those glasses and still kept that camera stable. There were little snippets of experiences on that trip that stick with me to this day. When we walked into the Russian officer Vlad's apartment on that first day I was somewhat surprised that they had color TV, but I was flabbergasted to see an episode playing of the American soap *Santa Barbara. Mason Capwell* speaking in Russian was humorous, but I hope that the Russians didn't think we all lived the opulent life styles of our soap characters; perhaps the supply officer, but not the rest of us.

For folks who were never allowed the legal use of the free enterprise system it was enlightening to discover that after fifteen minutes of trading with a hard bargaining Russian 13 year old it was possible to get enough military adornments to put *Idi Amin* to shame. What they needed at the time were the niceties of life. Communism provided them with all their basic needs such as military medals and officer's daggers, but the extravagant items like pay checks, food, adequate housing, and dental care were still somewhere on the horizon.

We also discovered that when we had our dinner party that it was actually the first time the Russian wives had ever set foot on a warship. It seems that they were not permitted at that time to go aboard their husbands' vessels. I thought it ironic that here were these Russian Navy wives and the USS YORKTOWN was the first ship many had set foot upon.

After dinner when they tried our ice cream for the first time they were gifted not with any ordinary dessert. No way, I had to make them the ultimate Z-Man special; The *Pittsburgh Manly Man's Banana Split, or*

PMMBS Special. The *PMMBS Special* was a dieter's worst nightmare. Packed with fresh bananas, Breyer's ice cream of varying flavors, assorted goops of chocolate, pineapple, strawberry, caramel, and topped with whip cream and walnuts. They were also laced with sprinkles and topped with a Maraschino cherry. The *PMMBS Special* was truly a work of art representing Western decadence at its indulgent best.

These Russian folks required calories and in the YORKTOWN CPO Mess they were going to get some. I only wished I had brought sparklers to stick in them like the Greeks did, but nonetheless they were the Picassos of ice cream concoctions. Our Russian guests were in large-eyed awe of these monstrosities appearance, but when one of the wives tasted the creation she screamed in unbridled joy at her first taste of a Yankee banana split in her entire life. Right then and there I postulated that in the Russians' hearts they knew with conviction and certainty that any people who could make something as delightful as a *PMMBS Special* could not possibly be an enemy.

Scenes like this were being played out all over Severmorsk as the YORKTOWN and OBANNON were ensuring *World Peace* with Yankee good will and engaging humor. As much as we brought, we could have used ten times as much and still not filled all the needs of these people. This was a great trip of epoch proportion. It was living history and the YORKTOWN once again was part of a significant world event. In this instance it wasn't a call for harm's way, but for something important and profound nonetheless. Many of us had spent our entire careers counter balancing the power of the Soviet Navy. To be here, in their back yard sharing bread and making *change* was something that none of us will ever forget. It was an amazing week. Then I had to do the weekly TAGOUT audit.

When we did our basic maneuver with the Russian ship and the OBANNON that was another historical statement that became a record of fact. The YORKTOWN and the OBANNON were the first ships in forty years to operate in a coordinated effort performing a joint operation. Put that one on *Jeopardy* and see who gets it right.

We were now in route to Edinburgh Scotland after a short day or so of watch standers only, so the crew could recover from our Russian adventure. Before we arrived there we had to take care of a small matter called the *Blue Nose Initiation.* Yes, Captain Mullen was in need of certification and he would be participating in the initiation process, to gather a proper license for operating in the *domain of the polar bear*.

I was pleased that we waited because now we had a wide assortment of Russian style Blue Nose attire to wear, as we intimidated those who dared to enter our realm. After a week in dress blue uniforms it was nice to be wearing khaki work clothes again, but when the *invaders from the South* were mustered on the aft missile deck for their judgment we resembled Siberian Blue-faced maniacs. We hit the scantily clad wannabes with a little fire main to get em nice and moist. They crawled up the starboard side into the break where they were graced with a smoke machine and blue muck. How the cook made that stuff is beyond me. By the time they made it to our bow to meet our biggest Blue Nose, King Neptune Curt, the nastiest looking Neptune Rex to ever adorn himself in blue ice, they were forced to cheer to our wishes.

The ceremony was a little challenging, but it wasn't hazing or beating people. It was fun and memorable. The captain addressed the crew on the 1MC and said we did it with class. I never thought I would get a BZ for hosing down the skipper with fire main in the Arctic but we do what we do and its all in the day's SOE, or schedule of events.

After our Russian visit we were about liberty tired, but Edinburgh Scotland is just too intriguing of a place to pass on. The huge castle could well take you a month to tour and you still wouldn't see everything it had to offer. Max, our resident German submariner became strangely addicted to bag pipe music while we were there. Every morning as we crossed the Atlantic in a westward track home we were greeted to the Scottish Highlander favorite bagpipe tunes blasting away on the CPO mess stereo, courtesy of Max's recent music purchases. I had witnessed guitar airbands from American Sailors before, but a German bagpiper doing airband was a new and strange twist of a creative pursuit. Yes, only in the United States Navy could one wake up in the middle of a strong North Atlantic storm being pitched and tossed while you witnessed an animated German dancing around your breakfast table in a ritual of ecstasy to Scottish bagpipers.

While in Edinburgh we did what most tourists do. We drank beer, toured the castle, and bought warm wool sweaters for the family. The castle is impressive; within its protective walls are hundreds of years of history. The tour guide would inform us with a tale of an incredibly heroic figure in Scottish history whose likeness would be displayed in paint before us. Invariably after listening to a litany of the hero's epoch accomplishments, the tour guide would conclude with the hero's beheading due to some change of command issue. They certainly left no loose ends in their power struggles and I would guess that *Met Life* wasn't a profitable proposition at the castle.

The military ceremonial guards were just as talented as the San Francisco mimes. They moved less than the Pittsburgh quarterbacks who played in the years between Bradshaw and Ben Roethlisberger (Kordell excepted). Those guys don't even blink, and they look very physically fit.

I wouldn't advise messing with one. He just might catch up to you in a pub after his shift. Those Scottish guards would absolutely clean your clock.

The real fun in Edinburgh though is the people. Never ask a Scottish person a question unless you really want an answer. Their national past time is verbal communication. My guess is that they watch very little television in Scotland. They seem to be way too engrossed with old fashioned conversing.

When we queried a Scottish policeman for directions to a good pub, he left his position of directing traffic and escorted us to his favorite watering hole. This marked the first and up to the present only time I ever received a police escort to a bar. The patrons there formed the nucleus for the Scottish version of *Cheers.* They were mostly a forty plus crowd and their life's mission as a group was to exchange spoofs with their Yankee guests. Mark, Mack, Pete, Dave Ballance, and Me, the regular Louds loved this atmosphere. The Louds enjoyed the verbal sparring, in spite of the fact that the Scotts were much better at it than us. We were going to stay the night in Edinburgh and we asked for a recommendation. Ten minutes later a driver herded the Louds into a car and carried us to the coziest bed and breakfast you could imagine, for a price much lower than you would ever expect.

This is how Edinburgh went. If you wondered into a small shop it often took an hour to get out. People wanted to talk. It was like having *Oprah* at each address. The double decker buses were also fun and the tour guides were hilarious in the way they had of understating what was at times a rather brutal history. I would recommend this place as a vacation to anyone, however, if you are planning to stay for a specific length of time it is wise to double that estimate for planning purposes, you will be detained by the Scotts for conversation purposes.

We packed up from Edinburgh and set sail for the East Coast, what a trip, what an adventure. At this juncture, I had enough time in to retire, and to be honest, if some employer came up to me and offered me a big wad of sweaty cash I may have said goodbye as a senior chief, and I would have continued on to a quiet life with *Universal Widget* or some other job in a large square shaped establishment with a foundation and a street address. But I found a billet at a repair facility at the Amphib base in Little Creek and that convinced me to hang and around and try to make master chief. A few years of shore duty would do my family life some good. Iris had reentered the work force and was also a drilling reservist and chief petty officer, and she could use my help for a change. If the YORKTOWN was anything at all, it was gone. In the three years I served as a crew member we had deployed three times and had done several Law Enforcement

Operations. There was also GITMO and all that goes with that adventure.

I was leaving the YORKTOWN with a great deal of mixed feelings. This was a great ship with an excellent captain. Captain Mullen was in my opinion the standard of what a leader should be. When Sailors talk about the *Real Navy* it is a concept that I equate with the USS YORKTOWN. I can honestly say the YORKTOWN was the most rewarding tour in my career. Captain Mullen was the best CO I ever served under, while the YORKTOWN CPO mess and crew were the reason we were simply *"The Best Ever,"* and, "*They no longer painted in the rain.*"

Chapter Six:

The Creek, Basketball, & Old Faithful Again

Naval Amphibious Base Little Creek was the home to Gators, SEALS, Special Boat Units, and our repair facility SIMA. Today it still is with the exception of SIMA or Shore Intermediate Maintenance Activity. They have a new and more cost effective method in place for repairing ships. In the early nineties SIMA was the tender in a building; there specifically to keep the gators and small boats operating.

I arrived at SIMA where I was assigned as the LCPO of the IC shop, 51G. That was exactly where I expected to be. I never became a planner or a ship's superintendent. It was my fortune to always be with the blue shirts in every command I was a part of. I liked it that way. I've spent my whole life around twenty year olds, but SIMA actually had a slightly older group of technicians compared to a typical shop on a ship. This was normal because most shore duty types had already completed at least one sea tour in order to gain eligibility to go to a shore command. Most if not all Sailors get an initial jolt of sea duty. Consider it a paying your dues process. It's also an enticing method of getting Sailors to stay beyond their first enlistment. A nice easy going shore command tour prior to getting out is often preferable to stepping off of a ship's brow after a six month deployment and walking straight into the civilian world with no job lying in wait. It always struck me as odd that our very best Sailors seem to worry about this the most. Our most under achieving (and we always had a few) forever possessed that most influential rich uncle who was straining at the bit, appetent to hire them once they were released from active duty. These rich uncles were all poised, anxious to fill their underachieving nephew's pockets with vast quantities of wealth and prestigious responsibilities for their labors. I hope it worked out.

For the rest of us mere mortals with modest connections, shore duty allows for a Sailor to make a smooth transition to the civilian work force. In all honesty, that was one of my reasons for being at SIMA. As a YORKTOWN Sailor, planning for civilian life wasn't an option. On a cruiser every hour of every day is usually chock full of fun and good times. You live in the moment and if there is time for planning, it is usually a plan for passing your next inspection.

At SIMA, we were at times referred to as a *Retirement Farm.* We always had a multitude of chiefs and officers passing through, charting a final leg to their life's next great adventure. This was actually an excellent place to retire from. We did so many retirement ceremonies that we became very good at coordinating and executing the events and we did develop an impressive level of expertise.

The command had attributes for many reasons. Most of the shop personnel were mature E5s; (second class petty officers) and above. They had already mastered a decent level of expertise in their prior duty stations. In the IC Shop I had two very sharp first class petty officers, John Williams, and Mike Buckler. Behind those two were a group of fix it men and women who made life rather facile. In the motor rewind shop our short in height, high in talent electrician, Chief Gerard, referred to himself as *The Master of Rewind,* and deservedly so. His group handled the busy volume of their shop, problem free. He had that place running like a business operating in the black.

Whenever you go to a shore command of some size it is a safe bet that you will bump into a few ghosts from the past and duty at SIMA was no exception. Over at the electrical repair shop I found now Chief Jesse Santero from the YORKTOWN along with funny Lenny Singleton, now an EM2. EMC Joe Giffear from my YELLOWSTONE days was in the Planning and Estimating Department. Mike Huebner, now a senior chief HT was in the ship's superintendent office. I knew Mike as a third class from way back in the LAWRENCE days. After being there a few months, now Senior Chief Dave Hales showed up as a leader in the safety department. This was the same Dave from the *Wanderer years* on the YELLOWSTONE. As a final bit of good fortune, along came CWO3 Dave Owens who I made chief with on the SCOTT in 82. To say I was pleased was an understatement. In many respects this was an excellent command to be a part of.

As with the success of any command and its accompanying command climate it all starts at the top. Commander Kathy Miller provided the type of leadership that encouraged innovation and teamwork. It was evident that she actually liked being the captain, and she was both competent and personable. Along with Commander Miller was her XO Lieutenant Commander Joanne Fish, another name from my YELLOWSTONE days. Both of these Navy women were capable thoughtful leaders and neither would hesitate to enforce accountability or to give recognition. They were top notch and made a great team.

My division officer upon arrival was a warrant officer who originated in the ET rating. He was about to retire so I really didn't know him that well. The master chief electrician who worked along with him was also about to retire also, and that occurred soon after I arrived. I was destined as a senior chief to be in the division office as one of the administrators. I even got the title division LCPO or assistant division officer. Titles are humorous. However; it was a significant position seeing that we often had over 120 people to account for when you combined R3 with R4 as we did. One might say I had become a *Great Watubah.* Our division consisted of the IC men, the electronics techs, and the electricians with the rewinders, the balance shop and the electrical repair techs. We also had a group specifically for cableway inspections on ships. Can you guess this one? They were called the cable way inspection team.

Our R4 division chief was a favorite of mine. He was an extremely hard working stalwart athletic type named Andy Martin. It also didn't hurt that he was a Steeler fan, as bad as the Steelers had become. He was a Western Pa boy, so we had common ground. We also had an ET Chief named Tim Wendorf who was one of those high energy types who seemed to know how to do everything. Tim was so competent that you often had to be careful so as not to take advantage of him.

When the *Great One* came to be the R3/R4 Division Officer all the pieces were already in place for an outstanding division. Chief Warrant Officer Harry L. Daggette was the final piece of the puzzle. We had good chiefs, great petty officers, and knowledgeable allies throughout the command. It didn't hurt that we could fix ships.

Harry L. Daggette was the perfect fit for the division. He had a sense of humor along the lines of some of Hollywood's funniest wits. This was now a division where the work would get done and people still had a great time at work. We ended up with some real superstar Sailors in this division. Jay Mallette, a hard working electrician I knew from my Nea Makri years showed up and could be counted in that group. We also had Gordy Bightbill who was a true leader and definitely on the fast track to chief petty officer. It didn't hurt that he was also a Steeler fan and had a deadly jump shot on the basketball court. Gordy looked a lot like pro player *Dan Marjele*, of NBA fame and as you may suspect, that became his name, for the duration of course.

The warrant could also play some ball and he would at times go unconscious on the court. Not that he passed out but unconscious in the sense that his jump shot was deadly accurate. He was also as eaten up with the Boston Celtics as I was with the Steelers. His idol as one would surmise via an intelligent guess, the *Great Larry Bird.* We changed Warrant Daggette's name to Bird. He liked it. We had a collection of great athletes in R3/R4; one young ET, Jody Gonzales was exceptional. Jody was fast enough to play cornerback for the local semi pro football team and when the base had an Olympic challenge he swept all the events with his blazing speed. This was rather significant considering his competition had a large contingency of Navy SEALS in the mix. They were all waxed by an ET3 from a repair facility, a slight to macho pride.

We had some female athletes as well. One of our young second class ETs, Marilyn Bowen was a regular gymnast and could be found at Rockwell Hall doing back flips and showing some gymnastic skills you would rarely expect from a hard working Sailor out of one of your shops. If you ever take the time to go to a Navy gym sooner or later you will observe someone who makes you wonder why that person wasn't on TV huddled up with some Division I college team. There are always a few who slip through the cracks.

The IC shop gained a female second class named Dawn Anderson, a real character. She was an Alabama girl who worked like a solitary sled dog pulling a gang of Suma wrestlers uphill in a blizzard, and she could she fix any device made by man. If she would have stayed in she would have become another Keesey. I am sure of it. She was also very close in attitude to that old great icon from the LAWRENCE days, Stebare. Yes Anderson could talk wad cutters, hollow points, stopping power, and hunting techniques. She actually shot her first husband for beating on her, his mistake, her notch on the barrel.

We gave her the name *Taclkeberry* from the *Police Academy* series. It fit perfectly and she was Tackleberry for the next few years until she got out. The last we heard about her, she and her husband went off to New Mexico. I feel sorry for New Mexican varmints with Tackleberry around. Coyotes beware.

If this sounds like a good tour of duty, it was. We had good people here. Folks enjoyed coming to work each morning. Harry Daggette was forever doing reenlistments. Everyone wanted him to be their reenlistment officer because of his engaging personality and easy going sense of humor. Not only was this true for our division but Harry Daggette was a command wide phenomenon. Everyone loved Mr. Harry L. Daggette.

We ended up with three more chiefs in the division. Rene Brown, from South Philly was a dead ringer for Barry Bonds, with just a touch of Richard Pryor thrown in. An awesome guy Rene had one great burden to bear, he owned a Renault Alliance. Yes the poor unsuspecting chief owned a Renault Alliance. Rene Brown had one mood, good, and truthfully most of us had that same trait. We welcomed another chief who was with us for a short while in a limited duty status. ICC Dave Baker was quick witted and funny. I would love to put up Dave Baker on a talk show and have him joust with that certain element of privileged people who think military folks are cerebrally challenged idiots who only enlist because they can't get a job in the civilian work place. He would intellectually shred them to pieces, you would die laughing; their public humiliation would be complete, all the while Dave would maintain a trademark straight face and sober countenance. Dave was raising a few young girls on his own. He married a nice lady with several girls of her own. They all banded together to form their own cheer leading squad in Virginia Beach. I know Dave needed that great sense of humor over the years to deal with all that estrogen.

With a great division in place we received a final piece to our mosaic of folks. Jeff Baston arrived as our senior chief ET, or ETCS, and he fit like a glove with the rest of us. Harry and I used to have these contests whenever it was a male only environment in the office. We held flatuation follies followed by ratings. *Nice one, ooh, damn! Weak, or non-manly* were some of our rating criteria. Jeff said nothing then, calmly biding his time, but mentally he thought; *these guys have no idea what they are getting into*. And indeed, we did not. We had carelessly opened the locks to a formidable although formally shackled monster that would make us pay a thousand fold for our weak attempts at bodily function humor.

Jeff had a wife from the Philippines who was a wonderful cook. Jeff maxed out on roughage and he thoroughly enjoyed beer. It was a combination that created toxic clouds that were beyond hideous. Jeff simply called an attack, *the Jeff Stream.* Harry L. Daggette and I surrendered. We were weak and Jeff was strong. From that time on, the mere threat of a release would send us scampering faster than the Republican Guard being chased out of Kuwait by the American Army. Jeff was a gaseous legend; a real man among mere boys.

SIMA Little Creek was a command that bought into physical fitness. Commander Miller expected the command to meet the standards. I have strong opinions about the subject of physical readiness. To this day I see many Sailors who are fit and trim but I also witness many who have nurtured their girth beyond the boundaries of most standard uniform garments. The standards still get ignored by some who are positioned to enforce. If a PRT coordinator is a second class petty officer and he is measuring a captain's waistline; is he really going to write down that the captain is above the body fat standard? Brave lad if he does. If the Navy is going to have standards and enforce those standards then do this. Have all senior people (E7 and above) go to a designated digital photo lab get photographed in gym clothes and have the image transmitted to a central computer. The computer will analyze the pictures to determine if someone looks out of standards. The key here is do they look out of standards? It is very possible to be out of standards but look fit. Why worry about a number, if appearance and health are what counts? If they do look overweight then they are informed via message to their commanding officer and they get sent to an impartial medical location for human measurement. No pressure on the E5 PRT coordinator and everyone has to participate. With the Z Man method no one can hide in the shadows. Well that was my two cents. I am sure that twenty thousand people are now willing to explain to me why this can't be done, but save it because I believe it can. All commands who actively participate in a physical readiness program; those commands that painfully enforce the standards have a right to demand equal treatment across the board, Navy wide.

I still did my running routine everyday. Our new command master chief, Terry was an accomplished marathoner so he was onboard with physical fitness. Commander Miller motivated the entire command into a momentum and mindset of fitness. We started aerobics and a medley of activities that forced up the heart rate of the entire command. Commander Miller herself would participate with enthusiasm. The old adage stood. If the captain can find the time to exercise so can you. We were not the *Retirement Farm* that some would label us in the sense that we just sat around. We got our butts in gear with everything from weight lifting, to basketball, to step aerobics. I was nearing the end of my career and I was feeling good health wise with the Navy's new physical requirements. There was only my one remaining vice.

I wasn't isolated from my old running mates on the YORKTOWN. We still kept in touch on occasion. This is the story of how Captain Mike Mullen saved my life. I had heard from Pete or Beno Miller that Captain Mullen was going to put the smoking lamp out permanently on his ship. Some folks were a bit bitchy about that I was informed; but I went into a panic over at SIMA. I could not fathom Pete and my other old shipmates being off the nicotine while I remained addicted. I had to give it up and kick the evil habit once and for all. Only this time I was going to assemble all the forces and assets necessary to win this war. Battle plans were laid; I was tired of my enslavement to the evil toxin. Demon of nicotine I swore to cast him out.

I attended the Little Creek clinic smoking cessation class. I saw pictures of cigarette executives who were dead from cancer. I watched footage of the *Marlboro Man* with his iron lung. I procured a stack of nicotine patches. I was ready to go to general quarters on this scourge. There was no way I was going to endure the entire YORKTOWN weaned from nicotine while I sat at SIMA puffing away like an antiquated dragon, sullen and addicted. I was ready with an impavid determination to tame the beast.

I returned to the shop wearing my patch and went into anti- smoking battle mode. With the patch on my shoulder and a huge bag of lollipops on my desk I sat there as the others went out to the gazebo for a smoke break. I sat there alone for what seemed like an interminable amount of time. I began to understand how the non smokers were affected by our smoke breaks. I answered a lot of phone calls while people were out smoking.

I began to feel like failure was imminent, but rethinking my strategy I adapted a new more aggressive and proactive plan of action. Making a tactical change I gathered up my lollipops and left with everyone else whenever they took a smoke break. It was a cursed environment being around smokers at the gazebo, but I had my candy and it was easier than sitting in the office thinking about cigarettes. The war raged on for a week. One day the patch fell off and I didn't bother to put it back on. It remained stressful for a few days but eventually I won, sealing the victory, ending the long bondage to poison. Iris was very proud. The YORKTOWN had to allow the smokers their rights. The complainants won. Captain Mullen couldn't make them all quit. A noble idea, that quite frankly saved my life even though I was no longer stationed there. Without the Mullen attempt to end smoking on YORKTOWN I have no doubt that my addiction would have continued unabated leading to a hideous and early death. Since that time I have tried to use my circle of influence to encourage others to kick the habit. Where I have succeeded, and the numbers have been more than a few, brings further tribute on that thwarted YORKTOWN attempt that was in retrospect more successful than anyone would surmise.

We had a unique method of holding division quarters. In the morning the chiefs mustered the division. Mr. Harry L Daggette in accordance with his normal routine met with the repair officer and then gathered us at quarters to put out all the latest and the greatest information. After that the division was dismissed, tasked to go off to their shops and get hopping on the day's repair activities. The chiefs and leading petty officers then met in the office to discuss plans and other outstanding division business. We kept a boom box and a cassette tape that a division member thought we would enjoy. The tape was preliminary music to the old and most popular television shows of the past generation. Harry loved singing to the *Mr. Ed* song and he actually was an excellent singer, sounding exactly like the guy who sings for *Dire Straights.* I was partial to the theme for *Gilligan's Island* because of the fond memories I held for the big bags of beer in the back alleys of Toulon. One of the songs we had on that tape was the lead in for *Johnny Carson* from the old *Tonight Show.* After Quarters we would assemble in the office. I would hit play and *dad a dad a dad dadadadda dahhh! Dadad a dad a dahh daddadadadahhh... The Tonight Show Theme* would run. Harry would walk in, move around the office nodding to his assembled audience, I mean chiefs and LPOs. Very smooth, Mr. Harry L Daggette would draw a cup of coffee, stir, and I would hit stop while Harry would roll into division business for the day. At the conclusion of quarters after Harry dismissed everyone, I would hit play again and out would sound the concluding music from the old *Three Stooges* episodes. Na Na Na Na Na NANANA .... We had fun in R3/R4 division, and it started at the beginning of every day. We liked to get folks in a good mood right from the opening bell, the days work goes better that way. So remember the wisdom of Harry L Daggette when you come to work weaned on a pickle because your ass sat in traffic for an hour and a half. I know; it's time to get off that soap box, right?

One day someone came down and said "*Way to go"* you made master chief. This was indeed a great day. Jeff Baston had also made master chief, as did Mike Huebner my old LAWRENCE buddy. I had planned on seeking a civilian job after SIMA figuring all the fun was going to finally have to end. I was figuring out how to be a; *whatever.*

No civilian job really seemed appealing to me, *Myron Cope,* the great Pittsburgh sportscaster already had the one I wanted. I also discovered that being a U S Navy Master Chief automatically makes one look wiser. Making senior chief is a great accomplishment; making master chief is a tremendous honor. I had traveled a long way from that day cousin Gary and I flew out of Pittsburgh together, but to say the journey was all work and no play was ridiculous. Now was a chance to do a little bit more before I walked away from it all. I was getting to the point of negotiating orders and now that I was an electrician instead of an IC man I thought that orders would actually be more manageable. Not to confuse what I am writing here, but at the master chief level, electricians and IC men combine into one rating. By this point they're both supposed to know each other's rates. There are a few other rates that also do that. For IC men it is a good thing because ICCM would be a super difficult plateau to achieve because of a lack of billets. Attaining ICCS provided enough difficulty.

At SIMA we were preparing at this juncture for a major command inspection and certification. Commander Miller wanted to loosen up the troops so she mustered us all in the parking lot, prior to the inspection. We believed this would be a typical go getum *rah rah* speech. Instead the captain, dressed in hip hop attire with a do wrap stood on top of some crates doing a little harmonica rap tune. A very credible performance too, I might add. *Snoop Dog* would have been rather proud. We got loose. I couldn't have pictured Mike Mullen or Pete O'Connor doing that, but it worked for Kathy Miller. And we kicked ass on that inspection.

A plan was beginning to take shape in my mind now that I was a master chief. It wasn't a thought I took for action until people who worked for me in the division suggested it. A few subordinates offered the thought that I should go for the command master chief program. Hearing that from the troops meant a great deal to me and their advice I must admit directly influenced my decision. As a CMC I would be working for both the crew and the captain. It would have great deal to do with personnel issues, but the involvement with equipment would be far less. It was a big challenge and there was a process in getting selected.

Initially, when the program began, your rating detailer had to release you to the program. You were required to attend the Senior Enlisted Academy in Newport Rhode Island and then negotiate orders through the Command Master Chief Detailer. At the time, a key for the volunteer master chiefs was getting your rating detailer to release you to the program. If he had a valid billet for you, he may well decline to allow that to occur. This process ended near the time I was negotiating orders into the program. However, because of the time line involved I still had to transfer to a ship as an electrician. Of all the ships available to me there was one in particular that fit into what I was trying to achieve. That was none other than *Old Faithful* herself, the USS YELLOWSTONE.

Under the guidelines of a new message; command master chiefs were now selected via a written package consisting of photos, the commanding officer's endorsement, and a personal interview with the Force Master Chief. This process was similar in some respects to the method of choosing warrants and limited duty officers. The package submission process may have been a little bit of a pain in the tush, but it did take away the detailer's power of telling you a point blank not only no. but hell no.

With all the bureaucratic t crossing and i dotting that I needed to complete, coupled with waiting for an answer in the selection process, it made sense to choose the YELLOWSTONE over the ENTERPRISE which was my other choice of ship. If I were selected I would be PCS transferred any way. So it actually made sense to go to a ship that was decommissioning; yes, the YELLOWSTONE was decommissioning within months after my arrival. My detailer didn't object. As far as he was concerned his requisition showed a valid billet so that was fine with him. To my way of thinking being on YELLOWSTONE short term made better sense than to go to ENTERPRISE, get involved for a few months, get picked up for the CMC program and then leave on a PCS transfer. The roll of the dice was getting selected to the program. If not, I would soon be negotiating orders again with the electrician detailer.

My good friend and right hand man, Rene Brown had weathered an awful accident in his Renault. When I visited him in Portsmouth Naval Hospital we joked about the evil luck we had with those damn cars. To Rene's credit, within months, and before I left the command he was out on the basketball court once again mixing it up. You can bang Sailors around and beat them up; you just can't make them quit acting like teenagers. After awhile they just get locked into being twenty year olds. Every now and then, an old salt will gaze in astonishment in the barber shop's mirror. The barber spins you around and in shock he'll wonder, "*Who is that Old Shit staring at me*?" It all goes by so quickly.

I departed the repair facility after a cheery farewell cookout at Little Creek. What a great division it was. I knew a lot of these folks were going places. There were a lot of future chiefs and officers in this group. The R3/R4 Division presented me with a Steeler ring. I was dumbfounded. Commander Miller had written an awesome CO's endorsement for my CMC package. She wrote some powerful message about my unique abilities and how I was exactly the type of master chief to help the Navy into the next Millennium. The write up she did for me was so good that if I were a schizophrenic I would have asked for my own autograph. I appreciated her taking the time to do that write up.

With all the bureaucratic checks required for my transfer to a decommissioning command; as I awaited a package process decision in order to immediately leave where I was going to for a third tour, the detailer sent me to a school I probably wouldn't be using. Did you catch all that? That wasn't his fault.

I arrived at the Material, Management, and Maintenance Coordinator's School where I spent a few weeks researching an endless repertoire of reports in big fat books. We were instructed by a first class petty officer who was nearing a retirement date. He thought we were all insane to be getting into maintenance management. He was a crispy character, slightly burnt on the edges, but overall he was actually well versed in the content of those big fat books. When I finished that school I reported to the YELLOWSTONE for the third time. Once there I was told that they already had a Material Maintenance Manager or 3M Coordinator and the chief doing the job really enjoyed it and was quite capable. Now I wasn't at all sad about the prospect of not being inundated with maintenance reports for the next four to six months. I have always been a part of a group and my final tour on YELLOWSTONE would be as E Division Officer. I breathed a sigh of relief. Having characters was always much more accordant with my skill set than paper. I'm not knocking the folks who excel at reports, tracking, and being meticulously accurate in those functions. I would and could do those things, just not joyfully.

For me it was always better to muster, instruct, and inspect, so I was ecstatic to be the E Division Officer. My boss, Mr. Grady (that may have been his first or last name), the Cheng, was a great people person, very cordial. In his youth he was an athlete of some notoriety from the Charleston Low Country. He was an avid sports fan and he reminded me of Tony Gwinn, the Padre baseball great. It was also turnaround time and once again it was great to be a Steeler fan. The Back and Gold had once again surged to prominence under the leadership of their young, aggressive coach, the *Jaw,* Bill Cowher. It was true that we still had to contend with the always loud, forever obnoxious Dallas Cowboy contingencies, but at least the Steelers were once again a powerful force, and were not to be taken lightly.

Gordy Brightbill the Great and I made a pilgrimage to Mecca for the AFC Championship game of the 95 season. His good wife Debbie had performed a miracle and obtained two tickets from her job. Gordy with his bad back acting up, rode shotgun in pain as we traveled the 450 miles north for a game against the vastly overmatched San Diego Chargers. It would be a slaughter. The Chargers had no chance. Well, Cornwallis met Washington, Napoleon had his Waterloo, the SERAPIS met the BON HOMME RICHARD, and the Steelers met the Chargers.

The Steelers fell behind in the game when the corner, *Tim McKyer,* slipped on the turf allowing the Chargers to score a go ahead touchdown. Tough as they were the Black and Gold, known that year as the *60 Minute Men* came back strong at the end and were poised to win the game near the goal line on the games final play. Three Rivers Stadium was so loud it was impossible to hear your own screams. *O'Donnell's* pass to *Barry Foster* fell incomplete, the Steelers lost. The stadium went from frenzied pandemonium to dead silence, the exception, a tiny group of Charger fans off in the distance who were extremely nauseating in their screamed jubilance. Sixty- six thousand Steeler fans left that stadium wordlessly, in confounded shock. The Steelers had looked unbeatable. Outside of Three Rivers Stadium venders were hawking Steeler AFC Championship T shirts for a dollar, they were twelve three hours earlier. There were no buyers.

My black and yellow wig now appeared limp and idiotic on my forty two year old grizzled head. Hours earlier it had looked powerful and ominous as Gordy and I rode into battle debating on whether the Chargers could even score. Fans had waved as we passed; fellow *Steelerites* decked in festive battle attire; as they too headed west on the Pittsburgh Parkway. We had known assuredly that a championship was about to occur. Pittsburgh was poised for a party that would rival Times Square on a New Year's Eve. Even the news casters on local TV were delivering their broadcasts adorned in black and gold outfits; while billboards greeted you in brazen confidence with the words *"Welcome to Blitzburgh."* There was no way that San Diego could win that contest.

Gordy and I drove home in silent shock that evening keeping company to the soothing words of a *KDKA* radio talk show host speaking on the 50,000 watt super station. I feared that the elevated expectations coupled with the sheer shock of the emotional roller coaster drop may have caused severe psychological implications or perhaps brain damage. My fears were probably well founded. There would be a required lengthy period of healing needed. Being away from Pittsburgh on a U S Navy ship did not afford a warm environment for a damaged psyche. At least the people of Pittsburgh could band together therapeutically in dealing with the resultant *shoulda couldas* of the disheartening event.

A similar event occurred a few years prior to that Steeler loss that still haunted me. Back on a particular October evening a high fastball to an unrenowned hitter named *Cabrera* had sent the Atlanta Braves to the World Series as the valiant Pittsburgh Pirates came up short in a crucial game seven. It was excruciating the following morning when the IC Shop at SIMA Little Creek greeted me in a formal circle doing an Indian chant as they choreographed that absolutely awful chopping motion practiced by the Atlanta Braves fan base. To this day I patiently wait for baseball redemption. It may be nothing like being a Cub fan, but as the years roll by without even a single winning season one wonders.

In the more rewarding world of the Steeler fan, we expect them to win every year. It's who they are and even with players who can't stack up to the status of Lambert, Harris, and Bradshaw, the fans still expect to win every game. It's in their DNA. To understand it, just go to a local Pittsburgh tavern and tell someone that Steeler football is just a form of entertainment. A little word of advice, get life insurance first

The YELLOWSTONE, although it was losing people every day to transfers, was tasked to execute an important mission. The naval base at Charleston had shut down as a cost saving move. The *Maximus* build up seemed to be heading into reverse as new countries, friendly to the West formed out of the Soviet Block faster than *Jerry Springer* got transvestites running from their duped lovers. Some thought the threats facing us were vaporized, after all *Gorbachev* actually did tear down that wall. The political thinking was down size and save money.

What the soon to be decommissioned YELLOWSTONE was faced with was to rescue the USS NICHOLSON from the Charleston Naval Shipyard. The Shipyard was closing its doors and the NICHOLSON still needed fixin, so as a final hurrah, the YELLOWSTONE was heading to Charleston, South Carolina to fix ships. The YELLOWSTONE may not have been savvy about the political situation, but it still knew how to fix ships. She had been doing it for fifteen years and was about to do it one last time.

The weirdest thing I ever saw (or at least it cracked the list) was the Charleston Naval Base right after it was closed. We entered the port and tied up to a beautiful multi level pier to receive hotel services. Off to our port side, a quarter mile away was the USS NICHOLSON and then there was us. Surrounding us was expansive emptiness. There was only this vast empty parking lot and rows of piers without ships. It was emptier than the parking lot at a Montreal Expos home game. What it still had was the infrastructure. It still had the base police and the base landscapers. You still got a parking ticket for nesting in officer's parking, despite the fact that crew members who found a way to get their cars down could each claim 70 or 80 of those spots with plenty left over. Frequently the bureaucracy doesn't change as quickly as the environment. It was strange watching base police write traffic tickets in an empty parking lot.

We had the run of the Charleston base except for one critical issue. Our commanding officer, Captain Ron Bogle was a great man. He liked people to fix ships and he liked sports. He felt the same way about the Boston Red Sox as I felt about the Pittsburgh Steelers, and all of that brings me to the critical issue, cable TV. With the base contract discontinued and the facility now isolated, cable TV was no longer available. If I were the captain I would have given the exact same order that that Captain Bogle gave. "*Get cable TV.*" It wasn't a question.

We ended up running about a mile of coaxial cable through the abandoned shipyard area; up, over, and around buildings trying to route it such a way that it would avoid being cut in order to get to the closest connection point off of government property. Soon YELLOWSTONE had cable TV in Charleston. The Captain got us the Red Sox, and other sports channels and we were a happy crew as the NICHOLSON got fixed.

I noticed that my old age of forty two was beginning to get the best of me. I found it much more difficult to remember names from 1995 than I did from 1975. I can remember names from that earlier era, but it is frustrating to draw a blank with names because I did meet some very interesting people from that final abbreviated tour on YELLOWSTONE.

One of my favorites was the senior chief from A gang. He didn't resemble a typical A Ganger at all. He was very polished and well spoken; very different from the blue collared hard nosed Pete from my YORKTOWN days.

We had a female warrant who ran the HTs. She was feisty as junk yard dog if someone riled her, but I enjoyed talking sports with that lady. She knew as much about the Green Bay Packers as I did the Pittsburgh Steelers and I respected her ability to communicate about sports. Packer fans always seemed to be knowledgeable and the *Cheese Heads* were less obnoxious than those from some of the other successful teams. Mike Huebner, the HT master chief, another Wisconsin *Cheese Head* who I had known in my LAWRENCE days and at SIMA was also assigned to YELLOWSTONE. Mike and I saw eye to eye on a great many issues and he was an excellent ally in the mess.

The months we spent in Charleston provided us with a critical mission and we eagerly accomplished it. Many were busy figuring out future assignments and were busy planning where to go after decommissioning. I was interviewed by the Force Master Chief while in Charleston and my package was sent on for consideration for the Command Master Chief Program.

Completing its Charleston mission, the ship returned that fall to Norfolk to begin preparations for decommissioning. There was a tremendous amount of work to be completed in preparation for the deactivation of the ship and a pair of old civilian guys from the inactive ships world came by to brief us on the entire process. One of those gentlemen I recognized as soon as I saw him. Master Chief Alvie Reid, King Neptune from our 1973 Shellback initiation on LAWRENCE. He looked about twenty five years older, as indeed, he was.

I had to go fetch Mike Huebner and together as two old grizzled master chiefs we flanked him, one of us on each side. I said, "*Master Chief Reid, Do you remember us*?" He looked at us and said, *"Hell no Master Chief."* When I told him we were his firemen in engineering from 1973 on the LAWRENCE he got a big kick out of that. I think he was glad to be remembered, and glad two of his youngsters did OK.

W deactivated the YELLOWSTONE by packaging, moving, preserving, and securing. Step by step in a choreographed process we secured the YELLOWSTONE one space at a time. When the ship was finally locked up by the end of 1995, it actually looked great. I know it sounds conflicting, but YELLOWSTONE was being placed in storage, like your Grandma's most precious Christmas ornament. If the country ever called on her again she could be quickly activated and made ready to answer all bells. YELLOWSTONE and the other tenders like her were retired for cost, not because they were old and maintenance intensive. It would give me pleasure to once again see AD41 out there making turns or fixing ships. A lot of great Sailors served between her life lines.

That January in 1996 when YELLOWSTONE decommissioned there was a huge ceremony at the pier in Norfolk. It was cold, Minnesota cold, and many of us had chemical packs in our gloves. Captain Bogle's speech unfortunately couldn't be heard from my station where we stood manning the rails, but I was told he acknowledged that I was there for both the commissioning and decommissioning of the great ship. The sixteen years that YELLOWSTONE served the fleet may seem like a long time, but in retrospect it was a *blink of the eye*. It seemed like two weeks and not sixteen years since I was laughing at Yosemite Branch and California clog wearing Tim go at it with each other. The time between being a young first class petty officer and a brine encrusted master chief was mentally negligible. Where did all that time go? Even now when I look into the mirror from that barber shop chair I expect to see that young first class. Often I wonder, "*Who in the hell is that thin lipped, bald headed, big eared geezer with the abundance of ear hair staring at me*?" I once read a quote by someone to whom I can't give credit due to a failed memory. That person said, "*It's a shame that youth is wasted on the young*." Once I would have scoffed at that. Today I consider it as one of the sagest comments I ever heard. But on that day of YELLOWSTONE'S decommissioning, I wish I could have been more reflective and thoughtful, it was just too damn cold.

The YELLOWSTONE chapters were finally closed once and for all. Great memories would remain. I loved the smell of a tender, the oil in the machinery, the welder's torch, the noise of enthusiastic activity. A Navy tender was a snap shot of why America was great. It was a perfect microcosm of the country at work. The destroyer tenders did their duty. Now they sit dormant somewhere on a dark pier, getting remote flooding alarms checked by a security patrol. But they are neatly stored and wrapped tightly hoping the day will come again when some leader will remember their versatility and create for them a new mission. Until that day they sleep, waiting for that glorious moment when a group of Sailors will arrive to bring them back to life, to once again, *Fix Ships.*

Chapter Seven:

Self Actualization

I was selected to the CMC program and I was extremely excited about that. The electrician detailer had to send me somewhere awaiting the start of the Senior Enlisted Academy now that the YELLOWSTONE was closed for business. It would be unwise to place me in a three year billet just to have me transfer within a few months. He found me a spot at FASOTRAGRULANT. FASO was an airdale school house with a really neat acronym. It has more letters in it than your average disease, but the people who worked there were bright, energetic, and passionate about properly training the Fleet. After all these years of being on cruisers and destroyers this was my first visit with the *Brown Shoe Navy.* Realistically they may think they are different but they *ain't.* A Sailor is a Sailor and back in Greece Bubba Martin was right when he wrote, "*We are all still one Navy.*"

In all likelihood I was going to be assigned there for a few months at best. I volunteered for the Total Quality Management Team as a trainer. I knew something about it from my SIMA Little Creek days and I knew a lot of Sailors didn't like it, understand it, or felt that it was of no use to the military. I personally liked some of tools they used in process measurement and evaluation. The trouble is that most of the work processes that commands were attempting to measure seldom got to the point of taking good statistics and meshing them into a standard deviation formula which would provide them a true result of how a process was in fact functioning. Crews turned over too often rendering it difficult to hold the gains. It was often reinvention of the wheel over and over again. In the end, I believe it created a sense of purpose in some commands. COs wrote their mission statements and ship crews or shore commands developed a better sense of what they were attempting to achieve.

From a personal standpoint I was introduced to the work of Stephen Covey and his *Seven Habits of Highly Effective People.* I like the manner in which he presents lessons, such as the expanding circle of influence. Covey is quite brilliant with a huge following. I became an instant fan.

Mainly though, what I enjoyed the most about my several months at the FASO training facility was working with a few excellent fellow chiefs. Two of them were Ocean Systems Techs turned Sonarman due to a rating consolidation. One was an Aviator named George, possibly an AWC. We also had a Master Chief AZ named Tom who was right about ready to retire. Mitch Ditterbrand was the younger of our two sonarmen. He was an up and coming chief who had the smarts and drive to really go places in his career. Tom was our other sonarman in the group. Have you ever racked your brain and realized that you were just unable to remember something that should be readily accessible? Well that is the way it is with my memory of the senior chief sonarman, Tom. I can't remember his last name. He was by far the most knowledgeable and best informed of our group. He was a true total quality management expert, very bright, and very deep in his thought processes. I learned quite a bit from senior chief. One would think that this *Old Fart* could at least remember his name. But alas, the ginko biloba has not worked and I'm drawing a blank. The sad part is that he is probably a millionaire and I could request a loan if I could remember his name. To me he was the Godfather of Navy total quality and I really enjoyed teaching those classes with this group. I must say though, if I never see the Dr. Demming *Red Bead Experiment* again, it will be too soon.

I was enjoying these days at home to be sure. The shore duty Sailor is permitted to live a somewhat normal life and mine for the time being was like everyone else's, filled with kid's soccer games, martial arts lessons for Andrew, and little league baseball. They were good ages and happy moments. I also got some time to get to know my nephew Greg Olszewski, an up and coming second class petty officer, an IC man at that who had served on both the JOHN F KENNEDY and the AUSTIN. I saw a younger version of myself and I thought he would someday make a great chief. He also had that excellent IC man innate ability to fall sound asleep on a hard floor regardless of the surrounding noise level. Greg had very real possibilities. Perhaps with Iris, Greg, and myself I thought we may well develop a little U S Navy family tradition. The trouble is that time really flies when life is that good, and ours was. We were fortunate with a nice home, good schools, two vehicles, recreational facilities, and an occasional vacation to Disney World or Newport Rhode Island. Many fellow Americans do not have those blessings and I for one felt an obligation to the U S Navy for all it's given to my family and me. The longer you are in and the closer you get to the end, the more you begin to realize how much the Navy really means and how inseparable you are from it. One becomes woven into the mosaic until the U S Navy is a large undeniable element of who you are. When you hear about crime committed by Sailors you cringe. When you see ships reacting to disaster and saving lives you shed a tear of pride for your shipmates. When tragedy strikes, it is felt, directly.

I was selected to the command master chief program. I was leaving for the summer session of the Senior Enlisted Academy in Newport Rhode Island, class number 73. That fall I would report to the USS KAUFFMAN (FFG-59) as the command master chief. It was the pinnacle of my career. I was unsure about staying on for thirty years or if I was going to do this tour and take my chances in the world of evil civilians. Time would tell and I could decide that issue later.

When I arrived in Newport I received the training I expected. But the entire experience was above and beyond my highest expectations. I was assigned to the Brown Group and met soon after with our facilitator, an Army master sergeant from the Army Chemical Corps named Gary Edmondson. Gary was a good natured halcyon leader who, like me was highly evolved from a lack of hair aspect. Perhaps the Army Chemical Corps causes hair loss in the same manner as Navy electronics. The possible correlation bears further investigation. We had both exchange instructors and students at the SEA from the other service branches which explains why we had an Army facilitator. All the facilitators at the SEA maintained a titled acronym that was strange indeed. They were endeared to us as our *FUGM*s. Telling folks that I really enjoyed my FUGM Gary was just wrong in retrospect, but it truly was a catchy title.

Our class had about ten folks in it, all senior chief and master chief petty officers from all parts of the Navy. In our class we also had a guest student from the Air Force, a master sergeant named Larry. It was an opinionated group, although the curriculum guided the group, the dynamics of our round table discussions was where the real learning took place. All had real life lessons to share and this was the type of environment where adult learners flourished. Whoever invented this school was a genius. I know that time brokers change, but I sincerely hope that bringing these groups together continues. I fear that something would go amiss if the school went to a 100 per cent on line format.

I am sure that it occurs with most classes but Brown 73 bonded well. We went through the physical training, compelling guest speakers, exacting written assignments, public speaking and introductions, heated class discussions, and very annoying tests. It was a place I would say was *special.* Today I wear two pieces of jewelry, a wedding band on my left hand, and my class ring from the Senior Enlisted Academy on my right. Whenever I think of AVCM Ski Venisky, or the athletic EOD MTCS Mark, Air Force Larry, Submariner Mike McCalip, Big CSCM Ski from the Navy Reserve, and the others, I have very fond memories for a group I truly respected. I felt that this was the overall best Navy school I ever attended and I certainly recommend it to all senior enlisted. It is truly time well spent.

I reported to the KAUFFMAN (FFG -59) in the fall of 1996. When you're new to a frigate the first thing you discover is that if you want something done you better look in the mirror because that is normally who is going to do it. The KAUFFMAN was a clean ship with a solid reputation. The two captains whom I served there, while vastly different from each other in their methods of management still had a common thread which applied to both. I always felt that in each decision that they made they were doing their best to do the right thing in the interest of the training, morale, well being, and safety of the ship and crew.

I did not always agree with their decisions. My point of view on an issue was often rejected. That came with the turf. I had some good allies on the KAUFFMAN and I also experienced some resentment and acerbity. Command master chief is not a job for the thin skinned. Although stirring the pot a little may ruffle a few feathers, and although change may often have to overcome inertia in attitude, it does act against the evils of complacency.

I convinced the first captain to write a mission statement and his was awesome. Maybe it was the guidance in that mission statement that propelled the crew to win the Battle E against our larger squadron competitors in that year 1997. The KAUFFMAN was a stout man of war. The ship made turns and boldly accepted all assignments with enthusiasm. I enjoyed this job. It was different not being up to my arm pits in equipment issues, but social issues and personal development were of a priority. I knew I would spend time counseling the crew. The surprising group was the officers who made their way to my tiny office. You discover that even the most intelligent leaders need someone to sort things out from time to time.

I used all the lessons I had learned over the years to help me succeed in this job. I took on management of the FSA (food service attendants) and organized that thankless job. I learned that lesson from Jack Lewis. I ensured that all the Sailor of the Quarter Boards were held and the recipients awarded in a timely manner. Hank Davis and Curt Cook were both very big on that program. If I had to correct a chief, a time came for a Frank Caron special. For reenlistments and ceremonies I drew on the skills I saw in Warrant Officer Harry L Daggette. When I took over the equal opportunity program in its entirety once again I relied on the methods I learned from Curt Cook. I had worked and learned from great Sailors and mentors and the observations through all those years came in useful at critical moments. I made sure I managed all the newly reporting personnel, the same way I remembered Jack Lewis doing it. I got out there and PTd with the crew every day as I had myself with Jack Lewis and Hank Davis in earlier years. Whatever talents I had developed along the way I could in some way credit those skills to a great Sailor from my past that I emulated.

If you asked me who I worked for I would tell you not only the captain but for every man in the crew. One of the best complements I ever received was from our young XO the gung ho Commander Brian Nunenfeldt. The Captain asked, "*where's the master chief been lately*?' The XO told him, "*Captain he's everywhere, Sir*." That was how I wanted it to be. The ubiquitous CMC was a most worthy label.

When we were preparing for our deployment in 1998 I wrote a letter to on the captain's behalf to all the family members of the crew. It summed up everything we were trying to do on KAUFFMAN. That letter in many ways described to the families of our crew why it was a good choice that their sons had joined the Navy. It informed them of how they would travel the world, learn a skill, save some money, and become responsible citizens. It let the families know that there was a cadre of seasoned professionals who would be looking out for their sons, nephews, and grandsons. This is what we try to do, regardless of the mission and even going into harm's way, that mission still holds true.

There are those of course who can't accept what we have. On occasion a political figure or someone in the media, or even a professor from the academic world will make a statement about military members. They may say that the only reason the all volunteer military is able to recruit and keep people is for economic reasons. There is a little truth to that as it pertains as a reason to join. Sometimes it takes a while for a young person to discover that their potential is unlimited. Someone may have to go through a few hard knocks prior to gaining the insight to lead a hundred young people in a division. It may take some training to repair a thirty million dollar piece of equipment or to operate the helm of a three billion dollar ship. All these successes begin to pile up as a Sailor begins to grow a confidence level that may just carry him to a special program resulting in a commission as an officer in the United States Navy. They will build a common bond with like minded individuals that will last a lifetime. So tell me who has this issue right, the old salts or the polished media?

Certainly there were good people on this tight little frigate. There were friends I had fun with like Senior Chief Dave Martin and Chief Kevin Sheerin. We traveled one final summer Med cruise together, soaking up the sunshine and making a few memorable toasts with the Brits, the Dutch, and the Germans in a prolonged NATO exercise. We went to more liberty ports than the crew had money to spend. I fell in love with the revamped city of Barcelona. We took advantage of the opportunities to tour Rome and the Vatican.

I even had the opportunity to test my running skills when I chased down a pickpocket who snagged Dave's wallet on a Roman street. It was euphoric when the thief realized she could not outrun the old man who was gaining on her. Finally she tossed the wallet in order to get this geriatric jackrabbit off her heels.

Kevin, Chief Martinez the aviation chief aboard with our helicopter crew, and I did the Mediterranean jogging routine and once again we logged a thousand miles from Bulgaria to Spain, much the same way that Jack, Pete, and I had several years before. I noticed that those of us who participated in distance running were in a perpetual good mood probably from the enhanced levels of serotonin, dopamine, epinephrine, and beta-endorphin that entered our oxidized brains. All in all aerobic exercise is a great alternative to alcohol, and fitness equipment on ships along with command support of a vigorous program is a key element in the evolution of today's Sailor from what I experienced in my LAWRENCE years.

It was a great way to say farewell. The KAUFFMAN was in social demand, and there was a constant procession of dinners and ceremonies. KAUFFMAN was a polite and well behaved crew. Our frigate was an excellent choice to represent America in public; we cleaned up nicely, not only the ship but us. Our crew attempted to do charity projects in every port, and led by Chief Ralph Seutter, our damage control chief and his affable HT1, Larry Cherry there was never a shortage of volunteers to perform a civic service. The crew accounted themselves well. I took a great deal of pride in the manner they performed each and every day of that cruise. There were many young men who left the east coast of America inexperienced and came home six months later with their chests out, seasoned veterans. We had a few mentors who taught the skills and challenged subordinates to exceed their own personal expectations.

My final Med cruise wasn't all serious business. Even during the final cruise of a twenty- six year career there were there were things to be remarked about.

We were steaming with the Brits on July 4th 1998. We had a full schedule of events that day and for the KAUFFMAN it was well…… a day. We steamed past the British frigate and we observed them up on deck doing a little sun bathing, fully engaged in a realistic Fourth of July holiday. Later that day they watched *Will Smith* battle evil aliens in *Independence Day.* We didn't take that day off to celebrate. I'm appreciative that the Brits did it for us.

We had a very pleasant port visit in the picturesque Spanish coastal town of Calpe. The city had two very unique things to see. One was the huge mountain of a rock that marked the entrance to the harbor; it was impressive enough to be pictured on sixty per cent of their post cards. The other was a small bar owned by an entertaining and authentic Comanche Indian who had the entire establishment decorated in fashionable American Indian style. He was a one man entertainment show and the crew thoroughly enjoyed the Native American atmosphere. There is never a better way to spend an evening than with a Comanche Indian on the Spanish Riviera.

On the eastern side of the Med the crew had fun in one of my old favorites, Antalya Turkey. I couldn't find the Professor, although I did seek him out. What we did find was an engaging American gent who had a karaoke tavern in the center of the city. The crew swarmed to his place like gators on an antelope carcass. Crew members often say they just want to get away from everyone on liberty. Then you see them out in town and who are they with? That's right. All those shipmates they wanted to get away from. So it was with the American's karaoke machine. We chiefs were fine with having everyone in a set location. The tavern owner probably made enough money to retire. Like I always say, "There is never a better way to spend an evening than with American karaoke in Turkey.

There comes a time in every Sailor's career when an internal voice says, "it is time to go." For me, it wasn't anything concrete, or something I could pinpoint in particular. I just knew that it was time for me to move on. I had no great motivating reason. I wasn't on an agenda that required me to jump into a well thought out plan of action. Actually, I wish I had thought it out a little better. I always felt that could make the transition to the civilian world seamlessly. In many ways a retiring military member is facing many of the same anxieties as a graduating college student. No matter how sure you are of a plan's success, there is still a feeling of apprehension.

Most military members find a way to make ends meet. They often find ways to remain relevant with the Navy. Some will say they miss it, most say they don't even if they do. A lot say they don't miss the *Bullshit.* The definition of that term seems to have as many meanings as there are snow flake designs in nature.

I had brought some excellent new chief petty officers into the fold in the years I was on KAUFFMAN. With PNC Brent Benlein (my right hand man), FCC Will Gardner, and the sonarman from Pittsburgh, STGC Semachko (a personal favorite of course); I knew the Navy would be fine without one forty- four year old Z Man. I was looking forward to the next round of life's challenges with a great deal of excitement. At forty- four I wouldn't be the oldest person in my organization any longer. People I talked with would actually know that Paul McCartney once had a great voice. I could immediately go from dinosaur to slowly ripening.

The ship was alive with activity after our return from the Med. There were preparations for inspections, training plans, I division, enlisted surface warfare boards, and hundreds of other time consuming tasks. My favorite JO and running partner, LTJG Morelli had me provide him with some pertinent information for the naval base paper, the *Flag Ship.* He was tasked to do a little farewell article, and truthfully it was nice to get a parting paragraph.

The ship's schedule was so packed in its agenda that the current XO, John Wayne clone, LCDR Joe Murach, struggled intently to find a window for my retirement ceremony. The KAUFFMAN Duke finally found that hour and on a late November day in 1998, I retired from active duty, moving on to the Fleet Reserve. It wasn't a large ceremony. It didn't have a band but the ship was dressed out. The crew was splendid. Iris, Kelly, and Andrew were alongside. Some important Sailors were in attendance, Gordy Brightbill, Dave Hales, and Bill Moran. There were some good neighbors like Bob and Paulette Carlson, and Jim and Debbie Rasmussen, who were like us, Navy families

The ceremony was what you read about in the beginning. It was a time of reflection; a time of thanks, and a final moment to enjoy the kinship of my other family one last time. And then someone else had to do the *Tagout Log Audit.*

Author Biography

Jeff Zahratka is a retired command master chief petty officer who entered the Navy in 1972. He remained on active duty until his retirement in January of 1999. The story is essentially an autobiography of his adventures and his personal slant on the social issues of the era. The author was initially a technical type known as an interior communications electrician, normally assigned as part of the engineering or combat systems departments on most navy ships.

He readily communicates in the language that Sailors understand and educates the curious about ships and Sailors having been a member of five different crews. The author earned the title of Command Master Chief and spent his final tour aboard the USS KAUFFMAN (FFG-59). One of his primary duties was counseling the ship's crew on all matters of personal and professional issues.

Once retired with experience as a counselor the author pursued and obtained a degree in psychology from St Leo University graduating Magna Cum Laude as a forty eight year old in 2002. From there he went on to an inner city assignment as a group home counselor.

Since 2003 the author has instructed young Sailors and their family members at a computer learning facilitator at the Navy's Master Jet Base in Oceana, Virginia. There he is able to keep his pulse on how the force is progressing and as the cliché goes, "once a master chief, always a master chief."

His wife, known in the book as the Heroic Iris, is also a master chief. She is a reservist who is currently assigned to Fleet Forces Command in Norfolk, Virginia.

The Zahratkas are in the fullest sense of the term, a Navy family. They have two children, Andrew Tomas and Kelly Rachael. They reside in Virginia Beach.